The Today Show, CNN, Larry King, CNBC,
The New York Times, The Chicago Tribune,
National Public Radio, The Wall Street Journal

. . . are just some of the places you've seen, heard and read
about The Five O'Clock Club.

What They Say About Us

Letters to Kate:

"Kate, I've known you and your organization since the late 1980's. You have brilliant coaches, and I've worked with two of them, one for the past 7 years as I have advanced my career over the years.

"The long-tem relationship I have with him is testimony to his top-notch expertise and the value of working with a coach while you are happily employed. There is no better way to grow professionally than to proactively work with a coach like him to plan your next move and deal with current on-the-job hurdles.

"Keep up the great work."
Regards,
D.G., Business Development and Marketing Manager, major law firm

"I am a very satisfied customer of The Five O'Clock Club and I'd like to properly acknowledge the effort of the two expert coaches who worked with me over the last year."
H.G., information technology executive, financial services industry

A Sampling of Letters from Clients to Coaches

"I wanted to write and say thanks for all of the help and encouragement that you gave me over the past year. I think that you are a terrific coach and that The Five O'Clock Club has the best methodology. I wish that I had found out about it sooner and had not wasted so much time."
A.S., Head of Applications Development, major healthcare organization

"It was so valuable to have a trusted adviser to provide guidance and bounce ideas off of. The Five O'Clock Club process added structure and a proven strategic approach, vs. going it alone and hoping for the best. I was especially pleased to share my marketing plan with a coach, which forced me to brainstorm prospects. The specific feedback I received from you made me more realistic in my expectations and gave me energy."
SVP, Business Development, insurance industry

"It was more than a pleasure meeting you today. I can't describe how excited and energized I felt after leaving your office. To be honest, you made me feel like a million bucks! I'm thrilled at the prospect of working with you and seeing how things progress. Thank you again, and I'm looking forward to our next session already!"

K.P., Marketing Director, publishing company

"Thanks to [my employer] for making The Five O' Clock Club available to me. After 18 years of working, I didn't know where to begin to handle the new problems I was facing."

T.F., Head of Investor Communications, major insurance company

"As I have my 6-month anniversary in my new assignment, I feel so humbly grateful to you for the support I received from you and The Five O'Clock Club. I just wanted to say thank you for providing me with new skills. I intend to refer people to your organization when the need arises. Every time I spoke with you, I got another boost of motivation and new ideas. During a very uncertain time in my life, it was nice to know that The Five O'Clock Club methods were there for me. Thank you again for your support."

C.J., Business Affairs Director, healthcare organization

"Thanks so much. Our meeting has actually opened my eyes. I learned a lot and am beginning to feel confident that, with your assistance, things will turn out great."

T.O., Chief Financial Officer, major not-for-profit

"I think of you often and am very grateful to the Universe that I met you at that time in my life. Your inspirational words are what my soul needed."

G.B., Editorial Director, major magazine publisher

"It seems that I have absorbed and successfully applied everything that you and the other coaches have taught us to do in our careers. An added bonus is that what I have learned will also apply in my relationships with our internal clients too!"

E.K., Computer Operations Manager, major law firm

"As I approach my one-year anniversary of my first call to The Five O'Clock Club, I really appreciate the wise advice and kind words of encouragement that you and the other coaches offered me. The project that I am managing is fun, challenging, and a great opportunity; and I really like this area of the country. I look forward to keeping in touch as I endeavor to keep my career on track!"

K.S., V.P. Leasing, real estate firm

What Human Resources Executives Say About Five O'Clock Club Services

"I appreciate all the work you are doing on behalf of our employees."

"I'm happy to hear that our former employees are making such progress. It must be very gratifying to your coaches to help people tap into other talents/interests from which they can make new careers."

"I'm so glad to hear that our employees are realizing the benefit of the small-group sessions."

"A number of our employees have told us how impressed they were with The Five O'Clock Club. Of course, I already knew all of you are terrific. I'm so glad others are finding out too."

"All the folks here at [company name omitted] have been very impressed with the services of The Five O'Clock Club. So thank you for all the great work."

"I continue to be impressed by The Five O'Clock Club's work! Thank you!"

"Our employee has indeed given us great feedback about the care she has received from The Five O'Clock Club. Your methodology seems to have inspired her boosted her confidence as she prepares to embark on this new chapter of her life."

www.FiveOClockClub.com

WORK SMARTS

BE A WINNER ON THE JOB

- Build Relationships to Achieve Results
- Navigate Politics and Personalities
- Manage Conflict with Style

edited by

Kate Wendleton and David Madison, Ph.D.

Five O'Clock Books
www.FiveOClockClub.com

The
Five
O'Clock
Club

WorkSmarts
Be a Winner on the Job
Edited by Kate Wendleton and David Madison, Ph.D.

President, The Five O'Clock Club:
Kate Wendleton
Chief Operating Officer:
Richard C. Bayer, Ph.D.
SVP, Director of the Guild of Career Coaches:
David Madison, Ph.D.
Cover Design:
Andrew Newman Design

Here's to your great career!
We'll be with you every step of the way.

Quotes to Inspire You

If you haven't the strength to impose your own terms upon life,
then you must accept the terms it offers you.

—T.S. Eliot

He means well, but he means well feebly.

—Theodore Roosevelt (speaking about a political rival)

Concentration is the key to economic results. No other principle of effectiveness is violated as
constantly today as the basic principle of concentration.

—Peter F. Drucker, economist and author, pioneer in social and management theory

The problem is not that there are problems. The problem is expecting otherwise and thinking
that having problems is a problem.

—Theodore Isaac Rubin, American psychiatrist and author

Happiness is love. Full Stop.

—Dr. George Vaillant, who followed 268 men for 72 years, from the time
they entered Harvard in the late 1930s until now. In a video interview
based on the article, "What Makes Us Happy?" Atlantic, June 2009.

There is a vitality, a life force, an energy, a quickening that is translated through you and into
action. And because there is only one you in all time, this expression is unique. And if you block
it, it will never exist through any other medium. The world will not have it. It is not your busi-
ness to determine how good it is, nor how valuable, nor how it compares to other expressions. It
is your business to keep it yours clearly and directly, to keep the channel open.

—Martha Graham, American modern dancer and choreographer

In times like these it is good to remember that there have always been times like these.

—Paul Harvey, broadcaster

Foreword

A Five O'Clock Club coach is often the "secret weapon" behind an executive's success, and executive success is what this book is all about. You may heave heard about us though the *New York Times, Fortune, Black Enterprise, Business Week*, NPR, CNBC, ABC-TV, or other media. They've checked us out and you should, too.

The original Five O'Clock Club, founded in the 1880s, was one of Philadelphia's famed social clubs. It was made up of 35 leaders of the day, a group that met regularly and formed close bonds. The Club included executives from the Pennsylvania Railroad and Pennsylvania Hospital, the British Consul to Philadelphia and others from politics and the judiciary, shipping magnates and theater moguls, and executives from newspapers and industry.

Today's Five O'Clock Club, started a century later, cultivates the same bonding among members. Forty percent of our Club members earn over $100,000 per year. Almost 20% of those earn over $200,000 per year. Members are focused on their own career development and work closely with their coaches on whatever issues they face. Many of those coaches have contributed to this book.

This book covers a wide range of topics, including how to:

- understand the culture of your organization and corporate politics;
- handle performance reviews (your own as well as those of your subordinates);
- ask for a pay raise;
- handle conflict at work;
- make sure those above you know how good you are;
- use social media to advance your career;
- be an effective leader;
- retain the talent you have now;
- make ethical decisions;
- terminate an employee with dignity;
- be a mentor or mentee; and, in general; keep your job and do well in it.

Twenty-two of our coaches have contributed chapters, as have three members of our management team: Kate Wendleton, President; Richard Bayer, Ph.D., Chief Operating Officer; and David Madison, Ph.D., Director of our National Guild of Career Coaches. The coaches are from all over the country: Anita Attridge, Bill Belknap, Susan Bloch, Cecelia Burokas, Chip Conlin, Nancy Deering, Robert Hellmann, Peter Hill, Jim Hinthorn, Stacey Jerrold, Nancy Karas, Harriet Katz, Bernadette Norz, Joan Runnheim Olson, Ruth K. Robbins, Renée Lee Rosenberg, Hélène Seiler, Win Sheffield, Cynthia Strite, Margaret

McLean Walsh, and Mary Anne Walsh, Ed.D. You can find their full bios (and the bios of some of our other coaches) on our website in the *About Us* section (www.fiveoclockclub.com), and mini-bios following the Introduction in the *About Our Contributors* section.

Perhaps you are reading this book because you already have a Five O'Clock Club coach who is guiding you through your career. Today, it is tough to keep up. Organizations change, and they expect *you* to change quickly. Employees who don't are often left behind or pushed out. Whether you are new to an organization or have been there a long time, it can be hard to know what is expected of you. A trusted advisor (business coach) can help you or someone on your staff to understand the situation, anticipate and respond to the changes in your organization, and increase productivity and performance.

There has been a boom in business coaching, provided at the employer's expense. According to a recent American Management Association survey, companies that use business coaching report performing well on such measures as revenue growth, market share, profitability and customer satisfaction. Individuals who received coaching were more likely to (1) set work-related goals and (2) find that subordinates trust their leadership abilities.

Take a look at the chapter this book, *Is It Time You Got Yourself a Coach?* Maybe you should have a regular, trusted advisor to guide you. After all, you regularly touch base with your physician(s), dentist, financial advisor and maybe even a personal trainer. Add to that list someone who can give you regular feedback on your career—someone who will get to know you well and is completely on your side. And these days, many companies are paying for you to have a coach.

I worked with Sharon, the head of marketing for what was then a new company in a new industry. For the next dozen years, as the company and the industry grew and became more competitive, Sharon was able to stay on as the head of marketing, growing her staff and her salary at the same time. We met often in the very beginning and then infrequently, as the need arose. But she always knew she could call on me. Sharon knew I understood her—her strengths and weaknesses—and I understood the organization she was working for. Through The Five O'Clock Club's *Circles of Influence* exercise (in Chapter 3), I came to know Sharon's staff and all of those around her—inside and outside the organization—who could influence her career. I coached her on her Eight-Word Message as it changed over time. I helped when subordinates were trying to undermine her and bosses were trying to take over her position. I was on the journey with her, every step of the way, helping her to capitalize on situations, and avoid pitfalls and threats to her position and programs. And then, when she decided to leave, The Five O'Clock Club helped Sharon find a tremendous new job elsewhere.

In this ever-changing market, it's good to have a coach on your side to see you through the rough patches, to have someone with whom you can discuss your ideas and concerns—someone who can give you balance. If your employer is willing to pay for you to have a coach, it shows that your employer values you and your future contributions.

Our coaches help executives throughout their careers—to discuss problems they may have with bosses, peers, subordinates or clients. Since 1986, we've been helping people build great careers. We wish you the best in *your* career, and we'll be with you every step of the way.

Warmest regards,
Kate Wendleton,
President, The Five O'Clock Club
A national career coaching
and outplacement organization
Building Great Careers!
www.FiveOClockClub.com

The original Five O'Clock Club was formed in Philadelphia in 1883. It was made up of the leaders of the day, who shared their experiences "in a spirit of fellowship and good humor."

Introduction

Is workplace politics getting you down? This book was written by our coaches in response to our Members' requests about what we know about business coaching. After all, The Five O'Clock Club has always been focused on the career development of our Members—helping them to do well in their present organizations, as those organizations, and the world, change.

As organizations continue to flatten their hierarchies, eliminate permanent staff, rely on outsourcing and emphasize the bottom line to accomplish their goals, it is more critical than ever for employees to develop strategies that empower them to reinvent and position themselves for success in the workplace. The difference between advancing in one's career or stagnating in it often rests on one's ability and willingness to become a strategic thinker. An important step is to understand one's value and communicate that value to the company.

It has been well documented that the employee who can take charge of his or her career will be more productive, better satisfied, focused on results and relationships, and therefore prepared to impact a company's bottom line. It

is critical for individuals to manage their own professional development. Unfortunately, too many employees do not know how to develop strategies for success, whether they are new to the job or seasoned veterans.

The Five O'Clock Club coaches have identified winning strategies for success on the job and we have compiled them in this book to make it easier for every employee to learn how to be more effective at work. Each chapter is written by one of our experts. The chapters include self-help exercises and winning action steps, which can be implemented immediately. It is about helping employees to become change-resilient, more secure in themselves and their future as organizations continue to adjust to changing market situations. How can one improve his/her executive presence? What does it take to identify projects that drive revenue? Is change seen as opportunity? To increase value to the company, how can you focus on results, not activities? In a very diverse work environment, how can workers from different cultural backgrounds understand the impact of culture on doing business? Over the years, our clients have come to us for help while on the job. These are some of the common issues raised frequently, which will be addressed in the book.

Read what you need, but also read all of the other chapters that you think you may not need! The gems of advice that you will pick up will surprise you.

Remember: All Five O'Clock Club coaches go through a grueling, four-month certification process so they all speak the same language and have mastered the research behind what we teach. You're in good hands with a Five O'Clock Club coach and we hope to hear from you about your experiences. Write to us at hr@fiveoclock-club.com or call 1-800-538-6645.

—K.W., 2012

About Our Contributors

Anita Attridge, Branch Head and Certified Five O'Clock Club Coach

Anita Attridge is a Five O'Clock Club Master Career and Business Coach.

She manages and coaches at a weekly Club Branch and is passionate about helping clients to achieve their career goals.

She has held senior human resources positions with Xerox, The Nature Conservancy and Merck, working with leaders to develop their leadership skills and increase the effectiveness of their organizations.

Anita has worked with hundreds of clients to help them successfully manage their job search, effectively transition into a new position, and maximize their leadership potential in challenging situations.

She has a master's degree from the University of Rochester.

Richard Bayer, Ph.D., Chief Operating Officer, The Five O'Clock Club

Dr. Richard Bayer is an ethicist and economist and Chief Operating Officer of The Five O'Clock Club.

He is a frequent guest on radio and TV, having appeared on the *Today Show*, CNN, *Good Day New York*, *Fortune* magazine, *Bloomberg News*, and other major media. Dr. Bayer has a background of 22 years of teaching at the University level in economics and ethics. He has authored a book on labor economics (Georgetown University Press, 1999), and is the author of 18 articles and reviews in scholarly journals, and numerous popular essays on topics concerning business ethics. In addition, he has written a book for the general population, *The Good Person Guidebook: Transforming Your Personal Life*, which was widely praised by Amazon.com reviewers.

Bill Belknap, Certified Five O'Clock Club Coach

Bill has 30 years of senior-management and human resources experience as a Manager, Vice President and Senior Vice President in a variety of industries, including office products, consumer products and medical-cost containment. He specializes in coaching senior managers and executives, helping them find jobs at the right level, with the right company and at the right compensation. He is a Certified Five O'Clock Club Master Career Coach and the co-author of *For Executives Only: Applying Business Techniques to Your Job Search,* and regularly speaks to networking groups about the ins and outs of conducting an effective job search. Bill is considered an expert on networking and has taught networking to over a thousand executives. On the personal side, Bill is an amateur magician and fitness enthusiast; he has completed over 25 Triathlons.

Susan Bloch, Certified Five O'Clock Club Coach

Susan Bloch, Human Resources Executive, works with companies to shape their vision and create a culture that attracts, develops and retains key talent, while increasing employee productivity. With 20 years of human resources experience in a variety of industries, Susan is a highly skilled in problem solving, organizational effectiveness, employee relations, and management coaching and training. In addition, she has lived and worked abroad supporting managers and their staffs. She understands how to build an effective multicultural workplace. Susan has a B.A. from the University of California, Santa Barbara, and an M.A. from Antioch University.

Cecelia Burokas, Certified Five O'Clock Club Coach

Cecelia Burokas has directed her own consulting and coaching firm for over 15 years, focusing on executive coaching, strategic planning and change management. She has worked with individuals and organizations in manufacturing, energy, finance and agriculture, and with nonprofits in the arts, healthcare, education and social services.

Cecelia teaches in Northwestern University's MS in Learning and Organization Change Program. She holds a B.A. from Vassar College, a master's degree from Reed College and has completed the program in Client-centered Counseling at the Chicago Counseling and Psychotherapy Center. Originally from Connecticut, she has lived and worked in Chicago for many years.

Chip Conlin, Branch Head and Certified Five O'Clock Club Coach

Chip Conlin has been a coach with The Five O'Clock Club since 1996. He manages a major branch of the Club in New York City, plus maintains an active private coaching practice in which he advises clients at both the professional and executive levels. Chip brings 30 years' experience in human resources to his role at The Five O'Clock Club, in both the financial services and transportation industries. He has spoken on a variety of career topics to such prestigious groups as the New York City chapter of the Project Management Institute and appeared on National Syndicate Radio. He holds a master's degree in Sociology and is a member of the Association of Career Professionals and the Society for Human Resources Management.

Nancy Deering, Certified Five O'Clock Club Coach

Nancy is a coach and organizational professional. She is a practicing Certified Organizational Ombudsman Practitioner (CO-OP), working with organizations, teams and individuals on creating strategies to manage conflict. She has been developing win-win solutions for more than 25 years and is well-versed in handling complex conflict.

She holds a master's degree in Organizational Development from the University of Phoenix, a Bachelor's degree in Communications from Rutgers, the State University of NJ, an associate's degree in Management from St. Peters' College and is Certified to administer a variety of assessment instruments.

Robert Hellmann, V.P., Associate Director of The Five O'Clock Club Guild of Career Coaches and Certified Five O'Clock Club Coach

Robert Hellmann, Vice President, The Five O'Clock Club, brings a passion to coaching. He maintains a thriving private practice, helping clients to achieve career and workplace goals. Rob, who has an M.B.A., is also an adjunct Professor at NYU, teaching career development courses to mid-career professionals.

Frequently quoted in media outlets, such as the *New York Times* and the *Washington Post*, Rob has over 20 years of experience in marketing and career/organizational development. He's worked for and with organizations such as the Audubon Society, JP Morgan Chase, the Federal Reserve Bank of New York, and American Express, and has facilitated many organizational development initiatives.

Peter Hill, Certified Five O'Clock Club Coach

Known across the Asia Pacific as "The Career Doctor," Peter Hill is a Shanghai, China-based career and job search advisor to some of the region's most talented business leaders. He also shares his expertise with emerging executives as Professor of Lifetime Career Management at HULT International Business School in Shanghai, and he is a frequently invited guest speaker at other leading B-schools, international chambers of commerce, and organizations such as Harvard Business Review China. In addition to being certified by The Five O'Clock Club, Peter is a Certified Master Résumé Writer.

Jim Hinthorn, Certified Five O'Clock Club Coach

Jim is a Certified Five O'Clock Club coach and runs his own human resources consulting firm. He has spent his entire career in the human resources function, having occupied the top HR job at two major corporations,

Lightolier and F. Schumacher & Co. Jim started his career as a labor relations specialist for the New York State Nurses Association, followed by middle management and senior human resources positions at International Paper Company. Jim holds a B.A. in Sociology and a M.A. in Labor & Industrial Relations, both from the University of Illinois. Jim and his wife, Pamela, reside on Block Island, RI.

Stacey Jerrold, Certified Five O'Clock Club Coach

Stacey M. Jerrold, M.B.A., SPHR, is recognized as a leader in the field of Human Resources. She is known for "turning potential into performance." A strategic thinker who is able to see 360 degrees of any situation and has the aptitude for seeing change as opportunity, Stacey uses her talent for facilitation to effect positive transitions. Whether working on individual career-related issues or corporate business coaching, she provides her clients with the focus and problem-solving perspective so they can together create a step-by-step action plan to address the challenges at hand, allowing the client to release their untapped potential and realize the performance they have been seeking.

Nancy Karas, Certified Five O'Clock Club Coach

Nancy Karas specializes in facilitating change for people who need to move forward in their lives. She brings 20 years of corporate business expertise and over 15 years of coaching experience to the Club. Nancy holds an M.S. in Human Resources

Management from The Milano Graduate School of Management and Urban Policy, at the New School University in New York City. She lives in Southern California where she continues to facilitate change and help people to make smooth and positive transitions in their lives.

Harriet Katz, Certified Five O'Clock Club Coach

Harriet Katz is a seasoned coach and clinician with over 30 years of experience. She has worked with corporate clients from Bayer Diagnostics, Xerox, GlaxoSmithKline, Goldman Sachs, Merrill Lynch, The Bank of New York, The New York Mercantile Exchange, Time Warner, Adobe, and the U.N.

She is certified by the Centre for High Performance Development (UK), MBTI-qualified, and experienced in 360°, leadership development, and individual and team coaching.

Harriet is a Board Member of the Association for Psychological Type-NY, past Secretary and Board Member of Association of Career Professionals International-NY, and past VP of the NYC Coaching Center. She has a B.S. from the University of Michigan, M.S.W. from the University of California at Berkeley, and D.S.W. from Yeshiva University.

Bernadette Norz, MBA, Certified Five O'Clock Club Coach

Prior to transitioning to leadership development, executive coaching and career coaching, Bernadette held a variety of positions in healthcare over the course of three decades. As creator of her own unique career path, she has walked the talk of career transition, finding opportunities that fulfilled career goals, while balancing professional, educational and family choices and commitments. She has worked for hospitals, a state hospital association and for-profit healthcare organizations in technical and leadership positions. She is currently a credentialed coach with the International Coach Federation and is a Ph.D. student in human and organizational development.

Joan Runnheim Olson, Certified Five O'Clock Club Coach

Joan Runnheim Olson is an internationally certified career coach and workshop presenter. For 10+ years, Joan has worked in various venues to encourage nontraditional career paths for men and women, i.e., careers in male- or female-dominated industries. Serving as a project coordinator for a Federal Dept. of Labor grant, she helped move women into the auto service industry. As an assessment/placement specialist for a pre-apprenticeship training program, Joan helped women break into and succeed in jobs in the trades. Joan presents workshops across the country, sharing strategies on recruiting and retaining students in classes and programs preparing them for nontraditional careers.

Renée Lee Rosenberg, Certified Five O'Clock Club Coach

Renée Lee Rosenberg, M.A., is an author, Licensed Mental Health Counselor, speaker, trainer and facilitator. Renée has 20+ years in helping individuals to navigate organizational and personal transition. Her humor and sup-

portive coaching build trust and rapport on all levels. Her specialties include assessment, team building, coaching and leadership development. As a professional speaker, both nationally and internationally (Amsterdam, Paris, Munich), Renée's presentations are informative, creative, high energy and results driven. She is the author of The Five O'Clock Club book, *Achieving The Good Life After 50: Tools and Resources for Making it Happen* and frequently appears in the media such as MSNBC, ABC's *Eyewitness News*, NY1, the *LA Times, Health and Wellness Magazine, Washington Times, Chicago Times, US News & World Report*, Forbes.com and Fox.com.

Ruth K. Robbins, Certified Five O'Clock Club Coach

Ruth K. Robbins has been a Five O'Clock Club coach for over a decade, leading one of our weekly job-search strategy groups. She frequently co-presents with David Madison on "How to Lead a Five O Clock Club Group" for guild members in training. Ruth is also a member of our media team.

She holds an M.B.A. in marketing from Fordham University and a certificate in Adult Career Planning and Development from NYU. She was MBTI-certified in 1995. Ms. Robbins coaches at Columbia University Graduate School of Business as part of their Leadership Development program. Ruth has conducted numerous Five O Clock Club workshops and seminars on job search, career transition, career management and résumé development at industry and professional organizations, public venues and community-based organizations.

Hélène Seiler, Certified Five O'Clock Club Coach

Hélène has 25 years' experience in organization development and talent management in North America, Western Europe and South East Asia. She designs and delivers executive coaching programs and women's leadership-development workshops for international organizations.

Hélène joined The Five O Clock Club in 2003, and is the co-author of "For Executives Only," published in 2007. A Master Certified Coach with the International Coach Federation, she holds an M.S. in Management, a Graduate Diploma of Ontological Coaching, and is an Associate Coach for the Center of Creative Leadership. Hélène lives in Malaysia. She serves on the Board of the International School of Kuala Lumpur.

Win Sheffield, Certified Five O'Clock Club Coach

Win Sheffield is a career coach in private practice in New York. He offers strategies and guidance to support his clients to take their work to the next level or establish new careers. He coaches clients in delivering their message, runs workshops and delivers talks to many industry and alumni groups.

His background includes Citibank, JP Morgan and PricewaterhouseCoopers in strategy development and management consulting. He has an M.B.A. from Boston University and an undergraduate degree from Kenyon College. He has studied counseling at General Seminary and Myers-Briggs at the Jung Institute.

Cynthia Strite, Certified Five O'Clock Club Coach

In addition to being a Five O'Clock Club coach for more than six years and a former branch head, Cynthia Strite has over 20 years of management experience in human resources, education and coaching in the public and private sectors.

Her positions have included Human Resources and Education Director for NYC Comptroller Elizabeth Holtzman; currently she holds a senior management position in the Consumer Communications Department of a Fortune 500 company.

Her undergrad and graduate degrees are from Penn State, and Cynthia is in the final stages of completing a doctorate in adult education at Columbia University. She is an adjunct professor in the graduate department of The Fashion Institute of Technology, where she teaches management and leadership. Cynthia is Myers-Briggs and EQ-i certified.

Margaret McLean Walsh, Certified Five O'Clock Club Coach

Margaret McLean Walsh is a Certified Five O'Clock Club Career and Executive Coach, bringing 30 years of executive Human Resources financial services business experience to her coaching and consulting business. She is also a Columbia University Certified Executive and Organizational Coach, and holds an M.A. in Communications.

With a focus on strengths, solutions and inspiring breakthrough results, Margaret builds trust easily, and quickly gets to the heart of the agenda. She combines her coaching expertise with a passion for growth, renewal and fun. In a collaborative process, she unlocks a client's creativity to uncover resources, solutions and strategies for success.

Mary Anne Walsh, Ed.D., Certified Five O'Clock Club Coach

Mary Anne Walsh, Ed.D., inspires high-achieving clients to soar in their careers by helping them focus with laser sharpness on their strongest assets. She develops global talent by providing services for both individuals and corporations. She specializes in executive coaching, leadership development and cross-cultural organizational issues. Mary Anne has more than 20 years of experience coaching global leaders in a variety of industries in the U.S., Europe and Asia. She has worked extensively with clients in financial services, pharmaceuticals and consumer goods. Her offices are in New York City.

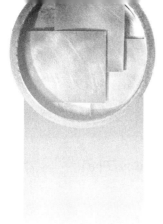

Contents

Part Three: Handling the Job

Part Four: Getting Ahead

Appendixes

Index   311

Part One

Starting Out

Chapter 1

• • • • • • •

"That's the Way We Do Things Here" Understanding Organizational Culture

by Anita Attridge, Certified Five O'Clock Club Coach

Custom, that unwritten law, by which the people keep even the king in awe.

Charles Davenport, biologist

Joining a new company can be like moving to a foreign country. You will encounter new customs, dress, language, ideas and rules, and you will need to learn about all of these in order to do well.

- You will be expected to work and interact effectively in the organization.
- You will be accepted and you will fit into the organization—or not!
- You will be assessed for recognition, compensation, rewards and promotion, depending on how well you perform in the new—and perhaps very different—culture. If you choose to ignore organizational culture, you do so at your own peril.

Yes, there will be the new customs, dress, language, ideas and rules, but, simply defined, organizational culture is the *set of written and*

"It's my newer, cooler look. I'm hoping my younger clients will dig it."

unwritten rules by which people function to get their work done.

What makes you successful in one company may not make you successful in another company. For example, at General Electric, the organizational culture is regimented and managers are expected to use the GE processes without question. At Xerox, the organizational culture is fast-paced, and continuously changing. Managers have considerable latitude in how they get the job done. At Merck, the organizational culture is consensus driven, with a strong emphasis on data analysis. Managers need a consensus to accomplish their goals.

What kind of environment are you accustomed to? If your new employer expects people to work differently than you did at your previous organization, you will be *expected to adapt* to the new culture.

Organizational culture is *the set of written and unwritten rules by which people function to get their work done.*

Case Study: Sara and the Hierarchy

Sara, a highly successful marketing director in an insurance company, accepted a marketing director position with a prominent healthcare company. The insurance company had strict rules about meeting with senior management. People were expected to discuss their marketing ideas in detail with their own manager, request permission to meet with senior managers, and *then* share the results of those meetings with their manager.

In her new job at the healthcare company, Sara's first assignment was to develop marketing ideas for a new product. She followed the process of meeting with senior managers that had been expected in the insurance industry. She was taken aback when her manager said, "Sara, why are you bothering me with all of this detail? And why haven't you met with the senior managers already?" The following day, a colleague explained that Sara didn't need permission to meet with the senior managers: "Everyone here has

access to whomever they need to talk with to get their job done. I'm surprised you waited so long to meet with them, too." Having the freedom to meet with senior managers whenever she needed was a new way of working for Sara.

Organizational Culture: Unwritten, Unspoken and Powerful

Organizational culture is powerful because it determines how a person will fit into the workplace. It can prevent a person from being promoted because, despite talent, skills and contributions, she chooses to do things "her way," going against the grain of "the way we do things here."

Unfortunately, organizational culture is:

- usually not discussed formally, and
- rarely found in written form.

But it does govern the way work really gets done.

We sometimes hear that a person was turned down for a job because the interviewer felt that he or she would not be a good fit. In other words, the interviewer knows organizational culture well enough to gauge who will succeed and who won't. If the job hunter has little idea about the culture of the hiring company, it will be hard to grasp why he was not hired or, more importantly, what he could have done differently in the interview.

Case Study: Bart Knew His Stuff, but That Wasn't Enough

Bart, a finance manager who worked for a large telecommunications company, landed an interview for a similar position with a computer company. During the interview, Bart was asked about his accomplishments, how he interfaced with department heads and how the work was done in his company. The telecommunications company had automated financial systems honed to meet the company's needs, and prided itself on how well the processes worked. Changes were carefully thought through before they were implemented.

The computer company, however, had a different attitude about how to get work done. Responsiveness to changing customers' needs was key and their financial systems were continuously modified to keep up. Managers in all functions were expected to anticipate changes and be prepared to respond rapidly.

When Bart was not invited back for the third round of interviews, he called the hiring manager to find out why he had not made the cut. The manager told Bart that his financial skills were impressive, but that she did not think he was *a fit for their organizational culture*. Bart met with his Five O'Clock Club Career Coach to discuss what had happened. When pressed by the coach, he admitted that he didn't know much about the culture in the computer company. He'd gone on the interview unprepared. With a little research and reflection, Bart realized that the expectations of a finance manager in a computer company differed greatly from those in a telecommunications company. On his current job, the pace of change was moderate. The computer company was fast-paced; chaos was accepted and the ability to change at a moment's notice was crucial. Bart now understood the cultural differences, and saw that he had not positioned himself well during the interview.

A company is judged
by the president it keeps…

James Hulbert

Organizational Culture Isn't Right or Wrong: It Just Is

The culture of an organization is commonly determined by the founders. It may evolve over time, but the processes and ways of working together become deeply embedded. The unspo-

ken rules, based on shared values and beliefs, become *the reality of how the organization gets work done.* Those who join the organization are expected to adapt and accomplish their work in accordance with the culture. Here's a checklist of questions to guide the newcomer in adapting:

- What it's really like to work here? What are the realities of working "our way"?
- What behaviors and attitudes are expected?
- How are co-workers expected to communicate and deal with each other?
- How are decisions made and problems solved?
  How are employees and customers expected to be treated?

Change is not made without
inconvenience, even from worse to better.

Richard Hooker, Renaissance English theologian

How Should You Choose Where to Work? Know Thyself!

All of us have preferred ways of working, although many of us don't give much thought to it. If you're working in a company culture that supports your preferred style, you are usually content. If you land in a company culture that is different from your preferred style, you may be compelled to change the way you work—or change jobs. We often fail to closely question how an organization works, even when we're in the interview process.

It is vital to understand your own preferences. The clearer you are about how you like to work, the more likely you are to choose wisely—and you will become attuned to how an organization really gets its work done and expects new members to work. Use the following *Working Style Preference Exercise* to assess your desired work environment.

This exercise should help you to see what is really important to you—and where you will fit.

If, for example, working in a fast-paced organization that encourages risk-taking is highly important to you, you probably will become frustrated working in an organization where the pace is slower, and risk-taking is not encouraged. Neither style is right or wrong…they are just different and require different approaches. In The Five O'Clock Club book on understanding yourself (*Targeting*), there are additional assessment exercises that will give you insights about how you like to work.

Working Style Preference Exercise

Think about an organization where you have enjoyed working and were comfortable— or imagine an ideal organization where you think you would enjoy working. Then review the choices under the following 11 topics and select the one that most closely matches your working preference. After you have selected your preferences, rank the importance of each. *Use a scale of one to five with one being not important and five being very important.*

Interactions in the organization:

- How do people interact with each other?   Ranking __
  - ✓ Are they direct and freely discuss their views?
  - ✓ Are they non-confrontational and don't openly disagree with each other?

- How are people expected to react to others in the organization? Ranking__
  - ✓ Are they expected to stand up for themselves?
  - ✓ Are they expected be a team member and not stand up for themselves?

- How accepting of questioning is the organization?
  Ranking__
  - ✓ Are you encouraged to question current practices?
  - ✓ Are you expected to accept current practices without question?

- How do people do their work?
  Ranking__
  - ✓ Do people work together collaboratively?
  - ✓ Do people work on their own with minimal involvement of others?

- How are decisions made?
  Ranking__
  - ✓ Are decisions made quickly?
  - ✓ Are decision made slowly?

- Who makes the decisions?
  Ranking__
  - ✓ Is decision making driven by the manager?
  - ✓ Is decision making consensus driven?

Organization attire:

- How do the majority of people dress?
  Ranking__
  - ✓ Traditional business attire?
  - ✓ Business casual?
  - ✓ Very casual?

Organization activity:

- How does the organization operate?
  Ranking__
  - ✓ Is it a fast paced organization with lots of activity and change?
  - ✓ Is it a moderate paced organization with a minimal amount of change?

- How does the organization deal with risk taking?
  Ranking__

✓ Is risk taking encouraged and rewarded?

✓ Is risk taking discouraged and often punished?

- What is the working style in the organization?

Ranking___

✓ Is it collaborative with people working together?

✓ Is it competitive where people are pitted against each other?

- What is the operating style in the organization?

Ranking___

✓ Is it formal where hierarchy is strictly observed?

✓ Is it informal where people have easy access to others?

Investigating Organization Culture

Understanding yourself is a good beginning. The next step is to uncover as much as you can about the organizational cultures of the companies you may be targeting to get interviews. At The Five O'Clock Club, we tell clients they can learn about companies in three ways:

- Primary Research: talking to people who are in the know—or who *know* people who are in the know. That's what we mean when we say, "Network, network, network!"
- Secondary research: reading as much as you can about companies, *e.g.,* articles in business publications, trade journals, websites, blogs.
- Your own direct observation.

Make use of all three methods to find out about company cultures as you prepare for interviews, or even as you start a new position. All three can also help you to gain deeper insights

into the culture of your *current* organization.

Actually, secondary research comes *first*, because you don't want to network intensively (primary research) until you already have a lot of background information—so that you will sound knowledgeable when you speak with people. You want to be prepared to ask good questions about the company culture during the interview, so you need some information and a grasp of realities before your networking and job interviews.

A good place to start is learning about the company founder(s). These people exert an extraordinary influence on the company culture. It's *their* company and they determine:

- the beliefs and values of the workplace
- the company's focus of attention
- the decision-making and problem-resolution processes
- the conduct and achievements that will be rewarded

If the founder is no longer with the company, find out about the leaders who replaced those who were present at the beginning. Who succeeded to the leadership roles, who failed, and why? How has the company culture evolved over the years?

There are usually many sources of information for your secondary research:

- Read the latest annual report to learn what is important to the company.
- Review the company website to learn about the company's history, the founder and the current CEO. A website presents an idealized portrait of the company; however it provides insights into how the company wants to position itself in the marketplace.
- Dig up as many articles as you can about the company in business publications. You'll likely find a variety of materials, some with information about how the company culture is viewed. In these days of blogs very little can be hidden!

- Look and listen to the marketing messages. Ads and slogans often convey underlying beliefs about the company's identity and views about its customers.

With an understanding of the company based on secondary research, you've made a good start, and are positioned well for your primary research, *i.e.,* speaking with people who can shed even more light on your targeted companies.

> *There is guidance for each of us,*
> *and by lowly listening,*
> *we shall hear the right word.*

Ralph Waldo Emerson, American essayist, poet

Network, Network, Network: The Critical Next Step

After gaining an initial understanding of the company, getting in front of people is one of the best ways to learn about what really goes on there. So, who can you network with to learn about the companies you're interested in? If you've never done this before, you might be suprised at how many resources you actually have:

- Make a list all of the people you know and the companies they work for. This list should include friends, relatives, present and former colleagues, neighbors—even the people you run into when you're at the gym or out walking the dog. There might be dozens of people you don't realize you have fairly easy access to.
- Also list the professional, community and religious organizations to which you belong. There are all those people you know from church, synagogue, mosque, PTA, Little League, etc. Professional associations have lists of members and their workplaces. These lists are invaluable tools for identifying people to call. Even if you don't know the people, you

can contact them and tell them that you're a member of the organization and would like to have an informational meeting. Members like to help other members.
- Scour your alumni directories. Fellow alums are excellent for networking.

Use *all* of these networking resources! The more people you talk with the more you'll learn, and since you're asking for information—not a job—people are likely to be cooperative and generous.

> *The eye sees only what the mind*
> *is prepared to comprehend.*

Robertson Davies, novelist

Personal Observation: You Can Be an Eyewitness

At The Five O'Clock Club we have always recommended arriving early for interviews. This gives you the chance to see and hear what's going on in the workplace. You can ask for water, and may be directed to the water cooler or to the employee kitchen. You can observe:

- how people are interacting with each other.
- how they're dressed.
- the energy level and activity.
- items on display in the company reception area. What company symbols are visible and how are they used?
- how the physical space is designed. Are there offices and cubicles of varying size? Are there cubicles in a large bullpen area, or are offices accessible by corridor?
- the awards, certificates of recognition and employee photos on display. These offer clues to the company values.

As well as observing, you can also ask questions. If you meet someone at the water cooler, you can say, "There's so much hustle and bustle here [or: This place seems so calm], what's it like to work here?" Of course, you're trying to get a feel for the company culture. You may be surprised at the answers. (See our book on interviewing and salary negotiation by Kate Wendleton.)

Ask Questions about Company Culture During the Interview

Based on your research and networking, you should have questions that relate to the culture. Having done the Working Style Preferences exercise, you have a better grasp of the kind of environment you'll do well in, and you can probe as to how the work gets done. It might be too confrontational to ask, "Is it appropriate to question current practices in the organization or is it best to just follow the practices in place?" Nor would you want to say, "According to what I've been reading on the blogs, your CEO is a real tyrant." But you can ask, "What's the tone here? Is it okay to make suggestions about improving procedures? What's the company culture like?"

Case Study: Doris "If Only I Had Asked"

Doris, a marketing researcher, interviewed for a position at a research consulting firm. She met with her prospective boss, the president and several colleagues. The projects sounded interesting and challenging, so Doris was delighted to receive an offer. In her previous jobs she had enjoyed collaborating with colleagues, and she looked forward to doing the same in her new role.

On her first major project, she did extensive research, summarized her findings and asked a colleague—who was working on a similar project—if he would like to compare notes. He told her that wouldn't be necessary because

everyone worked alone for the most part, and had the freedom to present projects to management and customers without consulting others. Research was the key, not collegiality. Doris soon found that everyone liked to work alone; no one was interested in collaborating or even sharing information. In fact, they considered collaboration a waste of time.

Doris realized that this culture was different from those she had worked in before. Collaboration was important to her and she assumed that most organizations operated on this basis. It had not even occurred to her to ask—during the interview—about how people accomplished their projects. Now she would have to adjust to a lonely way of working, or move on.

Starting a New Position: Adjusting to "How Things Are Done Here"

Up to this point, we have focused on finding out about company culture before accepting a job offer. But what can you do on the job to learn even more? If you start from Day One on your new job to quickly learn about the "way things are done here," that will ease your transition. How well you fit in will be established in the first few weeks, so learning the culture—as it is, up close and personal—is as important as learning policies and procedures. To be successful, comply with both formal and *informal* expectations.

Pay attention not only to what needs to be done but how it should be done. Every new employee knows he or she must figure out what must to be done, but you may not achieve desired results if you don't also figure out how it needs to be done.

"What" needs to be done includes:

- the objectives or goals I need to accomplish
- my work priorities
- the technologies and systems used

- the information I need to accomplish my job
- the resources available to me

"How" the job needs to be done relates to the culture:

- How do people work: independently or collaboratively?
- How are decisions made?
- Who needs to be included in the decision-making process?
- What is important to senior management?

Case Study: Jeff
The Intersection of Two Paths

Jeff was excited about his new position as VP of Human Resources at a prestigious consumer products company. At his previous job Jeff was known for his creative ideas and ability to develop HR programs to meet business needs. He enjoyed identifying and solving problems, had a lot of ideas and worked well with his staff and clients to incorporate their ideas. He worked with senior managers to ensure that his solutions would work in their areas within budget and headcount.

After a few months on his new job, Jeff felt that he was not making progress and that he was not being well received. He ran into continuous roadblocks about his ideas. He was told that he was moving too fast, even though he *thought* he was moving too slowly.

Jeff's Five O'Clock Club coach asked him to watch and listen more carefully as to how his peers operated in the management committee meetings. He then noticed that his peers always asked for permission before starting new projects. There was usually a lot of discussion about *if* the project should be done instead of *how*. Once the project was approved, each step was reviewed in excruciating detail.

When Jeff was ready to initiate a new project, his coach convinced him to discuss his ideas with the management committee, even though

he thought it was a waste of time. At the meeting, he suggested implementation of the project. After much discussion about whether the issue should even be addressed at this time, a decision was made to go forward.

Although he was hired for his creativity and innovation, Jeff saw he would need to spend much more time gaining project approval, as well as approval for each step. He was now in a consensus-driven culture in which executives didn't have much freedom to make decisions.

Learning about the Culture from Within: Observe

Now that you're on the job, observation and networking are keys to your success. Discover the unwritten rules of organizational life in your new workplace. Observe:

- Who talks to whom?
  - ✓ Do people interact with others at all levels of the organization?
  - ✓ Do people primarily interact only with their manager and peers?
- What language do people use when talking about their work?
  - ✓ Do they use acronyms or terms specific to the organization? If so, learn these rapidly.
  - ✓ Do they use more easily understood terms?
- What is the preferred means of communication?
  - ✓ Email?
  - ✓ Telephone?
  - ✓ In person?
- What is the style of written communication, via memos and email messages?
  - ✓ Are they formal?
  - ✓ Are they informal?
  - ✓ Are the messages usually brief?
  - ✓ Or are they detailed?
- Who is copied on the communications?
  - ✓ Are numerous people copied?

✓ Are only people directly involved
    copied?
- How are meetings conducted?
  ✓ Are they formal with agendas set
      prior to the meeting?
  ✓ Are they informal with agendas
      developed or shared in the meeting?

Case Study: Steven Waiting Alone

At Steven's former company, everyone was expected to be early for meetings, the meetings started on time, and latecomers were not welcomed. When he moved to another company, Steven was always the first to arrive for meetings, which never started on time. No one seemed to care that people wandered in 10 or 15 minutes late. He found this irritating, but when he voiced his concern he was told, "We don't start meetings here until everyone is present." Steven learned to accept that meetings would not start on time at his new company because "that's the way we run meetings here."

Learning from Within: Networking

Networking and building relationships will help you to understand the nuances of how work gets done in your new workplace. Be sure to network with:
- direct reports
- co-workers
- your boss
- peers in other departments

Begin networking on your first day with the company, starting with co-workers and direct reports. They can help you to understand how work gets done in your areas, as well as in the company as a whole.

For example, finance, sales and marketing, manufacturing and HR will have their own functional sub-cultures within the wider context of the company culture. This is why there is often a "we" vs. "they" feeling among functions within a company. The employees in each of the sub-cultures may dress differently, have different physical work spaces and different ways of accomplishing tasks.

If you don't like to network, do it anyway! And become good at it if you want to understand organizational culture and build relationships that can help your career in the long run.

Your networking meetings can and should be interesting. After all, you're learning about the culture when employees tell stories about people and events that have taken place in recent years or decades. And the company lore reveals a lot about what is distinct and unique about the organization. Listen to stories about:

- the heroes and how they rose to the top of the organization.
- crises encountered and overcome.
- milestone events in the organization's history.
- anecdotes about senior management.
- management's reactions to blunders and mistakes.
- the handling of firings and layoffs.

Each story gives you additional insight into some aspect of the organizational culture. For example, in one company the story is often told about its response to a bad economic downturn. The company was strongly committed to no layoffs, so employees and management worked together to reduce everyone's hours. As a result, no jobs were cut during the recession. The story reinforced company values regarding the importance of employees and the efforts the company would make to support everyone. This story was often told, particularly to new employees.

As you network, ask questions and listen carefully. Tell people that you are genuinely interested in finding out the insider's view of how the organization works. Some of the questions you can ask:

- What should I know about how to act?

- How is success defined here, and how does one succeed?
- What is the biggest mistake one could make?
- What are the sacred cows that I need to be aware of?

The answers to these questions will help you to master the subtleties of corporate culture and avoid pitfalls.

Advice from Veterans

I asked a few of my Five O'Clock Club clients about the most important lessons they had learned in adapting to new workplaces. Their advice can serve as a summary of the points made here:

- Do an assessment of your own needs. Know yourself, so that you will understand the kind of corporate culture that best aligns with your preferred working style.
- Do your homework and learn about the cultures of the organizations you will be targeting.
- Ask candid questions about the organizational culture during the interview and after you're hired.
- During the first couple of weeks on the job, observe carefully, meet as many people as you can, and ask about the culture.

You will have many challenges when starting a new job: Understanding your job responsibilities, learning what your new boss is really like, figuring out how best to get along with new colleagues. Make sure that learning and mastering the corporate culture is a top priority—*to achieve the fit you want.*

Chapter 2

• • • • • • •

Starting Out on the Right Foot in Your New Job

by Kate Wendleton, President, The Five O'Clock Club

. . . be patient toward all that is unsolved in your heart and try to love the questions themselves like locked rooms and like books that are written in a foreign tongue.

Rainer Maria Rilke, poet

Starting out can be tricky: You are *on board* but *the jury is still out* on you. It is a time of trial. You are often being watched to see if you will work out. Here are some things you need to do to start out on the right foot and keep moving in the right direction.

Before You Start

• **Say thank you**. Contact all the people who helped you get the new position. Often people don't make this effort because they feel they'll be in the new job for a long time. But today, when the average American changes jobs every four years, the odds say you're going to change jobs again soon. You need to keep up those contacts. Then think about ways to keep in touch with these contacts—if you read something that someone on your list would appreciate, clip it and send it.

• **Don't cut off other job prospects**. The

"I, along with some of the other employees, feel you're abusing the break room."

new job might not work out, so hedge your bets. Don't cut off all of the people with whom you have been exploring positions. Don't take yourself off the market. Instead, tell people that you are "doing work for" a certain type of company, but want to stay in touch with them. You never know. Three months into the job, you may find out that it is not a good fit or that the hiring manager misled you. Protect yourself by staying in the market until you feel you understand the situation there and are somewhat secure.

• Cultivate your relationship with your boss. If your peers, subordinates and clients all wind up loving you, but your boss does not, you will not survive. If you are senior level, you must take extra care because more will be expected of you. Between the time you accept the offer and actually start the job, work closely with your boss to develop your onboarding plan. Make sure you know what your boss expects you to get done during the first three months and beyond.

The price one pays for pursuing any profession or calling is an intimate knowledge of its ugly side.

James Baldwin, *Nobody Knows My Name*

José, an executive and Five O'Clock Club member, could not start at his new job for a number of months. He would have to sell his present home, find another one a thousand miles away, and he and his wife would have to find new schools for his children. José flew to the new organization once every few weeks. During that time:

✓ José worked with his new boss to develop an onboarding plan (of how he would learn and become integrated into the organization) and a work plan (of goals and objectives to be accomplished after he arrived). He also confirmed that he would have the resources he would need to do his job well.

✓ He intentionally forged a strong relationship with his boss.

✓ José scheduled individual as well as group meetings with his soon-to-be staff members to get feedback, iron out expectations and to make sure

they were on-board with the work plan. He also led the discussions on major projects that they were tackling.

✓ He made sure he formed relationships with his peers.

✓ To make sure he thoroughly understood who was likely to play key roles in his success, he attempted to complete the exercise in the next section, "Circles of Influence."

By the time he actually started in the new job, it felt as if he had been there quite a while and all went smoothly.

It is not the critic who counts; not the man who points out how the strong man stumbled or where the doer of deeds could have done better. The credit belongs to the man who is actually in the arena, whose face is marred by dust and sweat and blood; who strives valiantly; who errs and comes up short again and again; who knows the great enthusiasms, the great devotions; who spends himself in a worthy cause; who, at best, knows in the end the triumph of achievement, and who, at worst, if he fails, at least fails while daring greatly, so that his place shall never be with those timid souls who knew neither victory nor defeat.

Theodore Roosevelt

Right Away

• Don't fix things or do anything *big* for the first three months. That is one of the biggest mistakes people make. Take time to learn the system, the people, and the culture. You cannot possibly understand, in those first months, the implications of certain decisions you may make. You may be criticizing a project that was done by someone really important. Or you could be changing something that will affect someone on the staff in ways of which you aren't aware.

- Change agents, beware. If you were hired to make major changes, take it slowly. I worked as the Chief Operating Officer for a small company and was brought in to make major changes. When I was pressed to do things quickly, I asked: "How long has this been broken?" The CEO said, "Four years." "Then," I said, "it can wait another three months while I study the situation."
- Make yourself productive immediately. This does not contradict the point I just made. Do things that are safe. For example, install a new system where there has been none. This is *safe* because you aren't getting rid of some other system. What isn't safe? Firing half your staff the first week!
- Introduce yourself to everybody. Be visible—walk around and meet people as soon as possible, including those who work for you. Meet everybody. Too many managers meet only the *important* people while ignoring those who will actually do the day-to-day work. It may be that your best source of information — the person who will tell you the hidden landmines — is a lower-level professional or an administrative assistant. These are people who watch everything but are not caught up in the day-to-day politics. Figure out who your best sources are.
- Don't make friends too fast. Someone who befriends you right away could also be on the way out. That doesn't mean you shouldn't be friendly, however. Go to lunch with several people rather than becoming known as someone who associates only with so-and-so. Get to know everybody, and then decide with whom to get closer.
- Take over compensation of your subordinates immediately. Look at review and raise dates, and make sure no one

is overlooked. You can't afford to wait three months to get settled while one of your people is stewing about an overdue salary review.
- Get your budget—quickly. If it isn't good, build a better one. If you spend some time at the beginning trying to understand the budget, the things you hear over the next few weeks will mean more to you.
- Consider hiring an Executive Coach. Even before you smell trouble—and especially when you do, you need someone outside the organization to give you some perspective and advice. Otherwise, you are in danger of getting way off course. For 12 years, I worked with Cecilia, starting when she became the new head of marketing in a fast-growing organization. As the organization grew, she grew. We met a number of times in the very beginning of our relationship, and then once or twice a year for the next twelve years! The "Circles of Influence" exercise in the next section made it easy for her to tell me the changing situation she faced and helped me to understand and help her figure out what to do next. I became her trusted advisor whom she could turn to whenever she wanted to discuss a situation. I believe that having an Executive Coach helped her keep that important job as that turbulent organization grew. The Five O'Clock Club has an executive coach who is right for you and will help to steer you through the troubled waters that lie ahead.

....

**Try not to do anything too daring
for the first three months.
Take time to learn the system.**

....

Destiny is not a matter of chance, it is a matter of choice; it is not a thing to be waited for, it is a thing to be achieved.

William Jennings Bryan, American politician

What we anticipate seldom occurs; what we least expect generally happens.

Benjamin Disraeli, 19th century British Prime Minister

In the First Three Months

• Learn the corporate culture. People new to jobs lose those jobs often because of personality conflicts rather than a lack of competence. Keep your head low until you learn how the company operates. Some companies have certain writing styles. Some expect you to speak a certain way. In certain companies, it's the way they hold parties. Do people work with their doors open or their doors shut?

All those things are part of the culture, and they are unwritten. To learn them, you have to pay attention.

Tom, for example, lost his job because his management style rubbed everyone the wrong way. Tom was a *touchy-feely* manager who, when he wanted his employees to do things, schmoozed with them, saying things such as, "You know, I was kind of thinking about this and...." But the corporate culture was such that the employees liked and expected to be asked straight out. Tom's style made them feel patronized and manipulated. And his own staff did him in.

Pay your dues before doing things at a variance with the corporate culture. After you build up some credits, you have more leeway. Let your personality emerge when you understand the company and after you have made some contribution.

• Learn the organizational structure— the real structure, not the one that is drawn on the charts. (See the Circles of Influence exercise in the next chapter.) Ask your assistant to tell you who relates how with whom, who knows what, who thought of this project, who is important. You could be surprised.

• As far as subordinates are concerned, find out other people's opinions and then form your own. Consider that you may have a different perception because you have different values.

• Find out what is important in your job. For example, when I coach people for a corporation, coaching is not the only important thing in my job. The people who come to me are sent by human resources, and I must manage my relationship with these people. It doesn't matter how good a coach I am if I don't maintain a good relationship with human resources.

• Pay attention to your peers. Your peers can prove as valuable to you as your boss and subordinates. Do not try to impress them with your brilliance. That would be the kiss of death because you'd cause envy and have a very large reputation to live up to. Instead, encourage them to talk to you. They know more than you do. They also know your boss. Look to them to teach you and, in some cases, protect you.

Sharon, an executive, found out that her last three predecessors had been fired. She knew from talking to people that her boss was the type whose ego was bruised when someone had ideas.

He had a talent for getting rid of these people.

Pay attention to your peers. Look to them to teach you and, in some cases, protect you.

Know how to ask. There is nothing more difficult for some people. Nor for others, easier.

Baltasar Gracian, *The Art of Worldly Wisdom*

To protect herself, Sharon built relationships with her peers, the heads of offices around the country. After a year and a half, her boss' brother took her to breakfast and told her that, unlike her predecessors, she could not be fired: It would have been such an unpopular decision that it would have backfired on her boss.

• Don't set up competition. Everyone brings something to the party and should be respected for his or her talent, no matter what their level. Find ways to show your respect by asking for their input on projects that require their expertise.

• Set precedents you want to keep. If you start out working 12-hour days, people will come to expect it of you—even if no one else is doing it. When you stop, people will wonder what's wrong.

• Set modest goals for your own personal achievement and high goals for your department. Make your people look good, and you will, too.

The character of a person is formed as well as revealed by his own concept of self-interest.

John Lukacs, *A History of the Cold War*

You'll be busy in your new job and may not keep up your outside contacts. In today's economy, that's a big mistake.

Three Months and Beyond . . .

• Continue to develop contacts outside the company. If you need information for your job, sometimes the worst people to ask are your boss and the people around you. A network is also a tremendous resource to fall back on when your boss is busy—and you will seem resourceful, smart, and connected.

• Keep a hero file for yourself, a hanging file where you place written descriptions of all your successes. If you have to job hunt in a hurry, you'll be able to recall what you've done. You will also use it if you stay. If you want anything, whether it be a raise or a promotion or the responsibility for a particular project, you can use the file to build a case for yourself.

• Keep managing your career. Don't think, "I'll just take this job and do what they tell me," because you might get off on some tangent. Remember where you were heading and make sure your career keeps going that way. Be proactive in moving toward your goal. Take on lots of assignments. If a project comes up that fits into your long-term plan, do it. If one doesn't fit into your plan, you can do it or you can say, "Oh, I'd love to do that, but I'm really busy." Make those kinds of choices all the time.

*To act with confidence, one must be willing
to look ahead and consider uncertainties:
"What challenges could the world present me?
How might others respond to my actions?"
Rather than asking such questions, too many
people react to uncertainty with denial.*

Peter Schwartz, *The Art of the Long View*

Thank-You Note after Getting a Job

Anita Attridge
400 First Avenue
Dayton, Ohio 22090

May 8, 2013

Mr. Jerry Iannaccone
3450 Garden Place
Des Moines, Iowa 44466

Dear Jerry:

The happy news is that I have accepted a position at Ohio State Trust as Controller for their Ohio branches. I'll be responsible for financial reporting and analysis, loans administration, budgeting, and planning. I think it's a great match that will make good use of both my management skills and banking experience, and the environment is congenial and professional.

I really appreciated your interest in my job search. I very much enjoyed speaking with people like you about your career, and I appreciated your advice and encouragement. The fact that you so willingly gave of your time meant a great deal to me, and it certainly was beneficial.

If I can reciprocate in some way, please feel free to be in touch with me. I will also probably be in contact with you in the months ahead. My new office is at 75 Rockfast Corner, Dayton 22091. You can reach me at 200-555-1212.

Sincerely,
Anita Attridge

Chapter 3

• • • • • • •

Conducting Your Quarterly Review of Those Who Influence Your Career

by Kate Wendleton, President, The Five O'Clock Club

Woe to him that is alone when he falleth,
For he hath not another to help him up.

The Wisdom of Solomon—Apocrypha

When you are brand new in your job, this is the time to get to know the players—the real players who influence your career. They may or may not be on the formal organization chart. Some may even be clients. Give a copy of this chart to your career coach, so you two can save time when you bring up a problem and so your coach can ask you how it's going with certain people.

Every three months, review this list of your bosses, peers, subordinates (and clients). "Bosses" are people at a higher level who can influence your career. Don't go strictly by the organizational chart. "Bosses" would include your boss and your boss' boss, perhaps some of your boss' peers, and maybe even one or two people outside of your organization who are in the position of influencing your career. Remember that

"influencers" may even be in other geographic areas.

Most people have six to eight "bosses." Make a list of yours. Each quarter, go through your list and ask yourself: "What does this person think of me and what should they think of me?" If your bosses forget that you had extensive marketing experience before you took this job, you can easily remind them of this. If they have not noticed that you have been working seventy hours a week on an important project, make sure they know.

Always know your Eight-Word Message so that if you run into a boss in an elevator you can quickly slip it into the conversation, however brief it may be. You have many opportunities to communicate with people who are more senior than you, but you have to plan your communication. This is a way to manage informally the impression that senior bosses have about you. Don't let things build up until it's a major problem and you have to ask for a formal meeting. Instead, manage your internal PR as you go along:

- For bosses, ask yourself, "What do these people think of me and what should they think of me?"
- For peers, ask yourself, "What is my relationship with each of these people and what should it be?"
- Don't forget those who are lower down. Brenda, an assistant in Detroit, may try to do you in.

Now, make a list of your peers—usually 12 to 14 people who are at your level. Here again, you are not simply plucking the names from your division's organization chart. Certain peers may work right up the hall; others may be in other cities, or other departments or divisions. Review the list every quarter and ask yourself, "What is my relationship with each of them and what should it be?"

You don't have to take everyone to lunch or go out for drinks! Often, simply saying "hello" is all it takes to have a decent relationship. Or perhaps you want to ask certain people how they enjoyed the weekend, or the status of a major project. With others, you may want to exchange information about the projects you are each working on.

If your peers are out of town, you may have to pick up the phone for a brief chat. The relationship you have with your peers is critical to your success. And having a good relationship usually takes very little effort.

In addition to reviewing your relationships with your bosses and peers, also make a list of your "subordinates" (those at a lower level than you in the organization). They may include your assistant or your boss' assistant, for example. Do you treat your subordinates well? Do they complain about you to their bosses? Gee. Brenda, the boss' assistant in Detroit, may be the one who decides to try to do you in.

Also make a list of your clients—those that you service inside or outside your organization. Most people are conscious of focusing on their clients, so this may not be an issue for you. However, to be thorough, make a list of these as well, and review your list at least quarterly. In addition, when an issue comes up, just give your coach a call.

Circles of Influence

Fill in the real organization you're dealing with—not the one on the formal organization chart. These people may be in your organization, outside of it, in a different location, or even a vendor. Write each person's name in the circle. Also include the person's title, age and tenure.

Start with those above you who influence your job:

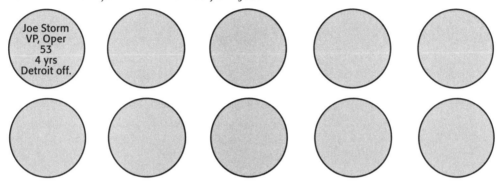

Joe Storm
VP, Oper
53
4 yrs
Detroit off.

Now, fill in peers: those who are at your level and influence your job:

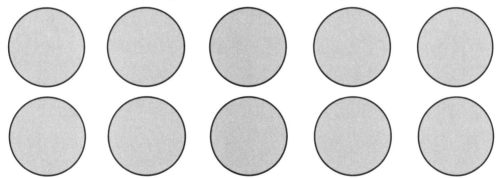

Finally, fill in those who are lower-level than you (not necessarily your direct reports):

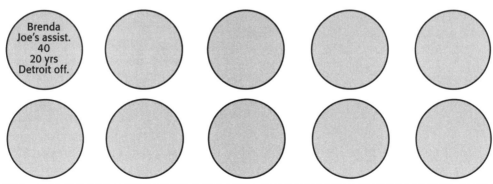

Brenda
Joe's assist.
40
20 yrs
Detroit off.

Chapter 4

• • • • • • •

Being Happy at Work: The Puritan Work Ethic and Beyond

by Richard Bayer, Ph.D., Chief Operating Officer, The Five O'Clock Club

Flourishing is the meaning and the purpose of life, the whole aim and end of human existence.

Aristotle

Philosophers and other great thinkers have always believed that there are just two major questions in ethics: "What am I to do?" and "Who am I to be?" I want to talk about the latter question here, since it is the more basic one, and it really is about our character. Certain character traits are overwhelmingly important for success in our personal lives, and in business.

We're all familiar with the Puritan work ethic, which was historically, the ethical underpinning for American life, both in the home and at work. The Puritan ethic answered the question, "Who am I to be?" with: "I am to be honest, hard working, reliable, sober, mindful of the future, appropriate in my relationships, successful, and thereby give glory to God."

Today, these character traits are usually thought about, but are only paid lip service. This is because their roots in giving glory to God are no longer as widely accepted (to put it mildly). Since many Americans have given God a back

seat, this makes it hard to instill these ideals in others, especially in the young. Without a belief in glorifying God, it's difficult to give others a reason why they should be ethical. Virtues today are like dying plants that have had their roots cut. Virtues are no longer nourished, and are even being deeply challenged, especially in our materialistic and selfish society. The Puritan virtues are dying on the vine almost everywhere—except in some small communities.

People who base their ethics on theological ideas should, of course, keep doing so. This is not to say that we should return to days when there was a greater unity in the belief about God and in business ethics. There are, however, issues of "overlapping consensus"—that is, matters in which almost all of us can agree upon what is ethical.

What this all boils down to is human dignity. Dignity in one's personal life and dignity in the workplace. Protecting and supporting human dignity is the guiding principle behind ethics for many writers, institutions (including the United Nations), philosophers, religious leaders (such as the Dalai Lama and the Pope), and theologians. So, in the 21st century, we can answer the question, "Who am I to be?" The answer is, "I am to be respectful of human dignity in all of its material, emotional, and spiritual aspects."

In the workplace, this means being cooperative, responsible, socially conscious, hard working, fair minded, and honest, so we can protect and promote human dignity. Acting this way at work doesn't solve all of our ethical work-related problems, but it's a start, and a good way to think about difficult issues. For example, when an employee is about to be terminated, the employer should be clear about what is necessary to protect the dignity and future of all parties involved. This includes other workers in the company, as well as the employee's family.

Human Dignity in the Information Age

A key to ethical behavior is the virtues to nurture shown in the table below (as well as the vices to avoid). These virtues and vices are consistent with a meaningful work-life. Like the Puritan work ethic, these virtues concern themselves with both character ethics and efficiency. They contribute to a thriving and productive work environment.

Question(s) to consider: It's often difficult to assess ourselves and our progress. Imagine a scale rating ethical behavior from 1 to 10, 10 being the most ethical. Anything above 5 is positive; anything below it is negative. As you go through the day, rate your behavior on this scale. Don't nit pick and rate every little thing, but every so often, ask yourself, How would I rate myself so far? Doing this for a week or so can give you a clearer perspective on how good/ethical you are, and how you are progressing.

A Matter of Responsibility

It is easy to dodge our responsibilities, but we cannot dodge the consequences of dodging our responsibilities.

Josiah Charles Stamp

Our age has produced two types of generally unhappy people: workaholics and those with an entitlement mentality. An exaggerated sense

Table of Virtues vs. Vices

Virtues: Consistent With The Vision	Vices: Inconsistent With The Vision
Cooperation	Excessive Competitiveness
Hard work, persistence	Entitlement mentality; Workaholic
Creative and optimistic	Zero sum mentality
Planning	Indifference and haphazard method
Regard for the welfare of others	Out-of-context behavior
Trust in the future	Siege mentality
Flexibility	Rigid, unable to cope with change
Activity based on knowledge	Disconnected activity
Sharing, generous, patient for long-run results	Closed and possessive approach. Focused on (short term) interests

of responsibility for one's future produces the workaholic; a failure of responsibility produces someone who feels a sense of entitlement. Both types can hurt an organization's culture, not to mention those in the person's personal life.

Ideally, we all should take on the appropriate amount of responsibility in regard to our jobs and personal lives. But, remember, taking on responsibility for *everything* in our lives is just too much to handle. Though it may seem strange to say this, its truth is clear when we recognize our inability to control much of what happens to us, and how paralyzing it is constantly to worry about the future (however, for those who are believers, there is solace in being in God's care). So, today, to live a happy life, anyone who is irresponsible or lazy should try to work harder and develop him/herself professionally. The reverse is true for workaholics—which means giving up some of their control. Our goal must be to stay in between these extremes—to stay at the center, to achieve a balance. (See Table below)

Social Virtue

In ancient times, land was the basis for production and economic power. To own land meant being able to meet the need for food and shelter, as well as being in power. Indeed, even today severely uneven distribution of land is still a problem in underdeveloped countries. Because

of this, many of the world's poor go without food or shelter.

In more recent times, however, capital became the basis for production and economic power. Those with it have had an advantage over labor, that is, people who have only their own labor to sell. The uneven distribution of capital remains a problem in many modern economies.

These days, we sometimes call the U.S. economy a "postmodern" one. This means that knowledge and access to it are becoming the main bases for productivity and economic power. In a real sense, we have entered a new era.

· ·

Question(s) to consider: Quickly list the ten most important things in your life, such as your job, time with your kids, keeping up with business, helping out your spouse, etc. Now, rank them and see how much time and attention you pay to each. Ask yourself: Am I living the kind of life that I want to? Am I happy? Don't spend a lot of time on this—it's just to raise your consciousness a bit.

· ·

Sharing knowledge is sharing productive capacity and power. Such sharing allows others to

Two Types of Generally Unhappy People

Two Types of Generally Unhappy People			
Type of Person	Attitude Toward the Future	Sense of Responsibility	Most Likely Long-Run Prospects
Workaholic	Fearful	Very High	Burnout
Entitlement Mentality	Reckless Indifference	Very Low	Failure
Well Adjusted Person	Confident	Strong	Sustainable progress and success

grow and advance, while those who share it also prosper. This is not only a worthy goal in human relations, but it is also a practical necessity, especially considering what's available on the Internet. Partnerships are formed—frequently without money changing hands—to share information (and access to it) to the advantage of both parties.

. . . .

Question(s) to consider: Pick a topic or skill at work. Do you give as much to others as you get? For example, someone gives you a tip on how better to make travel arrangements. When a new computer system is installed, do you tell him/her about a shortcut you have found?

. . . .

Land, labor, knowledge. Human power and prestige have been, and continue to be, tied to all of these commodities. And, still, there's the continuing need for ethical systems to promote and protect human dignity—no matter what the source of power or environment.

All human beings are born free and equal in dignity and rights. They are endowed with reason and conscience and should act towards one another in a spirit of brotherhood.

On December 10, 1948 the General Assembly of the United Nations adopted and proclaimed the Universal Declaration of Human Rights

. . . .

Group Discussion Questions:

• Discuss the Puritan work ethic. Do you agree that its virtues are "dying on the vine?"
• Do you think that centering a new work ethic around "human dignity" makes sense and that enough people would agree to this?
• Critically discuss the "new" virtues and vices for today.
• Of course, there are many types of unhappy and happy people. However, relating to work, do you agree with the "happiness" table in this chapter? Do you fit into one of the categories? Do you know others who do?

. . . .

Chapter 5

• • • • • • • •

Mirror, Mirror on the Wall: The Importance of Image

by Cynthia Strite, Certified Five O'Clock
Club Coach, with David Madison

*When you are dressed in any
particular way at all, you are
revealed rather than hidden.*

Anne Hollander, *Seeing Through Clothes*

Is there really anything more that can be said about the importance of image? Since the publication of John Molloy's book *Dress for Success* in 1961, we all get the concept—don't we? Certainly that three-word title has become part of our business lexicon, and has even become a cliché. Who doesn't know, for example, to dress up for an interview?

But we have decided to say something about image for three compelling reasons:

Believe it or not, some people didn't get the message—at least it didn't sink in as well as it should have. We do have to keep talking about it.

Some people resent and resist the message; they actually put up a fight at the thought of conforming to a certain image, since image is a 'superficial' concern. However noble such a sentiment may be, these folks have failed to come

to terms with the real world—the real *business* world, and the importance of image. The truth is that image counts—in all areas of life. Why wouldn't it count at work? In other words, to put it bluntly, they're wrong.

And finally, there's far more to dressing for success than having the right clothes. We also need to talk about the behavior and demeanor required to match the outfit, i.e., it's vital to dress up the way you present yourself in all aspects. Whether you are a man or a woman, the total package you present to the world matters.

• •

**Image counts—in all areas of life.
Why wouldn't it count at work?**

• •

Let's take a brief look at these three realities—and then move on to talk about guidelines and suggestions.

1. Missing the Message: What Can I Get Away With?

When we coach people at The Five O'Clock Club to get ready for interviews, we say, "It's show time!" That is, when you walk in for the interview, you will actually be on stage—so you want everything to be just right. But guess what: every day that you go to work, every time you attend a meeting—even outside of work—where you'll be mixing with colleagues in your industry, it's show time.

And from my experience, plenty of people have missed the message that success hinges on dress and presentation, no matter where you are. This was demonstrated one evening at The Five O'Clock Club when three successful job hunters came back to report. While all of their stories provided insights on proper job search, their *appearances* illustrated how different people relate to the world—and how some people fail to get basic messages.

The first person was "buttoned up" in all respects; he wore a suit, crisp shirt and tie—everything was in place. He looked professional in all respects.

The second person's presentation was borderline. She was definitely not dressed in a very professional manner; rather, she looked more like what she would wear on casual Friday.

The third person was a disaster. His hair looked like he had just crawled out of bed, he had not shaved, he had on a rumpled, un-ironed t-shirt, and his pants were baggy and unkempt. While he apologized for his appearance, he had known he was going to be in front of an audience that night—it was literally show time—so I was mystified why he had not bothered to look better. Furthermore, he was reporting on landing a consulting position—so he planned to continue his job search. Anyone in The Five O'Clock Club audience that night could have been a potential source for referrals. I would imagine folks would be reluctant to refer him for informational meetings given how he looked. I know I would have

hesitated. This job hunter hadn't really internalized the message about dressing for success. I am hopeful that he knew enough to clean up for interviews, but he failed to understand that, in a sense, you're *always* being interviewed—especially in a setting like The Five O'Clock Club where people are keen to offer help.

There aren't too many places where you can let down your guard and the office is certainly not one of them. Should you dress every day the way you would for an interview? Not necessarily, but that doesn't mean that dress codes do not apply. We all know those who follow the *letter* of the dress code, but not the spirit. They follow the dress code, but still manage to look sloppy or frayed around the edges. They send the message, "I really don't care," but the truth of dress for success is that bosses and managers are always looking for the people who do care. Is there ever an excuse not to look your best within the guidelines of the dress code?

....

Every day that you go to work, every time you attend a meeting, it's show time.

....

2. Rejecting the Message: Appreciate My Skills, Not My Appearance

In addition to those who do know the importance of image—but just try to get away with too much—there are those who simply resist the whole idea of paying attention to image. They resent that something as "shallow and superficial" as external appearance should count for so much. In fact, we hear moral indignation from these folks: "With all that's wrong with this world, with all the misplaced emphasis on glamour and beauty, the workplace should be exempt from such standards." We also hear: "Why should we care all that much about how people dress? Please reward me on my accomplishments, my GPA, my MBA, my IQ, my EQ—not on what I wear."

There would be no problem with this idealistic approach if everyone agreed that image is unimportant—and if the universal human inclination to evaluate people on how they look could be erased. For better or worse, we do size people up based on what meets the eye. As a species we always have done this, and we always will. Taking pride in appearance was not invented for the office! It's hard to argue that the workplace can be a free-for-all, and we can be sure that the emphasis on image is here to stay. In truth, dress is a gauge of self-esteem and respect for the surroundings. For example, in the overwhelming majority of circumstances, potential clients will feel disrespected if a salesperson shows up looking sloppy or dressed inappropriately for the role.

The argument that image guidelines for work violate individuality doesn't hold water either. Even in the most casual environments, certain standards always apply. And most of us, when we walk into our offices, give up certain freedoms as part of the deal—and may not even think very much about the fact that we do. The language, vocabulary, posture and pastimes that we freely indulge in at home are simply not allowed at the office—any more than we can bring our pet boa to work. And, generally speaking, if we've signed on for an eight-hour day, even our freedom to come and go without accountability is limited. We're employees—we really can't "do as we please" on someone else's time and turf. Hence, expectations and standards concerning dress cannot usually be construed as violations of individuality. The reality remains: The tendency to judge people on how well they dress and act will continue to impact promotion decisions.

. . . .

Dress is a gauge of self-esteem and respect for the surroundings.

. . . .

3. The Full Scope of the Message: It's About More Than Clothes

Look around you at work….consider your closest colleagues, your boss, your boss' boss: How would you sum up each one of these individuals in just a few words? You can be sure that they all do the same with you. The way people describe you is based on your dress and speech, your demeanor, your way of relating to others, your moods, your sense of humor or lack of it. Dress is absolutely part of the equation, but be aware that your image, and your chances for success, are based on far more than the clothes you wear. It doesn't do much good to dress well—but then have people grumble about you behind your back.

I have found it helpful in working with executives to speak about *personal branding*: the total package that you present for others to see. This is not about becoming a famous brand name, e.g., Martha Stewart, Howard Stern (all of whom work hard to define their brands), but about establishing your over-all image in the context that most matters to you. What message does your personal brand send out to the world? When the people around you think of you, what *do* they think? Chances are, these are the people who can influence your career the most. It is largely up to you to determine how the world perceives you. You are responsible for your brand's total marketing package.

What is at stake, after all? When we coach those who are in search of new jobs or careers, we stress the importance of outclassing the competition. When you get the offer and start a new job, you've won the race—you've outclassed the competition. But once you're on the job, you're in another kind of race. The focus shifts to managing your career astutely and advancing according to plan, which also require outclassing the competition. Image should remain a primary concern—every day on the job.

So just what are the components of image? What's the total package that we need to be aware of? In the seminars and workshops that I give on this topic, I explain to executives that they need to concentrate on the three "V's."

....

The language, vocabulary, posture and pastimes that we freely indulge in at home are simply not allowed at the office.

....

The First Image Component: Visual Appearance

When people address the issue of image, the question that comes to mind immediately is *what do you look like?*—a major component of which is *what are you wearing?* Hence clothing is a primary factor. Of course the fundamental role of clothing—starting presumably long ago with the fig leaf or the loincloth—has been to *hide* our bodies. But I began this chapter with the observation by Anne Hollander (in her book, *Seeing Through Clothes*) because of the paradoxical nature of clothing: "When you are dressed in any particular way at all, you are revealed rather than hidden." One interpretation of Ms. Hollander's message is that *we have control over much of what is revealed.*

The bad news about image and appearance is that there are some things over which we have little or no control, e.g., height, bone structure, eye color, the color of our skin. However, the good news is that there is much that we can control: weight, hair color and style, grooming in general, and, of course, what we choose to put on our bodies. But the elements that are under our control go even beyond these: what about posture, attitude, demeanor, mood, eye contact? Without a word being spoken, we give impressions to others. How many times have you described someone as "having a great upbeat attitude" or, conversely, "she always look down and depressed."

Social psychologists who have studied the dynamics of first encounters have found that it takes just about 30 seconds for people to *form impressions based mainly on what they see:* these impressions run the spectrum from social and economic status to education, occupation, marital status, ancestry, trustworthiness, credibility and potential for success. Most of these impressions, of course, are based on how you look and how you act.

Job applicants *can* essentially destroy their chances of being hired by doing poorly on a first interview: they don't get called back. They can destroy their chances by showing up in wildly inappropriate dress—or lack of dress. For example, I found quick consensus among my colleagues after we had interviewed a candidate who appeared with a bare midriff—complete with navel jewelry. Did we really want to start from scratch educating her about how to dress for an interview with a Fortune 500 company or what it means to work in a professional setting? No, we did not.

If the visual impression that you make is positive, people will assume that other things about you are positive as well. Psychologists call this the "halo" effect. If the visual message is negative, however, people may promptly lose interest, and may not make the effort to discover the talents and virtues that lie beneath the not-so-impressive exterior.

....

Once you're on the job, you're in another kind of race. The focus shifts to managing your career astutely.

....

As far as the dress component of image is concerned, there are several initial suggestions:

- **Be observant:** Make an effort to tune in and notice things you have previously overlooked. How do the people one or two levels above you dress? What is the standard of dress and grooming for those who have more power and responsibility than you do? You may see immediately that there is room for improvement in your personal style and presentation.

- **Ask for advice and feedback**. Your spouse, partner or best friend may or may not be sources of constructive criticism, but it doesn't hurt to start with them. However, since the stakes are pretty high, why not pay for a session with an image coach? You'll get an objective evaluation of the *brand* you're projecting every day in your professional environment—and whether you're helping or hurting yourself. You may leave the session with a list of minor and major changes to make with respect to clothing, hair style and grooming.

- **Upgrade your wardrobe**. *This absolutely does not mean* spending large sums on designer labels. Look for bargains and shop smartly. You can get great style without spending a fortune. Savvy shoppers no longer exclusively shop in upscale stores. "Mastige" (a new word blending "mass" and "prestige") has become the name of the game: searching out the best value and the best look, no matter where. Regular customers of upscale stores like Saks Fifth Avenue are now seen walking the isles of WalMart and Target. We have heard of bargain hunters finding great clothes as well in thrift shops and on eBay. If you hate to shop or do not feel confident in selecting new clothes, seek help. One Five O'Clock Clubber adopted a truly strategic approach to changing his image: he signed up for a weight loss plan and hired a personal shopper to help him select his new wardrobe.

- **Pay attention to the details**. Little things can ruin an otherwise great presentation. How long has it been since you've had your shoes shined? Are your nails clean and manicured? The little touches can make a big difference. A woman who interviewed with one of my colleagues was eliminated from the competition for several reasons, including the fact that her fingernails were dirty!

- **Remember that "casual Friday" doesn't mean sloppy Friday**. How many employers have come to regret dress-down days?—because too many people think that dress down means anything-goes. Just remember that every day when you go to work, it's show time. So be sure that your casual always translates to looking your best.

If the visual impression that you make is positive, people will assume that other things about you are positive as well.

The Second Image Component: Verbal Skills

The main plot line of *My Fair Lady* is the long hard struggle of Professor Higgins to transform the cockney flower-seller Eliza Doolittle into a lady who can be presented in society. It turns out that dressing her up to look like a lady isn't even half the battle. Higgins' primary challenge is to get Eliza to speak English properly—and the project took many months. Eliza was ready for the embassy ball when the words that came out of her mouth matched her elegant gown. The lesson here: it won't do much good to show up at work every day looking like a million dollars, but not be able to speak and act like you belong in the board room.

There are many elements involved in achieving excellence in the way you express yourself: tone of voice, enunciation, vocabulary and word choice, powers of description, animation. Absolutely fundamental, of course, is the mastery of grammar. When a boss hears Daniel, one of her best employees, say, "Me and Tom finished that project last night," she knows that there are gaps in Daniel's mastery of English. Would she have confidence promoting Daniel to represent the company? Of course, depending on the industry or profession, such grammatical errors may be of no concern. But in some contexts the use of proper grammar is vital. The problem, of course, is that Daniel doesn't know that his English is flawed, and most people won't say anything. If you suspect that your usage of the English language isn't all that it should be, hire a tutor, take a course, or get a copy of *English Grammar for Dummies*. Decisions on promotions or coveted assignments may very well be based on such details, which are, in fact, part of your presentation.

However, a grammar book might not address all potential verbal issues. While in the last decade or so the use of the word "like" as a filler word has become popular among younger generations, other words such as "you know" and "basically" also detract from a professional image. Your image will take a serious hit if you pepper your conversation with "like," "you know," and "basically." I recently overheard a conversation that illustrates the point; this was a well-dressed junior executive speaking: "Robert was like you know really upset when he found out that report wasn't done on time. He was like shouting at all of us. I was like this is really not happening. He even like asked the manager to come to the staff meeting. It was like really embarrassing." You might not even notice that you're speaking this way—but others may, especially in professional environments. Recently a client, who is a vice-president in the advertising industry, told me—as we were discussing image and presentation—that a close colleague pointed out that she used "like" too much and it made her sound immature. These filler words will never serve you well, so you are smart to concentrate on eliminating them from your vocabulary.

Notice how the people one or two levels above you dress.

Regrettably, some accents can also detract from one's presentation. Regional or foreign accents might be a problem for some roles and in some industries. If you suspect your accent may be holding you back, look into an accent reduction course. This is not a matter of giving in to regional or ethnic biases; it's a matter of becoming the best possible communicator. In the 1988 film, *Working Girl*, which is a modern variation on the *My Fair Lady* tale, Melanie Griffith's image transformation—from secretary to corporate professional—included hiring a speech coach to rid herself of an accent that would not serve her well as she climbed the corporate ladder.

And what can be said about cell phone etiquette? This certainly falls into the category how you speak. You can speak very softly into a cell phone and the person on the other end will hear you. Most of us do business by cell phone—in the company of colleagues, and commonly in the company of many others as well. Chances are, some may question your judgment if you speak so loudly about company business that half the people in the commuter train can hear you. Your image as a professional is diminished if you disregard proper cell phone etiquette.

"Casual Friday" doesn't mean sloppy Friday.

The Third Image Component: Visual Aids, the Documents that Support Your "Brand"

We all know the horror of discovering an error on our résumé—after 25 copies have gone out. We know there's little chance that any of those résumés will result in interviews—so we kick ourselves for being so careless. Yes, we made a mistake, but it's important to realize that this is actually an image issue. *Every document that leaves your desk represents you and your brand.* People draw conclusions about you—and the quality of your work—from the documents that you produce. It's up to you to set the standards and tone for the materials that leave your office. They speak volumes about how you do business.

We have all seen PowerPoint presentations that are an embarrassment because of misspellings and egregious grammatical errors; or so much information is crammed onto each slide that the message is dense and unintelligible. The presenter is demonstrating carelessness or incompetence to 50 or 100 people at once! How could this not be an image issue? So give your presentations a test run with trusted colleagues; ask for suggestions and corrections. Be vigilant in proofing all written presentations for which you are ultimately accountable.

Email is another source of potential misrepresentation of your brand. We love email and cannot live without it, but because of the speed of this modern medium, it is so easy to make presentation mistakes. By quickly hitting the send button, too often emails inadvertently are sent to the wrong people, sometimes with disastrous or embarrassing results. Or they convey the wrong tone. Taking time to read messages several times—and reflect on how they'll be perceived—is vital. Because they are too hastily done, email messages are often misconstrued and perceived to be negative, when, in fact, that was not the intention of the sender. It's a good idea to be overly cautious to insure that you are conveying the proper tone; this is a key to effective email communication.

While we tend to be somewhat more forgiving of typographical, spelling and grammatical errors in emails—given the speed with which they are written and sent—if you want to continue to set yourself apart from the competition and present your best possible image to the

world, take time to make sure your emails are error-free.

Producing great documents rests ultimately, of course, on your skills as a writer; many careers have stalled because of the failure to write well. It takes a lot of reading, hard work and focus to learn how to write well for business. If you need help, get it. There are lots of resources to draw upon: Hire a tutor, take courses or read books. A place to start is *The Complete Idiot's Guide to Writing Well* or *Grammar Essentials for Dummies.*

....

Your image as a professional is diminished if you disregard proper cell phone etiquette.

....

A Final Thought on Image

So, these are the three "V's". There's a lot to pay attention to. You may have your work cut out for you in terms of polishing your image. Of course, it can be argued that there are much more important things to worry about in this world than good grammar, shined shoes and manicured nails. But one could just as easily argue that it's a waste of time to keep the house clean or paint the shutters every few years. The truth is we all devote a lot of time and energy to our own personal needs and making things better in our daily lives.

And most of us have a vision of how we'd like to have our lives play out. At The Five O'Clock Club we urge people to have a Fifteen- or Forty-Year Vision, depending on your age and where you are in your career. If a significant part of your vision involves career, then a certain amount of planning is usually required. Having things go your way usually depends on making the right choices at crucial times—and by *looking and acting the part.* You may still find yourself arguing that image is a superficial concern. But whether we like it or not, how we look and act is part of how we are judged by others. They are watching, and in business it is part of the game. It is your choice to play the game or not, to be concerned about your brand or not. It's always show time. Shakespeare's words apply to the business game: "All the world's a stage, and all the men and women merely players; they have their entrances and exits and each in his time plays many parts…" Will you be ready when the curtain goes up? You never know when you will be influencing the influencers.

Achieving your Forty-Year Vision may not depend on being the most beautiful, but I guarantee this: How you choose to look and present to the world will definitely have an impact on being selected for the roles you choose as you go forward.

Clothes and manners do not make the man; but when he is made, they greatly improve his appearance.

Arthur Ashe, tennis champion

Part Two

Managing Relationships at Work

Chapter 6

• • • • • • • •

Handling Conflict at Work

by Nancy Deering, Certified Five O'Clock Club Coach

It is not stress that kills us. It is effective adaptation to stress that allows us to live.

George Vaillant, psychiatrist

At the core of all anger is a need that is not being fulfilled.

Marshall B. Rosenberg, American psychologist

In Greek the word *utopia* literally means *no place*. For us it means paradise, a place of bliss and peace, but the irony was probably intended: *there is no place* without worries, problems and conflict.

So, in this life no one has discovered or established utopia. Escaping conflict is not an option. We have all experienced conflict at home, indeed from the earliest age. We've faced it on the playground and in sports. Even when you go to the movies, conflict is always there: especially in films such as *Twelve Angry Men* and *The Contender*, but even in *Snow White and the Seven Dwarves* and *Cinderella*! Hence, you've probably heard this wise counsel many times: "The issue is not whether or not you will encounter conflict, but how you will deal with it."

Each one of us could probably write a book about conflict *at work*. Since we spend many hours each day in the workplace, and since our livelihoods depend on surviving on the job and working well with others, it is imperative that we learn to deal with conflict in the workplace. A lot of people hate their jobs because conflict is not acknowledged and dealt with. They don't hate what they do: they hate the stress, the emotional tug of war.

It is almost a foregone conclusion that conflict will ensue when two or more people with opposing opinions are unable to find middle ground. And needless to say, when people operate with intent to deceive, conflict can be taken to whole new level. But when conflict is managed effectively, it can provide valuable lessons.

So How Do We Manage Conflict? Where Do We Begin?

The first step is to assess the situation as objectively as possible, so that you can position yourself to communicate from a position of awareness. It is important that everyone's position and *stake* be understood as clearly as possible: (1) Person A has an opinion and a vested interest, (2) Person B has an opinion and vested interest, but there is (3) that place in the middle that represents an agreed-upon solution.

One of my clients, Timothy, is a senior learning and development professional, responsible for identifying and placing administrative managers; he ended up putting himself in an uncomfortable situation. His role was to review the job requirements and compare the skills, experiences and relocation preferences of qualified candidates. New to his position, he was eager to impress, and wasted no time finding and contacting the individual whom he thought was the ideal candidate, Connie, an administrative manager with more than 10 years of experience. Connie was ready and willing to relocate to Atlanta, even if it resulted in settling for a lower salary. But after Timothy had recommended Connie for the position, he discovered that Connie had been in her current position for only six months. He informed her that she was not eligible for the Atlanta transfer, because of her length of service. He thought that his call to Connie to inform her of this had ended on a positive note. That was the end of the story for Timothy, or at least so he thought.

A few days later Timothy got a call from a senior branch manager who had been on the team that hired him. Getting on this manager's good side would do wonders for his career, but disappointing him could mean exactly the opposite. This is how the conversation unfolded:

Timothy: "Hello Mr. …"

Branch Manager: "Are you the person who called a member of my management team about a position in Atlanta?"

Timothy: "Yes, but the position has since been filled. What else can I help you with sir?"

Branch Manager: "You can help me by not interrupting me again. You called a member of my team about another position without my knowledge or consent?"

Timothy: "Yes but…"

Branch Manager: "And, did I just hear you say that the position has been filled?"

Timothy: "Yes, but I…"

Branch Manager: "Let me see if I've got this straight. You contacted a manager of my management team to discuss a position in a location that she has been wanting for years. And, to add insult to injury, it's no longer available. Is that about right, Timothy?"

Timothy: "Yes, but…"

Branch Manager: "Young man, you need to consider a new line of work. Your actions are inexcusable. I don't think you are cut out for this type of work. And truth be told, you were not my choice. When you and I are done, I'm going to have a conversation with your manager. He needs to know what a debacle you just made."

Timothy: (Hoping to ease the tension, but his attempt at humor failed miserably). "I beg your pardon. The last time I checked, I believe I am older than you are. Didn't your mother tell you to respect your elders?"

Branch Manager: "What is your name again?"

Timothy: "You don't remember me. I am Timothy, the newest member of Phil's team and I really don't feel there is cause for your condescending tone. I don't understand why you are raking me over the coals, especially since I was trying to do what's right for the firm. I would think you would be pleased that someone would consider Connie for the position in Atlanta because she is a reflection on you."

Branch Manager: "And you would be wrong. That's your problem young man. You didn't think. You don't have to like my tone, but if you want to stay in your role, you'd be careful how you speak to me. Do you understand?"

Timothy: "Is there anything I can do to make this situation better?"

Branch Manager: "I didn't get this far in my career by not knowing how to deal with these types of situations. I think I have enough experience to clean up your mess. You've already done enough."

As you can imagine, Timothy could not believe what just happened to him. He replayed the conversation in his mind over and over, and each time came to the same conclusion: he had done everything he was hired to do. He was upset because the branch manager questioned his integrity and qualifications, and would possibly derail his career. From his perspective, he felt he had found the ideal candidate with the perfect background and skills—and one who would jump at the opportunity to relocate.

What went wrong here?

As I reviewed this episode with Timothy, he was sure that he knew that the branch manager had been wrong. I could see that the incident consumed him, and he rattled off the mistakes the manager had made:

Branch Manager's Contributions

1. Decided that Timothy was wrong before he made the call.
2. Was inappropriately condescending.
3. Interrupted more than once.
4. Questioned his qualifications and threatened his job.
5. Did not respect him.
6. Used fear and intimidation as weapons; threatened to call his manager.
7. Did not give him credit for doing any part of his job well.
8. Refused to accept his offer to assist.

Timothy was convinced he was not a contributor to the confrontation, and he did not deserve any of the blame. He stressed that he would have not changed a thing if he had to do it over. I then asked if he could have acquired more information about Connie's profile from HR or another source—before telling her about the Atlanta position. And wouldn't it have been politically correct and strategically wise to get approval first from the branch manager—before contacting Connie? I could see the light bulb

come on as he experienced a major break-through. He hadn't been an innocent bystander: he had been a major player in a stressful episode.

Timothy's Contributions to the Crisis

1. Did not contact the branch manager or the regional administrative manager (RAM) prior to contacting Connie.
2. Word choice and tone may have been inappropriate.
3. Assumed a defensive posture and lost control of the conversation.
4. Should not have attempted humor.
5. Took it personally and internalized the conversation.
6. Presumed the branch manager was calling him to welcome him to his new role.

Timothy finally admitted that he had made some big mistakes, but he continued to believe that he was less wrong than the branch manager. It wasn't until we reviewed how the situation had unfolded that he began to see how both parties had contributed to the escalation.

Shared Contributions

1. Use of inappropriate tone.
2. Decided the other was to blame.
3. Inability or unwillingness to understand the other's perspective.
4. Branch manager had adopted the role of the bully, while Timothy was defensive.

I reminded Timothy that the only thing we have complete control over is our behavior. Conflict, whether handled effectively or poorly, can be life altering, and can provide an indelible lesson for life. And this was the case with Timothy. If he had taken a moment to make one call, he could have ruled Connie out as a viable candidate and the ensuing conversation with the branch manager may have never taken place, or it would have been a very different exchange.

Timothy's Life Lessons

1. Always do your research before diving head first into a situation.
2. It's okay to admit that you were wrong.
3. When you discover that you are wrong, apologize sooner rather than later.
4. Accept responsibility for your actions.
5. Well-intended humor is not always appropriate.
6. The best strategy in a tense situation is to stop, listen and learn before responding.
7. Avoid jumping to conclusions before having all of the information.
8. Don't assume you know why someone is contacting you.
9. Mistakes can be corrected.

Timothy had no problems in apologizing to the branch manager and planned to do so. But he also understood the importance of time and distance. So upon realizing the significance of his contribution, he chose to contact the RAM to give him a heads-up. He apologized for not connecting with him prior to or after the conversation with Connie. He then detailed his interaction with the branch manager. Timothy explained that he offered assistance, but the branch manager refused. The RAM did not like the way things had unfolded. He gave Timothy some feedback, sighed heavily and thanked him for the call.

Although the first call was to the RAM, it was still not easy to do it, but Timothy knew that it was the right thing to do. He felt a sense of relief and new-found confidence.

Tips for Handling Conflict

- Assess the situation and identify your contribution.
- Don't exacerbate the situation by letting the other person control how you respond to conflict.
- Confront with courage from a position of knowledge. This can take the form of knowing when to admit you are wrong and extending an earnest apology.
- Knowing when to walk away can be the best strategy.
- Know your triggers.

Pitfalls That Contribute to Conflict:

- Talking more than you listen: "Take the cotton out of your ears and put it your mouth. You need to listen more and talk less."
- Interrupting is rude, disrespectful and contributes to negative energy.
- Having a defensive posture can prevent the other person from wanting to work through the issue.
- Failing to admit your contribution to the problem.

At the end of the day, don't run from conflict. Position yourself for success; always take a moment to reflect before you respond and when in doubt, close your mouth.

Which hurts the most, saying something and wishing you had not, or saying nothing and wishing you had?

Javan, American poet

Chapter 7

• • • • • • • •

How to Manage Your Boss

by Susan Bloch, Certified Five O'Clock Club Coach

If you think your boss is stupid, remember: you wouldn't have a job if he was any smarter.

John Gotti, American mobster

What comes to mind when you hear the term *"managing your boss?"* Does it conjure up thoughts like "tell the boss what to do," "keep the boss happy," or "keep the boss out of my hair?" These could all be true—depending on you, the boss and the situation. There is a lot to gain from having the ability to manage your boss and definitely a lot to lose if you don't.

We all come to work with different sets of experiences, skills, behaviors and values that often cause friction in the workplace. The skill of *managing up* enables you to work with your boss' style by focusing on your shared goals and the results you are both trying to achieve.

A good boss can motivate you to perform, improve your work-life and job satisfaction and help you advance in your career. To have this kind of relationship takes effective communication and attention. For example, knowing when to interrupt or disagree with your boss is a skill that savvy employees need to develop. This

kind of attention can also help you avoid those irritating behaviors that rub the boss the wrong way and cause you to fall out of favor. Without properly managing your relationship with your boss, you put your professional development and success at risk.

Below is an example of what can happen when a relationship is not properly managed.

Case Study: Sam New Hire Style Clash

When Sam interviewed with the team, it was clear to him that Don, the hiring manager, had a very different work style and it could be a challenge working for him. Don required a lot of information to make a decision. He liked to ponder ideas out loud and usually he got side-tracked and went off on tangents. He was a loner and didn't like spending much time with others. Sam, on the other hand, liked to look at the facts, make a decision and move forward. He also valued building relationships; people, not information, were the most important resource for Sam.

Sam quickly tired of Don's endless demands for more information. He'd tell Don he'd get back to him but then get busy with something else and not follow through. After a few months, Sam noticed that he and Don weren't communicating very much. He was actually happy about that since talking to Don could get tiring. Sam felt he was doing a good job; he was working hard building relationships and people really seemed to like him. Sam thought things were going well.

When it came time for Sam's 90-day review, he was shocked to hear that his performance was not satisfactory. Don went on and on about the reports Sam had neglected to turn in and his lack of attention to detail. Don suggested that perhaps Sam should think about looking for a different position since this didn't seem like a good fit.

Where did Sam go wrong?

Although Sam picked up quickly that his style was very different from his boss', he never focused on what he could do to bridge that gap. Instead of trying to manage the situation, Sam ignored it, resulting in serious consequences for his future at that company and perhaps even his career.

Sam's situation is an example of what can happen when you don't manage the relationship between yourself and your boss. Ignoring your boss' style or his priorities is never a good strategy for success. Sam knew from the beginning that Don was detail oriented and deadlines were important to him. Instead of adjusting his own work style, Sam decided to work around Don and try to be successful by demonstrating his strengths. Sam missed an important first step when starting a new job: understand the value of your relationship with your boss.

In this chapter we will consider several topics: understanding who you are, where you are in your career and how you can develop in your career. We'll provide some tools to help you understand your boss and guidance on how to deal with difficult situations. We'll close with some important tips to help you build a more effective relationship with your boss.

Understanding Yourself

You have a mutual dependence with your boss. You depend on your boss for direction, feedback and support while your boss depends on you for new ideas, hard work and cooperation. You both have needs and both benefit from working together. So start building a strong relationship with your boss by developing a good understanding of yourself. What gives you job satisfaction? What upsets you? Are you an extrovert or an introvert? Are you detail oriented? Understanding yourself will give you a major advantage.

To do this you need to collect some data. Many organizations have made it a customary practice to ask managers to participate in a process called 360-degree feedback. This process starts with you identifying a small number of people in all areas of your work-life (hence the 360 title) and asking them to complete a confidential survey about you that is sent to a third party for tabulation. You select a group of your direct reports, your boss and perhaps his or her boss, peers and sometimes customers. The survey provides information about you in a number of areas including communication, management style, leadership skills and technical knowledge. The results can be a real eye opener. You will learn what people at all levels experience in working with you.

If you don't have the luxury of participating in 360-degree feedback, think about creating your own tool to get the information. Depending on your work relationships, you might be able to set up a series of meetings and have a serious discussion with selected staff to learn about yourself.

Talk with your peers. You can put together a short list of important questions and, for the price of a cup of coffee, you should be able to get some valuable feedback. Questions that provide good insight include:

- "In working with me, what do you see as my three top strengths?"
- "If you were putting together a work team, can you think of an area where I would add value?"
- "If I wanted to improve one aspect of my communication skills, what should it be?"

These questions are specifically worded so they encourage the recipient to share information. People will usually provide feedback if they see that you are open to hearing it and are sincerely interested in making changes.

You could also contact your Human Resource Department to see what they offer or suggest. Many companies provide training and professional development. Classes are offered internally or through a variety of outside organizations, so it should not be hard to find something that gives you an opportunity to develop your self-awareness and receive feedback. It doesn't matter how you get the information to build your self-awareness *but it does matter that you get it*.

Case Study: Michael
Finding Ways to Get Feedback

Michael was feeling frustrated. He'd been in his new Senior Manager position for a year and he had no idea if he was doing well and if his boss, Sally, was satisfied with his performance. She was always so busy that it was hard to get business questions answered, let alone receive any performance feedback. He knew Sally was uncomfortable with any type of confrontation, so asking her point blank, "How am I performing?" would be too threatening.

On a day when he was feeling particularly isolated, Michael stepped into John's office and asked his colleague, "Do you ever wonder how you are performing in this job?" John, also a Senior Manager reporting to Sally, smiled broadly and said, "Yes, I wonder about it but I don't have a clue how to get Sally to take the time to give me feedback." As they talked, they realized that it would be very helpful to get some performance feedback so they could work on any deficiencies that emerged. Michael and John decided to write down a list of questions they'd like answered by their boss. Then they constructed a conversation that was very developmentally focused and non-threatening. They identified a more senior-level position in the organization that they would like to grow into and wanted to know what skills they needed to develop to be successful in that position. Michael thanked John for his time and went back to his office feeling reenergized and focused.

Later that week, Michael looked for an opportunity to catch Sally at a time that she was relaxed and available. He got his opportunity on Friday when they were both walking back from a meeting. Michael told Sally he was thinking about the future and shared that, at some point, he would really like to move into the director role in the Marketing Department. He asked Sally what she knew about the role and what skills he would need to develop to get there. She gave him a lot of information on what that role involved and provided feedback about his strengths and how she thought he would be a really good fit for that role. In a casual hallway meeting, Michael got the feedback he wanted on his performance and skills.

This case study is one example of how you can manage your boss. Unfortunately, it is rare to find a boss who takes the time to give performance feedback unless it is time for an annual review. *Taking responsibility to get this information becomes part of your job.*

Once you have information on your strengths and areas that need development, the next step is deciding what you want to do about it. If you go through a formal 360-review process, you'll most likely work with a consultant or coach to review the feedback and develop an action plan. If you are working on this process independently, there are many resources available including management development courses offered through universities or local business training centers. Hiring a management coach is very common today and this can be a great help in developing skills. Some organizations provide mentors to junior or mid-level employees. This can be a great resource since your mentor will know both you and the organization. You can get feedback on your skills, learn more about your organization and be introduced to contacts that can help in your career development.

The actions you take will vary, depending on the particular skill or behavior that you are trying to develop. For example, if you are weak in a technical skill like accounting, you could enroll in a class. If you are described as a micro-manager, however, you'll need an action plan that includes more than a training class. Talk to your Human Resource Department or other managers that you respect to get suggestions on resources.

What You Need from Your Boss

The type of support you require from your boss will vary with your own experience level and where you are in your career. For example, when you are just out of school or new to a profession, you require a certain amount of attention and direction from your boss. As you gain experience, your needs change. Some bosses recognize this, but not always. You need to take responsibility to get what you need and get rid of what you don't need. Below are three scenarios describing tips and strategies for getting what you need at various stages in your professional development.

Professional Development Level I Strategies

If you are in the beginning of your career, the best boss for you is one who acts as a mentor or coach. It would be very helpful to have someone who would give you feedback on your strengths and areas needing development and who would encourage you and motivate you to do your best. *How do you turn your boss into this kind of person?* Here are some steps you can take:

1. Ask for a regular meeting for which the agenda is simply, "Tell me how I'm doing and what you'd like to see me work on." During your first year on the job, this should be held once a month. After that, it can be held once a quarter. It doesn't matter if it's a casual lunch meeting or a more formal gathering in the office at 3 p.m. If your boss is not comfortable with giving feedback, you should prepare a list of questions that will get you what you need. For example, "How did I do on the presentation last month? Please tell me two things that went well and two areas that could be improved." "What did you like about my sales presentation? How could I improve it?"

2. Establish quarterly or semi-annual goals and give them to your boss. Make sure that you are both setting the same priorities for your work.

3. Find a way to share your career goals with your boss. Make sure he knows where you'd like to be in two years, what skills you'd like to develop and what future education you are interested in. At a minimum, you should have this conversation on an annual basis.

Professional Development Level II Strategies

By this level you probably don't need or want a lot of managing from your boss. You bring the knowledge and skills to do the job, so what you really need is a good understanding of the direction the company is going and the priorities of your position. To be successful, it is critical that your boss clearly articulates his expectations and that you clearly understand them. In addition, you need to understand your department's priorities and how you can help pitch in when needed. Steps to managing your boss at this level include:

1. Ask to be included in appropriate business meetings.
2. Look for ways you can support teammates.
3. Take a leadership role when possible.
4. When you present your boss with a problem, try to offer a solution.
5. Get on your boss' calendar once a quarter to review priorities and get feedback on how you are performing.

Professional Development Level III Strategies

Once you reach a certain level of expertise, your needs in a boss become very different from what you wanted at the beginning of your career. At this point, your boss is there as a sounding board, that is, someone to share ideas with, discuss strategies and define priorities.

Steps to managing your boss at this level include:

1. Set up a regular meeting schedule, at a frequency that supports enough communication so priorities are always clear.
2. Make it your business to understand what your boss is working on and how you can be of support.
3. On an annual basis, ask for feedback on your behaviors and identify what skills you need to develop. *Understand what it would take for you to replace your boss.*

Developmental Needs: How to Grow your Career

One area that seems to always get lost in the workplace is employee training and development. Smart companies have long realized that a key factor in retaining good employees is the ability to offer career growth opportunities. Unfortunately, most companies do not take the time to focus on this, so it becomes an area where *you must take responsibility to make things happen.*

Identify your developmental needs, clarify your career goals and communicate them to your boss. Think about the future and picture what you'd like to be doing three years from now. What skills and experience will you need to get there? Ask your boss for input and share any suggestions that you feel will help you reach your goal. For example, ask to be part of a committee or volunteer to run a project in order *to gain* valuable experience that will challenge you in areas that extend beyond your current day-to-day responsibilities.

Ask for a mentor or coach. Spend time with someone more senior in the organization to learn new skills and behaviors. It is also a way to be introduced to others in the organization that you normally would not have contact with.

Another path for development is through education and training courses. Discuss these with your boss. Talk about your future goals and what you think could help you get there. See if you can get any tuition reimbursement from your company. Be flexible if your goals are not in line with what the organization needs. Many companies only pay for courses that are job related, so it may be necessary to take a course on your own to move forward in your skill development.

Become active in groups to grow professionally. Ask your boss to steer you in the right direction. If your interests are in a different area, do research to identify professional groups in your vicinity and talk to colleagues and friends to see if you can get contact names in these groups. Networking with professionals in your field of interest is an excellent way to hear about learning opportunities or potential job openings.

Have a conversation about your development with your boss at least once a year, on your own initiative if necessary. Discuss the agenda ahead of time and come prepared to run this meeting. Keep your boss' communication style in mind and make sure that the format you choose is one that is compatible. For example, if your boss is casual, perhaps going for coffee and talking in a relaxing environment would be a good idea. However, if your boss is the quiet type and not a smooth communicator, providing a list of questions ahead of time and structuring a more formal meeting should get some results.

Understanding Your Boss

Now that you see the importance of having a good understanding of yourself, let's turn to developing an understanding of the person you report to. Here are some helpful tips to begin the process of understanding your boss:

1. Learn your boss' management style. One way to do this is by taking the time to watch and listen to what your boss does and says with other groups and individuals, peers, secretaries or assistants, board members, customers, etc. Does your boss work lots of extra hours in the office? Socialize with others from work? Communicate by phone, emails, and formal memos or in person? Prefer frequent updates or just an occasional briefing? By observing your boss in various situations, you will gain a good understanding of his values and what is important to him.

2. Recognize the areas where your management style and the boss' management style are complementary and where they diverge. It is your responsibility to strategize on how best to make your strengths, weaknesses and style differences work together well. If you think you're going to get the boss to adopt your style, think again. To have a positive relationship, you'll need to be the one who demonstrates flexibility, is able to compromise and shows a willingness to take direction.

3. Don't overlook the importance of little things in a boss' management style. Small things can be very helpful in developing and maintaining a good working relationship. For example, if the boss is a stickler about being on time and starting a 7:30 am meeting on the dot, get there on time (or even a few minutes early). If you arrive even a few minutes late, it may be a problem.

4. Choose your battles wisely and address them one-on-one with the boss, in a confidential setting. There is nothing more fruitless than watching a smart, skilled manager suddenly embark on a suicide mission by going head-to-head with the boss on a relatively small issue or wrong approach. And even worse, to do it in front of an audience. When you have differences to air or problems to resolve, take it behind closed doors.

5. Wherever possible, meet your deadlines; but if unforeseeable problems intervene and a deadline becomes impossible to meet, let the boss know this ASAP. Waiting to the last minute and hoping for a miracle isn't too smart, particularly when the boss may have built a schedule around your deadline.

Communication Style

Communication is a major component of your relationship with your boss and it is also an area where many employees fail. People communicate in a variety of styles and you should learn what your boss' style is and communicate using techniques that will prove successful.

If your boss moves at a fast pace, makes decisions quickly and doesn't make time for chit chat, your interactions should be concise, organized, fast-paced and to the point. This type of boss will appreciate your ability to articulate the "big picture" without long explanations. Learn to express yourself using bullet-point statements and speak with confidence.

If your boss is logical and analytical, you'll be better off providing a sufficient amount of data. Understanding your boss' communication style helps you speak the same language as your boss.

Some bosses are very people-orientated, and *face-time* with you is important. Others prefer to communicate through email and don't want a lot of discussions. Whatever the style, it is part of your role in managing your boss to become familiar with your boss' style and react to it in a way that will be productive and appreciated.

Dealing with a Difficult Boss

Successfully managing a difficult boss is a challenge. A good place to start is to try to understand the reasons for your boss' difficult behavior. If your boss is normally reasonable and the difficult behavior is the result of stress or work overload, there is a good chance that things can change. You should communicate your issues/concerns in a helpful, positive manner and try to create an atmosphere for problem solving.

However, if this hostility or chronic abuse is a regular occurrence, it is less likely that the behavior will change. If this is the case, you might need to seek counsel from a mentor or human resource professional to evaluate your options.

When talking with a difficult boss, never be confrontational. Try to carry out your conversation in a non-adversarial way so you do not further damage your relationship.

Criticism is tough to take, but try to see it as valuable information about how to do better. Try to separate your ego from your business persona. Although it will be hard, try not to react emotionally or defensively. Picture yourself as a business partner with your boss and try to see the criticism as an opportunity to grow.

Having a difficult boss is one of the biggest challenges you face in your career. Sometimes it helps to seek outside counsel or support to figure out the best approach in dealing with an unreasonable personality. Talk it over with a trusted colleague or a Human Resource professional to get a different perspective and to calm down. Remember, however, that every organization has its own culture *and it is important that you use your political savvy to determine what is acceptable in your organization and what is not tolerated.* For example, if bullies are looked up to and supported by senior management, it's a losing battle to try to fight it. You are probably better off looking for a new position.

Case Study: Hannah

Hannah was excited to learn that she received the sales position reporting to Kate. Kate seemed like a smart woman with much experience and Hannah was sure she could learn a lot. It didn't take long, however, before Hannah became disappointed.

When Hannah first started, Kate was very friendly and supportive. She assigned Hannah some clients and helped her prepare her first presentation. Soon after that, Kate became very hard to reach. She was rarely in the office and when she was, she was behind closed doors. Hannah approached her one time but received a harsh look that basically said, "Leave me alone." Kate did not hold back when she disapproved of something Hannah did. She would ask her questions in a manner that felt belittling and many times she did this with others around.

There were two other team members who worked with Hannah and it was obvious that they were having trouble dealing with Kate. One member was terminated after Kate accused her of not being able to perform her job. The other teammate confided that she could not work with Kate and was looking for another position.

After six months on the job, Hannah decided that if she was going to stay in her position, she needed to have a conversation with Kate and come up with a more comfortable way of working together. Hannah set up a meeting and went in prepared to make her points clearly and professionally without getting emotional. Hannah explained that although she really liked her job, she felt that communication between them needed to improve and she had some suggestions to share. Kate listened as Hannah gave some examples of when communication had broken down and she continued to listen as Hannah made suggestions on how to improve things.

Surprisingly, Kate seemed pleased that Hannah had stepped forward and raised these issues. She said she didn't realize how unavailable she had been and suggested that Hannah leave her voicemails when she needed something and she would make every effort to return the call that day. Kate shared that she was under a lot of pressure from her boss and she didn't mean to take it out on Hannah. She told Hannah that her work was excellent and that she had a lot of potential. Kate understood that it was upsetting to receive criticism in a public setting and she agreed to make sure that they were alone if she was going to say something that had a negative tone.

Hannah was pleased that she made the effort to improve her relationship with her boss. Although working for Kate continued to be challenging, Hannah felt she could handle the situation. Her self-confidence grew and she continued to be a strong contributor.

Tips for Success

Here's a list of how to be successful at managing your boss:

1. When your boss speaks highly about a project, report, organization, etc., use that knowledge to get a sense of what the boss rates as "good" in a variety of areas. Knowing the boss' definition of "good work," including content and process, is very important.

2. Observe which colleagues have a particularly good working relationship with the boss and talk to them. Find out what they think is the best way to work with the boss and get suggestions on how to be successful.

3. Avoid stepping into sensitive areas by carefully observing and talking to colleagues when you are new to a position.

4. Don't speak badly about your boss in public or private. It's okay to disagree but don't sink to a level that is unprofessional.

5. Make sure you get the information you need. If your boss is not forthcoming with it, ask for it. Communicate in whatever fashion is appropriate but don't sit back and wait for something to come your way.

6. Learn the corporate culture and use appropriate behaviors.

7. Review your priorities with your boss regularly and stay focused on them. Build credibility by addressing the boss' problems.

8. Learn to read your boss' body language so you know when it is an appropriate time to talk and when it's best not to disturb.

Managing up is a skill that every employee needs to learn. Think of it as YOUR responsibility to build the relationship. This attitude will get you the results you want.

Understand the boss' priorities, likes and dislikes, sense of urgency and style of communication and adjust your behavior accordingly. In many ways, managing up is simply having the right attitude and realizing you have the ability to make things better.

Chapter 8

• • • • • • •

Making Your Performance Review Work for You

by Cecelia Burokas, Certified Five O'Clock Club Coach

Apply yourself. Get all the education you can, but then, by God, do something. Don't just stand there, make something happen.

Lee Iacocca

A Positive Marketing Campaign

Why do so many of us get anxious when it's time for the annual performance review? First, we know performance reviews can have a significant effect on our career in an organization. We also know that they may determine promotions, pay increases and even whether we keep our job. We may find it difficult to separate judgments about our work from judgments about ourselves. Finally, when our performance is being judged, no matter how well we think we've done, we are often fearful and insecure about learning what others think and say about us and our work. For all these reasons, it's a good idea to give your upcoming review careful thought and preparation. In fact, try thinking of it as a positive marketing campaign—a way to highlight your accomplish-

ments and position you for your next job in the company.

Many managers are also apprehensive about reviews. Some know they need to give negative or "developmental" feedback and fear they will not do this well: "I'm always afraid of crushing someone's spirit by coming down too hard."

Others are uncomfortable putting judgments about others in writing: "I really have to think hard about what to put in writing and what to say in the review meeting."

Some are afraid of getting into an argument about performance: "Terry's very sensitive to criticism and tends to put up his dukes whenever he's asked about his work. These conversations never end well."

You can't control your manager's attitude coming into a review, but there's a lot you can do to influence the review and make it easier for both you and your manager. The techniques for making your review a positive experience include great preparation, lots of listening, and asking the right questions.

Prepare

Good preparation reduces anxiety. Some of the following preparation techniques are built into the review process at more progressive companies. If you are lucky enough to work in a company that supports these positive practices, be sure to take advantage of them. If you work for a company that follows a more traditional "top down" approach to reviews, these techniques will help you maintain some influence over the process.

- *Familiarize yourself with your company's review process.* Know the timing, as well as the standard procedures and forms used for reviews. You usually can get this information from your manager or a peer, from the employee handbook, or your human resources department.
- *Take the initiative.* When you know performance review time is approaching, assemble a list of your accomplishments over the entire past year. Managers tend to remember only your most recent accomplishments. If you haven't been keeping an accomplishment and activity log, this would be a good time to start one for the next year.
- *Focus on outcomes.* When you write, include the impact and outcomes of your work, as well as what you did. Frame your accomplishments to show the specific benefits your work provided to your company: "I changed the product mix I sold in a way that increased company profits, increased my commissions, and better met the needs of my customers."

  Whenever possible, cite numbers you can prove: "Redesigned the tuition assistance record-keeping process. Saved at least 20 hours per month of staff time."

  You also can note projects you've started but are not yet complete, with information on your progress and a fore-cast of when the goal will be reached. If you are running behind, explain, but do not make excuses. This information should be factual and outcome-oriented.

  Include ways that your performance has improved since the last performance review. This is especially important if your previous review had negative aspects.

- *Send your accomplishments to your manager in advance of the review.* This may happen automatically if your company uses a formal self-review process. But if not, once you've made your list, send it to your manager a week or two before the review is due. Use your own words, but include a short note saying something like: "I know performance reviews are coming up, so I'm sending you a list of what I've been doing for the past year. Please let me know if there's anything else I can provide that would be helpful."
- *Think in advance about your professional development goals.* If you know what you want, do some preliminary research into development opportunities, both inside and outside your company. This way, you'll be prepared to suggest alternatives to your manager. This will give him the chance to ask you to do more digging, or give him time to find other options for training, workshops, or special project assignments.
- *Prepare yourself to listen.* You've had the first word already by sending your manager your self-review or list of accomplishments. Let your manager open the conversation. This will give you a chance to gauge the tone and mood and set your expectations appropriately.

Listen and Respond

A face-to-face is always best, but if you work remotely, you may want to suggest Skype or another medium that allows you and your manager to read each others' expressions and body language.

- *First, listen to what your manager has to say.* A common mistake employees make in review conversations is to respond before listening to everything the manager has to say about an aspect of the review. This can cause you to sound defensive. When your manager begins to talk about your performance, let her finish each remark before you respond. In fact, paraphrase back to her what you are hearing before forming your response. This lets your manager know you are listening, and gives her a chance to correct anything you may have misunderstood. Paraphrasing also ensures that you are hearing what she intended and gives you thinking time to help you frame your response.
- *Respond positively to critiques of your work.* Most managers want their employees to do well. This means that feedback in the form of constructive criticism is given to help you do better. If you agree, be sure to say so. "I appreciate this feedback. You're right—I didn't realize that the timing of these reports was so important. I'll make sure my staff submits them on time in the future."

Ask Questions

If you don't understand any aspect of the feedback your manager gives you during the review session, be sure to ask for more specific information.

One of my coaching clients was shocked to learn during a review that her manager saw her as "inattentive" in department meetings. Jeanne asked what caused him to see her that way and learned it was her habit of slouching back in her chair throughout meetings. Jeanne saw this as relaxed behavior that hid (she hoped) her anxiety about speaking up, but her manager interpreted it as being disengaged. When she learned this, she was able to consciously change her posture in meetings. She also found that sitting up and leaning forward made it easier to speak up when she had something to say.

- *If you believe the criticism is unfair, state your case calmly and ask for a response.* Ask for a chance to collect additional evidence to support your view. This is your chance to show that you take your work—and the feedback—seriously and want to do your best work in the future.
  - ✓ "Have you had a chance to speak with the other team members? I got a lot of positive feedback from them about the value of my contributions."
  - ✓ "I have some additional information about what we accomplished with that project. After we meet, may I send that to you and then set a time to look it over together?"

- *Ask what you can do to perform even better.*
  - ✓ "What do I need to do differently to get to the next level?"
  - ✓ "Is there anything I'm not doing now that I should be doing in the future?"

- Ask what the company can do to assist with your development goals. You are responsible for your own development, but your manager may be aware of additional opportunities—a training class, team project, mentoring, or working side-by-side with a more experienced associate. If you don't ask, these opportunities may not come to your manager's mind.

- *Ask what you can do to make your manager's job easier over the next year.* Never forget that part of your job is to help your manager do well and look good. You don't want to sound obsequious, so think about how you want to word this. When talking with someone who is used to the direct approach, "What can I do to make your job easier?" may do just fine. But if not, you may want to frame this request in organizational terms:
  - ✓ "Is there something more I could be doing to contribute to our divisional priorities?"
  - ✓ "How else can we put my skills to work?"

Additional Thoughts

- *What to do if you start to experience strong emotions.*

  Anger, tears, and expressions of shock rarely contribute to a positive review conversation, but as human beings we can find ourselves on the verge whenever we feel threatened by new information. When this happens, take a time out.

  If you feel safely in control of your words and behaviors, one option is to admit your discomfort, name your emotional state (angry, sad, in shock) and gauge whether you and your manager both are comfortable enough to continue: "I have to admit I'm feeling very angry about this because I believe it's an unfair conclusion. I can continue talking, but would you prefer to wait until I've had more time to absorb this?"

  Another option is to ask to reschedule: "I'm really surprised to hear that and I'm not sure how to respond. I'd like some time to process this. Do you have some time tomorrow to continue our conversation?"

Remember that *performance feedback, whether considerate or tactless, is a gift*. We can change and improve only when we recognize the gap between what we are doing and what is expected—and performance review feedback provides the information needed to change both the reality and perceptions of performance.

Chapter 9

• • • • • • •

Performance Reviews: What Managers and Leaders Need to Know

by Robert Hellmann, Certified Five O'Clock Club Coach and VP, Associate Director, The Five O'Clock Club National Guild of Career Coaches

Criticism, like rain, should be gentle enough to nourish a man's growth without destroying his roots.

Frank A. Clark, American writer and cartoonist

Performance reviews are widely used, and yet often controversial. Do they work? What's the best way to implement them? Don't unfair grudges or favoritism, or other forms of bias, fatally compromise them? In this chapter, I'll share with you a few thoughts on these and other questions.

Part 1: How Performance Reviews Can Benefit Your Organization

Why should my organization bother with performance reviews?

Both research and experience show that organizations tend to succeed in what they measure. Performance reviews, when implemented

correctly, go a long way toward measuring and improving employee performance (or allocating employee resources correctly). A systematic, well-executed process can also help to protect employers in the case of employee disputes.

But there's a huge organizational benefit beyond that. Performance reviews can play a crucial role in communicating organizational goals, and engaging employees at all levels in the right tasks that will help the organization reach those goals. I've personally seen the tangible benefits in terms of both improved productivity and morale in an organization once a well-thought-out performance review process has been implemented.

What's the best way to implement performance reviews?

Performance reviews should be applied both *consistently* and *comprehensively*. Everyone should be reviewed, from the CEO in public companies (responsible to the Board) on down to entry-level clerk. Reviews should be given regularly at assigned times for the entire organization; typically, this means a formal year-end process, with a mid-year check-in. This kind of consistent, comprehensive approach helps to ensure that organizational goal-alignment benefits happen, and that both the perception and reality of individual bias is reduced.

What should the performance review measure?

Performance reviews need to measure both the *what* and the *how*. The "what" is where the money is in terms of organizational alignment. Half of the performance review should focus on whether specific agreed-upon objectives were attained. Each employee's performance review objectives should roll up to her or his manager's objectives, all the way up to the CEO, so that all employee objectives fit together laterally (like pieces of a puzzle) and vertically (like layers in a pyramid).

How an employee achieves an objective is very important for organizations where planning extends beyond the short term, and should account for 50% of the review. Holding employees accountable for how they get things done helps to ensure that individual goals aren't being achieved at the expense of larger organizational goals. An organization's "leadership competencies" (behaviors that an organization values) are often used as a guide to measuring this part of performance.

Case in point: I worked with an organization where a recently hired executive excelled at achieving short-term objectives. A year after being hired, business unit revenues were up and costs were down. It became apparent, however, that this person was, in the process, alienating colleagues, duplicating the effort of other departments, and causing a retention problem for productive employees! After a while, those initial, stellar results became quite tarnished. Unfortunately, the organization did not yet have a review process in place to deal with this situation, and

things were allowed to fester far too long. Don't make this mistake in your own review process!

Keep in mind that leadership competencies may need to differ based on the position's level or type. As an example, for more junior employees leadership competencies might include:

- Demonstrates commitment and knowledge
- Drives improvement

Competencies for more senior employees might include:

- Drives innovation
- Develops effective strategies

Part 2: How to Implement Performance Reviews

When should the performance review process start?

Reviews are most effective when the process begins right after the prior year's review. Starting 12 months prior means aligning with your employees throughout the year on how they are being measured. Not only is this fairer to the employee (i.e. no surprises), but you are more likely to get the performance results you want.

But how can we start 12 months prior when organizational priorities change frequently?

Yes, priorities change, but there's a huge benefit to putting a stake in the ground wherever you are, so you can get some traction around measurement and organizational goal alignment. That said, there's got to be room for reasonable movement of the goalposts. And when priorities inevitably do change, communication about how that impacts performance goals needs to happen.

In addition, have a six-month checkpoint, to help maintain organizational alignment and reduce the likelihood of unpleasant surprises. The review process in month-6 should mirror the final month-12 review process, with two important exceptions: (1) your employee's performance is not scored, that is, the words are there but the numbers are not, and (2) the six-month review does not become part of the employee's official performance record.

What kind of goals should be set?

Start with your own goals as a manager, and ensure that your employee's goals directly support yours (as your goals should support your manager's). You and your employee should agree on specific, measurable goals. "Improve the efficiency of marketing campaigns" is not specific enough— were they improved a little or a lot, and was the improvement above or below expectations? Much better is "Shorten marketing campaign processing time by 20%."

In other words, three categories should be considered in goal formation and evaluation for the review, the first two agreed upon with the employee at the start of the year, and the last to be discussed in the review.

1. Specific goal ("Shorten marketing campaign processing time…")
2. Criteria for success ("…by 20% or more")
3. Results/accomplishments (to be discussed in the review)

How do I rate performance?

Most organizations use a numerical scale to measure performance. Having a numerical scale helps both the employee and the organization understand the strengths and weaknesses of its most important asset, its employees. The scores ideally should fit together, so that your score as a manager is reflected in the score average of the people working for you.

A scale of 1 to 5 is common, where 1 is "exceptional," 5 means an "exit strategy" for the employee, and 3 is "met expectations." A smaller number of organizations use a 1-to-3 scale where 1 is the top 15% of performers, 2 is the middle 70%, and 3 is the bottom 15%. Having only three rankings helps focus attention on the outliers (those to promote and those to exit), at the expense of a more fine-tuned understanding of employee performance and potential. (Organizations using the smaller scale may supplement the performance review process with other processes for talent evaluation in order to keep track of the middle 70%.)

The ratings for individual goals and behaviors roll up to an overall employee score. In the "goals" section of the review, each goal should be rated, and weighted based on an organizational determination of how important that type of goal is. For example, goals might be weighted differently based on whether they are customer-focused or employee-focused. Similarly, each component of the "behaviors" portion of the review (how goals were achieved) should be rated as well.

How do I conduct the actual review?

First, ask the employee to write their own review, including the numerical scores, a couple of weeks before the actual review will occur. This way, you are encouraging the employee to engage in their development and performance achievement—so it's not just the manager telling the employee. Also, the employee will remind you of achievements throughout the year in their self-appraisal, helping to combat the "what have you done for me lately" bias that can easily creep into annual reviews.

At the same time, ask the employee for three co-workers to be references. Get these names from your subordinates so you preemptively address concerns about negative bias. I've seen many situations where making the effort to get this feedback has paid off in a substantially revised (for better or for worse!) perception of performance.

Then, set up a separate time, at least an hour, to go over the review. Make sure you are in a room with a door and you are not disturbed—

that is, communicate how seriously you take this, and respect your employee's privacy.

What should I bring up in the review?

Go over each of the goals step-by-step. Always strive to give specific examples to illustrate your point of view. Don't say, "You are annoying others in the department." Instead, say, "I heard from participants in that meeting about how you interrupted several times to bring up off-topic subjects." Specifics enable people to see the real issue, and reduce the likelihood that your observations will be perceived as unfairly biased. Make sure you use examples to both reinforce good performance and address sub-par issues.

Don't bring up salary—that should be in a separate conversation. Having the two in one conversation could hurt delivery of the message on performance and goals.

Additional guidelines:

- The write-up should NOT be a laundry list of all the steps taken to achieve goals.
- Instead include: (1) what the goal was; (2) what were the specific parts of the goal that make up success criteria; and (3) what was accomplished. Keep it concise.
- Included criticisms should be actionable; list the specific thing the employee needs to do to improve.
- Talk (giving supporting examples), then listen.
- Be open to making changes, but don't make them easily—it's not a negotiation. If something is factually wrong or has been omitted, that should have an impact.
- Discuss next steps, areas that might be in a development plan.
- Have an optional employee response section where employees can comment if they feel it's necessary.

- Get the employee to sign the review (or sign after any needed changes are made).
- Then you sign it.

Aren't reviews too subjective or biased to be of any use?

There's always the potential for bias in a review. Following the principles described in this chapter can go a long way to reduce that possibility. Other things can be done on an organization-wide basis, including (1) education on how to be alert to potential sources of bias in order to avert them, and (2) analysis of systemic problems within departments to identify problems, for example everyone getting top reviews or poor reviews. Managers should work closely with HR in conducting this type of education and analysis, as well as ensuring that performance reviews meet legal requirements.

A good performance review process can have a huge benefit for both individuals and the organization. I worked with a client who was having trouble with an employee on her staff. He was hired with high expectations, but was not meeting them. This particular client worked in a division that believed in a rigorous performance review process.

The review process forced all parties to focus on what the problem was. Where one organization might have said, "it's just not working out," and let the employee go, this leader was able to rely on the review process to take a far more productive approach.

In this case, the review process uncovered the employee's weakness with data analysis, but strength in more creative areas. The result was the employee shifted to a different department within the same division, and became a star in the organization!

Summary: Do's and Don'ts

Do:

- Make everyone accountable via the review process.
- Align on goals well before, and continue to align throughout the year.
- Have a mid-year checkpoint.
- Get employee input prior to your review, by having them write their own version.
- Use specific examples to support your review.
- Have actionable items in the review (continuing the good, improving on the not-so-good).
- Have uninterrupted privacy.

Don't:

- Discuss salary.
- Make your review points too general, with no specific examples.
- Give too much detail—the review should not be too long.
- Make it personal. Focus on facts, observations of behavior or actions, and their implications.
- Have vague phrases with no supporting information. e.g., "Susan is a results-oriented problem solver." Ok, now give examples.
- Implement reviews in your department in an irregular, inconsistent manner.

Chapter 10

● ● ● ● ● ● ● ●

Focus on Solutions to Boost Success

by Margaret McLean Walsh, Certified Five O'Clock Club Coach

There is an almost universal quest for easy answers and half-baked solutions. Nothing pains some people more than having to think.

Rev. Dr. Martin Luther King, Jr.

Identify your problems but give your power and energy to solutions.

Anthony Robbins, motivational speaker

Problems. We all have them. We want to solve them, understand them and avoid a repeat performance. We get great satisfaction in learning the cause, the possible solutions and the action plan to get it fixed. And, there is a better way!

Problem solving too often starts us down the problem-talk path. You might ask, "What are the usual questions?" You'll recognize them—our problem-talk questions may sound something like, "What happened?" and "Who is accountable?" and "How do we fix it?"

And, the problem with problem-talk is that it gets us focused on the problem when we would be better served focusing on the change or out-come. Actually, there is something very satisfying about understanding the problem, its causes and what will fix it. The more we look into it, discuss it, question it and come up with ways to solve it makes us experts on the problem. When we use our resources to clarify and solve the problem, we are very possibly missing an opportunity to create a new reality and innovate what could be—the post-problem future state.

So, what can we do to take a solutions-talk path? How would things be different if we focused on the solution? This is much easier than you would think. And the results are amazing. Simply by changing our questions, we can look at the situation through a solutions lens, and change our thinking and our outcome. Instead of staying with the problem and what we have to fix, we think about the outcome—what we want to be different.

Our focus becomes our reality. By changing our questions, we change our focus, and at the same time, change our reality. New questions bring new thinking—the questions we ask ourselves when faced with a problem influence the path we take and the reality we create.

If this hasn't convinced you yet, this next piece of insight might. *Using a solutions-focused approach can greatly quicken the path to results.* We immediately focus on the future and what we want as an outcome. Briefly, here are the steps to a solutions-focused approach:

Evaluate. What was already happening that was working towards their desired result? What they were already doing was making sales, just not enough. They thought about their recent sales success and brainstormed about what they did to close those sales. Using that knowledge,

Result	What you want to be different is . . .
Evaluate	What are you already doing that's working? How would you rate where you are (current) and where you want to be (result) on a scale of 1 to 10?
Expertise	What has worked for you in similar situations?
Verify and Action	Where are you and what is one small step you can take to bring you closer to your outcome?
Check-In	What's better—how did you do that?

Let's take a look at how Jack, a senior sales manager, put this into practice. Jack was head of a sales team for six years. His team always performed well and Jack was proud of their achievements. However, during the past six months, the team was consistently missing its monthly sales quotas. Jack needed to solve this problem—it meant his success, as well as that of his team.

When Jack's team met, they did what many of us do when faced with a problem. They analyzed data, identified things that interfered with their success, discussed problems, and made a list of what they thought they needed to do differently. After two months of problem-talk and action plans to fix things, the team's sales results were still below quota.

Luckily for Jack, Tai, a colleague of his, introduced him to the solutions-focus approach. After a brief introduction on how the process works, Tai guided the team through the solutions-focus process, using questions about what is and what's possible to inspire their commitment. Here's a summary of how that worked for Jack and his team:

Result. The team wanted to achieve their monthly sales quota and set this as their desired result or outcome.

the team focused on learning from their successes. Their goal was to discover what was already working and finding ways to do more of it.

To get a sense of where they were and where they wanted to be, Jack's team used a 10-point scale, with 1 being "no sales" and 10 being "meeting quotas." The team thought and discussed, and agreed at a rating of a 6. This helped them to see that they were more than half-way toward their goal and could break their work into manageable steps to move further up the scale.

Expertise. The team looked at past successes for resources and know-how. Jack helped the team to describe what they did to make their sales quotas in prior years and think about how to apply that knowledge to this situation.

Verify and Action. The team met weekly and continually scaled their progress. They were now at a 7. Their next focus was on committing to taking one small step to bring them closer to their desired result.

Check-In. After one month, Jack did a check-in with his team. What they focused on was their progress—what was better, and how did they do that?

By continuing to use the solutions-focus approach, within three months, Jack and his team were back on track and were meeting their sales quotas. The questions they asked themselves through the solutions lens helped them to discover what worked and how to do more of it. They created their new reality, reenergized their team and brought added value to their organization. Not a bad result!

Now, it's your turn. When you are faced with your next problem, and you know there's at least one out there, remember that your focus will become your reality. So, choose wisely and bring your passion, creativity, sense of humor and know-how to your future challenges. Just remember to find out what's working and do more of it!

Chapter 11

• • • • • • • • •

Younger Bosses, Older Workers

by Kate Wendleton, President, The Five O'Clock Club

Older workers generally report the most satisfaction with their job. A Gallup poll released yesterday found that older workers are the most likely to enjoy their work.

"Most Older Workers Have a Younger Boss,"
Money magazine, March 2, 2010

When I was a young computer programmer in the mid-1970s, I supervised a group of older males, a number of whom were in their mid-50s. They were smart and funny and productive. In addition, they brought common sense and solid advice to our discussions based on their many years in corporate America. We had a great rapport and accomplished a lot. Maybe I was lucky that things worked out so well.

> The workers in their mid 50s were smart, funny, productive and had common sense.

The Trends

More and more, there is this same reversal of the traditional model of older boss, younger workers—with those in their 20s and 30s now routinely supervising workers in their 40s, 50s and even older. This is happening more often because:

- Young people know more of the new technologies than a lot of the older folks—so they're getting jobs with rapid advancement potential.
- On the other side of the ledger, older people need—or want—to work longer, many into their late 60s and 70s. And many ambitious mid-career people are leaving retrenching industries to get into the high-growth fields where the younger people have more experience.

The Conflicts

This age difference can produce problems. When conflicts arise, either party can be at fault.

Many times older people think young managers are inexperienced. An older worker is tempted to meddle or be condescending or unwilling to learn. And older workers may deeply resent working for someone young enough to be their child—or grandchild.

Young people, on the other hand, think older workers can't learn new tricks. They may feel threatened by the older worker's knowledge and experience and prefer to be surrounded by others who don't know as much. They may feel uncomfortable giving directions to someone their parents' age, and they may assume that the older worker is not interested in getting ahead. A younger manager could sometimes think that he or she knows it all.

We had a Five O'Clock Clubber in her mid-40s, who went to work for very young twenty-something in a website development company. They needed her connections to bring in brand-name accounts such as AT&T, IBM and the like, and they promised her equity. She brought in a huge amount of business and made them a lot of money. But they did not give her equity, and the president brought in his 22-year-old girlfriend to be her boss. The 40-something left.

······································

**Many of the young bosses
are smart, mature, good leaders
and good listeners.**

······································

The Solutions

It doesn't have to be that way. Here are a few hints for working things out.

Do's and Don'ts for Both Sides

When the older person mentions how the font size in the phone book keeps getting smaller, laugh about it. When the young person says, "In my experience …" about something where he or she has no significant experience, let it slide.

······································

**Young boss:
Your success is not 100% your own doing:
you are at the right place at the right time.**

······································

Don't stereotype.

Young bosses are not all alike, nor are all older workers. Some of the young bosses are smart, mature, good leaders and good listeners. Some of the older workers are ambitious, knowledgeable, energetic and supportive. Don't put each other in a box.

Don't be afraid to discuss your concerns.

Schedule a meeting with your young boss/older worker to discuss the issues. Try to work it out. Get things out in the open. You both have a lot to gain.

Do's and Don'ts for the Younger Boss

Value those who work for you.

Listen to those who have been around a while: they have seen it before and can save you a few mistakes.

Don't try to assert control; talk to people.

Leaders listen, make use of the talent they have at their disposal and keep their promises. Give credit where credit is due.

Help your people to grow.

Leaders help all of their subordinates to grow—even those who are older. My brother, in his early 40s, became a computer programmer after many years as a hotshot in the retrenching printing industry. He started out near the bottom, but trust me when I say that he is ambitious and wants to get ahead.

"It's the economy, stupid."

Remember that part of your success is not necessarily your own doing: you happen to be at the right place at the right time. A dose of humility helps you to value others and to not think that your success has everything to do with you. You will be stronger in a downturn (which will come) than those who cannot separate internal factors of success from external ones.

Remember that the balance of power will change.

You may be working for one of your subordinates someday. Or your subordinate may be in a position to praise you—or to damn you with faint praise. Pick your enemies wisely.

Do's and Don'ts for the Older Worker

Learn new skills.

—or the younger people in your office will run circles around you. They'll get to manage the exciting new developments while you are relegated to the old-fashioned, often lower-level work. Change is the order of the day, and most bosses are obliged to be trail-blazers. By resisting change and constantly comparing the old ways to new ways, you'll get a reputation as a stick-in-the-mud.

Never claim that you're set in your ways—that's the kiss of death because the ways are changing. If you've been in accounting for 20 years, for example, you know that computers have changed everything—and the change is not likely to slow down.

Coach your boss.

No matter what your boss' age, it is every subordinate's job to support the boss. Make yourself a resource. Tell your boss the landmines you see, but don't be condescending or sarcastic. Remember that the younger people tend to move on more quickly, so you will probably have more knowledge of what went on in the area before your young boss arrived. Fill him or her in.

··

Older worker: "Coach" your boss,
and don't belittle "the kids" for
not knowing something.

··

Protect your flanks.

This is a day of revolving bosses. Make sure as many superiors as possible know who you are and what you do. When you see a vice president in the elevator and he says, "Hi, Jane, how are you?" Don't just say, "Fine, thanks" and keep walking. Say something like, "Fine, thank you. I've been working on the seasonal sales pitch and I think you'll be pleased with the results we'll see in the coming months."

Don't talk about the good old days.

. . . or constantly talk about your arthritis . . . or the old TV shows . . . or belittle "the kids" for not knowing something. Such talk only widens the generation gap. Spend more time listening than talking. Stay current with the new things that are happening.

....

**Leaders help all their subordinates
to grow
—even those who are older.**

....

Don't meddle

Keep out of your boss' and your co-workers' business. Do your job and do it well and you'll earn respect.

It's a changing, tumultuous economy, one that can use all of the talent available. There's enough for everybody. Respect what each person brings to the party and make use of all of the resources an organization has. We're all going to be here a long time.

Chapter 12

• • • • • • • • •

How to Manage Workplace Politics

by Win Sheffield, Certified Five O'Clock Club Coach

A politician is a person with whose politics you don't agree; if you agree with him he's a statesman.

David Lloyd George, U.K. Prime Minister, 1863 — 1945

Each of us wants to bring value to the workplace and to be rewarded for our effort. We want to be paid for what we do best. For many, this simple proposition falls apart in the face of "politics." Politics can involve aligning interests, cajoling and accommodating and/or sandbagging, lying and undermining. These are skills that we may not have, we may not choose to exercise and that we are not comfortable dealing with when they are used to undermine our efforts. Politics gets in the way of our providing value.

Politics is often seen in its most negative light:

"Our proposal was rejected because Sam has never liked our department."

"Terry only got that promotion because he plays golf with the head of marketing."

"Alex always takes credit for projects, whether or not she had anything to do with them."

People who act in this way are called "political." Being political is associated with individual prejudice, hidden agendas, saying one thing and doing another, backstabbing, scapegoating, sabotage, etc. If this is what politics is, no wonder we avoid it. Why would we want to be involved in something like that? Yet, by avoiding politics, we discard much of our ability to accomplish what we want to achieve on the job. Achieving our goals requires more than our simply doing a good job.

Our purpose in this chapter is to take a closer look at politics, its relevance to getting our job done, and perhaps surprisingly, to lay out how we can participate in politics— ethically, as a part of working smart. Not all of politics is destructive and bad. It can be used in the interests of shareholders or the organization as a whole and not be solely based on self-interest.

Let's look a little more closely at the distinctions between ethical politics, where the values of all participants are weighed, and unethical politics, where interests are narrower and the means of reaching decisions are manipulative or worse.

Understanding the nature of politics

"The savvy see the organization as a human system trying to act in a rational way—rather than as an economically structured entity that happens to need people to make it go. That may seem to be just a bit of semantics, but it turns out to be fundamental. When you understand people—and realize that an organization is a human system—then you know that you'll always do better if you strive to create win-win scenarios."

Joel DeLuca, Savvy Politics

According to the *Oxford English Dictionary,* politics is "the activities associated with the governance of a country or area, especially the debate between parties having power." Wikipedia more broadly describes politics as a process by which groups of people make collective decisions. In other words, politics is the process by which people get things done and how we get things done is by allocating time and resources (our own and others'). The ability to control the allocation of time and resources is the dictionary definition of power.

A formal organizational structure is the official expression of and conduit for power. People in organizations entrusted with leadership positions make decisions about how to allocate resources, how to produce and/or achieve things. Formal hierarchies and organizational structures serve their intended needs fairly well, but imperfectly, not always, for instance, getting the product out the door before you have to leave for your daughter's soccer game.

The full assessment of the interests of various stakeholders and accommodation of their views—to ensure the success of the project—is better suited to an informal structure, one that can adapt to individual quirks and requirements. Even when all parties are acting in the best interests of the organization, there are differing opinions as to any issue's relative importance, what resources should be allocated to it and when. Politics is about using power of relation-

ships, loyalty, personal charisma and access to formal power to affect the change we want (or do not want) to see.

When I first arrived at Morgan Guaranty in the late 80s, I was advised to be nice to our assistant, Ellie. I thought that was odd advice; why would it occur to anyone to do otherwise? I subsequently learned that important information flowed among the assistants and that an assistant's opinion of you affected the attention your information received.

Some information doesn't warrant going through official channels and yet is still important for management to keep an eye on. If there was a message you felt management needed to hear at Morgan, you could pass it by your assistant who could share it, for instance, with the assistant of the managing partner. Information went both ways. If you were dropping the ball, a quiet comment by your assistant could refocus you before the issue was raised in your annual review.

This informal network served as a way to be in touch with senior management and they with us. Working up the chain of command was still, ultimately, how decisions were made. The assistants' network served to provide a back door to the existing, formal command and control structure. It provided a mechanism for outside influence, and was, as such, political; ethically political and political, just the same.

Making the best decisions about impossible situations and a lack of resources, incorporating the needs of all stakeholders is always complex and requires more than a formal structure can provide. Not all informal structures are as clear as this one was. Some networks and alliances arise to address a single issue. The Morgan system represents one example of a place where people recognized that a formal structure could not bear all the needs for communication of differing interests. The resulting informal communication may not have had the precision and clarity of the formal system, but it let outside opinions influence decisions that were made.

Some networks can be toxic. Some unofficial

networks exist to serve narrower and counter-productive interests. There are individuals whose primary focus is on other agendas that serve to keep them in power, to undermine people they do not like. This is unethical politics. It is unethical not only because it is based on selfish interest and relies on deception, but also because of the strain it places on the organization.

Management may not acknowledge informal power structures, yet they will often choose to leave them alone or perhaps even access them on occasion. Because accommodating people's needs is complex and important, politics is often the most effective way to meet those needs, as uncontrolled as it is. What it loses in control, it makes up for in subtlety and comprehensiveness and complexity. Human beings are enormously complex and any system that fails to take that into account, will fail itself. There are as many ways to approach these complexities as there are people and situations. How you can practically and ethically build and exercise power and practice politics is the subject of the next section.

How you can usefully and ethically participate in politics

It should be borne in mind that there is nothing more difficult to arrange, more doubtful of success and more dangerous to carry through than initiating change.

The innovator makes enemies of all those who prospered under the old order, and only lukewarm support is forthcoming from those who prosper under the new. Their support is lukewarm, partly from fear of their adversaries, who have the existing laws on their side, and partly because men are generally incredulous, never really trusting new things unless they have tested them by experience.

In consequence, whenever those who oppose the changes can do so, they attack vigorously, and the defense made by the others is ineffective. So both the innovator and his friends are endangered together.

Nicolai Machiavelli, The Prince

So here you are, a part of an organization. Perhaps you have some influence. Perhaps you have an acknowledged position that allows you to make some decisions. Whatever cards you hold, you probably need more allies and/or resources than you have to realize your vision on the scale you envision it. You can stick your head in the sand by relying on someone else or ignoring anything outside the official organization structure, but this is not effective. To do your job, you need to be political.

Dealing with politics is a way of stepping up to the plate. By being political you demonstrate your commitment to your idea by fighting for it. Arguably, if you are not willing to fight for it (using your own and soliciting others' political capital), the idea isn't that good, isn't worth the resources needed to make it real. If you want to succeed, you need to enter into politics.

Why Politics is important to you

Politics is important for you because you are in an organization with others. For your plan, whatever it is, to succeed (for the overall benefit of the organization), there are going to be others in the organization who must be accommodated, negotiated with, befriended and perhaps even evaded or outwitted. If these other players are not engaged, you will fail to achieve your objective.

You will fail to fully achieve your objective or you will be at risk to be undermined in some future objective. It may be tempting to concede some of your success to avoid these realities (and that is part of organizational life), but by embracing politics and choosing to enter into politics in an ethical way, you will minimize unnecessary shortfalls and sacrifices. Doing this is not as difficult as you think.

What we will assume about you

We assume for the purposes of this chapter that you are accomplished in your field and have good things to contribute to your organization. You are master of your subject matter.

We also assume that you have the best interests of the organization at heart. Such assessments always involve judgment. You and those holding official positions of power may not have recognized the same interests. Nor do your interests have to be without self-interest. Just because something is good for you or those you are close to, does not mean that it is not also good for the organization. All of that notwithstanding, this is a guide for acting ethically in the political realm. Ethical politics is about achieving a result while working to minimize the places where you have to spend time and effort to keep secret.

Into politics one step at a time

The steps recommended here require work and attention. When confronted with resistance to an idea, it often seems simpler to battle it out or avoid a confrontation (fight or flight). If you are master of the subject matter, you may feel your expertise should be sufficient for your project to succeed.

One way of thinking about the political realm is that it recognizes human factors. If you are master of both the subject matter and human factors, then you are much more likely to achieve your goals. Some people who dislike politics characterize it as hard-working subject matter experts against the manipulative, lazy, credit-seekers. You do not need to think this way. If you take the time to see where people seem to be coming from, you may be able to present things in a way that avoids a pitched battle.

Step 1 – Shift your attitude

The first step is to recognize that human beings are involved and that that can be messy and that it is important to deal with their issues in one way or another. Dealing with an issue can involve sharing information, negotiation, sharing credit, delay, acceleration, avoidance or even, though rarely, attack. The point is to exercise pa-

tience and anticipate reactions (where possible), thinking through options rather than engaging in a tactic that may have negative consequences down the road.

Step 2 – Lay the groundwork

The second step, having realized that you give yourself an advantage by taking the time to think things through, is to start to build the currency you will need to engage and succeed in politics. That currency is relationships.

Having a relationship with those who have an interest in what you and your department are engaged in makes everything easier. If you have taken some time to get to know someone, what they are doing in their area, what is important to their success or simply what they want to tell you, you will have a better idea of what to approach them about and how to approach them.

With some people you get to know, you will go further and develop trust. They can become allies, providing a sounding board for new ideas or colleagues to whom you can turn for support in developing strategies for furthering the initiatives you think are important.

Others who you get to know may be less interested and some you will learn to avoid, unless you have more carefully thought through the potential consequences of sharing your ideas and plans with them. You don't trust them, so you will want to be careful.

Still others may be particularly important to develop a relationship with. There are people who are tuned into people's priorities and motivations and who can be hubs for information. If you are not attuned to the organization in that way, you may find these colleagues particularly valuable in executing your plans.

Whether the person with whom you build the relationship turns out to be an ally or someone you do not trust, building the relationship is the key. The relationships will be different. Whoever said, "keep your friends close but your enemies closer," was wise.

You may sometimes wonder why people

should be drawn to you. To some extent, they just like you. In a corporate environment, where people are working to achieve, people form relationships because of advantages they see you bring to them. You may have knowledge they need or a position or resources. Perhaps, you have relationships they see as important, perhaps to someone with influence or access. You may be seen as reliable, trustworthy or credible. Awareness of these factors will be useful in your developing relationships important to you. In the world of politics, these factors are seen as sources of power.

Supporting a colleague's interests and initiatives is a key way to demonstrate your commitment to them and your relationship with them. Demonstrating your support serves to strengthen the relationship, making it more likely they will support you in turn.

Lending your support to your allies is easy. It can be more difficult and often ill-advised to be seen to support someone whom you do not trust. If their idea is a good one in your judgment, you may want to find an acceptable way to support it. It is a good practice to maintain cordial relations with all.

Step 3 – Practice good politics

Step 3 begins when you have an initiative in mind. I say in mind, because this is not a process that begins when you have completed a plan that will save the organization a great deal of money and will need to be rolled out. When you have an objective in mind, that is the point when you will want to engage your allies. This does not mean you want to turn to them empty-handed, asking them how to proceed; have command of your facts and ideas about what you want to do and seek their suggestions. It is a well-worn truth that engaging people up front will engage them in the outcome.

Keep in mind and listen for what people are interested in, the ways they are (and are not) interested in supporting your project. Being sensitive to this is the essence of success in politics.

For any given initiative, there will be some people who are natural allies. Networks and alliances can shift with time and come together around particular interests. Once the change is in place, the network recedes. Sometimes when a person who is a hub for information loses interest, the network evaporates.

For those whom you don't trust, you will naturally share less with them. There will be times when dealing with those who like to take credit, where you will want to be out there ahead of them, letting people know about the project and what is going on with it before they are in a position to take credit.

Good practices back up your alliances.

- Give credit when you can to others who have earned it; find nice things to say.
- Document the work you do (a good career practice).
- Send notes confirming discussions (avoids misunderstandings and provides a paper trail).
- Prepare. Do your homework.
- Avoid unnecessary interactions with people with whom you have to be on your guard.

Three Steps summarized

The steps laid out above do not represent everything you will ever need to know about politics. There are many books written about politics and many more to be written. What these rule provide is a way to begin. Change is difficult as is pointed out in the quote beginning this section. Recognizing the human factors in bringing your changes to your organization will increase your odds for success.

Step 1 – Shift your attitude

Step 1, recognizing that human beings are involved and that that can be messy, is an attitude adjustment that sets a foundation and motivation for entering the political realm.

Step 2 – Lay the groundwork

Step 2, building a relationship, is an ongoing practice that makes any subsequent action more informed and easier to execute.

Step 3 – Practice good politics

Step 3, listening for and including the motivations and priorities of others in your strategy increases your likelihood of success.

Summing up:
Key factors to remember to become a more effective contributor

This chapter is designed to allow politics back into the conversation of people you want to be with, to show that politics needn't be done in the back room and under the cover of darkness. It is a bias towards openness and a willingness to deal discretely with human foibles that characterizes ethical politics.

However you decide to approach making things happen in your organization, I invite you to approach it as a game. The Five O'Clock Club recommends approaching the interview in this way and it is equally useful for politics. There will be days when you are up and days when you are down. There will be days when it is easier and days when it will be harder. Play it as a game and you will sleep a little better.

Chapter 13

• • • • • • • •

Office Gossip:
The Good and the Bad

By Kate Wendleton, President, The Five O'Clock Club

Gossip needn't be false to be evil—there's a lot of truth that shouldn't be passed around.

Frank A. Clark, American writer and cartoonist

Clairee: And I can also report that a mysterious car is parked in her driveway at least once a week...

Ouiser Boudreaux: There. My secret's out. I'm having an affair with a Mercedes Benz!

From the movie, *Steel Magnolias*

When you talk about someone behind that person's back, that's called "gossip." However, there's good gossip and bad.

Good gossip can:

- bond people together (such as spreading the word that Peter's son is getting married and he's happy about it),
- make people more productive or help them fit in, such as when you let a new employee know that people don't like it when someone is late to work or wears sneakers,

- solve a problem, such as when you let the boss know that someone seems depressed.
- keep people in the know about important things that concern the business, and
- help people vent about customers, clients and coaches.

Bad gossip damages a person's morale: such as telling someone, "I think John's a slacker. He doesn't seem to be doing much." (Who are you to judge? Perhaps John's job is brainier than others. It's up to his boss to decide.)

Bad gossip gives power to the disgruntled and solves nothing. For example, one employee felt empowered to file for unemployment—even though she quit—because of the encouragement she received from other employees who engaged in gossip with her.

Bad gossip sets up cliques. Everyone feels left out of the loop when two people are whispering in the kitchen. And when people are whispering, you assume they're up to no good.

Bad gossip sometimes takes the form of sniping right in front of the person so others can hear: "Hey, Jane, you're allowed to pick up the phone too." Sniping can also occur behind someone's back.

What you can do:

- Come to the defense of a person being maligned.
- Don't contribute to the gossip. Instead, walk away: "Sorry, I'm really busy." Don't listen when someone tells you that someone gossiped about you. ("Jane said she doesn't like the clothes you wear.") The person telling you this news is only trying to hurt you or create dissension—and is probably misstating the truth.

Remember: You may think you're a good performer, but you are also judged by the affect you have on the performance of the group as a whole. If you adversely affect the performance of another individual or the group, you are NOT a good performer.

Chapter 14

• • • • • • • • •

How to Have Engaged Employees

by Richard Bayer, Ph.D., Chief Operating Officer, The Five O'Clock Club

Homer: *You don't like your job, you don't strike. You go in every day and do it really half-assed. That's the American way.*

The Simpsons

Any good manager wants to have employees who desire to participate constructively in the mission of the department and the overall organization. On the other hand, feelings of alienation harm the organization and can create an atmosphere of negativity, low productivity, general misery and high turnover.

In an interesting survey of 3 million employees, The Gallup Organization (www.gallup.com) has done research into what it calls "employee engagement." The questionnaire contained 12 questions, and according to Gallup, three groups emerged: employees who are actively engaged; not engaged; and actively disengaged.

• •

**71% of the Americans
who go to work every day are
not engaged in their jobs!**

• •

The research concluded that: 29% of the U.S. workforce are actively engaged, 55% are not engaged, and 16% are actively disengaged. In other words, 71% of the Americans who go to work every day aren't engaged in their jobs!

According to Gallup, the "engaged" employees are builders who use their talents and develop productive relationships. The employees that are "not engaged" tend toward indifference; they take a wait-and-see attitude toward their work, their employer, and their peers. They do not initiate and move the organization forward. Finally, the "actively disengaged" feel and act out estrangement from the organization. This is truly poisonous for productivity. Indeed, Gallup estimates that the cost to the economy from this group is as much as $350 billion per year in lost productivity.

So a key to organizational effectiveness is to move as many employees as possible into the "engaged" category. The following Five O'Clock Club recommendations can help in this effort: Help employees see the connection between the health of the company and their own welfare.

• Help people plan for internal career management. Employees who have goals do better. Performance reviews should help set reasonable goals for the coming time period.

- Develop mentoring relationships between senior and junior members of the organization.
- Encourage employees to talk about their needs in their present position.
- Encourage employees to join associations; perhaps offer time and money to fulfill this objective.
- Provide for and encourage learning new skills:
- Have in-house training programs.
  - ✓ Provide matching funds for outside classroom instruction.
  - ✓ Encourage (reward) the application of newly acquired knowledge and skills.
- Empower your employees. Allow tasks to be managed at the lowest possible and practical level.

- Ask employees to write proposals for ways to improve things.
- Allow for the free flow of information within the organization. Unnecessary secrecy only alienates those who are not on the inside.
- Expand everyone's network within the organization. Allow access to more senior management for good cause.
- Treat severed employees well, offering them career counseling in their transition to a new job. This keeps morale high.

People can be educated, guided and mentored. I believe that most people tend to be relatively flexible. Given the right structures and (corporate) culture we are more likely to perform at our peak. This way employees serve their organization well, and nationally we can begin making up some of that $350 billion in lost productivity.

Chapter 15

• • • • • • • • •

Keeping and Maximizing the Talent You Have Now

by David Madison, Ph.D., Director, The National Guild of Five O'Clock Club Career Coaches

And I'd say one of the great lessons I've learned over the past couple of decades, from a management perspective, is that really when you come down to it, it really is all about people and all about leadership.

Steve Case, co-founder and former CEO of America Online

The following article is based on a panel presentation at the HR Network Breakfast at the CUNY Graduate Center in New York City. The HR Network is sponsored by the Five O'Clock Club and is a vendor-free venue for HR professionals to meet informally, network with one another, and hear discussions of important issues of the day.

The panelists were:
- Juan Brito, Associate Director, Staffing and Employee Relations at The Rockefeller Foundation and the former Director of Human Resources at the Foundation Center; currently president of PANO, The Personnel Association of Nonprofit Organizations;
- Geanie Villomann, Senior Vice President & Director, Human Resources for White Mountains Reinsurance Company of America, a property and casualty reinsurance company. Prior to joining White Mountains in early 2009, Geanie served as SVP/Director of Human Resources for North Fork Bank/Capital One Bank;
- Wendi Lazar, Partner and co-head of Outten & Golden LLP's Executives & Professionals Practice Group, which represents employees and executives both incoming and outgoing in the employment process.

• •

Stability and the capacity to formulate long-term plans are vital to every organization.

• •

Holding on…and Holding onto What You've Got

One of our coaches reported recently that his job search clients have told him that they have not been hearing the old interview question, "Where do you see yourself in five years?" Maybe this question fell out of favor some time ago, but the coach and the clients have speculated that, these days, interviewers are skipping this question because they don't expect new hires to stick around for five years!

Now this is anecdotal evidence, and we've not done research to determine if there is a trend here regarding interview questions, but a lack of curiosity about five-year plans seems to fit with the spirit of the times: there is so much upheaval and uncertainty in the workplace today, from both the employee and employer perspectives. Who knows where anyone will be five years from now?

> **The happiness index has been slipping for those Americans who have held onto their jobs.**

But surely such an attitude is not good for business, in either the short- or long-term. Astute human resources professionals, who are responsible for the human capital in their organizations, know that stability and the capacity to formulate long-term plans are vital. The events of the last decade have made any five-year future hard to sketch out in detail: downsizings, mergers, restructurings, hiring and wage freezes, budget cuts, increased workloads.

As we hope for normalcy, one of the major challenges for most organizations is maintaining the stability of the current headcount, and making sure that there is no unplanned and unwanted shrinkage. That is, what can we do to keep the people we have now—and keep them happy?

"Running a tight ship" and "keeping things lean" may sound appealing to the CEO and CFO, but nowadays these ideals usually mean that many people are working harder, with fewer rewards than they have in the past.

Fewer Happy Campers; Cross-Generational Workforce

The happiness index—if we can put it in such human terms—has been slipping for those Americans who have held onto their jobs. In a recent Conference Board survey (2011) of 5,000 households, it was found that only 45% of wage-earners indicated that they were satisfied with their jobs. In 1987, it had been 61%. There have been many factors during the intervening 23 years that have contributed to the decline, but we can hardly discount the negative developments of the last decade. Another survey conducted by People Metrics found that only 47% of employees described themselves as "engaged" in their work. For not-for-profits—here's a surprise—the figure was 44%.

So, more than half of the employees in these surveys admitted detachment from what they do in their hours in the workplace. Clearly, in such an environment, retention will be a major challenge: many of the unengaged are no doubt dreaming about greener pastures.

And even those who aren't—they're willing to put up and endure—perhaps they don't care all that much about how well the organization is performing. Many HR experts have been diagnosing these morale problems, and there are approaches and solutions—there are tools that are available to help organizations increase the happiness index of their employees through the lingering months or years of the recession.

Of course, there can be no one-size-fits-all solution: not only do organizations vary greatly, but the demographics of today's workforce mean that it will be harder to please everyone. As one expert has put it: "One of the challenges with employee retention is that all employees are not created equal. They have different needs, desires, values, habits and aspirations. In fact, we have four generations in the workforce."

- Those born between 1922 and 1945— the pre-baby-boomers—are called **veterans**. Their virtues include hard work, respect for authority and duty, and sacrifice.

- The **baby-boomers**, born between 1946 and 1964 are basically workaholics. They desire efficiency and quality, and question authority. During their careers they didn't hear much—or even care that much—about work-life balance. It was all work-work-work.

- The **generation Xers** were born between 1965 and 1980. They tend to value self-reliance, and work-work-work doesn't make sense when tasks can be efficiently eliminated. But they do want structure and direction, while remaining a skeptical bunch generally. They look at work and family issues and want balance.

- Those born after 1990, **generation Y**, tend to possess a what's-next mentality, which has implications for loyalty to employers; they appreciate multi-tasking, tenacity, the entrepreneurial bent. They are goal-oriented and are committed to the work-life balance.

....

Only 45% of employees describe themselves as "engaged" in their work.

....

Steps to Enhance Retention

Leadership Development: the Better Treatment of Employees

While the task is a daunting one for so many reasons, one authority states: "Keeping employees motivated, involved, committed to the organization and job-satisfied has become a corporate battle cry. An organization's greatest asset is its people, and maximizing that asset begins with the organization's leaders."

Just think about it: how many times have you wanted to leave a job because you didn't like your boss? If people face this kind of aggravation in the best of times, chances are it will be aggravated in the worst of times, when bosses are under pressure to get more work done with fewer people. As one expert points out, "Retention and engagement are not really about employees—they are about effective leadership. When employees leave, they don't leave an organization. They leave their managers."

In other words, in stressful times, when the headcount has been reduced, managers with poor people/management skills will produce too much drag on an organization's ability to remain competitive. If employees are muttering, "I can't wait to get out of here—where is my greener pasture?" retention becomes even tougher. It may be worth the investment, therefore, to arrange for management training and/or executive coaching for bosses who have not been accustomed to managing in stressful times—or who have reputations for being insensitive, abrasive or abusive. One expert warns, "If there is a toxic manager, you really can't ignore the situation. The bad manager will infect the workplace, and it's only a matter of time before talent starts walking out the door."

One HR professional, who recalls earlier times, says, "We've learned lessons from the past. Train your managers and staff on how to deal with change. Workshops geared to handling change have been invaluable. Recovery will happen sooner if there is education about the realities and difficulties.

"Whenever possible, use the resources of your EAP programs to help people let go of the old. We found that we needed to do a better job in anticipating employee reactions and anxieties."

Leadership Development: Helping People with Career Advancement

Most employees would probably give high rank to financial rewards, but "show me the money" is not the only way to enhance engagement and productivity. If people see that the roles they are asked to perform mean long-term career gain, that, too, can be an incentive.

Says one expert, "Don't overlook non-financial strategies. Organizations can actually separate themselves from the pack by a commitment to developing talent." One major study of recession responses found that "leading companies attributed some of their success to spending more money and effort on leadership development. They are confident that they are positioned for the rebound by holding onto leadership development programs during the recession."

For many employees, working harder because co-workers lost their jobs means taking on burdens and roles that they had not done before. One workplace expert advises: "Take steps to ensure that people have the training and skills to do their new jobs. A sink-or-swim approach is not very smart. The more employees feel they have control over their jobs and their performance, the more they feel secure, less stressed, less overwhelmed. They're going to more engaged and less likely to be eyeing a greener pasture somewhere else."

Communicate Better than Ever Before

Nothing can be more poisonous to morale than mystery and secrecy. It seems to be in the genetic make-up of corporate leaders to assume that it's best to keep everyone in the dark. But during a downsizing—and even well after one is over—one expert advises as much transparency as possible:

"Communicate the facts as honestly and compassionately as possible. This will help restore trust that has been lost—if cynicism hasn't gone off the charts. It is vital for leaders to listen, and use every opportunity for conversation to emphasize the reasons for a cutback or a reorganization. It is especially important to describe positive plans and visions for the future. This will allow everyone to move on and create a more effective workplace."

> Companies are positioning themselves for the future by spending money on leadership development.

One HR authority who has done a lot of work with traumatized organizations, recommends being creative in enhancing communication: "Most of the success stories in my experience have been based on doing a few things that haven't been tried before. How about setting up **breakfasts between leaders and employees**?—maybe one-on-one, or with a few or more. Arrange for **fireside chats**, that is, informal meetings of leaders with high-performers and high-potentials. Hold **quarterly town-hall meetings** for whole departments or offices. Of course, one of the goals is to reduce mystery and secrecy, but a primary focus has to be letting employees' voices be heard. Also set up **virtual suggestion boxes** and publish the responses. Employees like to know that they're being listened to. Create more open lines of communication with the CEO. Treat employees as engaged partners."

Especially in an environment where there have been salary freezes or smaller raises—and as people have seen their retirement portfolios damaged—employees pay more attention to compensation. No matter how much training and leadership development may be appreciated, remaining whole on money is a primary concern, and transparency here is also a virtue.

Says one benefits expert: "People were keeping a very watchful eye on benefits and rewards and required contributions. There has been a lot of confusion in the wake of new legislation. So we developed and rolled out an **interactive online total rewards statement**. Our objective was to encourage employees to be aware of, and think about, everything that impacted their pay and rewards. We wanted them to see the whole package—the value of their benefits, both cash and non-cash rewards. It really did hit the mark with employees. That has been our feedback."

Efficiency Isn't Such a Bad Idea After All

Efficiency experts have been the butt of jokes and ridicule over the years—maybe because they prompted unwelcome change, maybe because they were perceived more as meddlers than experts. But when people are overworked and underpaid, inefficiencies become obvious and painful, and "Isn't there a better way to do this?" becomes an obvious question. Says one HR expert, "How can we ask employees to do more with less when some things we're doing don't have to be done? Cut down on the annoying and useless stuff that may be on their to-do lists. **Take a look at your business procedures and streamline them.**"

There are examples to use as guides, this expert says: "After one downsizing that I was involved with, we established bi-weekly meetings with managers and employees to look at all of our core business processes. We got rid of non-essentials and time-wasters. We eliminated unproductive meetings, redundant steps or reports that no one ever bothered to read or use. Find ways to **eliminate anything that is no longer important to the business.** Be sure that employees are involved. This makes for greater engagement because people can see that they're part of something bigger than just their jobs. It helps them to focus on progress and the future, and creates trust in a culture where people are more inclined to take ownership of their responsibilities and problems."

Engaging and Caring on Several Fronts

We're all familiar with the exit interview—and more about that later—but one seasoned HR officer urges more use of *the stay interview.* It's good to find out why people have accepted an offer elsewhere—what made the other pasture greener?—but it's better to discover what will make people want to stay. Indeed, are you monitoring satisfaction or fulfillment? The stay interview is a meeting between employee and boss (or HR), the goal of which is get a conversation going: what is the employee most interested in, and what are his/her key challenges? What are the person's key motivators? Does he/she have a career vision for the future, and what does it look like?

"You're trying to find out what will make them stay with the organization," this HR expert points out, "and this should be done periodically."

Managers with poor people- and management-skills create a drag on an organization.

Using this approach, talent can be used to the best advantage. At one organization, a receptionist resisted the efforts of four bosses in 20 years to promote her. Why? Because being the receptionist was her calling.

"She loved the role," the HR officer reported, "It was her passion. She arrived at her desk an hour early, gathered her thoughts, reviewed company information on the website, and was ready to be the front-line customer service rep. She took great pride in what she did." The four bosses could have benefited from listening to what motivated and satisfied her.

One stay interview happened accidentally when an HR officer needed to find out why one of the mail room clerks was showing up late for work. "I'm sorry," he said, "but I get to bed so late." "And why is that?" "Because I'm going to night school…I'm studying to be an accountant." After a pause, the HR officer said, "I know there's going to be a clerical spot available in our accounting department soon—would you be interested?" Of course, the answer was Yes, and the mail room clerk was eventually promoted to an accounting role.

> To reduce the workload, see which tasks
> can be done better or eliminated.

It is important to make the best use of employees. "Try not to get confused," warns one HR expert, "about the difference between high-performers and high-potentials. Sometimes they're the same, but **high performers** are the people who can get the job done today, while high potentials are the people who can get you through the future—they can be part of the vision that will keep you moving forward. And be on the alert for managers who may want to hoard **high-potential** employees. They don't want to lose them, and will be reluctant to pass them on for bigger and better opportunities."

Improving the Exit Process

The way you fire people can have an impact on your ability to hire people. Word gets around, and corporate reputations can be damaged by undignified firings. But the internal damage can be just as real. Your true colors will be on full display when the survivors see how people are treated on their way out. "If you need to terminate people," says one expert on best firing practices, "Play it straight. I have seen the most awful mistakes made when it comes to terminating employees. Bosses have made up things that didn't really happen to justify a termination. If you emphasize failure when you're letting someone go, you're going to get an incredibly angry person, and that angry person is going to find a lawyer. If you don't want to make the mess worse, be nice to the departing employee's attorney."

And what about the famous exit interview? Much of the time these will be conducted on a polite and civil level: the departing employee is unlikely to unload all of his or her grievances. While exit interviews are probably a good idea, more time and effort should be devoted to conducting stay interviews with the talented employees who remain. "The exit interview," says one expert, "is not much more helpful than closing the barn door after the horses have run off."

Chapter 16

Golden Rules for Creating Win-Win Business Solutions

by Harriet Katz, Certified Five O'Clock Club Coach

The attempt to combine wisdom and power has only rarely been successful and then only for a short while.

Albert Einstein

Some people go through life without ever finding out what makes business work, or why some people get ahead and others do not. Yet the basic rules are surprisingly simple. Let's take a look at four key areas that absolutely affect all business people, no matter what business they are in, whether they work for a large or small corporation, or are in business for themselves.

These four areas are: *strategy, alliances, selling, and money.*

- Strategy is the plan by which you get to where you want to be.
- Alliances are what you need to help you get there.
- Selling yourself, goods and services is how you get there.
- Money is the measure of your success.

Power comes from unambiguous clarity of purpose, not from playing dirty.

I will share with you some of my insights on the golden rules of business that apply in these four key areas, developed from working with a large number of companies and individual clients.

Strategy: The Plan to Get Where You Want to Be

You are not a player if you do not have a game plan. A *career* game plan is used for guiding your progression, whether you're in an organization or on your own. It is the most practical and economical approach for achieving your goals. But no game plan should be static. It must be continually monitored and revised. And it depends on the ability to *achieve and use power ethically.* Strategy depends on power, and although *power* has negative connotations, it is vital to learn its positive meanings.

Power comes from an unambiguous clarity of purpose, not from playing dirty. Tell people exactly what you expect from them, and do it in a way that shows how they will benefit. In some contexts, power can be achieved by creating social distance. Personal dignity and a certain amount of formality indicate to people that you have things under control. Choose carefully the people with whom you share your vulnerabilities. For most managing situations, speak with conviction, be highly results-oriented, and quantify the measure of your success whenever possible.

Communicate clearly and frequently to important stakeholders about how well you are doing. Line managers turn sour if they are not constantly reminded of your beneficial presence. Your shelf-life diminishes rapidly when communication ceases. Your shelf-life is prolonged, even if you are not breaking new ground or putting out major fires, when you relay information about your activities. Frequent, brief contacts are far better than infrequent, cumbersome communications.

Remain in control. In business there are no winners or losers—there are only those who take control and those who lose it. When a situation arises that requires action, be the active party, the one who initiates. Set up a strategy and act upon it. If it doesn't work, change it. But make sure that it's your decision, and that you are the one creating the solution. Hence, always be the one who is going to get back to someone else. Do not sit around and wait for others to contact you. When you are getting into hot water, or when you do not have the information, or when it is simply not timely, take control with this handy phrase: "I'll get back to you," a phrase that covers a multitude of sins. You do not weaken your position by postponing your response until you have the advantage. Only a fool opens his mouth and advertises his weakness to the world.

Your shelf-life diminishes rapidly when communication ceases.

*"Jenkins and I worked it out.
He can have the office with the window."*

When faced with someone else's anger, diffuse it. First acknowledge the basis for the anger, even it if seems completely unjustified to you. The intensity of the feeling must not be denied. If it is there, it is there. The angry person cannot help but respond positively to your understanding and concern. It is a basic psychological tenet that if someone feels understood, that person feels cared about. If you have created this foundation, then you can approach him or her with an action to rectify the problem.

Always mind your manners. No matter how rude or unbusinesslike your opponent is, do not succumb to the temptation to respond in kind. Bad behavior is usually a power play, and chances are, you will lose if you engage in similar power plays.

Yes, there are people who gain by being obnoxious, but take a look at them. Why are they usually overweight, prone to heart disease, and smoke or drink like fiends? Because they are stressed. Because they lose so much sleep worrying about all the people who have the goods on them! And because deep down, they know that, inevitably, someone is going to do to them what they just did to someone else.

••

> **Always mind your manners. Bad behavior is usually a power play.**

••

Alliances: Everyone Needs Help and Support

An ally is someone with whom you have a mutually beneficial relationship, although the mutual benefits may not be simultaneous.

Business cannot be conducted in isolation. It is essential to build alliances, whether they are with peers, supervisors, clients or customers. These alliances are the very fabric through which business is conducted, and their importance can

supersede quality, performance and timing.

Alliances must be cultivated, not calculated. Think of them as plants in a garden that must be maintained and nurtured. Virtually anyone can become an ally and, ideally, everyone you come in contact with should be one. Though the benefits may not always be immediate, building a stable of allies is, in the long run, the most practical investment you can make.

Do not let misunderstandings destroy your alliances. Misunderstandings can almost always be fixed. In almost every situation, opportunities will come up in which you can correct a mistake. Or, you can create the opportunity yourself. A phone call, a meeting, a lunch, a letter—all are valid means by which you can repair and rebuild alliances.

However, it is sometimes better to wait for the opportunity to present itself. Do not try too hard. You do not have to spotlight an error, and you do not have to be too self-deprecating. A little time away from the mistake will cool you off and give you a clearer picture of how to handle it. Then you can take control again and redress the issue.

If you want someone to recommend you, by all means ask. A recommendation may be needed from a colleague within a company or outside. If you wait for a favor to come that you think is due, you may wait forever. If you do not ask, you may become angry and resentful, so that when you eventually do ask, your request might be unpleasant and awkward. Let your needs be known, instead of letting your resentment build—and emerge in ways that can lead to straining relationships or even making enemies. If you have cultivated and tended your alliances, you should feel free to draw on the benefits.

Never attempt to drive a wedge between people who have an alliance. It is Machiavellian to try to get them to turn on each other. You may be hoping for personal recognition, you may be trying to make one of them look bad, or you may be trying to get one of them to prefer you. But in the long run, it is more likely that you will be left out in the cold. Your temporary gain will back-fire. No one with decent judgment will easily trust you again.

....

Acknowledge all of the people who have contributed to your success.

....

Curb the jealousy of others by recruiting them into your winner's circle—and let them be winners. This will be much more beneficial than keeping all of the credit for yourself. Acknowledge all of the people who have contributed to your success. This can be written publicly, communicated directly, or announced in a meeting. When it is in the open, the contributors have a stake in remaining on your team. Your success now reflects well on them and they have every reason to want to be a part of it.

Is there someone in your circle of coworkers who appears to be an opponent? In order to head off strain and escalating conflict, treat him as a potential ally. If only he knew how you could *benefit* him, he would be part of your team. You need a strategy that creates a win-win situation. Do this by understanding what you want out of it, what he wants out of it, and how to package and sell the idea to him. How? By making him an offer he cannot refuse. Be astute in truly comprehending what he wants and needs. Be artful. You have only to gain.

....

Gossipers always lose. Gossip is tasty and intriguing—but resist it at all costs.

....

George, one of my clients in the pharmaceutical industry, found himself in a desperate situation. Nasty tension was building with Henry, a colleague in another department;

George was pressuring Henry to make decisions that directly impacted Henry's own department, and George was met with excuses and stalling. The tide turned when George resolved to stop asking questions, thus escalating the situation, and started listening instead. George came to understand what reality felt like from the other person's perspective. Armed with this insight, George was able to devise a strategy that addressed Henry's issues and also helped George to achieve his goals. This new understanding and win-win solution enabled them to patch up their relationship and move forward, pulling in the same direction.

When you have limited influence or power up the line, develop allies in upper management. Make suggestions to those who have the power to help you, and let the credit for your good ideas be shared. Acknowledge that they are directing and remain in control so that you do not seem threatening. Many supervisors will take care of you if you make them look good. The same is true if the person in question is a competitive coworker. Either way, you create an ally.

Gossipers always lose. Gossip is tasty and intriguing—but resist it all costs. Once you are known as a gossip, you will be a likely target for blame, even if you are innocent. No one will trust you, and with good reason. The real purpose of gossip is to falsely raise the status of the gossiper, or to assassinate the character of an opponent. Gossip may seem irresistible at times, but it is too costly.

Selling: An Aspect of Most Relationships Most of the Time

Selling is perhaps the most misunderstood aspect of business. Novices tend to see it as a shady form of trickery, a vulgar occupation that nice people simply do not do. The truth is that selling occurs every single day in almost every aspect of our lives.

Real selling, the kind that works and has the best long-term benefits, is the process in

*"I'm your best friend, not your employee.
I don't need an appointment to see you."*

which mutual needs are met. *The buyer's need* might be anything from a vacuum cleaner to a sympathetic ear—or more authority. *The seller's need* is simply to make the sale. Therefore, a good salesperson needs to determine the need of the buyer and meet it. If the buyer does not need what you are selling, listen to what is needed, and try to provide it. Eventually, if both parties are trying, you should find a common ground on which to make a fair exchange—and the sale is completed.

Helen, another client, reported recently on a situation that deteriorated because her vendor refused to listen. Helen had a three-year relationship with the vendor, and told him exactly what she wanted to buy next. But having his heart set on a larger sale, the seller pushed another product on Helen. She resented this approach and sought out another provider who listened—and

gave her what she asked for. If the buyer (Helen, in this case) does not need what you are selling, listen to what is needed, and try to provide it. Eventually, if both parties are trying, you should find a common ground on which to make a fair exchange—and the sale is completed.

Hence, the key to selling is listening. The goal of a negotiation is to find a common ground. Do not get bogged down in petty details, power plays, or ego trips. Listen intently to what the other person is trying to achieve, instead of busily planning a counterattack or becoming defensive. You cannot meet your potential buyer's needs if you don't hear what he or she is saying.

When you have a robust list of customers, advertise you accomplishments. Your track record has to come across loud and clear, because new accounts don't usually just fall in your lap.

Results achieved for one person or company are easily transferable to a prospective second person or company. Word of mouth works in your favor, but be persistent in telling your own story.

George learned to listen and resolved his problems with a colleague.

Do this by giving examples of how you solved a problem—in concrete, specific terms. Say exactly how much money you saved or made for the company, how many people you trained, how many people you reached with a message, etc. One impressive achievement is worth more than ten promises about all the wonderful things you plan to do.

Recognize a brick wall when you hit one. It's okay to attempt to get through, around or over it, but sometimes that isn't possible. If someone is bent on impeding your goals, you might have to take no for an answer, but then alter your strategy. This may mean changing jobs, changing bosses, or stopping a sales pitch. This will save you a tremendous amount of time and frustration. Soldiering on against a brick wall can cost more than the gains you had hoped to make. There are times when no amount of salesmanship or politics work. Move on to a more fertile ground.

Money: A Key Measure of Your Use of Strategy and Power

Everyone is in business to make money—even the most altruistic people who are in love with their work. All too often, people are woefully unaware of how directly and irrevocably money is tied to their day-to-day work. Some do not like to talk about money, have trouble asking for it, and cannot quote their value in hard dollars and cents. They have no concept that the work they do makes much more money for the company than the comparable amount the company pays them.

Asking for a raise or charging for a service is directly tied to your relationship with money and your personal level of confidence.

If you separate money from work, everyone loses. You become detached from the reality of business so that alliances are undermined, management problems develop, and the lifeblood of the organization is drained.

But if you see money as the stimulating force it is, you can use it as a source of energy. It will help you to take control rather than fall prey, because it is the most potent source of power that is yours to manage. The more comfortable you become with it, the better able you are to relate to its purpose, and to understand the business you are conducting.

Asking for a raise or charging for a service is directly tied to your relationship with money and your personal level of confidence. If you are uneasy talking about your worth so bluntly, transfer the accolades to your achievements. These can be separated from you personally. They stand on their own merits and can be your best advertisement.

The first salary or price you get becomes a foundation from which future increases will be measured. Newcomers often tend to under price themselves. They do this because they want the opportunity more than the money, and this might be necessary to gain experience. But be realistic about what lies ahead. It is commonly not possible to negotiate big increases as soon as you might hope. Your initial price tag can prejudice your chances for getting what you're really worth. If you want more money, you must be prepared to make your case powerfully—and perhaps look outside of your present organization for another position. Or if you make your living by selling, you will need to expand your client list.

....

It is not cost-effective to exploit or fail to deliver on a good deal.

....

No business person can be casual about receivables. Money is either in your hands or theirs. The side that owes the money holds the most power. But proceed with caution in your collection practices. Attempts to collect overdue money should be regular and conducted pleasantly. Ask how the client is doing, and ask whether there are any problems you can help with. But yes, ask for the money. You may have to work out a payment plan, but be firm that you expect to be paid. After all, you did deliver an excellent service or product.

And a final Golden Rule: A good deal means that everyone is happy. The person who skimps on delivering a good deal (a job well done at work, or a service provided by a vendor) cannot expect a good relationship to endure. Your gain will be extremely short-term. The other party will resent you—and may look for opportunities to repay you in kind. This may take the form of disloyalty, stealing, or undermining your goals. In the long run, it is not cost-effective to exploit others or fail to deliver the good deal.

Chapter 17

The New Diversity

Be Smart and Brave—Please Hire My Family

by Kate Wendleton, President,
The Five O'Clock Club

*If we were to wake up some morning and find that
everyone was the same race, creed and color, we
would find some other causes for prejudice by noon.*

Howard Aiken, mathematician (1900-1973)

I'm so lucky. My family would never be considered activists, but they have always been blind to race, color, religion, sexual orientation and whatever else there is. I rarely even notice hair color or height!

Yes, there was real-life segregation: When I was in grade school, we went to the white school and walked by the black school every day. But it wasn't that simple. In the little row of only six stores in my neighborhood, the pharmacist/pharmacy owner was black. His wife and grown children worked in the store. We had sodas at his soda fountain, in retrospect an ironic twist given that blacks were denied sodas at white-owned soda fountains at that time. The corner deli, two stores away, was owned by a Jewish family.

It might not seem like much, but these owners were some of the most visible people in our small community. There were only 13 people in my eighth-grade class, which included one African-American boy and one real-life Gypsy who lived in a Gypsy camp and took a bus to school. I visited that camp many times, watching them make chairs to sell and listening to them sing around the campfire.

What an interesting world. The people of my childhood—again, I'm lucky—were sweet and trusting. People did not need to lock the doors to their houses. I don't remember any negative incidents involving race or creed.

In my environment, the trusting and openness were broad-based. In 1980, my parents, who had already had nine children, took in a Vietnamese family (husband, wife and brother), who stayed with our family for three months while an agency and my parents found them an apartment near us. They remained part of our immediate family for many decades.

· ·

**Hire people who are smart, highly motivated
and grateful for the opportunity: You'll
wind up with a diverse workforce.**

· ·

Today, my family includes just about every race and creed. My parents are Catholic, and their extended family now consists of Catholic, Christian, Muslim and Jewish. We have black, white, brown, Asian, Hispanic and probably whatever else there may be. We have an Iranian head of Information Technology (who started as a waiter when he came to this country), an African-American brain surgeon (who went to Harvard for undergrad and the University of Pennsylvania for medical school), a Latina micro-biologist, others I'm probably forgetting, and all of their multi-colored children. My sister, Patti, who is a white, blonde Catholic, married Moe (short for Mohammed), an Iranian Muslim. They have three beautiful brown-skinned children who went to Jewish day school. When the girls were young, they would ask, "Aunt Kate, do you celebrate Hanukkah or Christmas?" So touching and innocent. My sister and her husband wanted them to be blind to color, race, and faith, just as we older ones were.

My husband and I volunteer on Saturdays with African-American males who have aged out of foster care (they are now 21 to 23 years old.).

And, as I have mentioned before, I have a brother who could have been classified as having a disability. However, he has done so well with his life and has so worked around his disability that it is not relevant at all. (See article below, "Do Yourself a Favor: Hire My Brother.")

I hope it's not relevant to you when you're hiring. I hope you will enjoy the pride and excitement I have when I am around my diverse family by having that pride and excitement from diversity in your workplace. I hope you intend to hire with diversity in mind. After all, if you hire with diversity in mind, you would be hiring my family. I will be grateful that you are not prejudiced against them, but instead are able to see their true worth and see them as just other qualified persons who happen to be of a different race, gender, religion, ethnicity, age, sexual orientation or have what might be called a "disability."

The New Diversity: A Broader Definition

By Kate Wendleton, President, The Five O'Clock Club

There will be 500,000 people coming back from prison or jail this year, ... They can come back marked as ex-offenders, unable to get a job, presumed by community to be the person responsible for the next crime to come down the road and they will be right back in prison again having committed another crime.

Janet Reno, the first woman to serve as U.S. Attorney General

If you are in a position to hire, now is your chance to be smarter about it. We at The Five O'Clock Club have found many superstars in the making when we make an effort to hire former offenders who are committed to doing something positive with their lives. The onboarding for some could take as long as six months because, after all, some had never seen a cell phone, used modern-day computer programs, or ridden on today's transportation system. But nothing can stop someone who is smart, highly motivated and grateful for an opportunity. It wasn't long before these diamonds in the rough began to shine and kept on moving up. Annual pay raises didn't make sense when a person was making such progress yet some received raises far more often. But the organization benefits the most!

··

Don't overlook hiring former offenders. That is, if you have the smarts and the guts to do the right thing.

··

Of course, now it is the law in many states that you cannot discriminate based on a person's criminal record, and I can tell you that you can get very talented and devoted people if you make an effort to hire the best and the brightest who are classified as ex-offenders. We never ask why they were in prison, although it may be relevant in some cases (such as a drug company hiring someone who was convicted of a drug-related crime). And some industries, such as banking, are not allowed to hire ex-felons. But that makes it so much easier for the rest of us to pick and choose the best.

Why consider former offenders for your workforce? First of all, they have paid their debt to society—so let's be fair. Please remember the number of people who have been unfairly convicted of crimes:

- The Innocence Project (www.innocenceproject.org) has freed 252 people who were eventually exonerated based on DNA evidence.
- 17 of the 252 people exonerated through DNA served time on death row.
- The average length of time served by exonerees is 13 years. The total number of years served is approximately 3,196.
- The average age of exonerees at the time of their wrongful convictions was 27. (Source: The Innocence Project website.)
- After serving an average of 13 years in prison, many were unable to get their lives back or even find a job, even though they were declared innocent. It seems that no one wants to hire someone who has been in prison—even one who is proven innocent. Life isn't fair—but we can be.

And what about other incarcerated people where DNA is not an issue? There is no equivalent Innocence Project to help them. The Five O'Clock Club has never regretted hiring any former offender. We work with organizations that refer the best to us. Because we are relatively small we can hire only a few, but it has worked to our benefit.

Hiring former offenders does not fit the stan-

dard definition of diversity, but why not develop some pride in having a truly diverse workforce—including former offenders? You can be a leader—ahead of the crowd. You can capitalize on the talent that's out there.

That's the way America is going. Immigrants keep on coming and, in the not-too-distant future, whites will be the new minority. This means that your customer base will not be white. Better to have a diverse population to serve your diverse customer base. It's smart business and it's the right thing to do anyway.

Be brave. Be good. Show others the way.

"...I bought my daughter a dress." A Lesson in Becoming a Moral Compass

by Jeff Cohen, VP of Labor Relations, Mount Sinai Medical Center

Children of incarcerated parents are six times more likely than other youths to end up in prison themselves. Helping former offenders helps to break the cycle of offense.

Casey Family Programs, *Children of Prisoners Empowered for Success (COPES) Mentoring Program*

Be the moral compass.

Dr. Norman Metzger, *a giant in HR in the healthcare field.*

In his role as VP of Labor Relations at Mount Sinai Medical Center, New York, Jeff Cohen has been a strong advocate of hiring people with criminal records. He spoke of one memorable case, in which he made the decision to hire a man who had been convicted of manslaughter and had served six years in prison:

My interview with this man was an eye opener. He was completely honest. He referred to the crime 25 years ago as a mistake of his youth. He said that, if he had not taken the other man's life, he would himself have died that day. It was chilling. He told me he had three young daughters, and lived in one of the worst sections of New York because it was all he could afford: no one wanted to hire him because of his record. He was grateful for the opportunity to talk to me, but he also understood that he would not get the job.

Here I was facing a moral decision. I went to my own mentor, Dr. Norman Metzger, a giant in HR in the healthcare field. He told me, "Be the moral compass." After all, a great employer is not measured by how well people at the top are treated—but by how people who need help the most are treated. We offered him a job. He passed probation and is doing a fine job.

Three weeks ago I got a call that this gentleman wanted to see me. I had not seen him in more than eight months, and I immediately imagined the worst. No one ever comes to see the VP of Labor Relations for anything good, ever. He entered the room, just as he had eight months earlier. He told me that he was truly enjoying working at Mount Sinai, and he was thankful that he had been given the opportunity. He had been working overtime and earning extra money. Then he looked up at me and said, "You know what I did? I bought my daughter a dress."

....

"During the interview, he told me he understood he would not get the job."

....

I have worked in labor relations for a long time, and pretty much nothing affects me. But this guy just hit me in the heart. He was so proud of himself. He had done something for his daughter and just wanted to tell me.

So…you want to talk about social responsibility? Just do the right thing.

Do Yourself a Favor: Hire My Brother

By Kate Wendleton, President, The Five O'Clock Club

It is a waste of time to be angry about my disability. One has to get on with life and I haven't done badly.

Stephen Hawking, British theoretical physicist and cosmologist, almost completely paralyzed, in an interview with *The Guardian*, 2005

Everyone has a handicap—something they think that will hold them back in their careers. It could be that they feel they are too young or too old, have too little education or too much, are of the wrong race, creed, nationality, sexual orientation or background, or are very aware that they have a physical disability.

In fact, serious prejudice does exist. The subject is so sensitive that there is rarely an honest discussion between people with opposing points of view. Yet, in managing their own careers, people must try to forget about discrimination. Those who are too self-conscious about their perceived handicaps will hold themselves back. To advance, they must simply plow ahead and find an open window when doors are slamming shut all over town.

I got this attitude from my family. My younger brother, Robert, developed spinal meningitis when he was two years old. The medical specialists could not help. We all loved him, but in his grade school years we assumed he was mentally deficient. What he actually had was an uncorrectable speech and hearing defect. Instead of sending him to high school, my parents sent him to a trade school to make sure he could earn a living.

There, he became brave and asked his teachers to face him when they spoke so he could read their lips. When they forgot, he reminded them, and he graduated first in his class.

To make up for his lack of a high school education, he went to junior college. Then he majored in metallurgy at the University of Pennsylvania—all the while insisting that his teachers face him so he could read their lips.

Now he runs a highly successful nanotechnology company and travels the world marketing his company's products. His physical limitation is barely noticeable, he works like a demon and, as it turns out, he is as smart as can be.

"No excuses. Do your best." Because of my brother, that's what I've always told myself and my clients.

To managers, I say this: "Most of you do not understand. You have no idea what it's like to be judged on something other than your skills, talents and personality."

Bruce Faulk, a young, clean-cut, gifted actor—and a Five O'Clock Clubber—learned our techniques and did well in his career. He played in *Hamlet* on Broadway and toured Europe with *Hair*. Then he played again in the U.S. One night after a show in Boston, Bruce went out for pizza. A few policemen stopped him and asked where he thought he was going. Bruce did not answer as respectfully as he might have. He was thrown in jail. Of course, Bruce is black.

To this day, many black male professionals and executives I know have been treated unfairly by policemen. Or they have been mistaken for messengers or delivery men.

When I ask white male executives if they have ever experienced this sort of thing, they can barely understand my question. It is so foreign to them. Dear Manager: Try to understand. Give different people a chance. Young people. Older people. People with physical limitations. People of different races, ethnicities, genders or backgrounds. You will find plenty who work harder and are smarter than you would have imagined. You will be the winner for it. And you will have hired my brother.

The Five O'Clock Club Attitude

 THE GARDEN OF LIFE IS abundant, prosperous and magical. ❦ In this garden, there is enough for everyone. ❦ Share the fruit and the knowledge ❦ Our brothers and we are in this lush, exciting place together. ❦ Let's show others the way. ❦ Kindness. Generosity. ❦ Hard work. ❦ God's care.

Part Three:

Handling the Job

Chapter 18
• • • • • • • •

When You're Feeling Overwhelmed at Work

by Ruth K. Robbins, Certified Five O'Clock Club Coach

I like work; it fascinates me.
I can sit and look at it for hours.
I love to keep it by me; the idea of
getting rid of it nearly breaks my heart.

Jerome K. Jerome, British author, 1859-1927

"It's a tough job," we sometimes say when we hear about someone doing a cushy job—"but somebody's got to do it." There probably are jobs that are as easy as they look. But most of us work in situations that put us under deadlines and pressure, sometimes to the point that we feel overwhelmed—and we do wonder, "How much longer can I take this?" Consider the following examples:

Ryan was a communications manager at a not-for-profit. He was asked by his boss, almost at the last minute, to put together an extensive presentation for a meeting to plan the development of a prototype newsletter to go out to all contributors and members. He had less than a week to prepare for this important meeting; he had a part-time assistant to help him do the research, gather information and put together

a compelling presentation. The week became a nightmare.

Gail was hired as a recruiter by a dynamic head hunting firm that specialized in searches for mid-to-senior level IT and finance managers. As a former administrator in a law firm, she had hired professionals, but never at this level or with such technical specialties. She faced a very steep learning curve, trying to understand and speak knowledgeably about various IT specialties, programs and platforms; it was vital to maintain credibility with both clients and candidates. She faced the demands of her boss to qualify and close business, the exacting specifications of her clients and the impatience of high-profile, demanding candidates.

· ·

Waiting for things to calm
down is not an option!

· ·

Do their stories sound familiar? Both Ryan and Gail are hard workers and are used to performing at high levels. But sometimes the work piles on and piles up, and the point can arrive when we ask, "Am I being asked to do too much?" Tough assignments, steep learning curves, increasing expectations from the boss to achieve more with less: These seem to be the features of the workplace today, which is increasingly technology-based and globally competitive. It's not uncommon that employees feel overworked, stressed and stretched to the limit.

But this is the context in which careers either get a boost or get derailed. Every day when you get up and go to work your career is on the line. Waiting for things to calm down is not an option! It is your ability to meet increased expectations with skill, grace and humor within your organization's formal structure and informal culture, that will enable you to navigate your career effectively. If you're feeling overwhelmed, there may be things you can do to change the boss or the corporate culture—but, without waiting for that, what can you do to make sure you're working in the best, most efficient way possible?

On the one hand, there is...

- the matter of mastering time management: many people become overwhelmed at work because they don't make the best use of every minute of every day.
- the matter of what might be called the lack of workplace savvy, *i.e.,* becoming overburdened because of failure to understand and use relationships and politics properly.

In the pages that follow, we'll consider both.

Managing Your Time and Workflow

The Calendar

We say to job hunters who are in a rush to get a new job, "Take the time to do an assessment, even if it seems to be a waste of time." Coming to a dead stop to think can be productive. Likewise, proper time management requires a pause to analyze. Take an hour every two weeks, or on some regular basis, to review your

"You may want to send a search party into Konklin's cubicle. No one has heard from him in three days."

daily and weekly schedule and workflow. Try to get the big picture of what is supposed to happen during the next month or quarter.

....

**The work piles on and piles up.
At some point you must ask yourself,
"Am I being asked to do *too much*?"**

....

Arrange tasks by urgency and importance, based on what you and your boss identify as your major goals and objectives, usually determined at periodic performance reviews. Routine tasks and assignments can be done early in the morning or at the end of the day, or be delegated to an assistant. Plan the week or month in sync with the goals of your manager and department. A boss' priorities sometimes shift due to changes from his or her managers, so be sure to keep alert and remain informed.

The feeling of being overwhelmed often comes from being taken by surprise, so the periodic careful review of the calendar helps you to visualize what lies ahead during the next week or month. This can be vital in keeping up with the furious pace of your office.

As you plan for the weeks and months ahead, insert "to-do" reminders well in advance of deadlines. These are the helpful pop-ups!—they keep you mindful of deadlines, clients to call, or projects to get started on. These can help to prevent you from being overwhelmed by things you "forgot to do."

A word to the wise: If you master electronic tools you can have a real edge, especially if all of your colleagues use hand-held devices to manage calendar and email, and carry hundreds of files. Gadgets alone can't get you organized, but you will find yourself at a disadvantage if you still rely on paper desk calendars and legal pads.

If you are of a certain age, the gadgets and technology themselves may seem overwhelming. The out-of date PDA that you purchased may come with 300-page user manual. But here are shortcuts: Instead of sweating through the manual, make friends with an internal technology professional, perhaps even an entry level techie who will help you to get up to speed. Get short-cut suggestions and guidance in a non-technical, user friendly way.

Of course, nothing is more overwhelming and devastating than loss of data. Be fanatical about regularly backing up all your files—and knowing where to find the backup disks.

The Email Problem

We all get so much of it! Who hasn't felt that being overwhelmed at work is partly due to the burden of email? Maybe your job requires that you check email constantly—or perhaps only once or twice a day. The problem is that each email requires some kind of action eventually. If 200 envelopes arrived on your desk every day through the mail, you would soon be immobilized if you didn't take action on each piece. An email inbox cluttered with hundreds of messages presents the same challenge, and can be dangerous (business missed or overlooked) and demoralizing ("When will I ever find the time…?"). Email especially demands a method because it just keeps coming!

Try to adopt the principle of the four "Ds" when looking at your email in-box every morning—or even every ten minutes. Popularized by Sally McGhee in McGhee's Productivity Solutions, the following actions are required:

- Do
- Delegate
- Defer
- Delete

Do means taking immediate action on something as soon as you see it. This often takes only a few seconds or minutes—or maybe an hour if it is complex and urgent—but it's done.

Delegate is usually essential in the campaign to reduce the feeling—and reality—of being overwhelmed. Many people can't let go; they have a knee-jerk reaction about responding to requests that reach their desks. It takes initiative and confidence to know how and when to let go. Take the time to analyze the workflow: aren't there others whom you trust, support staff or colleagues, to whom many emails can be forwarded? If not, train others to help you. Delegation requires that artful mix of empowering others to do tasks, while maintaining oversight responsibility for the outcomes and performance. The key here is to maintain accountability and follow-up, ensuring that delegated tasks do get handled and completed satisfactorily.

Defer means making a bargain with yourself to handle the matter later in a thoughtful manner. Leave the message in your inbox as a reminder, or set up a reminder on your electronic to-do calendar to take action later.

Delete means getting rid of it on the spot; spam, obviously, but also requests or questions you simply can't be bothered with.

Deciding what is urgent, important, and less important; having the wisdom not to take on everything that comes into your inbox—knowing when to defer or file or simply take no action

at all—can contribute dramatically to good time management, both on normal business days and during high pressure, crunch times.

···

Many people don't make the best use of every minute of every day.

···

Email: The Virtue of Brevity

Of course email can be used to write thousands of words or send thousands of pages. But in the ordinary exchange of ideas and information, brevity is a key to survival. Being overwhelmed can mean you're spending too much time on email. Streamline your emails, with an eye to flow and legibility. Bold and underline highlights you want your reader to focus on. Neither you, your boss nor your colleagues have time for wordy messages. Respond to questions pleasantly and succinctly, referring to handbooks, publications or internal resources if you don't have the time for extended explanations.

"Johnson, if you're going to have negative thoughts, I suggest you get rid of that thought balloon!"

Managing Your Information and Contact Files

There's no doubt about it: the information rushing at us on a daily basis is daunting. We are flooded with incoming messages and requests competing for some level of our attention. Sorting though, acting upon and archiving emails and hard copy documents require a logical and consistent storage and filing system. The feeling of being overwhelmed is common if you simply can't find something and waste valuable time searching through computer folders or the piles on your desk. Getting out from under this burden of disorganization can mean staying late for a week or two or spending weekends at the office just to get organized.

So take the time to logically categorize and sub-categorize computer folders and paper files (files, not *piles!*), and then *get items out of your inbox or off your desk*. If your system is logical and organized, your boss, colleagues and assistants should be able to locate important documents when you are absent or off-site. Optimal use of your time requires an intelligent and consistent filing system that supports you.

Try to get the big picture of what is supposed to happen during the next month or quarter.

Managing Your Day

We have looked at reviewing the calendar, reforming email behavior and organizing files. These are great first steps in taking control. It's also helpful to apply the four "Ds" mentioned above to how you manage workflow on a daily basis. Review a typical day at your work and see where you might want to improve your allocation of time and effort. You might even do this every morning, and keep the four "Ds" in mind throughout the day.

- What are the tasks that *must be done today*?
  1. _____
  2. _____
  3. _____
  4. _____

- What tasks or activities can be deferred for *later* action? (And how is that noted?—to take more action, spend more time, expend more effort?)
  1. _____
  2. _____
  3. _____
  4. _____

- What can be delegated to someone else?
  1. _____
  2. _____
  3. _____
  4. _____

- What can simply be deleted, eliminated— tossed in the wastebasket? (Just say no.)
  1. _____
  2. _____
  3. _____
  4. _____

The Unexpected Tough Assignment

No matter how well organized you are, no matter how well you have planned your day and your week, it's very easy to feel overwhelmed if you're handed a major project on top of your normal work load. The boss asks you to tackle a challenging assignment; perhaps there is a very tight time constraint, insufficient budget and staff—and new skills are required. Perhaps like Ryan, the communications professional, you are expected to prepare a major presentation on short notice, or like Margaret, you may feel like you're in way over your head (see below).

"I've fired the entire company except you, Jerkins. You'll have more work without pay, but you do have job security."

Margaret's Story

Margaret came to The Five O'Clock Club to get help with her job search. Too much was wrong with her current situation and she wanted to move on. Her small group at the Club helped her with the search, but also helped her deal with the crisis at work.

Margaret felt overwhelmed when the job she *thought* she had signed on for as a meeting planner at a financial company turned out to be a back office control and support position. The job required a high level of organization, attention to detail, knowledge of a specific scheduling application, Excel and desktop publishing software that she did not know well. The learning curve that she faced was indeed steep.

The first thing that Margaret did was to listen carefully to her boss, without communicating panic or a sense of inadequacy. She made arrangements to learn the new applications; she was willing to stay extra hours and work Saturdays to do so. She made friends with her predecessor, who had been promoted into another department, but who helped her when she could. Margaret acknowledged her help with small tokens of appreciation. *Still* things were going slowly; Margaret was not picking up as quickly as she needed to and could not continue to lean on others with frequent questions.

She went back to her boss with documentation of the efforts she had made. She demonstrated what she had learned and what she had already accomplished, but she let him know where the gaps were and where she needed additional support to complete the project. She even acknowledged that it might be appropriate to replace her. The boss didn't think that was a good idea, mainly because it would have been more costly to hire someone else at that point. He urged her to keep learning as she had been, and identified a couple of other folks that could help her. But based on her obvious effort and hard work, he challenged her to get the job done.

> The feeling of being overwhelmed often comes from being taken by surprise.

Margaret's Five O'Clock Club group helped her to brainstorm what to do and played a role in boosting her morale, because she tended to second-guess herself a lot. She stayed on the assignment for nine months, instead of backing out in panic within the first month. As a result she had something of substance to add to her résumé, and her boss was pleased with her performance. As shaky as her start had been, the company asked her to work for them part-time when she went back to school for an advanced degree.

> You are overwhelmed when you spend endless time searching for something.

Specifics for Handling the Overwhelming Assignments

"I'll never be able to do it," may be your first reaction. But there are ways to respond constructively. Here are a few suggestions:

- Listen attentively to your assignment or project description without jumping to conclusions. Don't offer protests of self-doubt or outrage. Don't voice panic, because your boss is under even more pressure than you are and doesn't need your negative emotion.
- Go back to your office and take time to analyze the assignment, the resources, and the timetable in a calm, thoughtful manner.
- Assess you boss' style and react accordingly, and try to get at least one initial meeting to describe your evaluation

of the challenges faced. Get to the point and avoid digressions if your boss is known for his/her no-nonsense approach.

- Be sure to obtain clarity on the *deliverables* and feedback about *your understanding of the project*.
- Break down the assignment into *manageable* segments, noting schedules, deadlines, available support staff and resources, while keeping your boss' priorities in mind. Use Gantt charts, Outlook calendars or Excel spreadsheets.
- Analyze both your capabilities and deficiencies to see where and how you can enhance your skills and efforts to get the job done.
- Figure out the assistance you'll need, and delegate to get the assignment completed. Will you be working alone or will you be able to mobilize staff?
  - ✓ Can you hire temporary help?
  - ✓ Can you enlist the assistance of a staff member from another department for a short-term effort, with the understanding that you will reciprocate.
  - ✓ Can you enlist a student intern to help with the project or with your routine tasks?
- Propose alternative solutions that might work if the assignment or task appears impossible to complete on time, within budget and with available resources. Calmly outline challenges that lie ahead and propose positive alternative solutions. Get your boss' feedback.

> The burden of email contributes to the feeling of being overwhelmed.

- Describe the biggest problems you foresee, i.e., where, when and how you might get stuck; outline the best case/worst case scenarios—so that you have a record of your projections, expectations and misgivings.

- Keep to the schedule as you outlined it, and alert colleagues and assistants if deadlines are missed.
- Make sure your boss knows the project status. Schedule regular meetings and provide a short written agenda; also prepare progress notes that document your efforts.
- Ask the people who are helping you to keep you posted—to assure you that they are helping you. Ask for periodic feedback and status reports.

Getting Help: A Key to Avoiding Being Overwhelmed

Sometimes people end up with too much to do because they fail to see that colleagues and subordinates can be resources and partners; they don't trust others to perform as well as they do—and end up not performing well themselves! It is vital to cultivate a network of relationships and alliances to handle routine business and for managing during the high pressure times. Here are a few suggestions:

- Nurture ongoing relationships outside of your department; include peers and subordinates who might be of service to you. Identify people who can engage in reciprocal relationships.
- Develop a network *outside* of your company to get information, suggestions, support, and feedback. Build a network of peers within industry organizations that might become an invaluable resource in tackling a tough assignment. Keep up the relationships. If you built a sound network of contacts while you

were job hunting, don't let the network die. Work hard to maintain it. Create reminders in your automated calendar to call or email key people frequently.

....

Delegation is usually essential.

....

- Maintaining the network means learning how to cultivate people: yes, the ultimate goal is to derive benefit, but professional relationships are cultivated by offering and providing help when called upon.

Who, *within* your company, can you cultivate for reciprocal favors when you're under pressure? (Think at all different levels within the organization including those subordinate to you.)

1. _____
2. _____
3. _____
4. _____

Who do you know *outside* of the company in your industry whom you can nurture as a mentor or be part of your outside resource network team?

1. _____
2. _____
3. _____
4. _____

When Being Overwhelmed Persists

If you find yourself on constant overdrive and under unrelenting stress—despite time-management improvements, and bettering relationships with colleagues and support staff—you probably need to take stock of your situation on a deeper level. The overload that you face may be *built in*—it's just the way that your company does business. One senior HR officer at a major international bank commented, "If you want work-life balance, don't come to work here." Some companies want workaholics who take "being overwhelmed" in stride. Or if your company has slashed staff to help the bottom line—expecting fewer employees to do more work—you may be in a situation that won't show improvement.

She stayed on the assignment rather than backing out within the first month.

But if you don't work for a company that values "overwhelmed," you can seek possible solutions—and some companies are more flexible than others. For example, you might ask your boss to work from home one day a week, demonstrating to her the improved results that can be expected. Would it really make a difference if you didn't have to commute to the office one day a week? Would it help you to complete projects by working non-stop from early morning until evening at home, without being distracted by the routine at your desk at the office?

Break down the assignment into manageable segments.

If, despite all efforts, your mental and physical health are being seriously compromised by work overload, it's probably time to change jobs. If you like the company—and don't want to add yet another employer to your résumé—use your network and influence to try identify other opportunities within your organization that might be a better fit. Of course, it takes time and finesse to develop relationships while not jeopardizing your current position. At The Five O' Clock Club we emphasize being tuned into the broader picture: find out what's going on in other departments and cultivate relationships.

As a last resort, if being overwhelmed remains a constant, it's probably time to look elsewhere. At The Five O'Clock Club, we help people with job search, of course. But for most of the professionals, managers and executives who come to the Club, getting a job is not really the issue. *Everybody* will get a job. Getting the *right job* is the issue. And because members of the Club take the time to do a thorough assessment, and give a lot of thought to what they want to do—and what kinds of companies will really suit them—they usually end up in jobs that they like. They reduce the risk of ending up in another overwhelming environment.

Chapter 19

• • • • • • • • •

Time Management: How to Become a To-Do List Conqueror

by Stacey Jerrold, Certified Five O'Clock Club Coach

Take care of the minutes and the hours will take care of themselves.

Phillip Dormer Stanhope, British statesman and man of letters

Do you always perform at your peak? Do you excel at giving full attention to projects and providing ample support to the people in your life? Do you routinely finish your work and leave your job at the end of the day with a clean desk and an agenda for the next day? If you have answered Yes to all these questions, congratulate yourself and move on to the next chapter.

However, if for any reason, you answered No to any of these questions—or if you feel that your life is out of control too much of the time—don't despair! Time management is a skill you can master. It can also be considered a mindset, or even a lifestyle. It can be mastered by anyone who wants:

- to feel more in control
- to attain more out of life
- to achieve success in business while having time to enjoy a personal life

- to reduce stress and achieve more balance in their lives

Your success depends, of course, on utilizing a time management system that works best for you. But you have to start by addressing your attitudes, feelings and habits. What are your fundamental values and goals? Without this foundation, any success you achieve might be short-lived.

· ·

Time is the great equalizer. We all have an equal amount, but not all use it effectively.

· ·

What Do We Mean by Time Management?

Maybe the term is actually an oxymoron. There really isn't anything to manage. There are a fixed number of days in a week, hours in each day, minutes in each hour. But our perception of time can make a big difference. Some days we are conquerors and complete everything on our

"Mr. Billings realizes you traveled a long way to meet with Him. However, he decided to change the meeting until next week."

to-do list, and yet other days we can barely get through the first few items on the list. If you look back on your conquering days, you very likely will see that the projects/tasks that you completed were directly related to your goals, which added meaning to your tasks: You went into high gear and time seemed to speed by.

This is a major clue about becoming a conqueror of tasks and projects. When you are able to define your purpose, establish your values and vision, and develop a success-oriented attitude, both direction and meaning are more likely to emerge.

The best way to decide what you want—and set goals accordingly—is to have an understanding of yourself. The Five O'Clock Club's primary tool for doing this is the Seven Stories Exercise. This enables you to carefully analyze your outstanding accomplishments and identify your strongest and most enjoyable skills.

Doing your Fifteen or Forty-Year Vision helps you to give shape and scope to what lies

ahead. Your dreams and goals from this exercise are the driving forces that motivate you.

When you have a clear vision, you can move on to set specific goals, and it might be helpful to keep the following acronym in mind when you formulate goals: SMART. That is, goals must be:

- **S**pecific
- **M**easurable
- **A**ttainable
- **R**ealistically high
- **T**ime-specific

Specific goals will enable you to prioritize options, and just the process of writing them down can activate positive thoughts. There is power in visualization; it can bring the necessary behaviors that will help you to accomplish all that you want in your life. Successful people have a passion for what they do, and usually have set goals that are harmonious with the vision they have created.

"I CAN go to lunch with you. I just clutter up my desk with blank paper so the boss thinks I'm busy."

Do You Want to Spend or Invest?

When trying to come to terms with time management, it is important to acknowledge and understand the difference between spending time and investing time. The definition of spend, according to the dictionary, is "to use up, exhaust, consume." However, when we invest our time, we do so with the expectation of some sort of ROI, return on investment. If we were to value time the same way we value money, we would probably be motivated to manage time better. We don't like to waste money, and while we all say that we don't like to waste time—it's hard to get out of the habit.

The cliché is right: time is money! You can expect returns if you invest it wisely—no matter what the current economic situation. How you use your time is a reflection of who you are. Not only is it an indication of what you think about yourself, it also reveals what you think of others. Your real commitment to the goals you have set for yourself is reflected in your use of time.

How you invest your time mirrors your purpose, your vision and your values. Each day set out to achieve the highest level of performance and gratification.

Fundamentals of Time Management

You'll go a long way in overcoming the waste of time—and meeting your goals—if you can master the following concepts:

1. *Get organized*: set aside time to organize all paper and projects; block the time in your calendar, smart phone or tablet.

2. *Remember the three Ds* when something arrives at your desk:

   • Do It; decide which category it falls into: (1) immediate, (2) this week, (3) next week, or (4) when I have the time.
   • Delegate it to the appropriate person.
   • Dump it; dispose of it in nearest recycling bin: get rid of anything that is not in alignment with your personal/professional goals.

   And create a filing system instead of a piling system.

3. *Do the right thing right*. Management expert Peter Drucker says, "Doing the right thing right (effectiveness) is more important than simply doing things right (efficiency)"—no matter what the things are.

4. *Timing*: Determine your most effective time of day and take advantage of your body's natural clock to achieve your tasks. Also decide the best time of day to plan your day (for many people the night before is the better option).

5. *Refine your to-do list*: Break the tasks into either must do it and should do it.

6. *Plan for interruptions* and build in buffer times that will allow you to get back on course. But try to minimize interruptions: pay attention to caller ID and let some calls go to voicemail; post a Do Not Disturb sign on your office door or cubicle wall.

7. *Make the most of waiting time*: It happens to all of us, and the odd five or ten minutes here and there can be used to get things done.

8. *Make your meetings as productive as possible*.

   • Provide a written agenda and include the purpose and objectives of the meeting.
   • Start and end on time.
   • Have someone take notes and send a summary with the action items to attendees.
   • Determine the best way to share the information communicated in the meetings.

9. *Strive for time management at home* to help maintain control, since our professional and personal lives are so intertwined.

10. *Learn to say No:* taking on too much can be a major derailer and causes stress.

Time is the great equalizer. We all have the same amount, but the effective use of time is no accident.

Good time management is rooted in setting goals that are aligned with your vision and purpose. Making it happen is a personal choice.

If you have time to whine and complain about something then you have the time to do something about it.

Anthony J. D'Angelo

Chapter 20

• • • • • • • • •

Work-Life Balance or Harmony?

by Bernadette Norz, MBA, ACC, Certified Five O'Clock Club Coach

The best and safest thing is to keep a balance in your life, acknowledge the great powers around us and in us. If you can do that, and live that way, you are really a wise man.

Euripides (484 BC - 406 BC)

In the last few years we've heard work-life balance mentioned frequently. Does it bring to mind the image of a set of scales, with work on one side and the rest of your life on the other? Or perhaps it conjures up the image of walking a balance beam or tight rope, at risk of falling off at any moment?

Let's face it: We don't really want to pit our work and careers against our families and personal lives. But we are all involved in a balancing act, because changes on one side of the scale can upset the equilibrium and bring unwelcome changes on the other side.

The definition of *work-life balance* varies from source to source. One that seems to meet the criteria for a good workable definition, leaving room for both positive and negative influences on equilibrium, is by Professors Jeffrey Greenhaus, Karen Collins and Jason Shaw (2003): "The extent to which an individual is equally engaged in and equally satisfied with his or her work and family role." They describe three components of balance: time, involvement, and satisfaction.

Some experts now favor replacing the concept of *work-life balance* with *work-life integration*, where integration is a more-holistic approach including community obligations. This concept, developed by Professors Michael L. Morris and Susan R. Madsen (2007), creates the vision of a three-point balancing act that seems to be more inclusive of those who are at life stages that are not so intensely focused on child rearing or caring for the elderly. It also offers the opportunity to factor in the benefits that community involvement can add to one's work and/or family life.

Another concept is referring to it as *work-life harmony*, developed into a model by Professors Heather S. McMillan, Michael L. Morris and E. Kate Atchley (2011). They view work-life harmony as occurring "when the resources gained through work/life enrichment are successfully aligned with, and serve to, ameliorate, or alleviate the stressors arising from work/life conflict." The authors refer to harmony as "an individually pleasing, congruent arrangement of work and life roles that is interwoven into a single narrative of life."

Moving from Out-of-Balance to Harmony

For a select few, work and the rest of life are actually balanced and in harmony. Their investment over the long haul of their time, energy and talent has created a whole that is greater than the sum of its parts. For them, work has purpose and life is good. Imagine if the many dimensions of your life came together to create a happy, well-rounded person of accomplishment! Career, family, friends, community involvement, spiritual practices and recreation are all important components of the whole.

Harmony can exist at the systems level, too, both in the family system and in the workplace. Family-friendly firms know that human resource policies and benefits pay off in terms of productivity and performance. Families that create workable schedules and share household responsibilities minimize the conflict created when work and home compete for the limited resources of time and energy. The dynamics of a team approach make balance, integration and harmony much more likely.

Take a few moments and envision what your life might look like if all of the aspects of your life were to actually create a symphony where each contributes to the overall harmony of your daily existence. Ahh—what a beautiful dream!

There's nothing wrong with dreaming, as a matter of fact, a lot of good can come of it. With an awareness of what your harmony might sound like, the possibilities begin to unfold. Where are the gaps between your life today and this ideal harmonious existence? By identifying the gaps and developing a plan to prioritize and address them in incremental steps, life can become more rewarding. A dual focus on reducing conflicts and on increasing the enriching aspects of life brings an integrated approach to the plan. (Ed. Note: See the Forty-Year Vision exercise in the appendix of this book.)

Five Steps to Work-Life Harmony

1. *Learn to Say "No"*

Improvements in time management and efficiency are helpful in addressing some of the basic obstacles to achieving life harmony. Yet nothing will add more hours to the day or more days to the week. It is simply not possible to be at a doctor's appointment or a child's school play, and at an important work-team meeting at the same time. A choice between competing commitments has to be made. Of what value is it to be physically present at one event, while being emotionally and/or mentally preoccupied with the other?

For time and scheduling conflicts, it becomes crucial to find support systems to help with family matters: Consider reducing outside activities and/or begin to research opportunities to rearrange work responsibilities. Perhaps just allowing others to take on some of the functions that an individual has assumed that only he can do well can create enough relief to keep things manageable. For example, is a single individual really the only one who can check on an aging relative every day? Perhaps only one family member is close enough to do so in person, yet someone else's phone call may replace a visit once in awhile. Sometimes, it just takes a good look at the assumptions that have piled up and created what seems like the only one "right" approach. Becoming open to the opportunities of other right solutions is a good first step.

Reducing time and scheduling conflicts requires a clear understanding of one's values and establishing priorities and boundaries. It becomes necessary to learn to say "no" to adding yet another commitment to an already packed agenda. Letting go can create breathing room in both work and home life. Perhaps you've taken on volunteer commitments, personal or professional, that you are reluctant to step away from. If your circumstances have changed or you have underestimated the extent of the time commitment involved, stepping aside with integrity can be a much better alternative than performing the function inadequately or letting people down at the last minute. If you don't make a habit of over-committing, people will generally understand when you give adequate notice that you cannot go forward. Consider that most people only give a few weeks notice before leaving a full-time position; how much notice should be required to leave a volunteer one? It's clear that when time conflicts between non-work and work respon-sibilities exist for more than a short period of time, stress is likely to be the result. Over time, if enough stress and fatigue occur, it becomes increasing difficult to be fully present in any important role.

2. *Transition Between Roles Consciously*

For some, the work-life challenge is not in time and scheduling conflicts, but in switching gears when transitioning from one aspect of life to another. When the mind-set and/or behaviors that are appropriate for one role are significantly different than what is required to be effective in other roles, harmony is not likely. Consider the stereotype of a drill sergeant by day who arrives home to young children and has trouble turning off the commando switch. How does one find common ground between these two opposite aspects of life? Connecting with the purpose behind the drill sergeant's work-life that will lead to benefits for his children is a good start. Reflecting on the bigger goals of provid-ing financially for his children, contributing to a safer nation, and developing the character and strength of his soldiers, prior to coming home to his children, can soften the rough edges. Har-mony comes into play when one role enhances the other and vice-versa. What can he learn from his children that will make him a better sergeant? What can he learn from the troops that will make him a better father? Connecting with the humanity of both and consciously choosing behaviors that are role-appropriate increase the opportunities for harmony.

3. *Establish Financial Priorities Consistent with Long-Term Goals*

When finances are at the heart of the con-flict, a hard look at lifestyle choices, long-term goals and personal and family priorities may be in order. The assistance of financial professionals may be helpful to learn to establish a budget and develop a financial plan. Conflicts over money that exist within a household may spill over into one's work-life, making day-to-day existence on the job less pleasant. Irritability and stress create obstacles to being a good team player on the job and to enjoying work-life satisfaction.

In today's economic climate and time of high unemployment, work-related stress and concerns about downsizing, layoffs, job searching, etc., can create a huge overflow of anxiety that throws work-life harmony seriously off-key. Worry-ing about what might happen is not useful; it is simply "suffering in advance." Developing a plan of action and becoming proactive due to concerns about finances and job insecurity have value, but worrying without action is an energy drain at a time when additional energy resources are needed.

4. *Be Flexible if Emergencies Occur*

The best plans for long-term work-life har-mony aren't terribly helpful when life's emergen-cies happen. When a family member becomes hospitalized, when the car breaks down, when a child gets in trouble at school, when a basement floods, etc., that balance scale really starts to tip and the music of life loses its harmony. Most of these life events are stressors whether one has to work or not, yet work demands make it so much more difficult to gain control of any parts that are controllable. Separating the actions required to address the crisis from the emotional com-ponents provides a framework for beginning to restore equilibrium and to move toward har-mony. When work also provides a social support system of friends and colleagues, asking for what you need from those who want to help is key.

Flex-time, job sharing, and family leaves of absence may all be options worth looking into. Short-term solutions to short-term challenges make sense. Employers have sufficient evidence that home-life stressors can result in productivity declines. Family-friendly organizations have suitable policies in place and the Family and Medical Leave Act exists to help too. The trade-off is a reduction in stress level, better health and a more productive worker.

Careers that offer intrinsic rewards like a sense of self-worth, enjoyment and/or fulfillment can be helpful in times of crisis, especially when there is little one can do about the situation at hand. Practicing gratitude, even in the most difficult of times, is valuable in maintaining a positive attitude.

4. *Celebrate Accomplishments*

What if the work-life conflict is stemming from things you're taking on in order to move forward to a better career, such as school, starting a business on the side or working a second job? Congratulations on your initiative and commitment to following your dreams! If you've established a reasonable timeline, keep your focus on the big goal while implementing incremental doable steps that bring you closer to it. Take the opportunity to replenish the energy levels, both physical and emotional, needed to keep going. Celebrate the accomplishment of small goals and build in some planned downtime for rejuvenation.

A Worthy Goal

While work-life harmony may seem like nothing more than a dream to some, it is a goal worthy of the journey. Most of us desire rich personal lives that include family, friends, community, spirituality, exercise, enjoyment and personal growth while we continue our work lives. Careers that are in alignment with individual values and purpose are important foundations to work-life harmony. Engaging in work that is meaningful and which provides personal satisfaction offers the opportunity for positivity to flow into one's personal life. And a life outside of the workplace that contributes to family, community or the world at large, leads to an overall positivity that flows back into the workplace. The ideal will not exist on a daily basis for most; but the journey itself offers many rewards!

Chapter 21

• • • • • • • •

Selling Your Value on the Job: How to Be a Winner

by Stacey Jerrold, Certified Five O'Clock Club Coach

It is easier for people to see it your way if you see it their way.

Jack Kaine

Have you ever felt stalled in your job? Perhaps you have been working at your company for a few years, getting good feedback and decent annual reviews…but you're not getting ahead. You and your manager have talked about your taking on more responsibilities and helping to implement organizational strategy. The first year you heard this, you were excited. During year two, you wondered if this will be the year. You thought: "Why doesn't anyone see my worth and my potential for the organization?"

But waiting for management to take action will get you nowhere. You need to stop the BMW routine (bellyaching, moaning and whining) and learn how to sell your value. Do you shrink from the suggestion that you have to sell anything—especially yourself?

Here's a little secret to help you get over it: You have been selling most of your life! In your childhood, you tried to sell your parents on a type of cereal or toy you wanted, and this kind of negotiation probably continues to this day in your daily relationships. So have an open mind about the selling process we will cover here, and win at selling your value.

First, let's discuss the definition of a sale. According to Zig Ziglar, a sales trainer, a sale is "the transference of feeling." This means that selling is something much more subtle than coaxing someone to buy something. In fact, selling is based on passion. Hence, if you don't have a passion for what you do and the service that you offer, then you will have difficulty in helping people to buy what you are selling; in this instance, your worth and potential.

The Selling Process on the Job

By following the steps outlined below, you will be able to develop and maintain relationships with decision-makers and others throughout your organization, expanding your network and opportunities for increased responsibilities—and that is the basis for selling.

Step 1: Introduction: No one wants to buy anything from a grump. From the outset, maintain eye contact with people and be a pleasant person to be around. Colleagues don't feel comfortable around someone who seldom smiles.

You want your buyers to smile—and you can be the initiator.

Step 2: Gaining Favorable Attention: At The Five O'Clock Club, we talk about using the Eight-Word Message. Don't waste opportunities to make points with bosses and other superiors. If you're asked on the elevator, "How's it going today?" chatting about the weather doesn't give you much of a boost. But replying, "Everything is terrific, now that we've wrapped up the widget project," makes the point that you were involved in the widget project. Occasionally your Two-Minute Pitch may also be appropriate. It needs to be powerful and concise. You can build rapport in this stage, and gain favorable attention.

Step 3: Discover Wants and Needs: There is a time to eliminate the use of words "I," "me" or "mine." Dig deeply into the issues facing the organization, management, etc. Focus on open-ended questions. Good questions begin with who, what, where, when and why. The best techniques for navigating include:

1. Listen 80% of the time and talk 20% of the time.
2. Refrain from evaluating or judging the information being shared.
3. Be alert to the behavior of colleagues. Their verbal, as well as non-verbal behavior, can guide you.
4. Resist the urge to talk too soon about solutions. This comes later.

Your goals during the discovery process are to:

- gain complete understanding of the situations at hand;
- help your colleagues see how you can help them;
- stimulate their interest in working with you; and
- reinforce rapport and credibility.

Step 4: Presenting Benefits and Consequences: Here you can talk about your capabilities and how you can help the organization.

Make sure you demonstrate the following points. You have:

- a thorough understanding of the situation.
- the objectives that you can help them to achieve and your approach to achieving them.
- the measurable outcomes to demonstrate a return on their investment (you).

Your goal is to help your boss—and other superiors—make a positive decision to use your skills, and thereby expand your responsibilities and exposure within the organization.

Step 5: Getting Commitment: If you navigate the selling process correctly at each step, you will receive verbal and non-verbal permission to proceed to the next step. Getting commitment is a natural progression from the previous step.

Step 6: Follow Up/Execution: Be sure you understand your role in executing the tasks that were decided upon and that management understands the results you are delivering. Become indispensable and create more opportunities for your own personal and professional growth.

So, selling is a matter of following a few basic steps that can come naturally to anyone. Take the initiative. Don't wait around, wondering why promotions and raises haven't been happening. As we are fond of saying at The Five O'Clock Club about job search: "The ball is always in your court!"

When people talk, listen completely.
Most people never listen.

Ernest Hemingway

You have to have confidence in your ability,
and then be tough enough to follow through.

Rosalynn Carter

Chapter 22

● ● ● ● ● ● ● ●

Don't Keep Your Head Down: Top Five Strategies for Moving Ahead

by Kate Wendleton, President, The Five O'Clock Club (as seen on FoxNews.com)

Do not be too timid and squeamish about your actions. All life is an experiment.

Ralph Waldo Emerson

Homer: *Kids, you tried your best and you failed miserably. The lesson is, never try.*

The Simpsons

What is wrong with this picture? You work hard, do everything you're asked to do—and more—and you still feel like you're in the slow lane. You ask for training, but no one gives it to you. The biggies don't know who you are. How are you ever going to move ahead?

Before you can take even a baby step, realize that business is a game and you're supposed to be a player. Don't be glum, chum. Lighten up and start playing. Here are five strategies that are bound to get you to first base—and beyond.

1. **Find out what's going on and become part of it**. What are the major trends affecting your industry, your organization and your field? If you don't know, you may be working hard on the wrong things. Read your company's press releases, find out the direction the organization is now taking and take assignments that help you to become part of it. Join associations having to do with your industry and field. Be on the program or membership committee to meet the key players in your field. Whether you know it or not, your company is changing and your job is changing. You've got to keep up.

2. **Manage your internal public relations campaign**. Volunteer for your organization's United Way or Blood Drive campaign. You'll be seen as a team player and will meet people in other divisions and departments. Make sure that those above you in the organization know how good you are. For example, when your boss' boss asks how you're doing, the incorrect answer is "Just fine. How are you?" The right answer is: "Terrific. We've been working 70 hours a week on the Acme project and I know you'll be pleased with the results." He or she has to ask you more about your work.

3. **Get the training you need**. Don't complain that you don't get the kinds of assignments that will help you to grow. Don't whine that

they won't train you. You are in charge of your own career. Do volunteer work that gives you the experience you need, such as learning how to run a meeting. Take courses. Learn a new technical skill. Join Toastmasters. Find out what people in your function do outside of your present organization (or the function you are interested in long term).

4. **Develop a career plan for yourself, and gradually move in the right direction.** Knowing where you would like to wind up broadens the kinds of jobs you would be interested in today. For example, if you have been in accounting in the education industry for the past 10 years and would like to wind up in sales in an entertainment firm, you could make your move in two steps: First, sell accounting software or accounting services to entertainment companies. Then, move into the entertainment industry itself. I've seen it done!

5. **Meet with your manager to get more mainstream assignments**. But don't just sit down and have a chat. Go in prepared. For example, make two columns on a piece of paper. In the left column, which would be short, lists your job responsibilities. The right-hand column could go on for a page or two, listing—in priority order—your accomplishments on the job. Point out that you have always been willing to take on extra work and help where it was needed. However, you would like to get some of the cutting edge assignments that are coming along, such as … Don't expect your boss to say "yes" right away. You have to overcome her inertia. If you're not satisfied about the outcome of the meeting, say that you'd like to meet again in a few weeks to discuss this same issue.

These are just some of the strategies that you should consider to move your career along. What you choose to do depends on you, your personality, your organization, and your level

of ambition. Remember what Calvin Coolidge said, "Nothing in the world can take the place of persistence… Persistence and determination alone are omnipotent." Learn to play the game and stick with it.

"I'll be honest with you. I'm only hiring you because I need someone new to abuse."

Akeelah: [quoting Marianne Williamson]Our deepest fear is not that we are inadequate. Our deepest fear is that we are powerful beyond measure. We ask ourselves, Who am I to be brilliant, gorgeous, talented, fabulous? Actually, who are you not to be? We were born to make manifest the glory of God that is within us. And as we let our own light shine, we unconsciously give other people permission to do the same.

Dr. Larabee: Does that mean anything to you?

Akeelah: I don't know.

Dr. Larabee: It's written in plain English. What does it mean?

Akeelah: That I'm not supposed to be afraid?

Dr. Larabee: Afraid of what?

Akeelah: Afraid of... me?

Doug Atchison, *Akeelah and the Bee*, 2006 film

Chapter 23

• • • • • • • •

Improve Your Performance in Your Present Position

by Kate Wendleton, President, The Five O'Clock Club

A man's work is in danger of deteriorating when he thinks he has found the one best formula for doing it. If he thinks that, he is likely to feel that all he needs is merely to go on repeating himself ... so long as a person is searching for better ways of doing his work, he is fairly safe.

Eugene O'Neill, playwright

The techniques you use for job hunting inside your company are often the same as those you would use outside. You can look at ads for ideas, network, write proposals, even do some outside interviewing to learn more about how to position yourself and gain a realistic assessment of your value.

Job Hunters at The Club Sometimes Stay with Their Present Employers –But in a Stronger Position

Half the people who attend The Five O'Clock Club are employed. Some think they are in danger in their present positions and want to start looking now; others are simply unhappy.

Although employed people come to The Five O'Clock Club because they want jobs elsewhere, a surprising number end up becoming more val-ued by their present companies. That's because these workers start exploring what is going on outside their companies, pick up new skills that make themselves marketable, and often take that information back to their present employ-ers. Because they no longer feel dependent on one company, they develop greater self-esteem and become more assertive in developing ideas and programs for their present employers. Their employers start to treat them differently.

Case Study: Marie On Her Way Out: Then Promoted

Marie is the head of the direct-marketing arm of a major not-for-profit. She felt that she was undervalued, and perhaps even being squeezed out. She wanted to get into the for-profit world. To learn more about this target area, her counselor and group at The Five O'Clock Club suggested she read the trade journals, join associations having to do with direct market-ing, and get to know people in the field. Marie learned so much in her intensive research that she went a few steps further: she spoke at the association meetings, began writing for the trade journals, and even appeared on the cover of one prestigious trade magazine.

This caught the attention of her current employer, who began to value her much more than before. Coincidentally, Marie's boss moved elsewhere in the organization. Marie was surprised that she was asked to take her boss' job. That promotion eased Marie's pressure to find a new job quickly. In addition, her résumé was looking better and better.

If she decides to look for a new job again, she will be helped by her new title and experience, and also by her new visibility as a guru in the direct marketing field. By the way, she continues to stay involved and improve her career—as well as her worth—at her present place of employment. And she continues to attend The Five O'Clock Club to stay sharp in her field.

Continuous Improvement

This process of staying aware and marketable is what employees are doing to keep their present jobs longer, or to make career moves within their present companies.

With all of the changes occurring in most corporations, your firm may be one of the important places to look if you want to make a career change—or if you simply want to get ahead.

Improve Your Present Job

Think of ideas for changing your present job to move it in the direction in which you want to go. If you know where you are heading, you can be open to new assignments or projects that would give you experience in those areas. Assume responsibility for new areas. Move away from old areas that no longer fit in with your long-term career goals. When special projects come up that would give you new skills or update old skills, gradually start working on those projects—feeling them out—and then taking over the whole thing if it seems right.

And if things seem not to be working out, be sure to slip out early in the game.

At the same time, be sure not to ignore the work for which you are primarily responsible. If you spend time on the new area and your old job starts to slip, you are in trouble. Do both for a while. Then, either ask for additional help while you continue to handle both areas, or try to unload the area that no longer interests you. Just be sure that the work that interests you is important to your employer.

A Mindset of Strength

People are used to being dependent on their employers. They say, "My boss won't train me in this new area," or "Only those who went to Ivy League schools get into that program."

Make your own program. Don't let "them" stop you. You operate from greater strength when you do not feel completely dependent on your present employer, and your employer is usually better off as well. If you are well-versed in what is going on in your field or industry, you are more marketable, and your employer benefits from your knowledge and contacts. Take better care of yourself professionally.

Making a Move in a Medium—or Large-Size Company

Many people think that job hunting internally in a large corporation consists of only two steps:

- responding to job postings, and then
- doing well in interviews.

Job postings are one path to a new job, but they are not the way most people move into new jobs within the same companies.

Ongoing Career Management and Career Exploration

People who are successful in their careers know that "job search" involves ongoing career management and career exploration: building relationships, researching areas inside and outside the company, and developing marketable skills. This approach is more work than simply responding to job postings, but it is a surer and faster way to getting ahead in today's market.

All of this fits in with what we have taught at The Five O'Clock Club since 1978: It is best for both the employee and the employer if "job hunting" is seen as a continual process—and not just something that happens when a person wants to change jobs. Continual job search means continually being aware of market conditions both inside and outside our present companies, and continually learning what we have to offer—to both markets.

With this approach, workers are safer because they are more likely to keep their present jobs longer: they learn to change and grow as the company and industry do. And if they have to go elsewhere, they will be more marketable. Companies are better off because employees who know what is going on outside their insular halls are smarter, more sophisticated and more proactive, and make the company more competitive.

How to Search for a New Job Within Your Present Company

You are more likely to find a new job within your present company if you use an organized approach, and if you do not "put all of your eggs into one basket." Follow these steps:

1. Find out which departments or businesses within your present company are worth your interest. You can do a preliminary investigation by:
   a. networking within your company to find out the best areas for you to explore; and
   b. doing research through your annual report and other printed materials.
2. List three departments, divisions or businesses you would like to explore within your present company.
3. Now you need to get to know people in each of those areas. For each one, list the names of four to six people you think you should get to know. If you don't yet know the names of the appropriate people in those areas, ask others for their advice,

or study the organization charts for those businesses. It may even be that people outside your company can tell you who to see inside.

4. Now you have to figure out how you will get in to see each of these people. There are three main techniques for getting in to see a person within your present company:
   a. **Network directly** to that person through someone you already know.
   b. **Build a network** into that person or in to that general area. Even if the people you know do not work in the areas in which you are interested, they can refer you to people in those areas, who can then refer you on to other people in the department or division.

If you don't know anyone outside your department, you can get to meet more people in your company:

- serve on committees
- volunteer for internal programs such as the United Way or the blood drive
- join task forces
- meet fellow employees at association meetings for the field you are targeting, or
- simply meet people in elevators or the company cafeteria.

You can tell them that you are curious to learn more about their area. Perhaps you could suggest that the two of you have lunch sometime.

   c. **Contact the person** directly, such as by writing an internal memo.
5. Next, figure out what to say to each person. Handle these meetings the same as you would any networking meeting. However, you may also want to ask some of the following:

- what they do there
- the plans for their area
- the kinds of people they tend to look for,

even though they may not be hiring at the moment
- how you stack up against the kinds of people they tend to look for. You can ask, "If you had an opening right now, would you consider hiring someone like me? Why or why not?"
- the skills and abilities you would need to move into that area someday
- how they think you might gain the skills / abilities you are now lacking.

As you establish relationships with people in specific businesses, get to know more about each business and understand what skills you need to make yourself more desirable. Just as in Stage 2 of an external job search, your goal is to have people saying, "I sure wish I had an opening right now. I'd love to have someone like you on board." Then when a job opens up, you will be the one most likely to get it.

6.   It is usually not enough to find out about an area inside your present company. To be strongly considered, also learn how that area functions *outside* of your company. You will be more knowledgeable and more marketable.

Many functional areas exist across industries: customer service, computers, purchasing, corporate sales, public relations—to name a few.

Still other areas may *seem* to be related strictly to your industry, yet actually are found in many industries. For example, banks are involved in "check transaction processing," which may seem like a function related only to financial institutions. Yet *many* industries—hospitals, large fund-raising organizations, direct-mail houses—are engaged in heavy transaction processing. Broadly define the field you are in. It may well exist in other industries—but in a very different way. This will open up the industries where you can transfer your skills.

Regardless of where you work inside your company, think of how your function is handled outside—especially in other industries.

You can learn more by:
- Joining professional associations.
- Reading trade journals.
- Taking courses.
- Networking to people outside your company—including those outside your industry.

The more you know about the areas you are exploring, the more information you can share with people in the departments or businesses you are exploring. This will put you in a better position to figure out how you can help them.

7.   As you investigate, you may find that you are lacking in certain skills that seem to be in demand. Acquiring these new skills will make you more marketable.

8.   Keep in touch (about every two months) with four to six people in each department or business:
- Find out what is happening in the department or business.
- Let them know what is happening to you, such as new projects you are working on and new information or skills you have picked up that would be of interest to them.

9.   Continue to research (using the techniques in Point 6, above) those areas you have been exploring outside of your present company.

10. Continue to take that information back to those departments or businesses in which you are interested.

11. All the while, respond to job postings for those departments or businesses.

Do Not Jeopardize Your Present Situation

At first, take the most cautious steps possible. Reading trade journals and joining trade organizations are usually among the safest. You can join simply because you are interested in the subject and because "I thought it would help me do better in my present job if I were more knowledgeable about this area."

Chapter 24

● ● ● ● ● ● ● ●

When to Blow the Whistle

by Richard Bayer, Ph.D., Chief Operating Officer, The Five O'Clock Club

Didn't at least one of the six hundred guys think about giving up, and joining with the other side? I mean, valley of death, that's pretty salty stuff ... I mean any fool can have courage. But honor, that's the real reason for you either do something or you don't. It's who you are and maybe who you want to be. If you die trying for something important, then you have both honor and courage, and that's pretty good. I think that's what the writer was saying, that you should hope for courage and try for honor. And maybe even pray that the people telling you what to do have some, too.

Michael Oher, speaking about *The Charge Of The Light Brigade* by Alfred, Lord Tennyson in the movie, *The Blind Side*

Employees are sometimes presented with a difficult problem: Do I report an ethical lapse by my employer, or do I remain silent and say nothing? To whistle blow or not is the question. The Sarbanes-Oxley law both requires and protects "blowing the whistle" when there is wrong-doing.

For example, an engineer may detect a safety problem in the design of an automobile. Let's say that if there is even a minor crash, there is a slight probability of the fuel line's rupturing and causing a fire or explosion. Human lives could be at stake, so our engineer goes to his superiors with the hope that they will listen to him and act appropriately. However, he is told that it is unlikely (but certainly not impossible) that the line would rupture. He estimates that redesigning and changing the manufacturing process would be costly, and the company would rather avoid the lost time and money. Should the engineer blow the whistle and contact the press, or the government regulators?

Safety issues can occur with the design and manufacture of almost anything, including cars, busses, trains, toys, electric appliance, and airplanes. Other issues also raise the question of whistle blowing: A business with a manufacturing plant can produce byproducts that pollute the environment. If this pollution is in excess of what is allowed by regulations, should the employee speak up or remain silent?

These situations are always complicated by the danger to the employee's legitimate self-interest. The employer could very well mistreat the employee after the whistle has been blown. Often times, the employee is seen as disloyal, a loudmouth, and a danger to the welfare of the organization. Indeed, the single event could have implications for the employee's entire career.

Question(s) to consider: Do you know someone outside of the organization whom you can bounce your ideas off? She doesn't have to be a lawyer, just someone you trust who has good common sense.

With lives and careers at stake, we need to have some method of thinking about this ethical problem on whistle blowing; the table below does just that. The process absolutely must begin with the FACTS. Without the proper facts, more damage can be done than good. One could jeopardize one's entire career over mistaken information. The issue must impact the common good and be significant enough to justify whistle blowing. All other methods of resolution must be tried and exhausted before doing something as dramatic as whistle blowing. It is, of course, preferable if the in-house managers take the appropriate action without external coercion. Since anonymous tips are rarely believed and trusted, ideally the employee would take responsibility for his/her whistle blowing.

You might some day be presented with this difficult problem: to whistle blow or not. These four criteria could make your life easier, since they offer a way to think and act about the problem. With these criteria and other things in mind, follow your best judgment.

Group Discussion Questions

- Name the hierarchy of people in an organization who might confront people about an ethical lapse.
- Is maximizing freedom always a good idea?

The Matter at Hand	Criteria
Get the facts	The employee must be absolutely certain of all the facts. This will involve research and speaking to other people. Be sure to keep records and preserve evidence.
The issue	The problem must involve a significant ethical lapse.
Other means	The employee must first attempt an orderly in-house resolution of the problem. The employee should visit the appropriate supervisors, managers, and executives to see if an internal solution to the problem is possible.
Responsibility	Since anonymous tips are rarely believed and trusted, ideally, the employee would take responsibility for his/her whistle blowing.

Chapter 25

How to Overcome Suffering—Especially in Your Career

by Richard Bayer, Ph.D., Chief Operating Officer, The Five O'Clock Club

From that hour Siddhartha ceased to fight against his destiny. There shone in his face the serenity of knowledge, of one who is no longer confronted with conflict of desires, who has found salvation, who is in harmony with the stream of events, with the stream of life, full of sympathy and compassion, surrendering himself to the stream, belonging to the unity of things.

Hermann Hesse, *Siddhartha*

At The Five O'Clock Club we participate actively in the career aspects of our clients' lives. This puts us in a great position to make suggestions that can help the employed and unemployed. These same lessons apply to a person's personal life.

Our coaches across the country have noted what we call the unhappiness factor. Many people are unhappy in their professional careers for a variety of reasons. Indeed, they often describe themselves as actually suffering in their present positions. These complaints can include:

- I need more money! $250,000 is simply not enough to support my family.
- I am single, 43, work very long hours, and like having things my way. I definitely intend to have children, but have yet to start looking for the right man/woman.
- Everyone else seems to be moving ahead of me. I live very nicely, but feel left behind and I want more.

Question(s) to consider: On a scale of 1 to 10, 10 being the unhappiest, where do you fall? What's the major thing that stands in the way of your being happier?

We can learn a lot by analyzing these situations in light of Eastern traditions. Buddhism talks about suffering as much as any religion does.

Many people love the story of the Buddha, which means "Enlightened One." He was born Siddhartha Gautama and lived in northern India from 560 to 480 B.C. Gautama's family was wealthy, yet he himself was unhappy with the pleasures of the royal life. So, as a young fellow, he left his wife and son, and sneaked out of the palace and into the woods to become enlightened about the true meaning of life. Pleasure did not seem to be the key to a happy life.

After practicing yoga under religious masters, he concluded that it is best to avoid extreme asceticism. These masters followed a life of extreme self-denial to the point of begging for food and dressing in rags. Buddha finally left this sect and came to his moderate approach (the "middle way" between extreme asceticism and extravagance) while meditating for 49 days under a bodhi tree. Once he had achieved such enlightenment, he returned to ordinary life for the sake of others.

He was a compassionate teacher with a cool head and a warm heart. Once enlightened, the Buddha came to understand four things:

First, suffering is a part of life. There are the traumas of birth, sickness, old age, fear of death, separation from loved ones, etc. There is passing, constant change, and mortality.

· ·

To be sure that your goals (desires) will bring you happiness and not suffering, analyze them for their wisdom and compassion.

· ·

Second, unreasonable desires or expectations cause suffering. Failing to show wisdom, restraint or compassion, people cling to what is either too much or can never be permanent. People can put themselves at the center of the world, and become intoxicated with themselves and their desires. They seek permanence and an ease of life that are impossible to have. They look out for their own welfare without having compassion for others, or regard for the rest of the world.

I slept and dreamt that life was joy.
I awoke and saw that life was service.
I acted and behold, service was joy.

Rabindranath Tagore, philosopher, author,
songwriter, painter, educator, composer,
Nobel laureate (1861-1941)

· ·

Question(s) to consider: Do you have any unreasonable desires or expectations that are causing you to suffer? What are they? Are you simply looking out for your own welfare without having compassion for others or regard for the rest of the world? Specifically, how do you look out for others? Are you satisfied with what and how much you are doing?

· ·

Third, the good news is this: Overcoming desire can break the chain of suffering.

Fourth, the way to overcome desire is through a life of wisdom and practical compassion (as taught by the "Eightfold Path").

So, a Buddhist would analyze the three complaints of our suffering employees in terms of the wisdom and compassion that they do or do not show:

- If you "need" more than $250,000, are you clinging to what is really unreasonable, unfulfilling, and passing? (The median per capita income in this country was after all about $40,600 in 2010!). Does your preoccupation show a lack of compassion for the 99.99% of the planet's population that have less? Have you considered the middle way, living in between the extremes of poverty and riches?

- If you are single and insist on having things your way, have you put yourself at the center of the world? Are you too used to seeing yourself falsely, as a separate and isolated individual? Have you abandoned being compassionate, making intimate social relations difficult? Does this make the desired goals of a happy marriage and family practical impossibilities?
- If you live nicely, but feel left behind compared with others, are you a victim of some false view of the world? One false view is that of the isolated individual locked in competition with others (American individualism) as opposed to being part of a larger whole. The perspective of isolation logically cuts off compassion and heightens envy.

We can see that the root problems as suggested by Buddhism are a lack of wisdom and compassion. These are exemplified in having the wrong views of the self and the world, improper individualism, extravagance, clutching at permanence, selfishness, and greed. All of these lead to suffering.

The Five O'Clock Club recommends that you look into your future to set goals that are right for you. To set your goals, write your own obituary (to see how your life would have gone), invent your ideal job, decide what you would do if you had a million dollars (and do it anyway), and write your Forty-Year Vision® (see the Appendix on how to create this vision). The above discussion should help you to do these exercises, since all of us have happiness and the overcoming of suffering as major goals. To sum up, analyze your goals (desires) for their wisdom and compassion to be sure that they will bring you happiness and not suffering. Even this small glimpse at Eastern thinking can challenge us Westerners in varied and positive ways.

What could I say to you that would be of value, except that perhaps you seek too much, that as a result of your seeking you cannot find.

Hermann Hesse, German-Swiss author

In the depth of winter, I finally learned that there was within me an invincible summer.

Albert Camus, French author, philosopher

Group Discussion Questions

- Discuss the common complaints of people who are unhappy in their work. Can you add more?
- Examine the Buddha's framework for dealing with these and analyze critically.

Chapter 26

Humility and Success

by Richard Bayer, Ph.D., Chief Operating
Officer, The Five O'Clock Club

My List of Virtues contain'd at first but twelve:
But a Quaker Friend having kindly inform'd
me that I was generally thought proud; that my
Pride show'd itself frequently in Conversation;
that I was not content with being in the right
when discussing any Point, but was overbearing
& rather insolent; of which he convinc'd me
by mentioning several Instances; I determined
endeavoring to cure myself if I could of this Vice
or Folly amoung the rest, and I added Humility to
my List, giving an extensive Meaning to the Word.

Benjamin Franklin

Benjamin Franklin, printer, author, diplo-
mat, philosopher, businessman, and scientist,
saw fit to make humility his thirteenth virtue
(his list: temperance, silence, order, resolution,
frugality, industry, sincerity, justice, moderation,
cleanliness, tranquility, chastity, and humility).
He concluded that to be humble to one's superiors is our duty, to equals is courtesy, and to
inferiors is nobility.

Certainly, Franklin saw business applications in this virtue, but does humility have any

currency today? If by humility we mean having
a poor image of oneself, and failing to present
a positive assessment of one's background in
interviews and résumés, then, on a practical
basis, the answer is no. And it would be just as
hard to reconcile it with The Five O'Clock Club's
methodology! Fortunately, that is neither what
Franklin nor what others mean by humility.

A good definition of humility is: *to have a*
proper and not egotistical view about oneself and
others. Andrew Grove, a founder of Intel and
author of, *Only the Paranoid Survive,* argues that
in business and career planning one ought to be
humble to the point of paranoia about market
developments. His basic point is well taken,
but perhaps we can replace paranoia with other
(happier) traits that keep one agile, in touch with
the economy and responsive to the market.

Successful people are generally highly
sociable. They are able to listen, learn, charm,
network, be genuine, make agreements and
diffuse difficult social situations. For example,
at The Club, people are likely to be long-time
members of their professional associations; our
best and most senior Five O'Clock Club Coaches

are usually the most frequent attendees at our professional Guild meetings.

Question(s) to consider: Are you able to listen, learn, be genuine and diffuse difficult social situations? What can you do to improve in any of these areas?

Of course, we can think of highly successful people in business and government who we could not call "humble." But we do not know if all ends well with them; and it is likely that such gifted individuals succeed in spite of their arrogance (not because of it).

We can hardly overstate the importance of vigilance in pursuing positive character traits. Duty, courtesy, even nobility, can be characteristics of highly successful people. The meek, as is often said, may inherit the earth for a number of reasons—the willingness of others to cooperate with them surely being one of the most significant of the reasons! The table below summarizes humility in practice.

Question(s) to consider: How often do I think about myself? About others?

If I have seen further than others, it is by standing upon the shoulders of giants.

Isaac Newton

Group Discussion Questions

- What is humility as used in this chapter, and how does it differ from the common meaning of the word today?
- Look at the table of "Humility in Practice." Discuss what is there and add your own insights, ideas, and applications of humility.

Humility in Practice

Character Impact	Manifestation
Insight into one's own need to learn.	• Join professional associations; follow industry trends. • Take classes; read books; subscribe to journals.
Ability to see other perspectives.	• Success at negotiation. • Problem-resolution skills (with clients/colleagues). • DUTY: able to take directions from superiors. • COURTESY: able to be collaborative with peers. • NOBILITY: able to give directions to subordinates in ways that elicit cooperation.
Ability for self-examination and critique.	• Keep careful records to critique and improve one's own work (so others always needn't do the critiquing!). Higher quality work is the consequence.
Pleasant demeanor.	• Nice to be around. Create an atmosphere in which people want to work and produce. Employers love this.
Prudence.	• Not taking unacceptable risks; looking before leaping when making executive decisions. • Compliance with laws and customs.

Chapter 27

• • • • • • • •

Attending Parties and Events: Tips to Shine and Help Your Career

by Nancy Karas, Certified Five O'Clock Club Coach

Go out on a Limb. That is where the fruit is.

Will Rogers

How you conduct yourself while attending company events can have a major impact on your career. In one night, you can destroy your career or you can create a bright future for yourself.

Skipping company parties and industry events, even charity get-togethers—whether holiday celebrations or summer picnics or association dinners—is something that too many people do because they feel that these get-togethers are not important. Whether you are job hunting or looking to advance your career, these settings provide an ideal setting for networking.

No matter how badly you want to stay home and sit on the couch, do not turn down invitations to these events. You never know whom you will meet or what can happen. Such events are excellent opportunities to get in front of

the people you may not otherwise have access to. These provide settings that are a little more relaxed: The mood is more festive and key people are more social and much more approachable.

The Holiday Season

Most people slack off on job search at the end of the year. The common belief is that all hiring comes to a grinding halt during the holidays. Not true! December is one of the best months to network and pursue job-hunting goals. Most of your competition is coasting over the holidays and waiting until after the New Year to resume their job-hunting efforts. This is an ideal time then, for you to step forward and shine! Many human resources teams and hiring managers want to start the New Year with crucial job openings filled and with new talent on board for the start of the year. December is the only month when you will have less competition and there will be less chance of your résumé getting lost on someone's desk! Requesting a transfer or consideration for an internal position or promotion may be seriously considered, as managers plan their staffing needs and budgets for the next year.

Follow these simple guidelines for your own career advancement at company or association events.

1. Meet the Movers and the Shakers:

At Your Own Company Party or Other Employer-Hosted Events: These events allow you to gain visibility and build relationships. Top management is always present at events. Use these gatherings as an opportunity to introduce yourself and connect with the senior management team. Make it your goal to meet the movers and the shakers and I don't mean the people with the lampshades on their heads out on the dance floor with a cocktail in each hand! Those movers and shakers may regret their behavior tomorrow morning!

At Holiday Events: If you are planning to attend holiday parties for various businesses and associations, be sure to find out in advance who the other guests will be. Choose three or four people on the list, and set a goal for yourself to meet and connect with them during the evening. Choose the decision-makers, the people who make things happen, who are successful and happy. Choose the people who you can really learn from.

2. Always Do Your Homework

Don't Skip This Step! Before an event, do some research. Using Google, LinkedIn and company or industry websites, read the bios and profiles of the people you would like to connect with. Take note of their backgrounds, interests, goals and accomplishments so that you can find a common bond. You will have something to talk to them about that will connect you to them. Your main goal in networking is to develop a relationship. You want to create a bond and build *trust*, paving the way for you to have the opportunity for further contact later. This is not the appropriate moment to whip out your résumé or to begin a lengthy monologue about your career goals and past accomplishments. Use this time to connect.

3. Find a Way to Help

Make the conversation meaningful so that you may contact the person again and feel comfortable doing so. Offer something to the person you want to develop a relationship with. Is there someone you can introduce the person to who would be beneficial to them? Can you help them to network with someone or some group that they may want to meet? Is there an upcoming benefit that you can help to coordinate or volunteer to work the event? If so, use that as an opportunity to offer to help. It is always easier to ask for help for yourself from people who already appreciate you and your contributions.

4. The Approach

This is your moment to shine! Stand up and be noticed! Introduce yourself with a sincere smile, extend your hand and give the firm steady handshake of a confident, professional person who is comfortable interacting with others. Be sure to thank management or another host for the party and then mention something you know will be a common bond and begin to develop a connection.

For example, you can introduce yourself, "Hello Mr. Harrison, my name is Francis Marion. I work in Operations and am the supervisor of the Procurement Department. I've been with the company for two years and I am really happy to be a part of the operations team. Thank you for such a great holiday party! It's a really special event!" Then, you might say to the CEO that you understand that he is an avid fisherman. You can say that you've read that he has caught the largest lake trout in California's history. Share that you have always wanted to fish that lake and intend to go with your family next summer. This provides an opportunity for you to talk about those things that will create a common bond. If the executive is involved in or a member of a not-for-profit organization, and is serving on the Board of Directors, express your interest and knowledge of the organization and your willingness to volunteer or participate.

5. Be Prepared

Prepare a Two-Minute Pitch. During a networking moment with a decision-maker, the goal is to focus the conversation on her rather than on yourself. The purpose at this point is just to create a bond. Such events are not the time to come on too strong. But you also don't want to get caught off-guard if the person does inquire about your own job or career goals. So prepare a Two-Minute Pitch and know it well, just in case you are asked about your career goals. If the chance arises to discuss yourself or your career, you will be well prepared, well rehearsed and very comfortable speaking to any of the key players.

6. Network with Individuals from Other Departments and Organizations

It is always easier to work together when you know whom you are working with. For example, take the time to re-introduce yourself to co-workers whom you don't see on a regular basis. If you work directly with people from another department, branch or office, find them and introduce yourself. Thank them and tell them how much you appreciate the support you get from them at work or from their department overall. If you have problems with that person or department, use the opportunity to find a nice way to say, "Perhaps we can put our heads together and find a mutually beneficial solution!"

If you are at a community or association event, approach people that are of interest to you. Meet the movers and the shakers, the decision-makers and those people you do busi-

ness with over the phone or computer and with whom it would be advantageous to network. Introduce yourself and strike up a conversation. Remember, your goal is to build relationships and create opportunities down the road!

7. Dress for Success

Always dress for business. Even if the party is casual, stick to business attire! When in doubt, keep it more conservative than wild, keep one more button buttoned, rather than one less. Never wear anything you would wear to a club, to a bar, or the beach! Never forget this is a WORK related activity. You will always do your best networking when you are well dressed, well groomed and well spoken. Be aware that what might look good or feel good at night, especially if alcohol is involved, may not seem like a wise decision in the morning as you are passing by the water cooler in the office.

8. How NOT to Ruin Yourself One Festive December Night!

As a Senior Vice President of Human Resources, I've been responsible for planning and hosting many of the company events and parties for the various companies I've worked for. Over all these years, I've definitely seen and heard it all! Don't be the young woman who is normally so tightly wound at the office, working so hard to advance her career, but on the dance floor has her skirt hiked up while dancing cheek-to-cheek with the guy from Accounting who is gyrating and trying to do splits in front of everyone! And please! Don't be that guy from accounting either! Why do some employees forget that the office party is not a discotheque or college party? With far too many drinks in their system, people loosen up too much. Certainly, you don't want anyone you work with to see you like that. You can put a huge damper on your career, as others watch in horror as your reputation and career implode.

9. Follow Up

Seize the opportunity to develop a great connection. This is the most important aspect of your networking efforts, following up and maintaining the new connection. Your goal now is to develop this new relationship! Don't waste time after a holiday event. Make notes when you have left the party to remember key conversations and key points made. If you have been handed any business cards, use the back of the cards to make your notes regarding that individual. Be sure to follow up within a few days of the event. Send a hand-written note or an email with an article attached that pertains to the conversation you had. Send a thank you note to Senior Management for hosting the event and use it as an opportunity to strengthen your new connection.

10. For Those of You with No Clue — A Summary....

Never treat a business event as a chance to "let your hair down." You can always plan to meet up with friends or family and continue your party later on, once you have left a company event for the evening. Never flirt with bosses, co-workers or your own staff. How many people are mortified the next morning, when they have to face co-workers, bosses or employees with whom they have crossed the line at the company bash?

No lampshades, no make-out sessions, no more than one cocktail or glass of wine. While mingling, hold a glass of sparkling water with either a lemon or lime. If a fellow employee is intoxicated, alert security or the event planner so that they can make arrangements to get an inebriated employee home.

Turn the event into a productive and fruitful experience. Events can take on a whole new meaning and lift your spirits when you have a networking goal. Use these events as a golden opportunity to advance your career!

Chapter 28

• • • • • • • •

Networking...
One More Time

by Bill Belknap and Hélène Seiler,
Certified Five O'Clock Club Coaches

*We are all connected; To each other,
biologically. To the earth, chemically. To
the rest of the universe atomically.*

Neil deGrasse Tyson, Astronomer and
Hayden Planetarium Director

Chapter Highlights

- The difference between *networking* and *direct contact*.
- Situational networking.
- How to quickly expand your network.
- How to remove your networking blinders.
- Networking Do's and Don'ts
- The "Golden Rules" of networking.

Overview of Networking

For many networking is only done seriously when they are looking for a new job. We hope after you read this chapter you will consider it as a proactive career management tool.

The difference between networking and direct contact

There is no question that *networking* has become a cliché; however when combined with *direct contact* they are still the most powerful tools available to you for finding a job, making contacts with other professionals in your field, meeting new friends, locating a new doctor, learning about a new restaurant or locating someone to redo your kitchen.

At The Five O'Clock Club we define *networking* as using someone else's name to make contacts and get a meetings or, of course, calling people you already know. We define *direct contact* as aggressively pursuing people you have never met or people you may have known in the past. In fact, when The Five O'Clock Club recently surveyed its members to find out how people *really got their meetings*, we uncovered an astounding statistic...our job hunters got 27% of their meetings through *direct contact* and nearly 30% of our executive clients got their first meeting through *direct contact*.

Situational Networking

The amount and kind of *networking* and *direct contact you do* will depend on where you are in your career. We like to use the metaphor of a *traffic light* so you can quickly decide.

Green Light Mode

In the Green Light Mode things are going well in your career so your networking efforts should concentrate on your longer term career goals. So what does this mean? It means you should be spending your networking time meeting with people who can have an impact on your career, or are experts in your field so you make sure you are on top of your game and the latest trends.

So who can make an impact on your career? A good first step is to take out a pad of paper or fire up your computer and create two columns. One column is all the people inside your current company that can make an impact on your career and the second column is all those outside the company. Here are a few suggestions to get you started:

Inside Your Company

- Your boss. We know this sounds like a no brainer but a number of our clients have told us they have not really had a good career path discussion with their boss; and worse, have never shared with their boss what their career objectives are. Myth: It is the boss' job to initiate this discussion. No! There is only one person responsible for managing your career...*you*.
- Your boss' peers. They can be invaluable in helping your boss formulate a positive (or negative) image of your performance and potential from their perspective. However, to be helpful relative to your career goals they need to know what your career goals are.
- Your boss' boss. In many companies this is part of an annual process, so if you

are fortunate to work in a company that does this, please take advantage of this time to ask a few pointed questions:

- ✓ Where do you see my career path going?
- ✓ Do you see any obstacles I need to work on?
- ✓ What do you feel is a realistic time-frame for getting there?

If you do not have this opportunity then we recommend asking your boss how *her* boss views your career. She may say, "I don't know but I will ask," or, if you are lucky, she might say, "Why don't you ask her yourself?" The latter opens the door for you to *immediately* schedule a meeting without any political fallout of going around your boss.

- Your peers. Many studies have shown that peer feedback is the most accurate way to understand how good you are at managing relationships, perceptions and at navigating the organization's politics. So take advantage of this and ask your peers how they view your career potential and for any suggestions they have.
- Your internal "customers." These are people you interface with or service regularly, often in other departments or functional areas. For example, if you are in finance, you may prepare the reports that monthly track another department's expenses, or if you are in IT, you may support all departments in a particular function(s). The advantage of this group is they see you in action frequently and can have some excellent input on how they see your strengths and weaknesses.
- Other divisions. Have you established contacts with your counterparts in other areas of the company both nationally and internationally? If not, pick up the phone and call them. Chances are they have been meaning to do the same thing!

Outside Your Company

We understand there never seem to be enough hours in the day to *network or make direct contacts* inside your company, let alone start to think about it outside. Here are some practical tips to make it easier:

- First, have a realistic *written* game plan. *Written* because it creates more of a commitment, *realistic* so you won't get discouraged. For example, scheduling one or two meetings, over coffee or breakfast, every month should be realistic. We don't recommend lunches because they have the highest cancellation rate.
- Whom should these meetings be with? There are three areas to focus on. One should be with an industry expert or a functional expert. They can help you assess whether you are staying on top of all the critical skill sets and trends in your area(s) of expertise. Another area is meeting with people who can impact your career either by being able to hire you or introducing you to someone who could hire you. The third is with people you just want to stay connected with. These could be friends, peers or old bosses. Notice we didn't suggest meeting with recruiters. You know the buzz that happens when someone sees you meeting publicly with a headhunter. The rumor mill goes into full swing and it is seldom positive. However, it is important to stay in touch with a few top-flight recruiters but best to do that over the phone.
- Phone and email are also effective ways to stay in touch. These can and should be done in the off hours. We define off-hours as before 8 a.m. and after 6 p.m. and suggest you target just one or two of these calls a week. They should also include the three areas we just covered in the previous bullet.

- Also please don't forget to give your time to people who need it. Return those networking phone calls. A few minutes of your time could mean a lot to somebody. And when it is your time to ask for help, they will remember.
- This is also a good time to join the Five O'Clock Club and order our books while you are in *Green Light Mode*. This is a significant step toward taking charge of your career!

We want you to stop here and think for just a moment. If you followed the above game plan and were successful just 50% of the time, how strong would your network be? How confident would you be about your knowledge of key trends, the job market, as well as your market value?

The good news is to do this well only takes five or six hours a month and none of these hours are coming from your prime work time or your family time.

Case Study: Vanessa Kicks Off Her Internal Networking Program

When we started working with Vanessa, she was a successful human resource manager who had just started a new job in a global consumer product company in New York. While she had received excellent feedback from her boss and direct reports, Vanessa was worried that she was not developing her internal network fast enough and might be perceived as an outsider from her peers in human resources and from the operating managers she supported.

We first asked Vanessa what her long-term career plan was and what she wanted to achieve in her current job. She said she wanted to continue her career in human resources and to be able to grow in her current company. To accomplish this, she knew it was important to have HR experience in several key divisions so internal networking was critical.

Next we asked her what she thought might help her peers and internal clients pay more attention to her? She said she wasn't sure. In fact, she had barely spent time with anybody outside of the daily business interactions.

We suggested she start having coffee or lunch with peers and internal clients and to spend a little extra time dialoguing after she completed a project or a task vs. immediately leaving their offices. We said "a little small talk" especially focused on a peer or a client's personal interests can be a nice way to strengthen relationships. We also suggested that she look for opportunities where she could demonstrate her proactive leadership.

A few weeks later, Vanessa came back to us with three opportunities about which she could be proactive. All were projects that were not directly in her job scope, but in areas she felt passionate about, could make a positive impact on the organization, and would give her visibility. The first project was organizing an African-American leadership forum, the second was starting a company alumni program, and the third was doing some research about a women's leadership training program.

While these projects certainly increased her workload, they were successful in increasing her visibility. In fact, soon after her involvement with these projects she was offered a position in a larger department, which put her on track for a director position within six months.

Yellow Light Mode

In the Yellow Light Mode, there are some clouds at the horizon. There may have been an unexpected reorganization, a new boss, a significant downsizing or a change in your performance-appraisal ratings. A change in your rating doesn't mean you received an unsatisfactory review; it just means there has been a change in either the overall review or in several categories. You could have moved from an "exceeds expectations" to "satisfactory" in one or more areas.

You need to take charge and networking is one of your most powerful tools to learn more about the situation and help develop personal strategies. Here the time commitment jumps to several hours a week. Our suggestions:

- Start networking within your own organization to understand who has more knowledge than you do about the situation or who can directly or indirectly influence it. Think about who the key decision-makers and influencers are.
- More than ever, you need to attend company gatherings. These can be great places to tap into the informal organization.
- Stay around for a little after important meetings so that you can chat.
- When you go to the coffee room for a refill, use the time to chat with folks. Ask them for their view of recent changes. They may have some helpful insights.
- Volunteer for projects, especially those that give you cross-functional or cross-divisional exposure. This not only raises your visibility, but also immediately expands your internal network.
- Attend relevant training programs; these are a great way to improve your skill sets and network inside your organization.
- Immediately start to network outside your organization. Focus on the people and organizations that know your company well, such as customers or clients, suppliers, industry experts, industry association members, former colleagues and former bosses who have left the company. Schedule phone calls or meetings with them to see what their perceptions are about what is happening in your company and what they suggest you do.
- Pick a group of trusted friends and colleagues to ask what they would do in your situation and to brainstorm possible next steps.
- And certainly try to have an open dialogue with your boss.

Experienced marketers are always telling us that increasing the loyalty of existing customers is a much more efficient and cost-effective than acquiring new customers. The same goes for a job search. We strongly recommend looking first in your own backyard. Explore all the areas in the company. The grass may appear greener on the outside, but it seldom is. It is also a thousand times easier to network effectively and schedule meaningful meetings inside your company than making those dreaded cold calls to people you don't know.

Case Study: Josh Deals With his Yellow Light by Re-building His Network Inside His Own Company

Two years ago, we received a call from Josh, a successful general manager of a $1 billion U.S. subsidiary of a European financial services company. Josh had been in the company for four years and wanted to leave. On paper he was successful, delivering above expectations, but he did not have time for anything but work. He also said his relationship with his European boss was courteous, but distant and he had no mentors or sponsors.

So what did we recommend? First, we discouraged him from leaving prematurely. Then we urged him to travel more frequently to the European headquarters and other subsidiaries in order to strengthen his relationships with his boss and other key operating people. This turned out to be a gold mine. He even re-connected with an old boss and asked him if he would consider his becoming a mentor, and to his pleasant surprise he said yes. His efforts really paid off. After just six months, Josh went to his boss and put his hat in the ring for a General Manager spot in a much larger business. Yes, he got the job and has now been there for over a year.

The important lessons here are the importance of building internal relationship and not immediately concluding that the "grass will be greener" outside.

Red Light Mode

In the Red Light Mode there are serious clouds on the horizon. The company may have filed for bankruptcy protection or missed its revenue and profit goals for the year. Or you may have been asked to leave due to a downsizing, received a performance warning or an unsatisfactory review. If any of these have occurred, you need to make a full-court press to explore outside opportunities. The key actions you need to take are:

1. Join The Five O'Clock Club and a Group or Insider Session (go to our website, www.fiveoclockclub.com, for exactly how to do that).
2. Order a set of The Five O'Clock Club books. These will become the foundation for your job search.
3. Update your résumé using our methodology.
4. Start building a list of specific companies you might like to work for.
5. Immediately reach out to:

- Bosses you worked well with.
- Mentors.
- The most networked people. We define this group as friends and associates who seem to know everyone.
- Trusted recruiter(s).
- Your significant other and other family members. The emotional support will be invaluable.
- Your best friend(s).

6. Expand your network. The next section covers this in detail.

Case Study: Corey Red Light Mode Calls for Immediate Action

Corey was Director of an Equity Trading Desk at a major bank. The day his boss told him his position had been eliminated, he went back to his office and did three things:

1. He called home to share the news and put the home renovation project on hold.
2. He called his major clients to tell them his company had decided to eliminate the trading desk and he would be leaving. The good news is that most of his major clients asked him to be sure and tell them where he was going because they wanted him to continue to manage their accounts.
3. Then he reached out to all the directors and VPs he knew at his current competitors and told them the following: the Trading Desk has been eliminated and he would like to explore whether there were any similar opportunities with them. And of course he mentioned that his major clients wanted to stay with him!

Just four weeks later, he was calling back his home renovation contractor and wondering which of the three offers he had received was the best to position him for his long-term career objective.

Quickly Expand Your Network

Here is a sure fire way to add a minimum of 50 names to your network. In fact, we have had clients who have completed this exercise and ended up adding as many as 200 names.

First we want to teach you how to take off your networking blinders. We all have them and in our experience the biggest blinders fall into three areas:

1. The functional or industry blinders.

This is where you only network with people from your functional area(s) of expertise or only those who have worked in your industry.

A classic example is someone in finance only networking with other finance folks and not calling someone in marketing or sales. It is as if no one in marketing or sales would know anyone who works in finance. And, of course, when you think about it rationally, it's kind of silly. The same is true with the industry blinder.

Why would I talk to anyone in healthcare about high tech?

The bottom line is that you are looking to talk to people who know people. Rationally, you know someone in healthcare can have lots of contacts in high tech and vice-versa. They could be married to someone in high tech, they might have worked in high tech themselves in a previous job or their best friend is a software developer.

2. The relatives blinder.

What we usually hear from our clients is, Why on earth would I call Aunt Mary? She has never worked in a company.

Well let's give you a true Aunt Mary story. One of our clients begrudgingly agreed to call some of her relatives after we coached her on networking. Guess what? Her Aunt Mary ended up introducing her to one of the most senior female executives at a well-known high tech company. What was the connection? Aunt Mary played bridge with the executive's mom. So dust off your list of relatives and let them know what you are looking for.

3. Your Alumni blinder.

Over 70% of our clients have not contacted their Alumni office(s). This is crazy!

Every alum who is in the alumni office database has had to agree, formally, to allow either students or alumni or both to contact them. This almost guarantees a return call. The other great thing about the majority of alumni databases is they are searchable. So if you are targeting IBM or The Home Depot you can look for all the alumni from your school who are working there. Talk about focus! This is truly a networking gold mine. Please note: In some alumni databases, they will list all alumni. However you will notice for some of those names listed there will be *no contact information*. This usually means they have not agreed to be contacted.

Now that you have your blinders off let's look at how you can easily add 50 to 200 new names to your networking list. We call it "re-scrubbing your network."

- Think about all the clubs you and your family belong to and we don't mean country, tennis or yacht clubs. Spend some time thinking about the less traditional clubs like the coin, stamp, bridge, poker, book or antique clubs.
- Your holiday card list plus your family and business email lists. While this is nothing new, we find very few of our clients have really sat down and thoroughly gone through them and then made calls or emailed them. Everyone on those lists should know you are actively looking for a job.
- How about all those sororities and fraternities you and the family have belonged to?
- How about neighbors, especially the ones you prejudged like the 80-year-old widower who doesn't appear to have many friends, but if you chatted with her you would find out that her grandson is now a manager at Microsoft.
- How about the parents of your children's best friends? How many can you reach out to? The same goes with the sports teams you and the family are (or have been) involved in. We bet most of the parents are professionals like you.
- Have you thought about sharing your target list with your doctor(s), dentist(s), barber or hair stylist? We had one client who mentioned one of his target companies to his barber and the barber said, "I cut the CEO's hair." He went on to say he would personally hand the CEO the guy's résumé the next time he is in.
- Think about all the professional people you do business with, such as your accountant, family attorney, real estate broker, banker, insurance agent or stock broker. Their client lists just may

contain some employees from one of your target companies.

- From your business life please think about:
  ✓ Vendors, suppliers, sales people you have dealt with on your job.
  ✓ Consultants you have worked with.
  ✓ Dust off those attendee lists from seminars or conferences you have attended.
  ✓ Don't forget your company's competitors; they would love to talk with you.
  ✓ Fund raising campaigns, such as United Way, that you were involved with.
- From your educational life please think about:
  ✓ Your grade school, high school and college friends. You will find it triggers a number of people you would like to reconnect with.
  ✓ We talked about connecting with the Alumni Office but you also want to contact your Alumni Association(s). They often sponsor networking events.
  ✓ Adult education classes you have attended.
  ✓ Now for all of these educational contacts you have gone through for yourself, do the same thing with your kids (especially your adult aged children), wife, husband, or significant other's contacts in these areas.

TIP: Expanding your thinking to the rest of your family can, by itself, double or triple your network list.

- From your community activities please think about:
  ✓ The Mayor and counsel members.
  ✓ PTA.
  ✓ The Chamber of Commerce.
  ✓ Community fund raisers.
  ✓ Girl Scouts and Boy Scouts.

✓ Community organizations you or the family have been involved in.

✓ Your house of worship.

For those who think they don't have a network...another case study.

Jean, a successful marketing manager had been out of the workforce for five years taking care of her twin boys. She was able to stay active by doing marketing work for a not-for-profit company.

When she decided to return to the workforce, she worked with us to develop her primary job target, marketing consulting companies in the Atlantic region.

Then she got discouraged. She felt having been out the workforce for five years would be a major drawback, especially since networking and direct contact would be her primary means for getting interviews. When we asked her how big her network was she said, "maybe 10 people who aren't even in the right industry!"

We told her nicely we didn't believe that number for a minute and challenged her to do a little networking audit of family, friends, business associates, social acquaintances, alums and everyone she met as a volunteer for the not-for-profit.

The challenge worked. It was like we told her she couldn't run 5k and she would do anything to prove us wrong. She came up with over 350 names!

Here is a list of her sources. Some you can see are obvious but others were highly creative.

• Last year's holiday mailing list.
• The invitation list to her 40th birthday party.
• The alumni office at her graduate school.
• The alumni office at her husband's graduate school.
• Her son's elementary school directory.
• She combed her Rolodex for all those business cards stuck in there.
• She thought about all the cocktail parties

she had attended over the last year and those with whom she had connected.

• She pulled out the list of the board members of the not-for-profit she was working for.
• She dug around and found the phone directory for the last company she worked for. She realized the majority of her contacts would have moved on but used Google to track them down.

Networking Do's and Don'ts

Here is a quick list of what to do and what to avoid as you crank up your network.

What to do…and these are *musts*.

• **Do reconnect** with **everyone** you have lost touch with and we mean everyone. And please don't tell us you don't know where they are. That old saw "six degrees of separation" has now dropped to "three degrees of separation" in the 21st Century. So with a few phone calls or a few Googles you should be able to track down most anyone out there.

Among the most common concerns we hear around the "reconnecting" theme are gut issues such as, "What do I say?" or "I feel so guilty."

Here is what you do first: Think about the last time someone out of your past called you after a number of years. How did it feel? Wasn't it almost instantly like they had never been out of touch? Well guess what? It is going to be exactly the same when they hear from you. **They will be delighted**!

Another excuse we hear is: Some of my good contacts are retired. First, when people retire today they seldom become inactive. We find while retirees may be playing a bit more golf or tennis, most stay very active. They often consult or are seriously involved in the not-for-profit sector. This means they still have active networks.

- **Always come bearing gifts**. As we have all read many times, effective networking is a two-way street. So what gift do you bring? Well it is not "a box with a ribbon around it" gift, but simply a current article or piece of news about something they are personally interested in. It can be about their company or a company they used to work for; it can be about their profession, their hobby or something you know they are passionate about.

What *not* to do.

- **Please don't be a pest**. Not that anyone reading this chapter would ever fall into that category. The best way to avoid being perceived as a pest is to follow one of The Five O'Clock Club principles which is, after your first voice mail... do not leave any other messages. However you can still be "seen" (literally) if you also don't block Caller ID. So please check with your friendly phone company on how to do that. For example, in the US you punch in *67 and your name and number will not appear on the Caller ID of the person you are calling and *82 to unlock it for another call where caller ID is no longer an issue

  Many of you are now asking yourself, then how the heck do I ever get to a real person instead of voice mail? Good question. We call it "bracketed calling" and it works like a charm especially for Type A managers and executives. You start calling earlier and earlier in the day and later and later in the evening. Sooner or later they will pick up. Remember the times you were in the office at 7 a.m. and the phone rang? The first thing that runs through your mind is, Who on earth would be calling at this

hour? Right? We have all been there. And most of the time we couldn't resist picking up the phone just to satisfy our curiosity. It is not unusual to make 10 to 12 calls before reaching a live person and we have had some clients that have reported making 30. The lesson, good old persistence will pay off.

- **Don't let your network get stale**. You should keep your name in front of your key contacts at least every 90 days and if you are in a full-blown job hunt, every month. Your key contacts are the people you want to stay in touch with throughout your search. They know you well and are in a position to either hire you or recommend you to someone who can hire you.

  One of the best ways to stay in touch to send them "gifts" as we discussed above. A tip on how to stay on top of this is to use the calendar reminder in your contact manager. We use Microsoft's Outlook and in Outlook it is the little red flag on the contact record. So all you have to do, after sending an article or if you just talked to them, is type in the next date you want to check in and your system will automatically remind you on that date as soon as you turn on your computer.

The Golden Rules of Networking

1. Be patient. Please remember, your networking calls are strategic, not tactical unless you are in Red Light mode.
2. The key to building a strong long-term network is your ability to develop relationships.
3. Maintain contact, at least quarterly, with everyone who has contributed to your learning and growth over the years.
4. Ask for advice and support, as opposed to favors.

5. Focus on those who have spontaneously given to you.
6. Try to always bring a "gift" to the table. It can be something as simple as a current article about their company or their hobby.
7. Graciously let go of any networking relationship where you are the only one giving.
8. Volunteer to become a mentor for someone else. Not only will it help your professional growth, but it is also the right thing to do.

Chapter Summary

- Our clients have found, if they "re-scrubbed" their networks, they always managed to add at lease 50 names and sometimes hundreds.
- Please pay attention to your career traffic lights. If you stay alert to them and take action as appropriate you will have gone a long way toward being in charge of your career.
- And remember, *direct contact* is a terrific way to supplement your networking. The last Five O'Clock study showed executives got 30% of their interviews by directly contacting someone, without being referred in by someone else.

Part Four

Getting Ahead

Chapter 29

• • • • • • • • •

How to Ask for a Pay Raise

by Kate Wendleton, President, The Five
O'Clock Club

*Homer: Bart, with $10,000 we'd be millionaires!
We could buy all kinds of useful things like...love!*

The Simpsons

Perhaps your salary has been held back
by the market for the past few years, years
when employees were just happy to have a job.
However, Five O'Clock Clubbers are reporting
substantial salary increases at their present or
new firms. This can happen when people ask
correctly, even though the job market might not
be on the employee's side right now.

Step 1: Get serious.

Prepare to justify why you should get a raise.
One way of doing this is by making a list that
clearly states your accomplishments. On an 8-1/2
x 11" sheet, draw two columns. The left column
lists your job responsibilities. The right-hand
column, which should be considerably longer,
lists what you have actually accomplished—in
rank order. It could be that Column 2 goes on for
another page.

Step 2: Request a formal meeting with your boss.

State your case using the chart you developed in Step 1. But be sure to start your meeting
my telling your boss: "I love working here and
want to stay here for as long as possible. I never
really loved any of my jobs quite as much as I
love this particular job. The only problem is this
..." Make sure you start with the positives and
make sure he or she hears this. This is the most
important message and protects you from any
negative reaction.

Step 3: Prepare yourself for rejection.

Your boss will almost certainly tell you "no,"
but keep your head up; this is to be expected. To
give you a raise, your boss must ask his/her superior, which is probably just as nerve-wracking
for your boss as it is for you. Sometimes, it is no
more than mere inertia that bars your employer
from asking for a pay increase on your behalf.
You must offset that inertia. And your boss can
use your prepared document when speaking to
his/her superiors.

Step 4: Develop a mantra.

When pressed, simply respond: "I just want to stay here forever and be treated fairly." Tell your boss you would like to meet again in a week or two. It's not over yet.

Step 5: Keep on truckin'.

If all else fails, ask your boss what you should be doing to get the raise. For example, suggest handling additional projects or participating in task forces. Also suggest a salary review in a few months. Remember though, keep repeating your mantra, "I just want to stay here forever and be treated fairly."

Professionalism and persistence, coupled with this proven Five O'Clock Club approach, have allowed hundreds of our members to get the salary they deserve. Good luck.

"Your hard work has paid off, Harold. I've decided to give you a $3 an hour raise. But it cost $4 an hour to process it. So I'll be deducting $1 an hour from your pay."

Chapter 30

• • • • • • • •

The Promotability Index
Will You Actually Get Promoted?
Or Are You Simply "Promotable?"

by Kate Wendleton, President, The Five O'Clock Club

Those who have cultivated persistence seem to enjoy insurance against failure. No matter how many times they are defeated, they managed to move toward the top of the ladder. . . . Those who pick themselves up after defeat and keep on trying, arrive. . . . Those who can't take it simply do not make the grade.

Napoleon Hill, as quoted by Dennis Kimbro
Think and Grow Rich: A Black Choice

When Is It Time to Move On?

People ask: "I've been at my current job six years. I'm killing myself, but I wonder when, if ever, I'll be promoted." How can a person tell? And certainly, since the 1980s (when the layers of management were dramatically reduced), many employees decided to move out (or over to another department) in order to move up!

But before jumping blindly from one job to another, reassess your situation. What are your chances of getting promoted where you are?

Half of the people who come to The Five O'Clock Club are employed—and have de-

cided it's time to move on. But before moving, ask yourself: Are you learning new skills that increase your marketability and fit in with your Forty-Year Vision? If so, stay.

If not, try to improve your present position. If you want to change fields, can you do it within your present company? If you need new skills so you can improve your promotability, get them on your own or get them where you are now. If you want to start your own business, keep your day job and start it at night. If there's no benefit in staying, *then* move on.

Case Study: Jim Moved Too Much

Jim had an amazing career—moving up every year-and-a-half or two by switching companies. He lost his most recent job because of a downsizing, but had no trouble getting interviews since all of his jobs had been with Fortune 100 firms. Then his job hopping caught up with him. Because he'd had five jobs in eight years, prospective employers were wary. Why had he not been promoted? After a lengthy search, Jim found a job in a city that was not to his liking. He could stay there awhile to offset the image of being a vagabond or consult there while continuing to search.

Sometimes Job Hopping Is Okay

In certain industries, job hopping is to be expected—many parts of the entertainment field, for example, or the Internet industry. But other industries want employees to be more stable.

Four Key Indicators That You Will Get a Promotion

When you think you are ready to move up, assess your chances and correct whatever may potentially hold you back. There's a big difference between being "promotable" (valued highly as a right-hand man or team member, but staying right where you are) and actually getting promoted. We all know people who have the qualifications to move up, but who just never do. Ask yourself these questions:

1. Are you READY?

- Are you considered a star? Have you developed a reputation in your field? Are you active in your industry? Do you help others in your department?
- Do you read the same publications as your bosses? Do you keep up with the messages put out by top management so you know where the organization is heading?
- Are you so known for your skills that people look to you for help?
- Is the next move an obvious next career step? If the move doesn't make sense to you, it probably won't make sense to others either.
- Have you trained your replacement? You'd better do that or bosses will be reluctant to leave a hole in the organization.

- Do you actually want to manage or would you rather be an individual contributor at a higher level? Not everyone should aspire to managing others. If you do want to manage, ask to manage projects, or manage as a volunteer for a not-for-profit organization.

....

If you don't like your boss, chances are that your boss does not like you.

....

2. Are you INCLUDED?

- Do you simply help out while the choice assignments go to someone else? Or do you get good assignments so that you're seen as being on the leading edge?
- Do you represent your department on important projects and task forces?
- Are you invited to meetings where your peers are excluded?
- Do you volunteer for critical responsibilities, including tasks for which your boss is responsible?
- Have you let management know that you *want* to advance within the organization? Have you asked them what it would take and are you performing the necessary steps? If they assume that you are happy right where you are and are not ambitious, don't be surprised when a promotion is announced, and it's not about you.

....

You work hard, are valued—even considered promotable—but maybe your boss would like to keep you right where you are. So ask yourself these questions.

....

3. Are you ACCEPTABLE to others?

- Do you get along well with your peers? Bosses want to make popular decisions. And if your peers do not like you, they could not support your promotion. Those who are disliked rarely become the boss because of the danger of having others resign.
- Do you get along well with your boss? Make sure your boss looks to you for input. If you don't like your boss, chances are that your boss doesn't like you.
- Have you supported your boss and never undermined him or her? Otherwise, you're doomed.
- Have you become part of the power center? Are you known to your boss' peers and others above you? (Use our "Eight-Word Message" in this book for this.) If no one knows your talents or likes you, you won't be promoted.
- Use The Five O'Clock Club's Circles of Influence exercise as a guide for building a network of influencers who are above you, at your level, and below you both inside and outside the organization.

If no one else is moving, you're probably not either. Your company is stagnant.

---

4. Are you in the RIGHT PLACE at the RIGHT TIME?

- If you are doing everything right, but your company is not doing well, you're not going anywhere. You will stay as a valued employee, but you are unlikely to get promoted.

- Is your boss going somewhere? If not, he or she may be a roadblock.

  When should you leave? Don't wait until you're so battered that you can barely think straight. Consider lateral moves into faster-growing companies. Big companies add credentials to your résumé; smaller companies add responsibility and experience.

When Is It Time to Move Sideways?

Consider a lateral move inside if it fits in with your Forty-Year Vision (in the back of this book). For example, if you know you would like to wind up as vice president of finance and administration, you could aim to get experience in finance, administration, accounting, operations, human resources or information technology. Experience in any one of these would advance your career in the right direction.

Furthermore, a lateral move from a department that is suffering to one that is growing gives you a chance to gain new experience and may protect you from future cutbacks. If you want to change fields, it is generally easier to make a major career transition within your present organization because they know you and you know them and their systems. You can gain experience in that new field through volunteer work, for example, or perhaps experience in your present field is transferable to the new field.

Get to know people in your targeted area — lots of people — and casually let them know of your interest. Read trade journals. Attend trade meetings. Get to know the field, and then create a proposal of why this lateral move would be good for the company, such as why your company experience coupled with your volunteer experience would make you a good internal hire rather than filling that job from outside.

Things may look stagnant, but there are many ways to assess your situation and gain the experience you need to keep your career moving.

Chapter 31

• • • • • • • • •

How We Respond to Life's Difficulties: The Most Important Factor in Success in Life

by Kate Wendleton, President, The Five O'Clock Club

It is not stress that kills us. It is effective adaptation to stress that allows us to live.

George Vaillant, psychiatrist

Books (and their electronic equivalents) have not lost their influence. Members read and re-read those that have affected them, and so do I. Beyond Shakespeare and the *Bible*, which both taught me a lot about human nature, the most important book in my life has been George Vaillant's *Adaptation to Life*, the forty-year study of 268 male Harvard graduates. The study analyzed who succeeded, who didn't, and why. Because of the homogeneity of the group, the study proved that "the relatively broad socioeconomic differences among the subjects upon college entrance had no correlation" with later success. Participants born to economic privilege did not do better than those from relatively poor backgrounds, such as those on need-based scholarships.

What a hopeful thought that the luck of the draw in how we were born is not so relevant to our future success. Everyone has a chance.

> **How we were born is not so relevant to our future success.**

Vaillant concluded that family circumstances are not the major determinant of future success. The study showed that **everyone has major setbacks, but how we respond to life's difficulties is the most important factor in success in life.** A broken love affair may lead one man to write great poetry and another to commit suicide.

We can choose how we react and those choices affect our success—in love and in work. Vaillant ranks 15 coping mechanisms by their relationship to successful results.

The study also observed that maturation continued over the span of a person's life. **We stop growing when our human losses are no longer replaced.** The study proved that it is "sustained relationships with people, not traumatic events, that mold character." **Without love, it is hard to grow.**

So I know that there is hope for each of us depending on our responses and our attitudes. Even a good book can offer hope.

You must find some way to hope in your future. Here's a quote I've saved for many years:

Optimism Emerges As Best Predictor To Success in Life

"Hope has proven a powerful predictor of outcome in every study we've done so far," said Dr. Charles R. Snyder, a psychologist at the University of Kansas. "Having hope means believing you have both the will and the way to accomplish your goals, whatever they may be . . . It's not enough to just have the wish for something. You need the means, too. On the other hand, all the skills to solve a problem won't help if you don't have the willpower to do it."

— Daniel Goleman, *The New York Times*, December 24, 1991

So **think long-term about your situation**. Do whatever you can right now to keep your body and soul together, and build for the future—regardless of how bleak things may seem right now.

Quotes to Inspire You

The most powerful arguments in favor of 'a tragic optimism' are those which in Latin are called argumenta ad hominem. Jerry Long, to cite an example, is a living testimony to 'the defiant power of the Spirit' . . . To quote the Texarkana Gazette, 'Jerry Long has been paralyzed from his neck down since a diving accident which rendered him a quadriplegic three years ago. He was 17 when the accident occurred. Today Long can use his mouth stick to type. He "attends" two courses at Community College via a special telephone. The intercom allows Long to both hear and participate in class discussions. He also occupies his time by reading, watching television and writing." And in a letter I received from him, he writes:

"I view my life as being abundant with meaning and purpose. The attitude that I adopted on that fateful day has become my personal credo for life: I broke my neck, it didn't break me. I am currently enrolled in my first psychology course in college. I believe that my handicap will only enhance my ability to help others. I know that without the suffering, the growth that I have achieved would have been impossible."

—Viktor Frankl, *Man's Search for Meaning*

Let me tell you something you already know. The world ain't all sunshine and rainbows. It is a very mean and nasty place and it will beat you to your knees and keep you there permanently if you let it. You, me, or nobody is gonna hit as hard as life. But it ain't how hard you hit; it's about how hard you can get hit, and keep moving forward. How much you can take, and keep moving forward. That's how winning is done. Now, if you know what you're worth, then go out and get what you're worth. But you gotta be willing to take the hit, and not pointing fingers saying you ain't where you are because of him, or her, or anybody. Cowards do that and that ain't you. You're better than that!

—Sylvester Stallone, author, *Rocky Balboa*

On Choosing One's Attitude:
Everything can be taken from a man but ... the last of the human freedoms—to choose one's attitude in any given set of circumstances, to choose one's own way.

—Viktor E. Frankl, Holocaust Survivor, *Man's Search for Meaning*

Chapter 32

Remaining Resilient and Achieving Success: Positive Thinking Can Provide a Boost

by Renée Lee Rosenberg, Certified Five O'Clock Club Coach

You must see your goals clearly and specifically before you can set out for them. Hold them in your mind until they become second nature.

Les Brown, motivational speaker

Do you ever worry about job-related problems? Do you express negative, limiting beliefs about a work situation? Maybe you're over-stressed and over-worked. These worries, beliefs and feelings can keep you from doing your best work and even hold you back in your career.

Earl Nightingale, known as the Dean of Personal Development, said: "We become what we think about most of the time." Negative, self-limiting thoughts create negative, self-limiting actions and can prevent us from being successful on the job and in our personal lives.

Every job environment has its ups and downs. Things happen on the job that you have no control over, and things happen as a result of wrong assumptions or errors you may have made. We're only human and have bad days and good days. However, it is important not to fall victim to the bad days.

Willpower and Positive Thinking

Research shows that the more positive your attitude is, the more likely it is you will be successful. It's very easy, when things are not going your way, to be overwhelmed by the **Terrible "Toos"**: too many stressful thoughts, too overwhelmed by work you dislike, too worried you can't learn new technologies, too certain you may lose your job, too sure you have made the wrong choices for your career, too stressed to see the opportunities for job growth at your company, too consumed by the negative chatter around you. It can be hard to see beyond the situation to grasp the big picture and move toward successful outcomes.

In 1991, Daniel Goleman wrote a brief article in the *New York Times* (Dec. 24, 1991), "Optimism Emerges as Best Predictor to Success in Life." Goleman quotes psychologist Charles R. Synder's statement that "hope has proven a powerful predictor of outcome. . . . Having hope means believing you have both the will and the way to accomplish your goals." Goleman explains, "It's not enough to just have the wish for something. You need the means, too. On the other hand, all the skills to solve a problem won't help if you don't have the willpower to do it."

Willpower can be best understood if we look at it through the lens of positive thinking, a term championed by Dr. Norman Vincent Peale (1898-1993). According to Peale, positive thinking can be broken down into several traits: Belief, Focus, Confidence, Calmness, Courage, Enthusiasm, Determination, Optimism, Integrity.

There is an additional important trait I like to add to the list: Humor.

The Positive Traits Awareness Scale

How do you rank on the positive traits awareness scale? Test yourself by asking the following questions.

Belief: Do you **tell yourself** that your work performance is your choice and that you can succeed in learning new tasks and can acquire the skills to handle stressful situations with ease?

Focus: Do you have a plan for your career, and can you break it down into small, specific, and achievable steps so that you can track your progress? Do you keep moving toward your goal even when obstacles appear? Do you also know when to stop and redefine your goal when necessary?

Confidence: Do you believe you are capable of achieving your job and career goals? Are you able to speak up and make your voice heard at meetings? Can you identify the decision-maker and share your ideas?

Calmness: Do you remain calm when things are not going your way? Do you use positive affirmations to keep stressful thoughts at bay?

Courage: Do you have the courage to take a risk, to make your voice heard when you have a good idea and take the extra step? Are you open to new possibilities at work, and speak up and ask for what you want? Do you redefine your goals when your original goals are not compatible with the goals of the organization? Do you constantly look for opportunities to express your

new ideas for organizational growth?

Enthusiasm: Do you appear energetic and involved in company events and new initiatives? Do you volunteer to help the team on special events and even mundane tasks?

Determination: Do you keep moving forward and view setbacks as challenges? Are you taking classes, and constantly looking for ways to upgrade your skills and stay current? Are you keeping track of new initiatives and opportunities at your company?

Optimism: Do you look at your job and career with a hopeful attitude and feel you are going to reach your career goals? Do you use positive language when describing your job responsibilities?

Integrity: Do you approach each day with honesty and truthfulness? Do you stay away from "water cooler chatter" (a/k/a gossip) and avoid being pulled into the negative complaints of others?

Humor: This is a trait that I believe plays an important role in helping contain stress and achieve a sense of well-being. Do you smile at others (especially when you arrive in the morning), not take yourself too seriously and look for humor and laughter in your every-day surroundings? Do you share jokes and funny experiences with co-workers? The comedian Victor Borge once said, "Laughter is the shortest distance between two people." A good laugh can relax a stressful situation and create a more productive working environment. Laughter does build connections, but make sure your humor passes the ATT test: appropriate, timely and tasteful. And even a smile can ease a bad mood and create productive energy.

Know Thyself: Moving Ahead with Positive Thinking

Here are some additional questions to ask yourself—if you suspect that you're being held back by a lack of positive thinking:

- Do you say, "I wish my job were different," but never take steps to change it?
- Do you stay at your current job because you are afraid to search for a new job?
- Do you give up when a task becomes too difficult or do you seek out a better way to complete the task? Do you know where to find help?
- Do you think your co-workers have better skills and are your competition?
- Do setbacks throw you off balance?
- Do you get annoyed when forced to wait for a reply?
- Do you get upset over a situation you can't control?

If you answered Yes to any/some/most of these questions you may need to work on your positive thinking quotient. Some suggestions for defeating negative thinking are:

- Explore who you are. What are your skills, interests and passions? Realistically analyze your personal style. How can you incorporate these attributes into your work situation? A great assessment tool to help you identify and articulate your skills and interests— perhaps for the first time—is the Five O'Clock Club's Seven Stories Exercise®. Many people drift because they've never learned to articulate their skills.
- Give serious thought to the clarification of your life goals. The Club's Fifteen-Year or Forty-Year Vision® exercise can help with this.
- Have a written plan that includes small achievable steps to keep you focused and moving forward. Ask yourself: what do I need to achieve this week, this month, this year to keep me moving toward the goals?
- Surround yourself with your most positive co-workers. Stay away from the complainers and the naysayers. These people are toxic and can sabotage your well-being and job success.
- Use positive words and phrases as often as you can to describe yourself—even when you may not feel like it—such as: "I know I can do it," "I'm terrific," "Wow to me," "Good job," "I'm proud of myself," "I can keep it up," "I'm tremendous," "I'm outstanding," "Nothing can stop me," "I'm marvelous," "I can master that skill," "I knew I could do it," "I can learn it."
- Regard setbacks as opportunities to learn and grow. Abraham Lincoln, who suffered from melancholy and had many setbacks in his career, saw the value of seeing things in a positive light: "The path was worn and slippery. My foot slipped from under me, knocking the other out of the way, but I recovered and said to myself, 'It's a slip not a fall.'"
- When you get up in the morning, remind yourself how lucky you are. Instead of, "Oh no, another day at the office," focus on your long-term goals and say to yourself, "This could be another day of opportunity to move toward my future. I can do good work and have a productive, enjoyable day." It might not work out that way, but you're less likely to be derailed if you have positive outcomes in mind.
- Create a schedule for your day. Record and evaluate your short-term successes, completing the tasks you find the hardest first and get them out of the way. Of course, some days the demands may be out of your control. But you can put effort into being in charge of your attitude. "Grin and bear it" is a cliché, but pausing, breathing deeply and remembering the bigger picture can help you to adjust to stress and frustration. Remember the research: successful

people are positive thinkers. Positive attitudes can improve your health, productivity, creative potential—and even help you live longer.

The choice is yours. Do you want to be a winner? Look and act like a winner even if you may be feeling the pressures of the day and the tasks at hand. Put on your best face and work on incorporating positive thinking traits into your daily routine. At The Five O'Clock Club we often say you have to outclass the competition, and that's more likely to happen if you remain a positive person.

Chapter 33

• • • • • • • •

Stay Focused; Take Control of Your Career; Keep Yourself Marketable

by Kate Wendleton, President, The Five O'Clock Club

If you look at yourself on the level of historical time, as a tiny but influential part of a century-long process, then at least you can begin to know your own address. You can begin to sense the greater pattern, and feel where you are within it, and your acts take on meaning.

Michael Ventura, as quoted by Peter Schwartz *The Art of the Long View*

Those Who Get Ahead Find a Way to Focus

Trevor, a 40-year-old Five O'Clock Clubber, was very excited about his career plan, which we had just developed together. He thought the direction was right and that it was comfortably attainable.

Yet as he was leaving my office he said, "But I'm afraid I may be offered work that would take me in a completely different direction. I may not be able to resist the challenge."

I told him he could "take the challenge" and give up his long-term vision. He would find himself headed in a different direction than the one he wanted.

Competent people get many once-in-a-lifetime opportunities that are impossible to refuse. As Garrison Keiller notes, "Once-in-a-lifetime opportunities come along all the time—just about every week or so."

Develop your long-term plan. It's okay if the details are murky. You still need even a blurry vision to help you keep on track. You can develop a Forty-Year Vision to be thorough, but the fifteen-year mark is often the most important.

When opportunities come your way, the decision is easier: If something fits in with your Forty (or Fifteen)-Year Vision, do it. If it doesn't fit in, don't do it.

In the early days of running The Five O'Clock Club, I posted a one-page sheet of my vision beside my computer. I forced myself to look at it every day so I wouldn't forget where I was headed. It seemed as though every week someone had an idea for me—good ideas, perhaps, but they were "off strategy."

There were still other threats to my determined focus. At one point, I was consulting part-time for a major corporation while running The Five O'Clock Club the other eight days a week. My boss asked me if I would like to be the next head of the department. It took me over a month to turn the offer down. Even I could be taken off-course.

Life has a way of sneaking up and distracting us. People are happy when they are working toward their goals. When they get diverted from their goals, they are unhappy. When they don't know what their goals are, they often feel lost.

So take the time to develop your Forty (or Fifteen)-Year Vision, perhaps by working with a Five O'Clock Club coach. Stay focused while remaining flexible in the market.

Your health is bound to be affected if, day after day, you say the opposite of what you feel, if you grovel before what you dislike and rejoice at what brings you nothing but misfortune.

Boris Pasternak, *Dr. Zhivago*

That's How You Take Control of Your Career

Decades ago, when a successful job hunter reported at the Club, he or she used to be relieved at simply landing a job.

Today, members' reports are more strategic, like this: "The Seven Stories Exercise and the Forty-Year Vision helped me figure out what I wanted to do with my life. I've landed a job at XYZ Company. Here's I how I got the job. Here's how the job fits in with my long-term plan. Here's what I expect to get out of the job. Here are the kinds of things I can see myself doing next: Within the company, I can see my career moving in this-or-that direction. But this job also positions me to do this-other-thing if I decide to move outside."

Five O'Clock Clubbers are taking control of their careers by continually thinking of how to keep themselves marketable. As usual, they are ahead of the rest of the country. Keep it up.

Keeping Yourself Marketable

Rhonda James, then 32-years old, attended our program in Harlem in the 1990s. Her experience is instructive. She started out as a temporary Administrative Assistant in the Information Systems Department of a leading mutual funds company.

Within four years, Rhonda rose to:

- a full-time administrative assistant
- then, Executive Assistant to the Office Administrator Strategic Planner Supervisory Paralegal
- then, a Risk Management and Compliance Officer, where she was the department's resident computer expert, was one of two systems administrators, and trained attorneys and paralegals in using the computer system.

Rhonda became an expert at keeping herself marketable. Here's what she did:

Networking Contacts She Made

She met with people and took information back to the Legal Department to solve some of the problems they faced. Here are some of the people she spoke with:

- the Information Systems staff, especially among people specializing in PC support, LAN network support, telecommunications, applications development, procurement and data security
- those who worked with mutual funds to better understand fund basics
- her husband, Ralston, also a member of Harlem program, who taught computers in the public schools

Television She Watched

- *Computer Chronicles* to learn new technologies, especially those using the Internet

Magazines She Read

- *PC Novice*
- *SEC Today*
- *Corporate Legal Times*
- *Compliance Reporter Law*
- *Working Woman*
- business articles, especially regarding the stock market and the trading area of compliance

Association She Joined

- Web Grrls (www.webgrrls.com)

Chapter 34

• • • • • • • •

The Eight-Word Message: How to Make Sure Those Above You Know How Good You Are

by Kate Wendleton, President, The Five O'Clock Club

Your security will come first and foremost from being an attractive prospect to employers, and that attractiveness involves having the abilities and attitudes that an employer needs at the moment.

William Bridges, *JobShift: How to Prosper in a Workplace Without Jobs*

The Eight-Word Message is one of the most effective tools any person can use to advance their career. You can use an Eight-Word Message to make sure that those more senior than you know what you want them to know about you—and the more that key decision-makers know about you, the better your chance of rising through the ranks—or keeping your job. The following are some examples of real-life accounts of how the Eight-Word Message has worked.

Case Study: Judy Not Getting Credit

Judy, Jim and Helen had worked 70 hours a week for the last three weeks to complete the Airbag Project. Judy was proud and relieved when it was done on time. Then she found out that Jim and Helen were getting all the credit. In fact, it seemed that no one even knew that Judy had worked on the project. There had been a pattern for her of not getting recognition for her work. Once more, she was being overlooked. She thought about looking for a another job and working for a company that would be fairer—someplace that would appreciate her hard work. Or she could go to her boss and complain about not getting credit. Instead, she decided to start using an Eight-Word Message whenever she wanted people to know something about her—especially those higher up. And right now she had a strong message to get across. The message was "I worked on the Airbag Project."

Most people miss everyday opportunities to get out information about themselves. For example, when Mr. Coyle, her boss' boss, is in the same elevator with Judy, he always greets her with his predictable "Good morning, Judy. How are you?" Judy, just as predictably, politely responds, "Fine, and how are you, Mr. Coyle?"

This time, however, Judy decided to say, "Great—now that we've completed the Airbag

Project." He almost *had* to ask, "Oh, were you involved with that?" This gave her the opening she wanted. "Yes. Three of us worked 70 hours a week for the last three weeks. I was in charge of all the marketing literature. I think it's an award-winning package."

As she came into contact with other people whom she wanted to know about her work, Judy gave them the same message. Gradually people were showing their appreciation. Her self-esteem went way up. If she continues to do good work, and makes sure the right people know about it, Judy's career will have a more promising future.

· ·

Most people miss everyday opportunities to get out information about themselves.

· ·

Selecting the Targets for Your Message

It's not enough to do a good job. People—especially those more senior than you—have to *know* that you've done a good job. Managing the message they get about you is even more critical in these turbulent times when those over you come and go, and you don't know who your immediate boss may be tomorrow. In the old days, you established long-term relationships and a long-term reputation. The management ranks changed more slowly. Now you have to make sure from time-to-time that people know your worth.

Case Study: Ralph Overcoming Career Stereotypes

Ralph used to be the head of a marketing department before he joined Lavaloc. Now he is in charge of all advertising—a smaller position—and is doing a good job. The management here forgets that he used to have much broader responsibilities and could contribute more than he currently does. For example, he could be on a task force to market a new Lavaloc product, or have another area reporting to him, such as the direct-marketing department.

Over time, Ralph became so frustrated that he was thinking of writing a memo to personnel to let them know that he had come from a bigger job. Or he thought about asking for a formal meeting with his boss and his boss' boss. Memos and formal meetings are often good techniques for getting ahead. But an Eight-Word Message is usually a lot less risky. Ralph decided to try it. His message was "I used to be head of marketing."

When Ms. Dolan, the division head, was in that proverbial elevator, she predictably said, "Hello, Ralph, how are you?" Ralph responded, "The energy in this place is just terrific. It reminds me of the energy at Galomar." She inevitably *had* to comment, "I forgot you had worked at Galomar." This gave him the opportunity to say, "Yes. I was the head of marketing there." If appropriate, he could have elaborated.

Ralph's goal, at this point, was simply to remind people that he has a broad background. Later on, he could change the message. And, at some point, he may even formally approach someone about being on a task force—once he has established a different image of himself.

Giving These Messages to Bosses

Part of the trick of managing your message is figuring out who your "bosses" are. You probably know who your immediate supervisor is (although, in some companies, it may be hard to tell), but who are the other people—senior to you—who can influence your career? Most people come up with a list of six to ten people who are senior to them. The list could include your boss' boss, some of your boss' peers, or your boss' boss' peers. It could also include a few people outside your organization, such as the head of an important industry association, your boss' peer in another company, or someone considered a guru in your field. These are the people who you want to consider when you have an important message to get across.

You can't constantly send out messages every time you run into someone, and you'd look like an idiot if you kept saying the same thing. You might, for example, want to send a message that supports your boss or your group, such as, "I think we have the best audit team in the industry."

Decide what message you want to send, and to whom you want to send it. Make sure your message is appropriate. In the course of promoting yourself, make sure you do not undermine your boss or say anything negative about others. You are simply trying to manage your own career.

Managing Relationships at Work: Bosses

Most people do not lose their jobs because of incompetence, but because of poor relationships at work. By definition, work relationships can be divided into those with people who are at a higher level than you (bosses), at your level (peers), or at a lower level (subordinates). Of course, one must also have good relationships with clients, but we will not be dealing with that issue here. Your career can be completely derailed by a boss, a peer, or a subordinate—but in very different ways. On the other hand, your career can be greatly enhanced by learning how to communicate well with the people in each of these categories—but, again, in very different ways.

Now, we'll take a look at the instructive example of someone who has totally ignored the importance of having good relationships up the line. And has suffered the consequences.

> It's not enough to do a good job.
> People have to know—subtly—
> that you've done a good job.

Case Study: Frank About to Be Fired

Frank's story is a common one: he forgot that it was his job to please his boss. Frank was the person in his company responsible for supporting computer departments all over the world, and his work was excellent. He and his boss, Mr. Williams, received many letters of commendation from happy clients who appreciated the work Frank did. However, Frank thought his boss was stupid and nasty, and deserved to be ignored. He would not tell his boss what he was going to say at meetings. What Frank said usually caught his boss by surprise, and that gave Frank pleasure. When Mr. Williams gave him an assignment, Frank was sure his boss was wrong and did it his own way. Sometimes Frank's clients agreed with him and sent more letters praising him. This only encouraged him to ignore his boss further.

Frank was doing such a great job that he was ready to have his duties expanded. He wanted new assignments and a promotion. In fact, Frank thought that he should report directly to his boss' boss! Because Frank served his clients well and did his job well, he thought that was enough. It wasn't. Frank was in trouble. He was about to be fired. Mr. Williams thought Frank was worth saving, and that some executive coaching could help change his attitude and behavior. Mr. Williams arranged for Frank to see me.

When I discussed the situation with Frank, he was adamant that, as a matter of principle, he would not show respect to his boss. Why should he defer to someone whom he thought was inadequate and who treated everyone so horribly? It had become a point of honor with him.

To keep his job, Frank first had to accept the fact that he was in trouble: he had no chance of reporting to his boss' boss; he was not going to get new assignments, given the way he was acting; and I couldn't emphasize enough that he was actually going to lose his job if he didn't change. The turning point came when he saw that it was possible to develop a good relationship with his boss without giving up his principles or his rapport with the people in the field.

....

If all of your clients like you but your boss doesn't, you're in trouble.

....

A subordinate cannot possibly know all the various pressures that affect his or her boss' decisions, and therefore is not the best judge of whether a boss' requests are valid. If your boss says that a certain assignment is the most important thing for you to do, you are in no position to second-guess him or her, in effect saying no. I told Frank that I know from personal experience as a manager that I don't want to always have to explain to my employees why I want them to do something. At some point, I get tired of explaining. Sometimes when I say something is very important, I simply want them to do it.

As we continued our counseling sessions together, Frank came to see that his point of view was not always accurate, and that perhaps it made sense to pay attention to the boss. If Frank didn't learn to deal with this boss, he would probably have the same problem with the next one—who might be one who would simply fire him, rather than trying to help him as this one was doing.

What could Frank do differently? He could find out his boss' priorities, let his boss know his agenda before he went into meetings, send his boss a copy of all memos (or show him the content of sensitive memos before he sent them). But even if Frank kept making these little changes, how would Mr. Williams tell if Frank was simply trying to placate him, or if he had seen the error of his ways and had had a real change of heart? Over the course of time, Frank's boss would have to watch carefully for signs of Frank's true intentions: Was Frank still trying to undermine him or was Frank now supporting him? This situation would create a lot of pressure on both of them.

Making subtle changes at this point would not be enough. Frank's boss was too frustrated. Instead, Frank would have to do something more radical so that his boss could see clearly that his attitude had indeed changed. Frank could make more dramatic and consistent changes in his approach, such as overtly deferring to his boss at meetings. An effective alternative would be actually to tell his boss that he had made a conscious decision to change, and that he was determined to become a new person. Then, even if his changes were not dramatic, Frank's boss would recognize the true significance of all of those small changes: Frank is now a different person. Things will be better in the future.

To let Mr. Williams know that he had had a change of heart, Frank needed to communicate a very simple message: "I was wrong. I've changed." So Frank said to his boss, "I can see now that I've been wrong. I'm sure that you have plans that I don't know about. I will make sure that I do what you want, and will also let you know my agenda before we go into meetings." Now Frank was consistently asking his boss for feedback on the things he planned to do, and filling him in before they went into meetings. He developed a good relationship with Mr. Williams. After a few months, Frank got a number of new assignments. After a few more months, he got a promotion. Frank is still working for the same boss, but now he loves it, and Mr. Williams is as happy as can be.

....

Changing your behavior is not enough. Those above you have to *know* that you've changed. You've got to *tell* them.

....

You Can Make Corrections Now

Stories about career crises are interesting and dramatic. However, it is better to manage your career to prevent the kind of crisis that you may bring on yourself. You don't have to wait until things get critical. You can make corrections at any stage. First, assess your situation. Make a chart of everyone in the organization with whom you have contact. Think through what your relationship is with each person, and what it should be. If you are in danger of losing your job, make a plan. The most effective ways to buy time for yourself are to make a dramatic change that takes the pressure off you, and to deliver a concise and consistent message.

According to the market paradigm, one's boss is really a major customer rather than an authority in the old sense.

William Bridges, *JobShift: How to Prosper in a Workplace Without Jobs*

I don't want any yes-men around me. I want everybody to tell me the truth even if it costs them their job.

Samuel Goldwyn

Chapter 35

• • • • • • • •

Forging Career Security: Things to Do When You're Not Job Hunting

by David Madison, Ph.D., Director, The
National Guild of Five O'Clock Club Career
Coaches

Those who have cultivated persistence seem to enjoy insurance against failure. No matter how many times they are defeated, they managed to move toward the top of the ladder. . . . Those who pick themselves up after defeat and keep on trying, arrive. . . . Those who can't take it simply do not make the grade.

Napoleon Hill, as quoted by Dennis Kimbro,
Think and Grow Rich: A Black Choice

It's not a big surprise that most citizens of the modern workplace worry a lot these days about job security—much more so than their parents did. It used to be the employers who were so concerned about hiring people who would stay put for years (beware of job hoppers!), but now candidates are eager to find the companies that won't shuffle them out of a job in two or three years. People know that job security has almost become a fiction; who is surprised when the next merger, corporate takeover, layoff or outsourcing is announced?—followed by headlines about how many jobs will be eliminated.

"Going up?"

Losing your job every five years could wreak havoc with your career plan.

With job security on the decline, it is important for people to be even more vigilant about career security. Isn't it pretty obvious that losing your job every five years could wreak havoc with your career plan? Maybe you don't even have a clearly formulated career plan—our members know that's not a good idea—but it's just good strategy to think about the consequences of forced job moves and minimize the impact of disruptions; obviously a derailed career can dash your hopes, plans and goals. A recent caller to The Five O'Clock Club lamented about how many wrong turns he had made—and at age 59 was facing the grim truth that he would never be able to retire. This might have been a failure to do proper financial planning (and saving!), but he was calling the Club because his career was a train wreck.

Let's consider some of the steps you can take to protect yourself. Career security—not just job security—should be one of your top priorities.

But what do we mean by career security? Let's give some specific content to the term. Successfully forging career security means:

- Being able to remain on track with your career goals even if your next job lasts two years instead of ten; even if you're out of a job suddenly when your company is sold; even if your new boss turns out to be toxic and blocks your advancement. In other words, having strategies to help navigate the unforeseen.
- Minimizing the time you spend in the job market, *i.e.,* reducing your "in-between jobs status" during a 20 to 25 year period. If you can put things together in such a way that periods of unemployment are brief, you're more likely not to be diverted from your goals. Long periods of unemployment often prompt job hunters to settle for jobs that are off-strategy. Career security means not having to settle.

People tend to think about job hunting and career goals when circumstances force them to—that is, when they're about to be out of work and they have no choice. But that's a bit like shopping for fire insurance after your house has started to burn down.

There are plenty of things you can do while you're on the job, hopefully for a period of several years. Here are a few suggestions—some of them may not apply to you…but you would have to come up with a good argument why any one of them doesn't!

....

Career security means not having to settle.

....

No. 1: Nurture the Network

If you have worked The Five O'Clock Club methodology properly during your job search, you have constructed a marketing plan designed to help you contact 40 to 60 people over several targets. The Club's mantra is "aim for 200 positions"—to get a lot going and get multiple offers. By the time you landed your new job, you may indeed have contacted 200 people—or maybe it was only 40, 50 or 60. But when you hear those thrilling words, "You're hired!" what do you do with the marketing plan? If you're thinking about career security, you don't put it in a file and forget about it.

Look at the this way: In the process of your job hunt you managed to tell at least a few dozen new people about your skills, accomplishments and goals—and these are the people to maintain relationships with forever. That's what we say networking is: building life-long relationships. Chances are, quite frankly, some of these people could play a key role in helping you stay on track years from now.

One Five O'Clock Club graduate, a senior bank auditor who hadn't looked for a job in 25 years, went through a long, stressful search. He admitted that he was shy and job-hunting didn't come easily. But where did he eventually get the lead that resulted in his new job? He contacted a former colleague with whom he hadn't been in touch for more than ten years. But the former colleague had a very positive memory of his work and character, and happily gave him the recommendation that paid off. In other words, it's overwhelmingly likely that he wouldn't have had a long stressful search if he had stayed in touch with important people. If you make a point of keeping in touch with former colleagues and new contacts forged during job hunt, the outreach during the next period of unemployment won't be such an uphill battle—and it is much more likely to be brief.

Keep reviewing your marketing plan and use it as a blueprint for your on-going networking efforts. These days there are so many electronic techniques to keep you mindful of calls or contacts to be made every week or every month. But you don't just need reminders: build a database of your contacts, and work to maintain and grow it; use an electronic format of some kind—Excel, FilemakerPro, Outlook, etc.—instead of a collection of business cards. You should have good written notes in this database on all these people (their projects, interests, areas of expertise), so keep feeding them information that may be helpful. Keep reminding people in your chosen career field where you are and what you're up to. Nurture the network by letting people know you are a resource and that you're at the top of your game (or working hard to get there!). Make your LinkedIn profile as relevant as possible and update it as frequently as possible, so that those in your Linkedin Network will see the updates.

> **When you get that first offer, don't put your marketing plan in the file and forget it.**

No. 2: Get Out of the Office: A Starring Role in Your Professional Association

We know that attending meetings of professional associations can give a boost to networking—and we have always urged career changers to get involved in associations to speed the process of being perceived as insiders. Thus, job-hunters are well served by showing up at monthly association meetings and pressing the flesh. But consider the impact that association participation can have on career security. It's one thing to attend from time-to-time—and it's very easy to argue that you're too busy to go to meetings—but career-minded people want to be seen as leaders, not just in their own companies, but in their fields. Join associations, accept leadership roles, and volunteer for projects and committees. Obviously, this means a commitment of time, energy and enthusiasm, but this can be part of your career security strategy. Is it worth it from that perspective? At the very least, your name, title and photo show up in the association newsletter or magazine—hopefully on a regular basis. Your boss and peers will see it, as well as executives in other companies. And you can add descriptions of your association accomplishments to your résumé.

> **Let your network know you are a resource and that you're at the top of your game (or working hard to get there!).**

One of our favorite case studies of the use of associations comes from Evan Gansl, a Five O'Clock Clubber whose story was featured in our magazine. As part of his intensive effort to move his career into elder law practice, he became active in a professional association. He signed on to work on a committee that included a woman who is a leader in the field, and who eventually was looking to hire someone for her firm. He applied for the job, and hiring Evan was a relatively easy decision for her. Because he was fully involved in the association, she knew him and the quality of his work.

You can become a star in your own company, but it would be nice—it would be strategic—if others in your industry can see your value. If you become easily recognized as an industry player because of your high profile in an association—appreciated for your hard work, perhaps on a research project or arranging a conference—it will be a lot easier in future interviews for hiring managers to recognize your commitment and contribution to the field.

. . . .

Career-minded people want to be seen as leaders, not just in their own companies, but in their fields.

. . . .

No. 3: Get Out of the Office: Building Your Reputation by Public Speaking

How about being the featured speaker at an association meeting? Or the keynote speaker at the annual conference? What better way to gain recognition as a thought leader in your field? You don't have to wait for your company to anoint you as a media spokesperson—that privilege actually falls to very few. In fact, if you end up speaking on topics of interest in your field, whether to industry associations or even to general audiences, you usually cannot appear as a representative of your company (unless authorized to do so). Rather, you can present as an expert in your field—perhaps on trends in the music recording industry, new reporting regulations for banks, or the areas of the biggest expansion expected in the hospitality industry.

The best protocol is to let your boss—and your company's PR department—know what you're up to, even though you are not speaking on behalf of your firm. In fact, you want your boss to know. Remember, this is part of your career security strategy; you want to enhance your reputation as a specialist and an expert. And the more speaking you do, the more you will be in demand.

Four times a year, the Five O'Clock Club sponsors the HR Network Breakfast seminars for human resources officers who can view it via video. We look for panelists for each event, people who have built solid reputations as specialists in their fields, with a knack for communicating well with audiences. A summary of each panel presentation appears in our magazine, *The Five O'Clock News*, along with photos and bios of the panelists. This all helps to build career credibility for the presenters. Bear in mind that the goal of *your* marketing plan (when you were job hunting) was to talk to 60 people who might ultimately be in a position to hire you. If you give speeches on hot topics in your field, people will be lining up to meet you. This will help you develop a wide network of professionals in your field.

It's very common for shy people and introverts to shrink from the idea of public speaking—and they may be tempted to take a pass on this technique for building career security. But any introvert can be inspired by the example of James Brown, a spokesman for the New York State Department of Labor. He often begins his speeches by admitting that he is a shy guy, and that the public speaking role was thrust upon him by his superiors. So he had to do what he had to do. But he is in demand as a speaker. His key for success is his amazing knowledge of the New York economy and labor market. His expertise allows him to get up in front of a roomful of people and talk from the heart to his audiences.

. . . .

Outside your company, it would be nice—it would be strategic—if others in your industry can see your value.

. . . .

Maybe you sense that you are not high enough on the corporate ladder to have anything to say or command attention. But one way to move up the ladder is to build your expertise and become known as someone who has something to say. The next time you hear a presentation at an association meeting, make a point of chatting with the speaker afterwards: "How long have you been doing this? How did you get into public speaking?" Maybe public speaking can become part of your plan five years from now.

No. 4: Build Your Reputation by Writing

One way to get asked to give speeches is to become known as someone who has a message or—like James Brown mentioned earlier—just a lot of useful information in any particular field. You can do this by writing for publication. Very few executives actually write books, so that is not the goal here. If you're at all aware of what your boss or CFO is reading, you'll know the industry newsletters you should be targeting.

We mentioned earlier that your name, title and photo will end up in an association newsletter if you're simply active on committees or at conferences; the same will happen if you're a contributing author.

Recall that a good networking technique is to email links of articles to people you've met with. It's a plus for you if people are sharing your article in professional circles. We have always recommended contacting authors of articles. If you are the author, people will reach out to you—people who can become part of your expanding network of industry contacts.

What about writing a book? Because writing a book requires so much work and typically pays so little, it's not really a practical option for most people who are strategizing career security. There are clearly cases where it provides a boost. Five O'Clock Clubber Anthony Politano is the author of *Chief Performance Officer: Measuring What Matters, Managing What Can Be Done,*

which enhances his stature as an expert in his field. He was a panelist for one of our seminars, "HR Metrics: What Your Board and CEO Want." At the end of the session, there was a long line of HR executives to get his book. Hence, at just one event he impressed a lot of people and expanded his network of contacts. The next time he looks for work, securing interviews won't be a struggle—and he won't have trouble adopting the stance of a consultant.

....

Build your expertise and become known as someone who has something to say.

....

No. 5: Take Courses or Teach Them, but Continue Learning!

If your company pays tuition reimbursement, take full advantage of this benefit. Even if your company doesn't, then consider paying out of your own pocket. Be on the lookout for courses offered by colleges, learning centers and professional institutes. It may almost sound like a cliché now to say that you should be "on the cutting edge," but you do want to be on top of the latest knowledge, trends and technology that impact your field. There's also a lot of talk these days about the importance of thought leaders, and pushing yourself to be perceived in this way can be a part of your career strategy. Being current and innovative—and taking the initiative to remain so—makes you a valuable member of your staff or team.

Coursework also looks good on your résumé, especially if the topics relate directly to important trends in your field. Effective interviewing, after all, is a matter of outclassing the competition, and you will have an advantage if you can list several recent courses that you've taken.

"The boss seems to think you have an unhealthy obsession with upgrading your computer. You're to check into rehab on Monday."

Write articles: It helps you
if people are sharing your
article in professional circles.

Naturally, teaching a course is even better. The hard work and research required for course preparation (reading a half-dozen books and probably many more articles) will push you to master new material and deepen your own understanding. What better way to achieve a reputation as a thought leader? Even if you don't take or teach a course, don't neglect the learning required to stay abreast in your field. Have there been five or six new books published in your field in the last six months that relate to your function and your goals, and have you read them? You want your peers and bosses to look to you as a source and a guide. Being well-read is a step in this direction.

No. 6: Taking Stock: Reviewing Your Résumé

If you've been through The Five O'Clock Club group process, chances are that a lot of blood, sweat and tears went into transforming your résumé into an effective accomplishments-based marketing tool. Most people find the job-search process so stressful that they just want to put their résumés away for a few years. Now that they have a job, why not?

One of the best reasons not to neglect the résumé is that jobs aren't permanent any longer! Of course, you may have every hope and expectation that a new job will last for five years or more—but we all know that job security isn't what it used to be. Hence, always keeping one eye on your résumé isn't a bad idea. "I haven't looked at my résumé in years," is a common refrain heard from people who have enjoyed a long run with one employer, but any Five O'Clock Club graduate should know that the résumé is a marketing tool to keep fresh. Get in the habit of reviewing your résumé every few months.

Presumably, you were hired to do something. A great interview question is, "If you were to hire me, what you would like to have me accomplish in the first three months?" Or: "Is there something keeping you up at night you want me to help solve?" After you've been on the job for six months, there should be new accomplishments to put on the résumé. If the months or years go by and you're not adding fresh accomplishments and skills to your marketing document, you may be stagnating. *You may not be building the kind of expertise that underwrites career security.* In other words, frequent résumé review is a way to gauge your career progress.

You want your peers and bosses to
look to you as a source and a guide.

Having your résumé current and fresh is a way of staying on the offensive. Always be saying to yourself, "If I had to market myself tomorrow, would I be ready?" Remember the importance of keeping job-search periods as brief as possible. You never want to have to dust off your résumé.

No. 7: Taking Stock: Reviewing Your Vision

Many people wander from one unsatisfying job to another because they skip assessment. Five O'Clock Clubbers know that we have tools for evaluating the past (The Seven Stories Exercise) and for figuring out where to go (The Forty-Year Vision). These are most commonly done when people are gearing up for a full-scale job search, but assessment can help people who may simply feel that they're in a rut, whose careers seem to have gone into a blind alley. The Seven Stories Exercise often drives people to a realization that they are simply in the wrong career—and something's got to give. A number of years ago a partner in a law firm realized he was off-course when his Seven Stories revealed that his most recent enjoyable accomplishment was in junior high school. Another member of the Club was reminded by his Seven Stories that he liked teaching. He went back to school to get instructor certification, and is expanding his job to include training responsibilities.

Reviewing satisfying accomplishments isn't something that needs to be done every year, but The Forty-Year Vision is clearly more fluid—and deserves repeated reviews, in light of how your life is actually unfolding. We always say that you should take the job that positions you best for the future you envision for yourself. At every anniversary of your start of a new job, you should review the vision, which should be in *written form*. Are you getting promotions and learning new skills according to plan? Are you taking on new assignments that move you in the right direction? Career security means paying attention to these issues on an on-going basis—especially

if you have been in your job more than two or three years.

....

You never want to have to dust off your résumé.

....

No. 8: Taking Stock: The Annual Checkup with Your Career Coach

This may not be something that you've given much thought to, but all of our coaches are certified by The Five O'Clock Club. That is, they are all graduates of our rigorous training program that ensures that they've mastered the unique Five O'Clock Club method. We don't entrust our clients to generic coaches. So it's no surprise that we get rave reviews about our coaches—those who lead the small weekly groups (either in person or by phone), and those who only see clients privately. The overwhelming testimony of successful Five O'Clock Club job-hunters is that the coach played a central role in seeing them through to the desired results.

....

The Forty-Year Vision deserves repeated reviews, in light of how your life is actually unfolding.

....

A powerful lesson to draw from this is the importance of staying in touch with your coach. Once people land new jobs, however, the tendency is to want to forget about the job-hunt struggle: "It's behind me now—I should get on with my new job and hope that it lasts a good long time." This commonly translates into complacency about career security as well. But the coach who provided such reliable guidance during the hard days of the job search should remain a resource. Just as it's a mistake to put the résumé in a file, it's a mistake to neglect thinking about and evaluating your career—in the company of an expert. Within a year after starting your new job, meet with your coach to review the long-term plan. Talk about complications or issues on the new job that may be pushing you off-course—or that may have opened up some new possibilities. Using your coach as a professional sounding board can help you to achieve perspective. Most of us are surrounded by professionals that we rely on to keep us sound and whole: an accountant, lawyer, doctor, dentist, pastor and a leader in your house of worship. It's a good idea to add your career coach to this roster—and arrange for a checkup periodi-cally, to guarantee that you'll make time for a few hours of focused attention on your career. And by all means, if you run into rough sledding on the new job, get in touch with your coach again.

....

Continue to rely on your career coach.

....

If your company purchased Five O'Clock Club outplacement for you, you may well have a few unused hours of private coaching—be sure to use them!

Chapter 36

• • • • • • • •

Social Media: Five O'Clock Club Coaches Talk about Using LinkedIn

by Kate Wendleton, President, The Five O'Clock Club

> Homer: *Oh, so they have Internet on computers now!*
>
> The Simpsons

For this chapter, we asked a group of Certified Five O'Clock Club career coaches to give us their opinions on Social Media in general and LinkedIn in particular. The coaches were: Damona Sain, Win Sheffield, Celia Currin, Mary Anne Walsh, Anita Attridge, Bill Belknap, Roy Cohen and Chip Conlin.

Technology changes, and you have to change with it, but the basic techniques and thought processes for career development don't change. As one of our coaches said, "I constantly give my clients this advice: even if you do not embrace social networking, you need to understand how business is using it because it will come up, sooner rather than later, in business conversations.

"So, please, for self-preservation, avail yourself of the data. By the way, www.mashable. com is one of the best sites for keeping pace with the business uses and business trends involving social media."

Yes, times have changed. In the 1960s and 1970s, if you left your house and the phone rang,

you missed the call. People did not have home answering machines. Nowadays, people are connected to their cell phones everywhere they go.

Twenty years ago, the Internet did not exist. Today, it can dominate our lives. We think that the new Social Media are meant to extend our relationships, but there are perilous risks, as well as benefits.

We can all build lots of connections, but let's be smart about it. Facebook is the cause of many relationship break-ups. A 2009 study makes the claim that "increased Facebook use significantly predicts Facebook-related jealousy" in romantic relationships.

While Facebook tends to be more of a personal medium, LinkedIn is more for professional relationships. Used correctly, it can help you to improve your current career, find a new job, or build a consulting practice.

Social Media in General
Keep up your contacts while working

Before Social Media came into being, we urged our clients who had landed jobs to make sure they had two networking meetings a

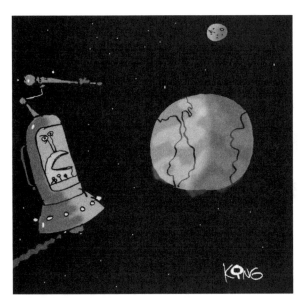

"I've located the source of all that annoying spam we've been receiving...preparing to destroy."

week—no matter what—to keep up their contacts, keep up with what was happening in their fields and industries, and to already have developed contacts if they needed information to help them in their careers or wanted to search again.

Be smart about building your connections.

Social Media can help you to keep up your contacts, particularly given how busy everyone is these days, but our coaches caution that "nothing substitutes for face-to-face contact. Don't ever forget the value of a phone call over an email." Meeting people virtually does not replace meeting people directly—either in person or via telephone. One coach advised, "Make sure that 20 to 30% of your time—whether in your job or job hunting—is 'in the field' meeting and connecting with people face-to-face."

Social Media are a serious part of the resources and tools that help people in their jobs and in job search. The basics of managing your career, looking for a job, or building a consulting practice have not changed—just the tools that help people to connect have changed—ranging from email, online search, to LinkedIn, blogs and Twitter.

Use Social Media as *one tool* to develop your career, build a consulting practice, or find a new job.

These tools help you to stay in contact with your network of people and companies, and to continue to build your network. You can use social networking tools to build your reputation as an industry or subject expert by blogging and tweeting—or every bit as important—responding and commenting on other people's blogs and tweets.

As one coach said: "Social networking should not be viewed as just a job-search tool. That's wrong and inefficient. This would be the equivalent of going to just one interview with the belief and expectation that it will produce a job offer. It's a resource for managing and navigating your career. Yes, you use social networking to conduct a dynamic job search, but it's so much more than that. Use it to expand your network, as a resource for information, and to build a community of like-minded people who will support you both on the job, as well as in job search."

Social Media Can Waste Your Time

Whether you are employed or not, we all know that anything on the Internet (or computer or handheld mobile devices, especially Smartphones) can suck up too much time. One coach advises that for one or two weeks, you should assess how much time per day you spend online. Track how often you click on interesting links and *surf to unrelated topics*. Then cut all your time in half for two weeks. Use that extra time to meet with people directly via phone and in person, rather than relying on virtual meetings alone.

As one coach put it: "Let's face it, it takes a lot of time and care to build Stage 1 and 2 contacts (getting to know people who know about your industry and field and then those who are more senior than you). It's easy to avoid the sometimes intimidating and anxiety-producing effects of reaching out to people in person. Social Media are also pretty much a '2-D' interaction. That can increase miscommunication possibilities."

Comparing Various Social Media

Facebook is generally for social purposes, rather than career development. Twitter can be very time-intensive and the tweets move so quickly that you can lose track of them easily if you stay away for a couple of days (even hours sometimes!).

Blogs are labor intensive, but can be effective if you like to write and write well. But check out the blogs you return to time and again, and figure out why they are appealing. Being too wordy with no graphics or other media (such as a short video) can be a recipe for a lack of traffic. Other media include verbal podcasts, but you need good recording equipment or no one will stay to listen. This coach notes: "I think well done video podcasts (NOT amateur YouTube versions!) on Twitter, Facebook, blogs, and whatever else there is, would likely appeal to more people—but ONLY if they are well done and if you are photogenic or a natural in front of a camera."

All of the above can take up so much of your time! Be sure to track the amount of time you are on the computer and what you are doing there. It is very easy to waste time digging through newsletters, blogs, junk mail, and it is important to keep the time invested *under control*.

What's more, Social Media can be a new way of "hiding out" instead of actually making contact with real people. The Internet in all of

its forms is a great research tool. But as we used to say, if you are spending all of your time in the library (or on the Internet), get out more. If you are spending all of your time meeting with people, research more. You need both for a successful career today.

Finally, Social Media are used more heavily in certain industries and professions than others. Here's one coach's thoughts on the subject: "Social Media are a tool to support your career. Like any tool it's best used when the audience you're targeting has embraced it and believes in it.

"Know whether your audience uses it so you don't waste a lot of time using the wrong tools to advance your career or your search. If everyone in your desired target is heavily invested in social networking then you should be, too. For example, I have a client who just became the president of a digital ad agency. He's on Facebook and LinkedIn to keep his universe of contacts—both professional and personal—apprised of his whereabouts and plans. He also uses and promotes other technologies to demonstrate his commitment to being 'wired.'"

"I'm sorry, but I can't hire you. I typed your name in on a search engine, and lazy, selfish and unmotivated were the categories that came up."

LinkedIn

Every professional needs to be on LinkedIn. We have well over 1,000 members in our Five O'Clock Club LinkedIn Group. LinkedIn has gotten rave reviews at The Five O'Clock Club. Wrote one Clubber to his group: "LinkedIn is a terrific tool that can help extend a person's network and simplify the process of identifying members of your network in target companies and industries. It's free to join so I've tried to recruit lots of other Five O'Clock Clubbers. As a quick anecdote, I received a cold call this morning from a distant contact in my LinkedIn network who is looking for help on a number of his projects. I was the perfect fit. A perfect lead! I wish you the same good luck, and pass it on. If you join, make sure you connect to me; the bigger your network the more effective it will be."

From one coach's point-of-view: "LinkedIn is being described as 'the best' online career-management guide around; and rightly so. There is a huge WOW factor knowing that at least 45 million others are on LinkedIn.

"Remember more than 85% of recruiters are trying to find you daily. Just a few years ago we thought of career management as a ladder: Get that first job and hang on that rung until you or someone else decides it is time to go. The current thinking is to visualize your career as a ramp where you are consistently, conscientiously and concisely moving forward up this ramp using all the tools available to you, especially the art of building and maintaining relationships on an on-going basis throughout your career. What better vehicle than LinkedIn to assist you in accomplishing this lifetime project of managing yourself?"

Another coach offers comfort to concerned employees: "Clients sometimes worry that their employer will see their activity on LinkedIn and assume they are looking for work. You can update your status on a quarterly basis, or at a minimum, when you complete each major project. You can even mention to your boss that you are tracking your accomplishments using LinkedIn."

Our coaches tend to agree that LinkedIn is simply a tool. As one said, "The key is to build relationships; to some extent LinkedIn can nurture or even extend a relationship. I think of LinkedIn as a fancy Rolodex and I rely on it as I would a Rolodex. It is not a substitute for developing the relationships. It is a medium, a sophisticated medium, but in the end, a medium."

***

Would you like to see a great LinkedIn profile? Look at Guy Kawasaki's. www.linkedin.com/in/guykawasaki

***

Get the Professional Headline and Profile Right!

One coach represented many of our coaches when she said, "Mainly, I work with two categories of people—those high-potential clients who are on the cusp of promotion and are ripe for business coaching, and those individuals who are interested in transitioning into a new career. The most important first phase of coaching is assessment or identifying one's career distinction, which is a cornerstone piece to crafting a dynamic profile. I strongly suggest working with a Five O'Clock Club Coach at this assessment-stage to help you identify your professional reputation or positioning. Keep in mind that it is hard to do these alone and much more fun to do in concert with a professional coach."

Before writing your LinkedIn Heading and Profile, re-read the section of our Interviewing book on the Two-Minute Pitch. As we say at the Club, "if your pitch—the way you're positioning yourself—is wrong, everything is wrong." As one coach said, "Whether you are looking to advance your career, build a consulting practice, or are looking for a new job, it's extremely important that your profiles on LinkedIn and other social networking sites be consistent in how they position you professionally. *It's amazing how many disconnects we see* between a member's profile on LinkedIn, the Summary Statement on their résumé, and even they way they talk about themselves in their pitch."

The LinkedIn Professional Heading is a small field, but the most important. As one coach noted: "It is your positioning statement and is the reader's first impression of your perceived promise of value—and we all know how difficult it is to change a first impression! Remember your positioning lives in the hearts and minds of others for a long time." This same coach developed the following list for you to consider:

Coaching questions to ask yourself:

1. What is the impression I want to create in the Professional Headline?
2. What do others say about my Professional Headline?
3. Are these congruent thoughts?
4. What is the feeling you want it to evoke?
5. What is the feeling others get when they read your Professional Headline?
6. What does it say about your career distinction that you bring to an organization?

Compare the feeling you get when you read these two very real Professional Headlines—Joe: "In career transition" vs. Jill: "Big picture visionary who gets the job done using creative nontraditional tactics." Which person would you want to get to know?

Most people decide they want to reposition themselves depending on *where they want their career to go.* A Clubber who had worked for the big consulting firms her entire life wanted people to instead see her as a "Communications Executive with 10 years of international experience." How do you want to be seen?

Would you like to see a great LinkedIn profile? Look at Guy Kawasaki's:
www.linkedin.com/in/guykawasaki

I know: Social Media are his job. The Internet is his life's work. But he is a good example of someone who has taken full advantage of what LinkedIn has to offer. Pay special attention to his summary statement. You can see that he's put a lot of thought into his. If you have been working closely with your coach, you may be able to simply insert your résumé summary statement onto your LinkedIn page. Every Five O'Clock Club coach would tell you that you want to *consistently* communicate your pitch in all of your communications: résumé, cover letter, your verbal pitch about yourself, email messages, and all other Social Media.

Develop your LinkedIn heading and summary *after* you've completed your résumé. That way, they both position you the same way.

By the way, if you are proud of your LinkedIn profile, be sure to list your LinkedIn address (see Guy's address, above) in all of your email correspondence, at the top of your résumé, and so on. If you've done a good job on your LinkedIn profile, you want others to see it. And, rather than using the address that is assigned to you, you probably will want to change your LinkedIn address and use Guy's format (with his name as part of the url).

All of our coaches echo the same thought: Complete your LinkedIn profile *after* you have completed your résumé. The Headline, 120 character limit, should define who you are and what differentiates you from others. The summary, 2,000 characters, should position you strategically for your career development, consulting business or job search. Start with the summary section from your résumé. Use bulleted points or short paragraphs so that it can be read easily. LinkedIn doesn't give you the option for bulleted points, *but* you can get them by using

"I've got to let you go, Johnson. But in honor of your service, I'm allowing you to keep you email address."

a copy/paste of bulleted points from Microsoft Word into your profile, or simply use dashes or asterisks.

Another coach suggested: "I understand that people who have completed most of their LinkedIn profile *are more successful in attracting employers* through the LinkedIn service that finds people for employers."

Recommendations

We asked our coaches about the number and kinds of recommendations a person should have. Here's what they said:

- Have at least three or four. Be careful not to have too many "reciprocal" recommendations (i.e., if you recommend me, I'll recommend you).
- People usually get a little suspicious about too many recommendations. (Even Guy Kawasaki has only six.) On this subject, when you ask people for a recommendation, it can be very helpful

if you tell them quite specifically what you are hoping they will be comfortable in saying—to the point of writing a "draft" of a recommendation that they might want to use as a sample and change or adjust in any way that suits them. This takes the hassle out of the process for the recommender and helps you get the recommendation you really want.

- Recommendations should ideally be from previous managers or colleagues. As with references, if there are key points you would like them to include, let them know.
- Many of my clients have been contacted by both internal (company) recruiters, as well as external. Several were told they were being contacted because of the quality of their references. This is because I try (not always successfully!) to have my clients:

1. Create a script for what they want said.
2. Make sure the content from the reference is performance-based or behaviorally worded, NOT just a rave about the person. For example: "When Mary led the XYZ project team we met all of our committed delivery dates and came in under budget. I don't think we could have done this without her leadership."
3. Choose the same people who are your job references; this makes the process much more efficient.

Too many recommendations make you look insecure.

Some people—especially consultants—regularly update something on their LinkedIn page so that a notice will be sent to everyone in their network and keep them top-of-mind. Whether or not you are a consultant, you can let people know what projects you are working on. What our coaches say:

- Check your profile regularly to see if there's anything you can add that will keep your name and expertise showing up via status updates. Also, LinkedIn keeps adding features. Make sure that you take advantage of any that will showcase your skills.
- Like all updates (e.g., on Facebook), it can be overdone.
- People change their headline and summary as they become clearer about what is important to their target markets.

"I'm sorry, but Mr. Roberts no longer takes meetings, phone calls, cell calls, faxes, snail mail, email, messages, notes or appointments. Is there anything else we can do for you?"

Using LinkedIn to Build a Consulting Practice

You can use LinkedIn to build a consulting practice by contacting companies or key people of interest to you.

Said one coach: "One financial client who wanted to work with small companies contacted all the smaller CPA firms on LinkedIn in his target market. He then met with them to let them know about his skills, since many small businesses contact the CPA firms to ask about recommendations for financial people." Excellent idea.

Another coach suggested using LinkedIn regularly to record your accomplishments and advertise your events.

Your LinkedIn Photo

I've seen some photos that were not professional looking. They were way too sexy. This is not a dating service. Our coaches say:

- Use a plain background, have a warm smile, use solid colors for background and clothing. Have your hair under control. Preview your photo and ask others for their input. If you have your own consulting business, it's best to have either a studio photo or one at high resolution so it can be reduced or enlarged for this and other purposes.
- The photo needs to be professional— ideally, professionally done. The photo is your business picture and should be as professional as your image and presentation would be at an interview.

· ·

Don't use a sexy photo. This is business, not a dating service.

· ·

Should You Put Personal Information on LinkedIn?

To repeat what we say at the Club, if it helps your search, put it in. If it doesn't help, leave it out. If you're interested in skiing, for example, a reader could have a positive or negative reaction to this information. Our coaches say:

- Be strategic about personal information.
- Don't think of LinkedIn as a place for any personal information. It seems out of place there—it's more appropriate on Facebook.
- The Club rule is right.

Joining Groups

Joining as many groups as possible increases your network base. Groups that can be most helpful are professional (industry and function), alumni groups, special interest groups and, of course, The Five O'Clock Club group. What else do our coaches have to say?

• Joining groups is a great idea, especially when you can participate in their discussions. Not only do they help you to showcase your knowledge and skills to a very targeted audience, but you can keep up-to-date in your field as you read others' posts. However, if you join too many groups, you can waste time with status updates; so prioritize the ones you think will be best for your purpose. Searching is all about finding the right keywords. I remember trying to help a client find groups related to accounting and the results were not what he was looking for. That might have been a keyword issue or simply that typical accountants don't set up these groups. (There were plenty of groups for CPAs, for example.)

• A footnote to the advice about not joining too many groups: If you are going to join a group try to be active in it and get to know the people in it. That's the point—not just having a laundry list of groups. As in all career development activities, you should be conscious of whether it is working for you. Are you seeing real results? Building a network? Study the metrics.

• Again, Club rules apply: if it works, do it, if not, stop.

> Use LinkedIn the same as you would any other medium. Use it in a professional manner.

How to Contact People through LinkedIn

I get requests all the time. The standard request that LinkedIn provides does not help me to figure out who this person is. Here's what our coaches have to say:

• Always customize your invitation to others you ask to join your connections list. The standardized invitation is very impersonal and shows you don't care enough to reach out personally.

• I absolutely agree that if you are building your network, you should personalize all correspondence—this is the chance to reach out and touch, and make it personal and leave an impression in someone's mind. Don't blow it to save two minutes.

• I am not offended if someone I know sends a standard request. Even so, I appreciate a custom note. If the custom note is from someone I don't know well, I feel it is a little pushy. In the end, I will only connect with those I know.

• Personalizing your LinkedIn request helps to make your request stand out from many other requests that the person may be receiving.

> The standard request that LinkedIn provides does not help me to figure out who this person is.

How to Build Your Network on LinkedIn

- Be sure you know the people you LinkedIn with—whether you are going to them or they are coming to you. Make sure that your network is full of people who actually know you and you know them.

- Check out the connections your connections have. If you find someone you'd like to reach out to, first check with your connection to find out how they know the other person, just as you would in a live networking situation. Then customize (always customize) your request appropriately.
- I stick to my contacts' contacts. I tried to go further and it fizzled out— no relationship, so no result.
- It's important to be selective in the invitations to accept. On most sites, as soon as you accept someone's invitation you become part of their network, and may get invitations from people who may really not fit within your network. If they cannot really help you, or you cannot be of help to them, why do it?

How to Contact Someone in a Targeted Organization

Should you simply contact that person directly (direct contact) or should you ask someone else for an introduction (networking)? Is contacting someone via LinkedIn any different from our typical advice?

- Most of our coaches agree: This is just like the Club's advice with other mediums: Contacting the person directly will provide you with the most control in connecting with someone. If you are trying to connect with a very senior person, you may want to contact a person you know before contacting the senior person. LinkedIn is the same as with any other medium.
- At The Five O'Clock Club, we advocate both ways to contact others. I'd look at the person's level. Unless you're a high-level executive, don't approach a CEO of a medium to large company directly. Remember our phrase, "contact people one to two levels higher than you are."

- Most job hunters I have observed are more successful when using LinkedIn and other sites to develop contacts and generate informational meetings. It's really about going after those Stage 2 contacts (people one or two levels higher than you are who are in a position to hire you or recommend that you be hired), then following up with a targeted mailing, and good old-fashioned phone calls.
- I have observed a trend among some job hunters using LinkedIn to identify the hiring manager, or someone of influence within the company for which they have applied online for a position. It's what I call the "one-two punch"—the same as if you were answering an ad, but also get your résumé bumped up because of your effective use of direct contact or networking.

Some General LinkedIn Suggestions

- I think it is important to regularly spend some time on LinkedIn and to be thoughtful about extending your network before you might really need to. LinkedIn makes networking quite easy and it lets you reach out and touch lots of contacts before you need the favor— and when you might be able to put some money in the favor bank.
- As for the time you might spend on LinkedIn, review it as you would ads, maybe look at it after the workday, once a day or look at it once a week.
- LinkedIn should be used as any other resource on an as-needed basis and with a purpose. It's important to build your LinkedIn network by including groups. With a rich LinkedIn network,

you can then use it to source candidates and companies. Like any of the social networking tools, it should be used with a purpose in mind.

- Check your privacy settings. Look at your progress bar and try to have it at least 75% complete. Look for groups pertaining to your industry/profession and join them. Follow discussions and contribute whenever possible.

Getting a Job Interview Through LinkedIn

We asked our coaches whether any of their job hunters have ever gotten a job interview through LinkedIn ads. Here are some of their answers:

- One group member did and was surprised to be hired for a position overseas.
- None of mine, but I have heard of people getting interviews through it.
- I have clients who have gotten interviews through recruiters. As many have noted, recruiters regularly troll LinkedIn for candidates.
- One client today said a recruiter called her about a position that he had posted, since her skills fit the profile. It appears that recruiters—both independent and for companies—are more aggressively using LinkedIn to identify candidates.

....

If you're not using Google Alerts, you're not a player in your organization, industry or profession.

....

Some Cool Advice

One coach suggested this very powerful LinkedIn technique:

"Use the counterintuitive approach of typing in your target company's name in the People box. If you type in Medco, as an example, the search engine brings up the names of all the people one, two and three degrees of separation from you who work [or used to work] at Medco. Very powerful.

"**You can also do this on Twitter and Facebook.** For those who are social-network challenged or cynical (believe it or not many of my clients are…but not for long!), this will quickly tell you if some of your targets are social-network savvy. For example, Medco and WebMD (and hundreds of Fortune 500 companies) pay for Twitter ads. Currently, many of the world's largest companies and consulting firms use Twitter as part of their recruiting strategy.

If you do the above on Facebook (e.g., type Medco in the people search box), it will give you a list of people who work or have worked at Medco and are on Facebook. It also give a hotlink so you can make **Direct Contact**! How cool is that?

Keeping Plugged into Your Industry and Profession

One problem is that we tend to focus on the next hot thing, but spending your time wisely matters! Whether you are employed or not, you need to conduct research to stay up with what's happening in your industry or field. Don't forget the basics that we teach at The Five O'Clock Club. If your only source of research is LinkedIn, that's not good. Consider the following basics for starters:

- Many members **use Google for industry, company or people information**, even if they're going after esoteric industries such as social service agencies, ethics, education policy, think tanks and nanotechnology. Key any industry name into Google and see what comes up. You may have to look through a few pages of information, but there will probably be a site that is a key one for your industry or field. Key in the people you are trying to research. Chances are, you'll find them.

- Make sure you **use Google alerts** for the organization you work for **and** your main competitors. If you're not doing that, you're not a player. Just go to Google, key in the word "alerts" and it will take you to the Google alert page. Key in the words you would like an alert for, see a preview of the kind of results you would get, modify the word if you don't like the results, and note how often you would like to get alerts on these keywords. You've probably already Googled yourself to see what the world would see. If not, you really ought to.

- Go to the **Google Blog page** and see what comes up. You might get some really good (but not necessarily trust-worthy) information about a person or organization.
- Take a look at our **Research Resources in the Members Only section of our website**: www.fiveoclockclub.com.
- Subscribe to online journals about your field or industry. You'll get their newsletters with the hot topics of the day.
- And, one of our tried and true favorites: **Join professional or trade associations.** You really do need to get out there and see real people.

Chapter 37

• • • • • • • •

No Matter What Your Age: The Value of Having a Long-Term Vision

by Kate Wendleton, President, The Five O'Clock Club

Where there is no vision, there is no hope.

George Washington Carver.

It takes courage to grow up and turn out to be who you really are.

e. e. cummings

We are living in a culture that emphasizes immediate gratification, does not value planning, and gives slight consideration to consequences. Hence, far too many people, young and old alike, are saddled with credit card debt and live as if there's no tomorrow. We are urged to live one day at a time, especially in the face of adversity, and that may be all some people can handle. But this is not healthy for most, and one-day-at-a-time does not qualify as a goal.

Many of our favorite clichés are wrong. To-morrow does not take care of itself. Not everyone learns from his or her mistakes. "Following your bliss" does not necessarily make you happier. And sometimes it doesn't "all work out." Instead, many people end up resigned to bad situations and "live with it." They say, "This is what fate had in store for us."

Ironically, Americans are action-oriented and like to think they'll figure things out as they go along. I've even heard very famous people brag that they don't have a plan, which adds to the mystique. But they *do* have a solid strategy, which they follow religiously. They may let someone else figure out their detailed plans, but they are not as haphazard as many would like to pretend.

For example, when I heard a successful children's book author give a speech, I was intrigued by her lack of candor. People in the audience were dying to know to what she attributed her success. She said it was pure luck, that she rarely got out of her pajamas, and the money kept pouring in. Yet, she wrote four or five books a year and had many deals for related items. I believe she was far more *planful* than she let on, and she simply didn't want to tell us any of her secrets.

I once appeared on the radio show of a major, nationally syndicated host. As we were waiting for the show to start, he asked about the contacts I might have at the prominent TV shows I had been on and what I thought of each. Then he bragged that he was lucky because he'd never had to job search in his life! He said things just happened to fall in his path. But that wasn't true: he was using me to network! He was actually job searching *continuously*, although not formally, and he had a *plan* for himself.

Many successful people don't like to admit that they plan. It ruins the aura. But most successful people are always aware and always planning—and modifying their plans depending on what they learn.

People are happy when they are working toward their goals. When they get diverted from their goals, they are unhappy. Businesses are the same. When they get diverted from their goals (for instance, because of major litigation or a threatened hostile takeover), tensions build and morale sinks. Life has a way of sneaking up and distracting both individuals and businesses. Many people are unhappy in their jobs because they don't *know* where they are going.

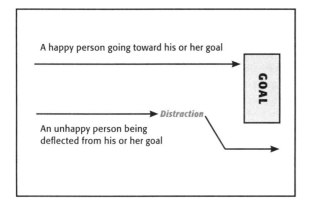

People without goals are more irked by petty everyday problems. Those with goals are less bothered because they have bigger plans. To control your life, you need at least a *tentative* vision of your future that encompasses your whole life.

Dreams and goals can be great driving forces in our lives. We feel satisfied when we are working toward them—even if we never reach them. People who have dreams or goals do better than people who don't.

Setting goals will make a difference in your life, and this makes sense. Every day we make dozens of choices. People guided by dreams make choices that advance them in the right direction. Dreams are the equivalent of the North Star. People without dreams also make choices—but their choices are strictly present oriented, with little thought of the future and are more likely to have bad consequences. When you are aware of your current situation, and you also know where you want to go, a natural tension (between what you face today and what you're trying to create!) leads you forward faster.

When you find a believable dream that excites you, don't forget it. Write it down. Look at it daily. It's less likely to slip out of your mind in the heat of day-to-day living. Happy people keep an eye on the future as well as on the present.

Lack of Vision and Depression

Herbert Rappaport, Ph.D., conducted extensive studies on the way people thought about time (temporal attitudes). His book, *Marking Time* (Simon and Schuster, 1990), is sub-titled "What our attitudes about time reveal about our personalities and conflicts." Dr. Rappaport asked various people to draw "timelines" of their lives: on a horizontal line representing a life span, make a dot to indicate the "NOW point" of life, noting your age. Then note your age at every significant event before NOW and every significant event after NOW.

In one poignant example, he notes the timelines drawn by two women in their early 70s. One, who was depressed, imagined *only two* significant events in her future. The second was fully engaged in life. She imagined almost as many events *after age 72* as she had before that age, and she noted the end of the line—her death. "Death for this woman is a motivator rather than a suppressor of goals and objectives. The acceptance of death as a 'punctuation' point in the life cycle signals her to 'crowd' the future with the unfinished business of her life."

Rappaport points out that although the two women are approximately the same age, they view life quite differently. The first woman seems to have little in her future to look forward to. She spoke frequently about aging and was considering moving into a retirement community. The second woman had a sense of urgency and planned to "work until it hurt too much."

Having a vision is important *at every age and stage*. Without a vision, we are on a journey without navigation. We are taking day trips and not heading toward a significant destination.

Since I read his book, I, too, have noticed this temporal difference in individuals. One elderly couple, in their late 80s, still has goals and milestones. They are determined to crowd the years ahead with events. They look forward to the marriages of six of their grandchildren who happened to get engaged at about the same time. They also look forward to the renewal of their wedding vows on their 60th anniversary. And they also picked out the plot where they want to be buried—with great cheeriness.

A second couple, in their early 70s and 15 years younger, said they no longer wanted to have photographs taken of themselves because they weren't going to look any better than they now did! They are cheerful but full of nostalgia for the good old days. Their only anticipated event is the high school graduation of the youngest of their eight grandchildren, which will take place in four years. Otherwise, they plan events one day at a time.

Both couples are aware of their future deaths, but one couple takes great joy in the details of their future. The other has their feet planted firmly in the present and past.

When a person focuses mainly on the past, that person is often described as depressed. Depressed people, experts say, often have a hard time thinking about the future. The present and its immediate extension are all there is. Rappaport has an opposing and compelling point of view about depression:

"Typically, it has been reasoned that the patient cannot relate to the future *because* he is depressed …While some individuals clearly become depressed in response to problems such as divorce, death, job loss and natural calamities, there are also individuals who seem to be depressed without a clear precipitating cause …

"Eugene Minkowski (1970), in his profound treatise on temporality and depression, suggested the opposite: 'Could we not, on the contrary, suppose the basic disorder is the distorted attitude toward the future.' The future and its possibilities are for Minkowski and a host of other existential theoreticians the force that energizes us and carries us forward in our lives."

Rappaport and others are suggesting that rather than being unable to relate to the future because he is depressed, *the person has become depressed because he is unable to relate to the future.*

And don't people know this intuitively? When a friend is having a down day, it comes naturally to encourage him or her to think about the future. We say that tomorrow is a new day and the possibility of a bright future is there. "This is just a bump in the road," we say. We all know to steer the person *away from the present and into the future*. "Things will get better." This applies, of course, only to those everyday "depressions" we all experience—not to clinical depression or depressions caused by a chemical imbalance.

An Ability to Move On

One interesting aspect of the Fifteen-Year and especially the Forty-Year Vision® is how they help people to overcome being programmed by their past. A woman whose parents both died in their 50s cannot imagine a life for *herself* beyond 50. We urged her to push her imagination a little and see what her life *would* be like if she lives until 80—which is probably what *will* happen to her if she stops counting on dying at 50!

Some people *overcome* traumatic childhoods and others are *bound* by them. Some people overcome by re-writing the past. They *choose* to remember certain things or interpret the past in a certain way. Others may choose a negative interpretation. One may become proud of one's poverty-stricken roots rather than feel deprived by them. As Alfred Adler (a disciple of Freud) said, "What an individual seeks to *become* determines what he remembers of his *has been*. In this sense, the future determines the past." (R. May, E. Angel, and H.F. Ellenberger, *Existence*, New York, Simon & Schuster, 1958). A Fifteen-Year or Forty-Year Vision can help a person to create a new future, and re-frame a person's past so that it no longer disables.

People must move on. We are sad not just because of some traumatic experience, but because we feel *tied* to it. It controls us; We can't get over it. One of my aunts in her 90s lost her husband of 70 years. She doesn't want to go out; she says she wants to "spend the evening with Frank." Even at her advanced age, we are trying to help her move on, because the years she has left *can* be brighter.

We must replace lost loved ones—those who are no longer in our lives for various reasons. When my grandmother was in her 80s but still vibrant, she volunteered to rock babies at an orphanage. Those babies perked up the minute she walked into the room. She knew that her efforts were worthwhile, and the babies satisfied her need for the everyday caring of children after her own children and grandchildren were grown. That was *her* bright future, instead of sitting home thinking about the past.

Her daughter, my now 87-year-old mother, makes hundreds of rosaries for the missions and volunteers at her church, helping others and making friendships at the same time.

> *Ultimately, man should not ask what the meaning of his life is, but rather he must recognize that it is he who is asked.*
>
> Viktor E. Frankl, author and Holocaust survivor

"We stop growing when our human losses are no longer replaced," wrote George Vaillant in *Adaptation to Life*. "Letting go" and moving on—making the replacement—is a healthy response.

When one's life has become unsettled, such as through the death of a loved one, the loss of a job, and other situations, to thrive again one *must* envision a new future. It takes hard work, and sometimes it takes years to figure out what your new life should be like. But it's the same result at any age: You will have a more satisfying future if you put effort into analyzing yourself and also exploring your options.

Work alone does not do it. Without love for others and from others, it is hard to grow. It is the continuity of those important relationships that keep us going over the decades. If you don't have them, you must make them.

The Impact on Older People of Imagining a Future

We say your vision should push you past age 80 so you can see what can happen if you live that long. People are sometimes emotionally scripted for bad health or unhappiness. But all of us *can* break away from the script and rewrite the future—as well as the past. We can rewrite the way we see our past. We can decide to have very different lives from those we grew up with or now have. That different life requires a different vision of our future.

No matter what a person's age, the process of imagining a future is difficult and can provoke anxiety. We would all like to "go with the flow" and hope it will all work out. Rappaport noted: "More so than individuals who are in their forties, for example, those who are over sixty have a great deal of trouble extending into the future." Yes, those who are over 60 may feel that imagining a future is wishful thinking. Even some career coaches titter at the thought of a 60-year old doing a Fifteen-Year or Thirty-Year Vision.

When Rappaport met with older people who were simply living day-to-day, doing what needed to be done and essentially wasting time, he asked them: "If you learned at the beginning of a two-week trip to Alaska that the trip had to be shortened, would you forget about your itinerary and aimlessly wander around your room? Would you pick up and go home, or would you accelerate and get as much done as possible?" The reality of death can make us get more out of the time that we do have, including making our wills and putting our houses in order. We're all going to die. *What matters is what we do with the time we have.* It makes sense to accept our future deaths and *make the most of the time we have.*

"Mr. Reilly, your 1 o'clock appointment is here. I took the liberty of cancelling your 2, 3 and 4 o'clock appointments."

When he asked someone over 60: "What would you do if you were told you had a few weeks left to live?," the question helped a person to explore his or her priorities. Rappaport found that, in most cases, people who had been wandering aimlessly became energized and focused on what was important to them.

Most of us do have a lot of time left. Being 60, 70 or even 80 is not the end of the road. The average life expectancy today in the United States is 29 years longer than it was in 1900. Because of better healthcare, these years have been added to middle age, not old age. You have the time to learn and be productive for many, many years. You could have your greatest life accomplishments after the age of 50 or even older. Why give up now? You have plenty of time to make great progress toward whatever you plan. When

Jean Calment of France was asked on her 120th birthday what kind of future she expected, she answered, "A short one"—but, guess what—she lived for two more years!

So, the after-retirement years may add up to 30 or more. We have plenty of time to make progress toward our vision of the future. Yet, people "retire" with no thought of how they will spend that time or how they will manage their lives through the decades. People may want to retire to get off the treadmill, but to do *what*? I have met too many retired people who are depressed and at a loss for what to do with their time. If a person was used to a vibrant career, this feeling of dislocation can go on for *decades.*

Often *unplanned* years are full of self-oriented pursuits: shopping, traveling and keeping physically fit. But many don't think through what their lives will actually be like. Some decide that they want to live in an adult community where there are no children around, but later become sad at being around all these old people. They think, "I'll travel or play golf." But 30 years of self-indulgence is a long time. Where is the sense of momentum and purpose?

Self-oriented pursuits are not considered the healthiest for the long haul. If you have been working hard for years and deserve a break, take a break. Cut back. But stay involved with life, especially in pursuits that *help others.*

Rappaport says that one of the common themes he sees among depressed adults in his practice is the deep sense of regret for not "stretching oneself" at different life stages. It is not too late to become deeply immersed in something that matters. Rappaport found that those who engage in meaningful activities are happier than those who engage only in self-indulgent activities.

Yet the evidence at hand suggests that ultimately life does not appear satisfying or socially valuable when approached as an opportunity to be free of responsibility.

Herbert Rappaport, Ph.D.

All of Those Years Ahead

People usually imagine retirement—if they imagine it at all—as one big lump of time. But 50 is *different* from 70, 80 and 90, just as 10 is very different from 30, 40 and 50. Each of the segments over 50 can be envisioned and planned for.

Let's take living arrangements, for example. You may want to continue to live where you do now until age 75, and then move to something smaller—say a two-bedroom apartment instead of a four-bedroom house. Then, at say age 85 or 90, you may have to move to a retirement home, and finally to a nursing home. If you don't like this vision for yourself, that's okay. Write your own! Where do you want to live geographically? What does your residence look like at each stage? If you live to be 90, your living arrangements will be worked out somehow, by someone. If *you* don't plan them, chances are, you won't be happy with how things work out. In the Fifteen-Year and Forty-Year Visions, you will plan this for each stage of life ahead.

Now, what about your preoccupations? Are you planning to travel when you retire? Thirty years is a long time to travel. How much time can you actually spend doing that? Many older people are depressed and bored. Life seems to drag. That's because the retirement dream was too vague and not well thought out, *i.e.,* "travel." They're not productive and contributing. More and more people are in great physical health and not as well off emotionally because they're *drifting*. They lack goals.

In the Fifteen-Year and Forty-Year Visions, we suggest that you push yourself to at least age 80 so you can see what can happen if you live that long. According to Kubler-Ross, while there is life, there is still potential for meaningful behavior. Rappaport, in a study of adults in a retirement community, found that those with an unstructured future ended up being present-centered, which is actually stagnation. For those in their 60s and 70s, there is a link between lack of

purpose and death anxiety. Planning for the rest of life and retaining a sense of forward motion are at the core of mental health. "Once we get people over the bias that it is frivolous to [plan] at these ages, there is usually ample time, focus and financial resources to face these critically important issues."

What would you like your pursuits to be? If you are now 60, for example, why not now imagine what your pursuits will be like at age 70 and get started in those pursuits now. This may take a lot of thought and exploration, just as it would for a young person choosing a profession. Would you like to raise dogs, for example? Then join dog-related associations now.

When I retire, which is many years away, I envision myself working with some disadvantaged population, perhaps continuing to teach in prisons. I have already researched the prisons and their educational programs in the geographic area where I plan to live—just to make sure the vision is doable. I also envision having an active role as a grandparent and have had serious discussions with my children about living in the same community. If that doesn't work out, I imagine myself doing something with young adults. I also imagine myself gardening, always my favorite hobby, and cooking more—although I do now cook just about every day. I also imagine myself writing another book, but probably not about careers. Working with young adults and inmates, gardening, cooking, writing books: I can research and plan now for all these activities, to assure that they don't remain pipe dreams, but can have real structure and content.

What kind of future would *you* like to imagine for yourself? You may have to work hard to make it happen, and you can plant the seeds now. The present is an opportunity to plan what we would like to do with the rest of our lives, but ironically that happens only when we accept that there is only so much time. Then we begin to worry that there is not enough time. Time becomes precious, not something to be squandered. We can still play bridge and go to the movies, but they become pastimes—just as they were during our "productive" years, and the foreground of our lives become areas of contribution.

Your Age: How Much Longer Do You Want to Work?

Age puzzles me. I thought it was a quiet time. My seventies were interesting and fairly serene, but my eighties are passionate. I grow more intense as I age.

Florida Scott Maxwell, writer and psychologist

I started this business at age 40; my brother started his business at age 55. With the Fifteen-Year and Forty-Year Visions, you realize that you have the time to start and be successful in whatever your pursuits are. Would you like to make an impact on an environmental issue? Your family? Other families? A community issue? Or just on the quality of life? Would you like to learn new things (you still have time to become an expert in something new)? Actually work for a not-for-profit? Do consulting work?

Culinary expert Julia Child, for example, brought joy to millions when she was past 60. She died at age 91, and is a striking example of those who don't really hit their stride until they are older. She was forced to abandon her first career because she married a fellow civil servant, Paul Child. After several years of searching, she discovered French cooking when her husband was assigned to France as a USIA officer. Starting at about the age of 35, Julia trained as a chef, founded her own cooking school, and worked on a cookbook, *Mastering the Art of French Cooking*. In 1960, when she was almost 50, the couple moved back to the United States, where the book was published. A chance publicity appearance on television led to her famous TV series.

At one point, by the way, after a double mastectomy, Julia was convinced that her life was ruined. But after many weeks of grieving and weeping, she snapped out of it. "After all, I could be six feet under," she said, "but I'm not."

She resumed her forward motion. She had a new lease on life and decided to make the most of it.

Any why not? At age 40, 50, 60, you will find that you are now using everything you have ever learned in your life and bringing it all together. You don't have the pressure of putting the kids through school. You can afford to take risks. Some fields, such as consulting, often favor the older folks. Who wants a twenty-year-old financial advisor?

The trouble with the future is that it usually arrives before we're ready for it.

Arnold H. Glasow, author, *Glasow's Gloombusters*

The Fifteen and Forty-Year Visions®

Our business is about helping people with their careers, but we have always urged our clients to do the Forty-Year Vision—or at least a fifteen-year version of it. You can't consider one part of your life without also considering its impact on the rest of your life: where you want to live, your relationship with your family, and so on.

Write down, in the present tense, the way your life is right now, and the way you see yourself five years from now and fifteen years from now, using the questions below.

When you have finished the exercise, ask yourself how you feel about your life as you laid it out in your vision. Some people feel depressed when they see on paper how their lives are going, and they cannot think of a way out. But they feel better when a good friend or a Five O'Clock Club coach helps them think of a better future to work toward. If you don't like your vision, change it—it's your life.

Start the exercise with the way things are now so you will be realistic about your future. Don't think too hard. See where you wind up. You have plenty of time to get things done.

The 15-year mark proves to be the most important for most people. It's far enough away from the present to allow you to dream. Here are the questions to ask yourself:

- What is your life like right now? (Say anything you want about your life.)
- Who are your friends? What do they do for a living?
- What is your relationship with your family, however you define "family"?
- Are you married? Single? Children? (List ages.)
- Where are you living? What does it look like?
- What are your hobbies and interests?
- What do you do for exercise?
- How is your health?
- How do you take care of your spiritual needs?
- What kind of work or work-substitute are you doing?
- What else would you like to note about your life right now?

We know that engaging in the Fifteen-Year Vision (at least) has energized many people to turn their lives in exciting new directions.

We are prone to judge success by the index of our salaries or the size of our automobiles, rather than by the quality of our service relationship to humanity.

Rev. Dr. Martin Luther King, Jr.

The Old-Fashioned Career Coach

In the old days of career coaching, coaches focused on what was called the "job-person match." They helped clients understand their values, accomplishments and interests—but did not discuss a person's goals or vision for a future. In fact, for some coaches, the entire assessment consisted of having the client write a lengthy autobiography—perhaps 30 or more pages long! Coaches simply helped people straight-line their past. A career change was an after-thought. The focus was to help the person get into an orga-

nization that matched his skills, abilities and values, but with an assumption that it would be in the same kind of job.

But Five O'Clock Club research in the early 80s proved that coaches had to help people not only analyze their past, but also *envision their future*, a future that looked at the whole person. We pointed out that coaches who did not do that were doing their clients a disservice. It took a decade to convince coaches—inside and outside the Club—of this necessity. But it makes sense. In the old days, people were stuck in their careers: once you were an accountant, you stayed as an accountant. Today, there is no reason for a person to feel stuck. It's easier to talk about the past than to plan for the future. But a coach can help someone envision a new future, regardless of that person's age. Today, 58% of the people who attend the Club make a career change, moving to a new industry or field. For example, one person went from being a high school science teacher in Canada to pharmaceutical sales in New Jersey. Another went from accounting to sales to human resources—two major career changes in under eight years. You, too, have a future. Try developing a vision and research it.

••

Quotes from *Man's Search for Meaning*

by Viktor E. Frankl, author and Holocaust survivor

On Choosing One's Attitude

"There is also purpose in life which is almost barren of both creation and enjoyment and which admits of but one possibility of high moral behavior: namely, in man's attitude to his existence, an existence restricted by external forces."

On Committing to Values and Goals

"Logotherapy...considers man as a being whose main concern consists in fulfilling a meaning and in actualizing values, rather than in the mere gratification and satisfaction of drives and instincts."

"What man actually needs is not a tension-less state but rather the striving and struggling for some goal worthy of him. What he needs is not the discharge of tension at any cost, but the call of a potential meaning waiting to be fulfilled by him."

On Discovering the Meaning of Life

"The meaning of our existence is not in-vented by ourselves, but rather detected."

"What matters, therefore, is not the meaning of life in general, but rather the specific meaning of a person's life at a given moment."

"We can discover this meaning in life in three different ways: (1) by doing a deed; (2) by experiencing a value; and (3) by suffering."

On Fulfilling One's Task

"A man who becomes conscious of the re-sponsibility he bears toward a human being who affectionately waits for him, or to an unfinished work, will never be able to throw away his life. He knows the 'why' for his existence, and will be able to bear almost any 'how.'"

"It did not really matter what we expected from life, but rather what life expected from us. We needed to stop asking about the meaning of life, and instead to think of ourselves as those who were being questioned by life—daily and hourly. Our answer must consist, not in talk and meditation, but in right action and in right con-duct. Life ultimately means taking the responsi-bility to find the right answer to its problems and to fulfill the tasks which it constantly sets for each individual."

Above quotations reprinted from:
Frankl, Viktor E., *Man's Search for Meaning*, Simon and Schuster, New York, 1963.

On Success

"Don't aim at success—the more you aim at it and make it a target, the more you are going to miss it. For success, like happiness, cannot be pursued; it must ensue, and it only does so as the unintended side effect of one's personal dedication to a cause greater than oneself or as the by-product of one's surrender to a person other than oneself. Happiness must happen, and the same holds for success: you have to let it happen by not caring about it. I want you to listen to what your conscience commands you to do and go on to carry it out to the best of your knowledge. Then you will live to see that in the long run—in the long run, I say!—success will follow you precisely because you had forgotten to think of it."

Preface: *Man's Search for Ultimate Meaning*

Chapter 38

• • • • • • • •

Virtue in Your Work-Life: What Makes a Meaningful Work-Life?

by Richard Bayer, Ph.D., Chief Operating Officer, The Five O'Clock Club

If a man is called to be a street sweeper, he should sweep streets even as Michelangelo painted, or Beethoven played music, or Shakespeare wrote poetry. He should sweep streets so well that all the hosts of heaven and earth will pause to say, here lived a great street sweeper who did his job well.

Rev. Martin Luther King, Jr.

While virtues contribute to productivity, they are also necessary to possess so as to make work meaningful. Let's look at the virtues and vices that foster this (see the table below).

Cooperation, hard work, creativity, optimism, planning ahead, concern for the welfare of others, trust, flexibility and patience characterize the new approach to work. These virtues also support having work that is meaningful. How can work be meaningful if there is ruthless competition, workaholism, disconnectedness, possessiveness and more? Work simply can't be. People should not be required to check their positive values at the door when entering the workplace. Clearly, most of us do not find meaning under harsh and oppressive conditions.

Meaningful Professions

As Reverend Martin Luther King, Jr., said above, everyone can have (or create) a job that is meaningful and satisfying. Examples abound in the professions. Think of entrepreneurs who strike out to do things that are from their heart. Think of the successful businessperson who manages employees by seeing to their professional growth, assuring fair treatment and, at the same time, striving to meet departmental goals. Think of the doctor who treats patients and sees them return to productive life; the lawyer who can help people to achieve justice (we hope); and the clergy who care for the soul and see to spiritual wholeness. It is not hard to see that the virtues in the table play a vital role in all professions to various degrees. These virtues make professional work meaningful.

However, aside from the professions, do meaningful jobs exist in today's labor market? Can *everyone* have meaningful work? How about truck drivers, waiters and laborers—can their occupations be meaningful, just like those of professionals? Yes, with one proviso (condition) that will be discussed later on.

A Question of Perception

It is sometimes a matter of perception whether or not a job is meaningful. It seems obvious that entrepreneurs, doctors, and other professionals mentioned above can have meaningful work. They should (hopefully) be walking testimonials to the virtues that were brought to light. But meaningful work can exist outside of the professions.

Perception is often the key. Reverend King's street sweeper is a prime example of how a working person can find pride and achievement in his work. So is a waiter who looks at his/her job in a positive way, rather than simply seeing the work as something that lacks the kind of control over circumstances and effect on people that are true of, say, doctors. The waiter is, one might say, a minister of hospitality. He is one who serves food, which is, of course, necessary for life. Further, the waiter's attitude helps to determine the quality of the meal. This is no small thing. Meals are a special time for us: they are times for celebration, important family gatherings or reunions, business dealings and just enjoying being with someone who means something to us. Nothing is small about this, even if we dine alone. Waiters certainly can show regard for the welfare of others, and demonstrate cooperation, trust, patience, and other virtues, besides just getting the order right.

Now, consider truck drivers. Their behavior on the road is especially important to city dwellers, both to drivers and pedestrians. Not only is there skill involved in driving a large vehicle, but also there must be regard for the welfare of others, patience, and cooperation (with other drivers). We have all seen truck drivers who allow people to navigate the road safely, as well as pull over to help other drivers in emergencies. If a trucker doesn't have these good qualities, the outcome could be road rage. People with road rage have even killed others. Further, given the grueling hours many people spend commuting, it's no small thing for truck drivers to show regard for the welfare of other drivers, as well as patience, and cooperation.

....

Question(s) to consider: Do you feel that your work is meaningful? Do you do anything to help those you work with to have more meaning in their jobs?

....

The Proviso

Working-class people are vulnerable in a way that professionals are typically not. Usually, doctors, lawyers and the like earn enough (or more than enough) to live comfortably, while, truck drivers, laborers and waiters, among others, face insecurity in this matter. It is not only the intrinsic nature of the work that counts, but also the extrinsic reward.

Compensation must be enough such that the individual is able to be self-supporting. Most of us can support ourselves (food, housing, transportation and others) through our wages. Few live off of interest income or an inheritance. It is for this reason that economic ethicists have so fervently insisted on a just wage. Such a wage is also an essential ingredient for meaningful work. Without it, there is gross injustice and really no chance that work will be meaningful.

Virtues and Vices for a Meaningful Work-life

Virtues: Consistent with The Vision	Vices: Inconsistent with the Vision
Cooperative	Excessively competitive
Hard-working, persistent	Entitlement mentality; workaholic
Creative and optimistic	Zero-sum mentality
Planning ahead	Indifferent and haphazard
Regard for the welfare of others	Out-of-context behavior
Trust in the future	Siege mentality
Flexible	Rigid, unable to cope with organic change
Activity based on knowledge	Disconnected activity
Sharing, generous, patient for long-term results	Closed and possessive; focused on short-term interests

*Management is doing things right;
leadership is doing the right things.*

Peter F. Drucker, American management guru

Group Discussion Questions

- What is meant by having a meaningful work-life?
- Give examples of a meaningful work-life.
- Can everyone have a meaningful work-life?
- What do you think of the Reverend King's quote at the start of the chapter?

Chapter 39

The Mentor-Mentee Relationship: Career Development Secret Weapon

by Peter Hill, Certified Five O'Clock Club Coach

If your actions inspire others to dream more, learn more, do more and become more, you are a leader.

John Quincy Adams

In 1994, I was living in central Japan. My wife-to-be and I decided that climbing Mount Fuji would be a fun dating activity. She suggested that we book a package tour to make the ascent. I was skeptical that we needed a tour guide to hike a trail that millions had used before us, but I gave in. In hindsight, it was an excellent decision because the guide had "been there, done that" countless times. He knew the little secrets to help us and our fellow hikers make it to the 12,389-foot summit with minimal hassle.

In our careers, we are all climbing our own Mt. Fujis, and a guide can help us get to the peak, whatever the peak may be for each one of us.

In the professional world, a mentor can serve as that guide. Regardless of your career situation, level of accountability, function, industry, or geography choosing to partner with a mentor (or

mentors) is likely to be the best decision you will ever make.

The potential mentor is someone who has depth of experience and superior insight. You will sense that this person is someone you can learn from, who demonstrates a high level of interest, commitment and confidence in your capabilities, and who is authentically interested in your professional development. Mentor-mentee relationships are sometimes quite casual. But formalizing the association is typically more valuable and rewarding for both parties.

Finding a Mentor

Mentors could be those who are senior to you in your current company, executive leaders in another division, customers, strategic partners, respected figures in your industry, or people who are doing the job to which you aspire. And there are many more possibilities.

After you identify someone whose example inspires you, and from whom you believe you can learn, the next step is to simply ask the person outright; "Would you be willing to be my mentor?" Most people will say Yes, and seasoned mentors know the immense satisfaction they get from sharing their experiences, insights and perspectives with others. The worst that can happen is the person will decline, but will certainly be honored that you asked.

When you pop the question, explain why you asked him or her, and what you hope to learn from the relationship. You should discuss the amount of time that you have in mind—and ask for the person's recommendation—and create an agenda of regular meetings.

Three Ways Mentors Can Help You

1. Navigating Your Career

Mentors need to know what makes you tick. At a minimum, they need to know your motivated skills (the things you are good at and enjoy doing) and your long-term career vision. Armed with this knowledge about you, they will be well positioned to support you along your career path. Their objective viewpoint is invaluable when it is all too easy for you to get caught up in the daily grind of workplace accountabilities. Good mentors help us remain grounded as we face the ambiguous reality of changing business environments, attitudes and market landscapes.

Seasoned mentors usually have a finger on the pulse of career opportunities and the most suitable ways to go after them, if you both agree that it is worthwhile. Mentors often know role requirements beyond what is listed in orthodox job descriptions. If you fall short, then your mentor can help pinpoint the gaps and together you can strategize how to fill them.

2. Developing Your Network

Mentors can also help move your professional network to the next level and beyond. In today's hyper-connected business world, you are less productive, less efficient, and less effective when you don't have a strong network. You should certainly be building your network

directly, but mentors can quickly expand the size and enhance the quality of your personal and professional connections.

3. Challenging Your Thinking

Lastly, and perhaps most importantly, superior mentors will challenge your thought processes in ways that make you uncomfortable, but in a healthy way. There is a wonderful 2007 essay written by Kirk Martini entitled *Usually Nice, Always Helpful: A Mentor's Approach* (you can Google it). As part of a fellowship program at the University of Virginia in the early 1990s, Martini was mentored by Professor Randy Pausch (1960-2008). Pausch later became famous for his "Last Lecture" delivered at Carnegie Mellon University while fighting a courageous battle with pancreatic cancer.

Martini wrote, "Being a mentor is not about being nice, it's about being helpful. Here's the difference: being nice is about making a person feel good; being helpful is about serving a person's best interest. The two usually go together, but the distinction comes into play when serving a person's best interest may mean making the person uncomfortable, a situation that arises easily when a mentor tries to be truly helpful."

Martini recalls how Pausch would hit him with pointed questions over lunch. "That project you talked about, is that really going to help you get tenure? If not, then *why* spend time on it? How many papers do you have in the pipeline now? How does your work compare to that of other people recently tenured in your field? That new course you are developing, is it going to move your research forward?"

You get the point. You will want to seek mentors who confront you with uncomfortable questions that keep you on track toward a far more productive career.

"It wasn't nice for him to ask so many pointed questions," writes Martini, "but it was helpful. Randy understood that my long-term future was more important than my short-term comfort. Our lunches would have been far more pleasant if he had just made a few sage statements mixed with casual chatter. But my career now is far more productive because he didn't take that soft approach."

Helping Your Mentor Help You

Here are some parting thoughts on how to help your mentor help you.

Be honest with the mentor and with yourself. The quality of a mentor's advice and guidance is heavily influenced by the information you share. Complete transparency is important here.

Strive for self-actualization. This means being fully committed to using your talents and achieving your potential. Mentors are more motivated to engage and support you when they believe you are authentic in your desire to persistently pursue excellence.

Trust the mentor. A career-coaching client recently said to me, "Trust translates into speed." That is brilliant! Think about that for a moment. Trusting that mentors are sharing the totality of their experiences—flaws and mistakes included—speeds up your learning and development. You can more rapidly learn to cope, to change course if necessary, and, most importantly, to achieve results.

Eighteen years ago I underestimated the task of climbing mount Mt. Fuji. Yes, we could have attempted the hike on our own, but why would we? If we didn't take that package tour and didn't follow that guide up the mountain, we would have wasted a lot of time and energy reinventing ways to make it to the summit.

When we rely only on ourselves, however unique and talented we may be, we often put ourselves at a significant disadvantage versus others who get help.

Chapter 40

• • • • • • • •

Mentoring: How it Can Help Your Career

by Rob Hellmann, Certified Five O'Clock Club Coach and VP, Associate Director, The Five O'Clock Club National Guild of Career Coaches

We make a living by what we get, we make a life by what we give.

Winston Churchill

At work it's easy to get caught up in the day-to-day—to react rather than plan, to focus energy on the immediate things that need to be done NOW! But there's a huge long-term career benefit to taking a step back. By making the extra effort to develop a more strategic approach to your career, in the long run you're more likely to get what you want! And mentoring can play a huge role in this approach.

So what is mentoring? It's a partnership between you, the mentee or "learner," and the mentor or "teacher." You get the personal support and experience of the mentor to help you to do your job better, while the mentor gains a new perspective, the intrinsic reward from helping you, and your loyalty.

Ideally you'd like to find a mentor who's both in a position you'd like to be in and in a position to help you—someone with experience, clout and connections.

So, are you ready to gain the benefits that a mentoring relationship has to offer? Before you move forward, you should be able to answer "yes" to all of these questions:

- The onus will fall on you as the "learner" to manage the relationship—are you willing to put in the effort?
- Are you open to hearing comments that may require introspection and self-criticism?
- Are you willing to try out new ideas or pursue new challenges?
- Are you realistic about what one person can do to help?
- Are you trustworthy? Are you able to keep the discussions in complete confidence?

How to Find a Mentor

Check to see if your company has an established mentoring program. Many medium to large companies have a structure in place that encourages employees to develop mentoring relationships, and take their mentoring programs very seriously. Why? Because companies reap the benefits from mentoring as well, in terms of improved employee productivity and retention.

If your company does not have this structure, or you'd like to pursue something less formal, professional associations, including alumni associations, are a great source for mentors. Contact the association and ask about this. If you are in business for yourself, there may be organizations in your area that can help you to find a mentor. For example, check out www.score. org, a non-profit national organization with local chapters that provides mentors and counselors for small business owners.

Here are some other things to consider:

- Know what you want from the relationship. The more specific you are, the easier it is for the mentor (and others in your network) to help you. Think about your three- to five-year goals, in addition to the day-to-day challenges you face, and be prepared to share them. Examples of ways your mentor can help you include:
- Navigating office politics.
- Developing a career plan.
- Communicating effectively with your boss or colleagues.
- Making new contacts in areas you want to explore.
- Preparing an effective presentation.
- Analyzing failures or mistakes so you can learn from them.
- Developing a business proposal.
- Improving your time management.
- Setting up a structure—agree on regular meetings, set up boundaries, and acknowledge that either of you can walk away at any time with no hard feelings. Have at least one meeting per month, or the relationship will wither from neglect.
- Showing your appreciation—saying "thank you" is a good idea. Small gifts as tokens of appreciation can also be appropriate. In this relationship, especially early on, the mentor is doing most of the helping, and it's nice to acknowledge that.

Chapter 41

• • • • • • • •

Isn't It Time You Got Yourself a Coach?

by Anita Attridge, Certified Five O'Clock Club Coach

We've found that 40 percent of executives hired at the senior level are pushed out, fail or quit within 18 months.

Kevin Kelly, Heidrick & Struggles CEO, discussing his executive search firm's internal study of 20,000 searches in the *Financial Times*, March 20, 2009

Today, it is tough to keep up. Organizations are changing—finding new directions—and expect management to get on board quickly. Those who don't are often left behind or pushed out. A trusted advisor (business coach) can help you or someone on your staff to increase productivity and performance.

More executives are asking for business coaching. You may want to ask your organization to provide you with a personal business coach, or you may want to hire a coach for yourself or for one or two of your employees. In fact, there has been a boom in business coaching. According to a recent AMA survey, companies that use business coaching report performing well on such measures as revenue growth, market share, profitability and customer satisfaction. Individuals who had received coaching were more likely

to (1) set work-related goals and (2) find that subordinates trust their leadership abilities.

In today's demanding work environment, leaders must effectively manage their organizations, adapt to continuous change and meet challenging objectives. As a leader, you know that the best way to manage is to use all of the resources available to you; however, you may be overlooking a critical resource...a business coach.

How could a business coach help you? Let's look at some situations where working with a business coach could be of benefit to you:

- You are in a new leadership position in your company or in a new company.
- You have a new manger with a different leadership style and new expectations for your organization.
- You are managing a significant change initiative while striving to meet performance expectations.
- You're passed over for a promotion that you felt you deserved or your work is not appreciated by the organization.

A business coach is a resource you can use to manage these situations so that you can:

- Assesses the realities of your situation.
- Define the core challenges to be addressed.
- Develop alternatives and actions to address these challenges.
- Receive support and guidance as you implement the actions.

Four Situations in which an Executive Coach Could Be of Benefit to You:

1. When You Are Starting a New Leadership Position

When leaders move to any new leadership position, leadership expectations change. What you do during the first 90 days in a new leadership position will determine how you are perceived by your boss, peers and staff. A new leadership position may be:

- a new management position within your company.
- a promotion from managing individual contributors to managing managers.
- a management position in a new company.

Regardless of what type of leadership move it is, you have approximately 90 days to establish your credibility, since you are working with people who do not know you.

Case Study: Sondra Managing the First 90 Days

Sondra was promoted to a new leadership position as Senior Marketing Director for a new product. Her previous leadership transition had not gone smoothly, so she decided to work with a coach as she transitioned into her new position.

As we began working together, we talked about her new boss and his expectations. She scheduled a meeting with him to clarify what was expected and how he preferred to commu-

nication with people on his staff. We used the *Circles of Influence* chart (in this book) to identify and prioritize the key stakeholders she needed to build relationships with to be successful in her new position. Some of these stakeholders were people she supported, so learning their perspective of her organization helped to identify what was working well and issues that needed to be addressed. When meeting with her direct reports, as a group and then individually, she again gained a perspective of what was working well, and what needed to be improved in her organization. Armed with this information, Sondra began developing her 90-day plan regarding the key areas she would focus on to gain "early wins" and creditability with her manager and key stakeholders. She then reviewed the plan with her manager. At the end of her first 90 days, Sondra had addressed a key organizational issue, was meeting project commitments, and was forming strong relationships with her key stakeholders.

2. When You Have a New Boss

As a leader, positioning your organization to meet changing expectations can be challenging; particularly when you aren't sure what is expected. When you have a new boss, you will need to again determine what is expected of you and your organization. When you're reporting to a new boss:

- Expectations for you and your organization may change.
- You may need to adapt your management style to that of your new boss.
- You may need to refocus how work gets done in your organization.
- To be successful, you will be expected to adapt to the new expectations and style of your new boss. A coach can help you to assess the situation and alternatives, and determine how you can best adapt to be successful.

Case Study: Sam
Managing the Transition with
a New Boss

Sam, a VP in Medical Affairs at a pharmaceutical company enjoyed working with his boss, who was a strategic thinker. When his boss moved to a new position, Sam was a bit anxious about what was in store for him and his organization. He had been through several changes with bosses in other positions and knew they could be tricky.

When Sam met with his new boss, the SVP of Research, he provided a status report about the organization's projects. Within the next couple of weeks, Sam's boss called regularly to ask for minute details about the various projects. Sam was frustrated by all the detailed questions from his boss; however, he began to realize that this would be the new reality. Since his style and his boss' style were very different, Sam called his Five O'Clock Club Coach whom he had previously worked with for help. When Sam met with his coach, they agreed that Sam would need to work differently to meet his new boss' expectations. Since extensive detail was important to his boss, Sam would need to provide much more detail about each project. As they discussed alternatives, they agreed that Sam would need to gain a better understanding of the project detail that his boss required. Based on that information they then developed plans about how Sam would work with his staff to ensure that the requested detail was obtained and included in all reports to avoid last minute fire drills. In addition, they developed strategies for how Sam would prepare for project meetings with his boss, since he would be expected to know much more about the details of each project then he had before. Sam and his organization were now working differently as they adapted to meeting their new boss' expectations.

3. When You are Managing a Major Change in Your Organization

Change is the constant in today's businesses. Managing change is an expected part of a leader's job. The greater the change, the more leadership time and focus it will take… and… you will still be accountable for achieving results. Change can include:

- Technology and major process changes in your organization.
- Organizational restructuring due to increased functions in your organization, or a reduction in headcount.
- New company initiatives that need to be incorporated into your organization.

Managing change can seem like having two competing priorities. A coach can help you to balance both priorities and avoid the pitfalls when managing the change.

Case Study: Vince
Managing a Technology Change

Vince, a Customer Service Director, managed a group of 30 people with three managers reporting to him. He had worked for his boss for several years, so he felt he knew what was expected.

The organization was transitioning to a new customer service system. Vince's boss made it clear that he expected the levels of service to be maintained during the transition process. Vince quickly realized that managing a major system change and maintaining the high service levels his organization provided would be extremely difficult and he was not sure how to mange it. His boss suggested working with a Five O'Clock Club Business Coach.

When Vince met with his coach, he identified the internal strategies needed to seamlessly implement the new system in his organization. In addition, his coach also encouraged him to develop a strategy to engage the customers he supported so that they would understand the impact that the new system would have on their organization. As the implementation occurred, Vince used his coach as a sounding board to be sure he was managing the unexpected glitches in the best possible way. What once seamed like an impossible situation, turned into a model of how to implement a new-technology system in the company.

4. When You're "Stuck" in Your Career

You are the manager of your career. Your career can become stuck through no fault of your own, such as when:

- The organization does not value the work you are doing.
- You find that the job is not what you thought it would be and it's time to move on.
- You are passed over for a promotion.
- You don't fit in the organization culture.

Candidly assessing where you are in your career and where you want to be is a way to ensure that you are managing your career.

Case Study: Judy Getting Unstuck

Judy was a Program Director in a prestigious niche consulting firm. When she joined the firm five years ago, she was excited to be a part of the organization. The firm was expanding and had added her area of expertise to their consulting services. She enjoyed the work she was doing and was well received by her clients and colleagues. As time progressed, Judy felt she was ready to lead the more complex projects coming into the firm; however, there was always a reason why she was not chosen, even though the performance feedback from her manger and clients was extremely positive, and she was often a major player in these projects, as well as in the projects she led.

Judy called me to discuss where she was in her career, and to assess what her next steps should be. She felt stuck and unappreciated, even though she was receiving very positive feedback about her performance. In discussing the background of the people who were receiving the leadership positions for the more complex projects, she identified that all of the selected leaders had a background in the firm's core competencies and had begun their careers with the company. It became clear to Judy that, although her expertise was important to the firm, it was not a part of their core business competencies and, therefore, she probably was not a strong candidate for promotion. She decided to initiate a job search for a position in an organization that valued her expertise, and is now a Senior Director in a major non-profit.

Managing your career is about accepting the realities of what is happening to you in your current position, and then deciding what is best for you and your career. A coach can help you focus on the realities of where you are and what are your options.

Should You Engage a Five O'Clock Club Business Coach?

Business coaching is becoming a part of leadership development in many organizations.

Many are working with The Five O'Clock Club to provide business coaching for leaders in their organization. It could be a part of your development plan.

If you are dealing with a business situation in which you would like expert, confidential business coaching, call The Five O'Clock Club and ask to talk with a Business Coach.

We'll want you to define the business situation and any expectations you have about a coach.

Our coaches have a variety of backgrounds and expertise, and you will be matched with one who meets your requirements.

It's then time to interview the coach to find the one you would feel most comfortable working with. Questions you might want to ask the coaches you interview are:

- How would we work together?
- Tell me about your coaching background.
- How will I be able to measure the results from our work together?
- What is your availability?
- What is your fee?
- How will we determine how long our coaching engagement will last?

Ask any other questions that would help you to determine if this person is the best business coach for you.

If you want to work with a trusted advisor and partner as you manage the various complexities of your leadership role, consider the question.....

Should I get a business coach?

Part Five:

For Executives

Chapter 42

• • • • • • • •

Achieve Success through Effective Leadership

by Rob Hellmann, Certified Five O'Clock Club Coach and VP, Associate Director, The Five O'Clock Club National Guild of Career Coaches

Leadership is a matter of having people look at you and gain confidence, seeing how you react. If you're in control, they're in control.

Tom Landry, Dallas Cowboys Coach

Leadership skills are needed by everyone. In this chapter you'll learn:

- why demonstrating leadership makes you a more valued employee;
- that leadership ability can be learned; and
- how you can lead from any position or level in the organization, whether you manage a staff or not.

....

Leadership is for everyone.

....

Those with the greatest work smarts exhibit leadership in their jobs, no matter what level they're at in an organization. In a previous era, just doing your job well may have been good enough. But in today's competitive global economy, taking the next step and displaying leadership is almost a prerequisite for getting ahead.

Let's use a real-life example to illustrate what leadership is and why it's so important.

Sharon managed a sales team. During her five-year tenure, she saw her job as:

- motivating the sales team to perform better;
- forecasting sales trends; and
- executing any other sales-related tasks that her bosses needed.

After Sharon left the company, her replacement Nellie came in. Nellie was told by her boss that she had "big shoes to fill." At first, Nellie did all the things that Sharon did. But she also

"You'll be happy to know, Johnson, that since I moved your desk out here in the alley, office morale has gone up 300 percent."

saw that the sales force was not as effective as it could be because there were communication barriers between her department and other key support departments, including Marketing, Pricing, Finance and HR. She was determined to break down these barriers, and began to enlist her bosses, her peers in these other teams, and her staff in pursuit of this objective. So Nellie saw her job as:

- influencing others to adopt her vision of better communication and information sharing between departments;
- motivating the sales team to perform better;
- forecasting sales trends; and
- executing any other sales-related tasks that her bosses needed.

So who's the leader, Sharon or Nellie? Nellie is, because in addition to the managerial responsibilities she took over from Sharon, she demonstrated the two key aspects of leadership. First, she had a "vision" for where she wanted to

take the department. And then she was able to "influence" others to support her vision and help make it a reality.

A year later, after successfully boosting her staff's performance through the pursuit of her vision, Nellie was told by the same boss who made the "big shoes" comment that "You've thrown away Sharon's old shoes. You're the best hire in at least ten years." Nellie had become far more valuable to the organization than Sharon because of the value she added as a leader.

So now we have these two underlying concepts that define leadership—*vision, and the ability to influence others* to adopt and support your vision. How do you develop your own visioning and influencing abilities? Many people feel that great leaders are born, not made, probably because these leaders are so successful. While some may be born leaders, you may be surprised to learn that these leadership skills can be taught.

In the next sections, we will dive deeper into the meaning of vision and influencing. Then we'll discuss some key competencies that you can focus on to help you become an effective leader.

> **Leadership consists of vision and the ability to influence others to adopt and support your vision.**

VISION

Anyone can steer the ship, but it takes a leader to chart the course.

John C. Maxwell, *The 21 Irrefutable Laws of Leadership*

As we saw in Nellie's example, she brought to the job something Susan didn't—a vision for the path her department should follow to make it more effective. A leadership vision is a goal or objective that you feel strongly about and that you want others to support you in achieving. It's an essential starting point for leadership.

Your vision will be most effective in influencing others to follow your lead if it is a simple, clear statement that everyone can understand, but specific enough to create a path for others to walk on. "We want to be the best" is not a strong vision because it's too vague. Here are some other examples for leadership visions in the workplace:

- "Our separate departments should be working closely together on behalf of the client, instead of being walled off from each other as they are now";
- "We need to start tracking every part of our process so that we can learn how to save time-to-market for the customer";
- "We should adopt a new strategy around using data and information to make marketing decisions, instead of just using our intuition."

The best visions incorporate elements of creativity, innovation and appropriate risk-taking. Nowhere is this more evident than at Google, where visionary leadership has built innovation and risk-taking into the corporate culture. As an example, a Google executive made a multi-million dollar mistake, but instead of being reprimanded, Google's co-founder Larry Page told her: "I'm so glad you made this mistake, because I want to run a company where we are moving too quickly and doing too much, not being too cautious and doing too little. If we don't have any of these mistakes, we're just not taking enough risk." (*Fortune*, "Chaos By Design," October 2, 2006.)

If you've read The Five O'Clock Club job-search books, you'll notice the similarity between the leadership vision and the Forty-Year Vision used in the job search. The same principle is operating in both situations. Whether you're articulating a vision for yourself in your career,

"The boss put his picture up to inspire us. But it just isn't having that effect on me."

or for others to follow in the workplace, setting that long-term vision is the first, essential step to realizing your goals.

INFLUENCING

So, now perhaps you have a vision for some aspect of your organization's effectiveness. How do you make it happen? Well, if you manage a staff, you can order your staff to carry out your vision, but that's not the most effective way—it would be better if they wanted to do it, or were even inspired to do it! And you certainly can't order your peers or superiors to support your initiatives. If you don't manage a staff, you definitely will need to rely on your ability to "influence" others. And, in fact, effective leaders are adept at influencing others to support their ideas.

Influencing Behaviors

As mentioned before, the good news is that you can learn the influencing skills that will allow you to build support for your vision. Some companies survey their employees to discover the skills that their own most-effective leaders possess, and then seek to develop potential leaders' skills in these areas. GE is an example of a highly successful company that has used leadership competencies to develop effective leaders. While the list of leadership competencies may vary among organizations, here are the most common leadership behaviors frequently seen encouraged in organizations:

- Communicate Effectively
- Inspire Trust in Your Leadership
- Invest Yourself in Your Organization
- Adapt Your Leadership Style to the Situation
- Focus on Goals/Winning
- Maintain Momentum

While all of these competencies help you to achieve results as a leader, the top three in particular help potential followers to buy into you as a leader, regardless of your vision. This concept

of leadership buy-in is key. John C. Maxwell, the noted author on leadership, has shown that people need to buy into the leader before they buy into the vision.

Communicate Effectively

Effective leaders use communication to focus attention on goals, to influence others to buy-in to their leadership, and to listen and learn from others. They do this by following these four principles:

- Communicate often.
- Deliver a consistent message.
- Listen to what others have to say in regular meetings and conversations.
- Emphasize an "influencing" communication style, as opposed to "telling."

By communicating often, you will keep the goals you're trying to accomplish at the top of everyone's minds. By keeping the message consistent, you build trust in your leadership.

Communication is a two-way street—a leader must be able to hear what others are telling her. The information you gain from listening will give you a reality check, on both the vision itself (does it make sense to pursue?) and the progress being made to achieve it. By listening, you create continuous opportunities to alter your strategy or tactics to ensure your ultimate success.

If you seek to influence others to your vision, you need to be able to hear them and learn from them as well. Being open to learning from others connects you to reality and eliminates dangerous wishful thinking, but it also reassures others that what they do matters.

As you listen to others' input, seek to constantly re-learn the answers to the following questions. If you answer "NO" to any of them, then ask yourself how you can change the answer to "YES."

- Is my vision viable?
- Am I succeeding in enlisting others to follow me?

- Is the path we're pursuing the best way to achieve the vision? (If you're not sure, what are the pros and cons of the alternatives?)
- Am I coming across positively in my interactions with others?

Lastly, effective leaders add to their position of authority by going beyond telling subordinates: "This is what I want you to do." Instead, they encourage others to buy-in to their leadership vision by saying "Here's why I think this is important—you have a key role to play in achieving these goals, and here's why."

....

Your vision should be a simple, clear statement that everyone can understand, but specific enough to create a path for others to follow.

....

Case Study: Fred Successfully Communicating His Vision

Fred started his new job as head of a dispirited division at a major bank. Under the previous head, the division was widely perceived as dominated by cliques, low morale and high turnover of valuable employees. The low morale was having a major impact on customer service and causing many high-performers to leave.

Fred had a vision of superior customer service for the division, and wanted to create an organizational culture where high-performers would want to work. Fred needed to get his message out to enlist others to follow and also wanted to make sure that he was getting the information he needed from his front-line employees.

Fred put in place monthly and quarterly meetings with different parts of his large staff where he did three things:

First, he clearly communicated his vision for the organization. Many initially were skeptical because they had heard it all before. But, in time, the consistency of Fred's message and behavior would win over the staff's trust in his leadership.

Second, Fred discussed the current situation in honest terms. In his monthly and quarterly meetings, the openness Fred encouraged resulted in many uncomfortable questions. For example, in one monthly meeting a questioner asked: "We're so used to management by 'flavor of the month,' why should we believe that what you're proposing is any different?" Another asked, "How can you expect us to deliver the customer service you want when we're overworked and underpaid?"

Fred directly answered these questions by describing various initiatives and reiterating his commitment to hearing out and solving employee issues like these. But it wasn't so much the specifics of the answers that began to win over the division's employees. Rather, it was his willingness—for the first time—to address questions such as these, and the respect this willingness conveyed, that began to win over the department's employees.

Third, Fred set up bi-weekly lunches with small groups of staff members at all levels of the organization. In these lunches, he did less talking and more listening. He made himself approachable with "open door" days, and made a point of attending social functions to chat with people. Through these forums he heard about important issues that were hurting department success, issues that had not been aired before. And every chance he got, he'd reiterate the goals he had for the organization, as a means of keeping everyone focused on the vision.

Through his openness to communication, Fred was able to completely turn around the organization within two years, transforming it into a leader in the customer service area. He also reduced employee turnover by roughly half.

Inspire Trust in Your Leadership

It's hard to maintain any positive relationship without trust, and the relationship between a leader and potential followers is no different. To influence others to follow, you need to generate trust in your leadership. Trust means that those you're seeking to influence know that you mean what you say, and that they can count on you to follow through. In the example above with Fred, his consistent communication of the direction he wanted to take the organization, encouraged employees to trust that the message was sincere. But obviously, words aren't enough, and his actions effectively backed them up.

A common problem encountered by would-be leaders in some organizations is a perception by employees that "we've heard it all before." You'll often hear this from employees who feel their leadership doesn't follow through on their words, and that every potentially worthwhile "vision" wasn't worth the bytes it was emailed on. They become so jaded by words that didn't match actions that a built-in inertia develops against following any vision, no matter how worthwhile. Building bridges through effective communication and trust will help to turn around this negative inertia.

Invest Yourself in Your Position

As a leader, the higher you move up, the more invested you need to be in the business you're in. At a lower level, it can be more about your work-life balance. As you move up, you have greater responsibility to others, and you may need to give up your entitlements for the good of the organization and the employees for whom you're responsible.

Adapt Your Leadership Style to the Task at Hand

Blanchard and Hersey pioneered the theory of "situational leadership," the concept that effective leadership is task-relevant. In our dealings with people, most of us will vary our style according to the person we are communicating with or the situation we're in. For example, we might communicate differently with an employee depending on whether or not they are motivated, or whether or not there's a severe time crunch.

As a rule of thumb, always strive to adopt an influencing and delegating leadership style to enlist others to help you achieve your vision. We've already discussed how the influencing style is a motivator, and delegating work frees up your time to focus on tasks only you can do.

There may be situations, however, when you need to adopt a highly directive style. You can determine whether the situation warrants this "telling" style by:

1. what your "rank" is relative to the person or people you're seeking to influence, i.e. you can't tell your superiors what to do;
2. what the employee's competency is around the tasks you need performed;
3. what the employee's motivation is; and
4. how time-critical is the task you need to get accomplished.

So, for a subordinate who isn't motivated to perform a task with a tight deadline, or for a new employee who doesn't yet have the competency, you will need to adopt a more highly directive style to make sure you get done what is needed.

> As you move up, you have greater responsibility to others, and you may need to give up your entitlements for the good of the organization and the employees for whom you're responsible.

Case Study: Beth
Adapting Her Leadership Style with Great Results

When Beth took on her new position as Sales Director, she initially tried to keep the reporting structure of her predecessor, so that all the sales representatives would report directly to her. Beth's predecessor had by all accounts used a telling/highly-directive style in his approach to all of his subordinates. He made sure he was involved in all decisions and told his staff exactly what needed to be done, regardless of their development level. Needless to say, morale was low, particularly for the highly motivated, highly skilled sales team.

But with a major expansion of the organization underway, and with 20 people reporting to her, Beth was feeling overwhelmed. She was so busy helping them put out their daily fires that she was having trouble performing the tasks that she was hired to do, including coordinating with marketing and developing new sales tools to help her staff succeed.

So Beth decided to adopt a more influencing/ delegative approach wherever possible. She did this by:

1. dropping the number of direct reports from 20 to six, giving these six (who had the greatest skill level and motivation) managerial responsibility over the others.
2. reducing her "open door" time to her staff, forcing them to come up with their own solutions to many of the problems they formerly came to her for.

3. presenting to her staff a "staff entrepreneur" model for how they can deal on their own with questions and problems.

The approach worked, and freed Beth up to focus on the strategic issues that only she could address. The change in style also resulted in an immediate boost in sales-force morale, with several top sales performers canceling their impending departures from the company.

Focus on Goals/Winning

In all your communication, you should be focused on the finish line. Keeping that goal top-of-mind helps protect both you and those you're seeking to influence from being sidetracked by issues of lesser importance.

Communication is key to keeping everyone's focus on the goal. But sometimes so much is going on in an organization that it's hard to keep focus. That's why effective leaders know how to prioritize. In fact, it's one of the most important things that effective leaders do. Use three parameters when figuring out your priorities as you seek to reach your vision, and prioritize them in this order:

1. What are you required to do?
2. What provides the greatest return on your investment of time or money?

"I know you both wanted the promotion to V.P. However, my dog has been a loyal and dependable friend, so he gets the job."

3. What do you find most rewarding?

Management guru Peter Drucker, in a Forbes.com interview, made a similar point in a slightly different way:

"Successful leaders don't start out asking, 'What do I want to do?' They ask, 'What needs to be done?' Then they ask, 'Of those things that would make a difference, which are right for me?' They don't tackle things they aren't good at. They make sure other necessities get done, but not by *them*." Successful leaders make sure that they succeed! They are not afraid of strength in others. Andrew Carnegie wanted to put on his gravestone, "Here lies a man who knew how to put into his service more able men than he was himself."

··

Always strive to adopt an influencing and delegating leadership style to enlist others to help you achieve your vision. However, sometimes a directive style is called for.

··

What has worked for me in my positions, as well as for my clients who have used it, is the "80/20 rule." This rule can be interpreted in the following way: You often spend 20% of your time getting 80% of the work done, and then the remaining 80% of your time getting that last 20%

done. Looking at this from a cost/benefit point of view, getting that last 20% done is usually not worth the time it takes. So one way to prioritize is to focus on the 80% you get done quickly, and then forget the rest or put it off for another time.

As Voltaire once said, "The perfect is the enemy of the good." Don't lose sight of your goal by focusing on the perfect, when the good will get you there as well.

Build and Maintain the Momentum

Look for the small wins and focus on the positive as you try to reach your vision. Celebrate the small wins with your team or colleagues—the audience you're seeking to influence. Building momentum is especially important in the early stages of a project, or when you and your team are going through a tough time and the goal may seem farther away than ever.

To help build and maintain momentum, consider doing some or all of the following:

- Ensure that there are milestones or stepping-stones that can be celebrated early along the way to achieving your vision.
- Use email thank-you's to individuals or the team to recognize achievements that bring you closer to the vision.
- Consider other ways of recognizing progress, including team lunches, sending "good news" notes to senior leader-

"It's signed by the entire office. You're not too popular around here, are you?"

ship that recognize individual team members, etc.

- If unexpected obstacles develop, work hard to find any opportunity for celebrating a success.
- Keep a project plan, keep it updated, and circulate it so everyone can see the progress being made.
- Work to keep sidetracking discussions at meetings to a minimum. An important way of doing this is to suggest taking the subject "off line" for further discussion after the meeting, without all the team members present.

Look for the small wins and focus on the positive as you try to reach your vision.

Case Study: Jackie
Starting With the Quick Wins

Jackie, a new director of Enrollments for a school, had a leadership vision of greater enrollments through collaboration between her enrollment team and other departments in the school, including Marketing, Financial Aid, and Housing, and the teaching staff. She inherited a department where morale was low and the staff had "heard it all before."

So Jackie started off looking for quick wins for her department to build morale and momentum for her goals.

She developed a periodicals rack in the department that contained marketing materials, financial aid information, teacher biographies, alumni locations, and international student visa information. Her enrollment team now had interdepartmental information at their fingertips that they never had before, and their sales effort became more effective. She chose one month to be a month of brainstorming new enrollment ideas, and her department came up with many new ideas that were easily implemented.

Jackie then began to tackle the harder tasks, meeting with Financial Aid and Housing, and with them developed a plan for faster approval of the most desirable students. Momentum and support for her vision began to build.

Lead from Any Level or Tenure

Sometimes new employees, more junior employees, or those without staff to manage, don't realize how much real leadership they can demonstrate in their jobs. If you are in this situation, put aside for a moment your specific job responsibilities as your boss related them to you, that is, the things you have to get done. Then take a fresh look at how your job and skills fit into the bigger picture. Start asking yourself questions about your role or specific job tasks, such as:

- Why are we doing things this way?
- How could this be done better? What are the pros and cons for alternatives?
- What are the obstacles to an improved way of doing things?
- Where is the proper place for these tasks?
- When should this be done, or how often?
- Who should be more involved to make for a better outcome?

In answering these questions, you may hit upon ideas for a better way of doing things that could form your leadership vision.

For example, say your new job is to run reports and distribute them. You might think that doing a good job simply means running the reports on time, making sure there are no errors, and then quickly distributing them to the recipients. This is all true.

But, in addition to performing your specific job tasks well, you might start to ask yourself questions about this task. For example, why are all these reports necessary—can we save money by eliminating some? What's the best way for a report to be sent out? Who should these reports go to? How could these reports be improved—is the correct information on them, and are they easy to understand? Do they really need to be produced weekly, or would monthly work?

From the answers to these questions you might develop a vision of more-efficient and effective reporting. When I was starting out in my career, a colleague of mine in a new job had these very tasks as part of his job description. And, although not consciously intending to demonstrate leadership, he developed a leadership vision based on his answers to these questions. He sold this vision to his boss and ended up leading a successful reporting task force that reduced reporting costs by half, and did wonders for his performance review!

....

Even more junior people can reexamine their jobs to see how they can be done better.

....

As You Move Up the Ladder

Executives are usually given more autonomy, and more time, than lower level managers to prove themselves. The danger of this additional flexibility for executives is that they could invest a lot of time and resources in pursuing a vision that is at odds with the CEO's outlook. You can counteract this danger by:

1. Striving for effective two-way communication up and down the ladder, and
2. Taking appropriate risks with the company's resources. (By "appropriate," I mean being careful with how much money and time you're spending, especially if support for your vision is uncertain and spending these resources eliminates the pursuit of other potentially viable options.)

I once witnessed an executive V.P. make this mistake at a company I was working in. Her leadership vision involved expanding internal computing resources by hiring staff and updating hardware, so that all customer-facing departments would have access to the most up-to-date customer information. This vision unfortunately ended up conflicting with the CEO's goal of outsourcing most technology capabilities. Clearly, there was a communication issue between the CEO and this executive, and much time and millions of dollars were wasted before these visions were in synch. This executive's career was essentially over at this company.

In Closing—The Importance of Achieving Results

Ultimately, leadership competencies and effective management techniques don't mean much if they are not accompanied by results. Great leaders and managers know this, and are always conscious of how well they can translate their mastery of leadership competencies and management skills into improved performance. But you need both the "what" (results) and the "how" (leadership) to be successful.

One manager I know was focused on results to the exclusion of how he was achieving these results. His lack of ability to effectively influence others and treat staff with respect resulted in short-term performance gains at the expense of long-term damage to morale and teamwork in the organization, and the departure of the most valuable employees.

You don't have to be born with the skills of a great leader or manager to become one. All of the approaches described in this chapter can be learned. So, whatever your level in an organization or aspirations for promotion, study and practice these aspects of successful leadership and your success at work will be greater. And if you manage a staff, these management ideas will help you to improve staff productivity, lower turnover and free up your time so that you can be more productive.

Chapter 43

• • • • • • • •

It's No Longer Business As Usual: How to Stand Out in a Time of Organizational Change

by Chip Conlin, Certified Five O'Clock Club Coach

Those who realize where changes are heading are better able to use those changes to their own advantage.

Charles Handy, *The Age of Unreason*

The world of work is changing. As organizations strive to "right size" after years of downsizing in the face of market and technological changes, employees need to find new ways to adapt, survive and remain marketable. For most organizations, it is no longer business as usual. Few employees are indispensable, and all need to stand out and be vital to their organization's mission.

As a career coach and human resources professional, I counsel many clients and employees who feel stalled in their jobs. They face an uncertain future if they cannot keep pace with the changes taking place. If they are to advance in their careers they will need to leverage their work experiences, skills, strengths and accomplishments to become resources to their organizations outside their normal realms of activity.

To stand out during times of change requires new mindsets, and most importantly, an ability to come to grips with the new reality: One's future as an employee hinges on not thinking about your job as you have in the past. Your role *will* change; you must focus on the organization's goals and what matters most to the key decision-makers. The employee's obligation is to figure out the goals of the organization and prepare to contribute to them.

It will become critical for people to learn new skills. Okay, that's easier said than done, but let's take a look at some steps employees can take to keep themselves viable contributors to their organizations, and take on more meaningful roles.

Here are some strategies to help you stand out in your organization.

Become Knowledgeable in more than One Area

After working more than 12 years in human resources for a major transportation company, I knew that I wanted to keep myself viable in the face of the changes I could see happening all around me. I explored opportunities in other areas of the company, specifically targeting departments with which I had closely worked in my role as a corporate recruiter. I met with the head of our Customer Service Department with whom I had worked in filling many of his department's jobs. A position eventually became available there and I ended up working another five years for the company in my new role as a Manager in Customer Service.

A key lesson learned is to think about internal clients or others outside your department with whom you work or do business. Having developed a good working relationships with various department heads while in human resources, these managers became important resources and advocates when I was looking to take on another role. Employees who work in marketing should think about those within and outside of their department, those with whom they frequently interact. For a marketing person it could be the sales group, the training department, or it could be a key relationship with someone in PR or IT. By building such relationships with others in the company, you'll better position yourself to support the broader goals of the organization.

Become a Strategic Partner

Lorraine, a client of mine, had had a successful career as a sales executive in the pharmaceutical industry. But she began noticing changes. She was no longer required to attend regular staff meetings, and she was not invited to attend educational and professional association events. The writing was on the wall: Lorraine was being written off by her company. She was no longer seen as a key player in its mission of meeting major changes in the healthcare field.

Lorraine could have avoided these developments if she had established internal contacts within her company, e.g., marketing, R&D, and even HR where her experience could have added value to these areas. She could have created more visibility for herself, based on the needs of her clients within healthcare. In short, she could

have realigned herself as a strategic partner within her company by building on these relationships, making her enhanced value known to everyone.

But we turned her situation around. We focused on the two or three issues most important to senior management, and then focused her work goals around those issues. Lorraine knew that she had exceeded her sales quotas in the past, and by exploring where else she could add value to the company, she was able to leverage her accomplishments accordingly. She became not only a survivor during a time of organizational change, but also advanced her career to a new level.

From Consultant to Employee

Be aware, however, that simply aligning yourself with the goals of the organization will not be enough to become a key player during times of organizational change. To be a standout employee you will need to be at the *forefront* of change—as opposed to just going along with changes as they come along. You need to be an advocate for your company and your company's senior management team.

Derrick, a Five O'Clock Clubber, worked as an independent consultant with a major consulting firm, and he quickly emerged as the team project leader for a new billing system that was being implemented throughout the firm. After working in this role for almost five years, the company decided to cut back on its consultants, and replace them with just a few full-time employees. In essence, Derrick had to outclass the competition to keep his job.

He was told by one of his managers that he lacked the level of managerial experience demonstrated by some of the other candidates. To make matters worse, only a few months earlier, Derrick had declined an offer to work full-time because he was still considering opportunities outside the company. However, as project team leader he had made all the right connections with senior management, he knew their priorities, and was seen by senior management as possessing the leadership skills needed to complete a multi-million dollar project. Because he had nurtured the internal network better than the others, Derrick was able to compete successfully with his internal and external rivals. He demonstrated in his interviews that he was the one best positioned to take this project to the next level, and he negotiated a competitive compensation package. Having an insider's knowledge of the company's major challenges—and knowing where his expertise would be most valued—Derrick landed the full-time position as team leader.

Formulate a Plan of Action

Employees are well-advised to have their own *written* internal marketing plan to best position themselves for other opportunities within their organization. I cannot tell you how many times clients have complained to me that their requests to take on new responsibilities (with higher pay) fell on deaf ears. Their only strategy seemed to be: "I work hard and put in long hours, so I deserve a raise." Most managers are not going to provide employees with new or broader responsibilities (not to mention pay raises) based on simple pleas such as these. "I'm ready for more responsibility or challenging work" should be backed up with a written plan of action outlining goals, strategies and the value that the employee brings. Remember, you add value by leveraging your experiences, strengths and skills toward the goals of the organization.

Scott had a promising career as a planner, working for a major transportation company. Previously, he had worked for city agencies, and he was ready to assume a broader role in his new position in the corporate planning and development department of his new company. When his expectations for the role were not met, he became increasingly frustrated, and blamed his manager for micro-managing him. Since I had hired Scott, he trusted me and often visited my office, complaining about how underutilized he was. He saw no prospect of advancing to a more

senior-level position.

Scott's problem was not his lack of ability or knowledge—indeed, he was incredibly knowledgeable. But he stumbled in developing a better relationship with his manager, and they disagreed over some strategic issues. He was used to doing things as he had done when he worked as a municipal planner. So, the first step in helping Scott was to eliminate his overt criticism of his manager.

When it became evident that Scott had pretty much sabotaged his standing in the planning department, we put together a plan of action to turn the situation around. Scott could build on his relationships with other managers in the company, many of whom he interacted with on planning-related projects. By exploring opportunities outside his department, and meeting with managers who were his internal clients, Scott was able to pursue a position in the company's industrial engineering department, using his planning skills in designing new office space for the company.

If Scott had initially built these relationships within the planning department, and advanced the goals of his manager, his advancement opportunities—and becoming a key player—might have happened sooner.

Recognizing the Realities of Today

Becoming a valued employee requires more than keeping pace with your current job. You may be able to cruise along doing what you have always done, but you will find yourself more and more on the periphery of your organization, less central to its emerging needs.

To avoid the cruise mode, be proactive in adjusting to and mastering change. At The Five O'Clock Club, we encourage members to complete the Seven Stories Exercise®. This is a great tool for identifying strengths, skills and accomplishments. Once you have assessed your skills, attend professional association meetings, and volunteer to get the experience and exposure you need to compete and stand out in your organization. Build relationships with key management personnel and find new ways to keep yourself open to new work possibilities, relationships, and emerging technologies. This approach will position you for taking on a more central role.

The changes that employees at all levels face can indeed be daunting. Assuring your boss, "Trust me, I *can* do other things" is not good enough. It is incumbent on you to take the steps outlined above to create even better opportuni-ties for yourself. It really is no longer business as usual.

Leadership is understanding people and involving them to help you do a job. That takes all of the good characteristics, like integrity, dedication of purpose, selflessness, knowledge, skill, implacability, as well as determination not to accept failure.

Admiral Arleigh A. Burke

Chapter 44

· · · · · · · ·

Ethical Decisions in Business

by Richard Bayer, Ph.D., Chief Operating Officer, The Five O'Clock Club

It's not hard to make decisions when you know what your values are.

Roy Disney, American film writer, producer, nephew of Walt Disney

Because business activity is human activity, it can be evaluated from the moral point of view, just as any other human activity can be so evaluated. The relationship of business to morality goes even deeper than this. Business, like most other social activities, presupposes a background of morality and would be impossible without it.

Richard T. De George, *Business Ethics*, fifth ed., Prentice Hall, 1999

Business leaders make ethical decisions every day. What if we were to assume that, "Let your conscience be your guide," is the simple tenet that most people follow when they grapple with ethical issues in organizations? It's actually far more complex than that—usually because the situations and issues in the workplace are complex.

···

"Let your conscience be your guide," does not provide the necessary guidance.

···

For example, what should hiring managers do about questions of diversity, quotas and affirmative action? How should a CEO go about deciding how much to spend to reduce air and water pollution caused by her company? When is advertising a forceful presentation of a product's strengths, and when does it claim too much and betray the public's trust?

How should a reduction in workforce be carried out, and how does the firm determine the right amounts for severance, career counseling (outplacement), and benefits coverage for those being terminated?

Question(s) to consider: When you make business decisions at work, how often do you consider ethics a part of them? Or are you only thinking about reaching a goal or implementing a plan? Always, sometimes, rarely or never?

"Let your conscience be your guide," falls far short of providing the necessary guidance in such matters. There are, in fact, *concrete methods for ethical reasoning.* Indeed, historically, there are several approaches that people have used.

Examining these can be fascinating, as well as aid in making ethical decisions in the organization. In the section that follows, we'll cover three of the most highly regarded, with emphasis on Economic Personalism, which is the most helpful and comprehensive (it includes the insights contained in the first two).

To prevent this discussion from sounding too theoretical, the best approach is presenting a case study, involving real people in a life-and-death situation—literally. Let's look at the inspirational Johnson & Johnson, Tylenol case. It provides a good example for analyzing the methods used to reason ethically.

On September 30, 1982, three people in the Chicago area died from cyanide introduced into Extra-Strength Tylenol capsules. The link between the deaths and the tainted capsules was made with remarkable speed, and authorities notified Johnson & Johnson. As the number of deaths grew—the final total was seven—the firm faced a crisis and, indeed, potential disaster. Tylenol, a leading pain-reliever, was Johnson & Johnson's single largest brand, accounting for almost 18% of the corporation's income. The executives involved in deciding how to respond did not know:

- Had the cyanide been put in the Tylenol capsules during the manufacturing process or afterwards?

- Were the deaths that had already been reported just the first of a large number?
- Would the deaths be limited to the Chicago area?

The U.S. Food and Drug Administration had issued a warning not to take Tylenol, but the government had not ordered the company to take any specific action. Perhaps the deaths would be local, and there would be no more than seven. Perhaps the authorities would not demand a recall. Perhaps a temporary cessation of sales until the source of the contamination was determined could prevent more harm to the public.

Against all these unknowns, the Johnson & Johnson executives had to weigh several certainties:

- A recall would involve a loss of up to $100 million.
- The loss was not covered by insurance.
- News of a recall could so damage the product that Tylenol might never be able to regain public confidence and its 37% of market share.
- The news and loss would surely result in a dramatic drop in the company's stock (it did, in fact, go down 15% in the first week of October).
- The competition in the analgesic market was fierce. Competitors would try to make Tylenol's loss their gain.

Public welfare and the company's reputation were both protected by ethical decision-making.

These were certainties; the rest was guess-work and speculation. But, being unwilling to expose consumers to further risk—and in making a decision that put it in the Ethics Hall of Fame—Johnson & Johnson ordered a recall of all Tylenol bottles. In the long run, public welfare and the company's reputation were both protected by ethical decision-making.

The Tylenol case obviously presents a major example of ethical reasoning. But ethical issues, large and small, occur every day. Business leaders need methods for dealing with them and arriving at reasonable decisions. There are three major approaches in ethics that have been fashioned by philosophers and theologians, *which are applied every day by many leaders who may never have read their works.*

> There are three major approaches to ethical decision-making.

Approach One: Universal Obligation

One way to look at it is this: *moral rules derive from our rights and duties toward one another.* The thinker most closely connected with this approach is the great philosopher Immanuel Kant (1724–1804), as expressed in his *Groundwork of the Metaphysic of Morals.* For Kant, actions are not good or bad based on the purposes for which we act. Rather than considering purposes, we should ask if the basis of our action could become a "universal law" for all moral actors in similar circumstances. If it is wrong for any company to sell a potentially defective product, it is wrong for Johnson & Johnson to do so—despite the considerable cost of a recall. The focus is on motivation, not on the consequences of an action. Further, since all human beings share this ability to reason about moral actions, Kant believed that no one must ever be treated purely as a means, but, rather, as an end in himself. We cannot use others purely for some benefit to ourselves.

This rule would prohibit seeing the consumer purely as a means to corporate profit—as could have been done in the Tylenol case (but was not). Johnson & Johnson correctly recog-

nized its duty to consumer welfare. However, the Kantian approach fails to consider the ends of an action. Indeed, it is often said, "The way to hell is paved with good intentions." Morality should, however, consider the consequences (not just the motives) of an action on the actual human beings who are impacted.

> *Universal Obligation*: **Never use others purely for some benefit to ourselves.**

A Modern Understanding of Universal Obligation

One of the foremost philosophers of the twentieth century, John Rawls, takes a position very similar to Kant. Now Professor Emeritus at Harvard, in 1971 Rawls first published *A Theory of Justice.* He argued that people choose proper rules when they are forced to reason impartially. Rawls asks people to reason from what he calls an "original position."

People should, in fact, imagine themselves behind a veil of ignorance. That is, they are free, equal, rational, self-interested, but, in the original position, they do not know their place in society. They neither have an idea about how well they will fare in the natural lottery of talents, nor do they know their likes, dislikes, religious beliefs and so on. They know only the general facts about human society. It is assumed that they have different aims (life plans), but they cannot advance them at the cost of others, since all knowledge is held behind the veil of ignorance. Ignorance of these things guarantees impartiality in ethical choice.

According to this method of reasoning (from behind the veil of ignorance), the management and stockholders of Johnson & Johnson would have reasoned impartially, that is, they would never have put the consumer at risk any more than they would have been willing to put themselves at risk.

However, the Rawls method has a serious flaw; few of us can reason so abstractly about concrete, everyday moral problems. This becomes especially clear when Rawls spells out what we must "forget" to reason ethically—our place in society, our talents, likes, dislikes, religious beliefs, and so on. The criticism made about Kant also applies to Rawls. The impact of any moral decision on real people never comes clearly into focus. The failure to consider consequences is resolved in the next approach.

The *Consequences* Approach:
Take actions that produce the most
good for the most people.

Approach Two: What Is the Impact of What You Do?

There are those, however, who believe that morality is about consequences, not rules and duty. This approach is known as Utilitarianism, and was argued most strongly by John Stuart Mill (1806–1873). According to him, actions are considered morally right if these produce the most good for the most people.

Utilitarianism seeks "The greatest good for the greatest number." Following this code, the decision-makers at Johnson & Johnson would have been forced to consider not only the interests of the company, but also those of the public at large. Determining the greatest good for the greatest number requires a cost/benefit analysis to be done for the public, as well as for the organization.

This reasoning method *probably* would have required a product recall. The protection of the millions of Tylenol users is the greater good and outweighs the financial costs to Johnson & Johnson.

But if only a few were to be poisoned, what then? *Unfortunately, utilitarianism would allow large and unfair burdens to be placed on the few (i.e., the risk of death), to the benefit of the greatest*

number. This runs against our ethical sensibility. It also says little about what is meant by the greatest "good." This flaw is remedied by the Personalist approach.

Approach Three: Economic Personalism

Personalism has human dignity at its center. Sources such as the United Nations, Christian social thought, and the Dalai Lama support this ethic. According to this approach, ethical reasoning asks, "Which action most leads to the protection and promotion of human dignity?" Of course, how one understands the human person is the key to answering this question.

The preferred approach is, *Economic Personalism:* Choose the action that most likely leads to the protection and promotion of human dignity.

Aspects of the Person to Consider

Those within the Judeo-Christian tradition believe that all persons were created in the image and likeness of God. This belief is the foundation for protecting and promoting human dignity. Catholic social thought, in particular, latches onto this approach to answer questions of business and economic ethics. (As already indicated, it is not only Jews and Christians who affirm human dignity, but also others—Muslims, philosophers and still others—who do so for their own reasons and within their own traditions. The reader who is neither Jew nor Christian should be able to find application for all or most of the ideas presented here.)

The following discussion covers the six basic aspects of the human person to consider when making ethical decisions in your everyday worklife using the Economic Personalism approach. After surveying these aspects, we'll

Characteristics of Human Being	Definition	Example, Application
1. Spiritual	A person must have "space" to practice spirituality.	Respect and encouragement for various belief systems. Time or days off for religious holidays is important.
2. Social	A person only develops to his/her fullest with others.	Employees should have opportunities to socialize, participate in groups, work in cooperative settings, and join appropriate associations.
3. Material	A person requires food, clothing, shelter, etc., to survive.	Payment of just wages and benefits. Safe and pleasant working conditions.
4. Free and Creative	We all want to move forward professionally, to exercise our creative abilities.	Assignments should assign creative responsibility at the lowest level possible.
5. Fragile	We are all prone to error; have our weaknesses; and failings.	Employees need oversight, second chances, extra training, or re-assignment.
6. Equal	Persons have a basic equality regardless of race, color, creed, etc.	There should not be discrimination on a non-performance basis.

look at how they would have affected decision-making in the Tylenol situation. These characteristics, which were presented earlier in this chapter, are now looked at in terms of Economic Personalism.

The six are summarized in the table above.

· ·

Question(s) to consider: So far, has reading this section in any way changed how you would go about making an ethical decision? If so, how?

· ·

Protecting Human Dignity at the Workplace

1. Spiritual. In Economic Personalism, all things on earth are understood as being ordered to human beings as their center and summit. Indeed, humans are spiritual beings, distinguished from other creatures by their capacity to know and love. In other words, God gives persons their true being, not simply in the sense of existence in time and space, but in the sense of life-purpose, meaning, and ethical structure.

To become truly spiritual, one must have "space" to delve into one's soul. This means that ethical decisions must respect and encourage various belief systems. For example, people need time off from work for religious holidays. It's a company's duty to help a Muslim be a *good* Muslim, for example, by giving her the space to practice spirituality.

> Human beings are distinguished from other creatures by their capacity to know and love.

2. *Communal.* Christians believe that God's being is not solitary, but communal (social). For example, there is a community of persons, Father, Son and the Holy Spirit, who all give and receive love. Humans, created in the image and likeness of God, also find their true being in giving and receiving love and in experiencing unity in the midst of difference. Since Economic Personalism says that a person only develops to his or her fullest with others, it is our ethical responsibility to encourage this. For example, employers can give employees the opportunity to socialize, participate in groups, work in coopera-tive settings, and join appropriate associations.

3. *Material.* In applying Economic Personal-ism, we need to consider the material aspect of a person. The basis for this is that God has created persons as body and spirit, and our everyday ma-terial processes should serve to reveal the hidden presence of God. Although, realistically speak-ing, the activities of caring for the body, provid-ing for the needs of family and self, participating in economic life, do involve some repetition and, at times toil, the more striking truth is that dur-ing these activities we can discover and recog-nize the workings and presence of the Creator.

Consider the act of eating. We eat and provide nourishment for the material needs of the body, but we almost always prefer to do this communally. Therefore, the material overlaps with the spiritual.

Eating can become almost a spiritual event. Indeed, for Christians, the Eucharist, a meal,

is the high point of worship. Therefore, ethical decision-makers should consider that a person requires food, shelter, and clothing to survive, and so should pay just wages and benefits, as well as provide safe and pleasant working conditions.

> Johnson & Johnson put people before money. Its executives understood their social responsibility to protect persons, whose unique value is inestimable.

4. *Free and Creative.* Economic Personal-ism also rests upon providing freedom for the individual, because only by exercising our freedom can we turn ourselves toward what is truly good. In our freedom and creativity, we may participate in and contribute to giving and receiving love, involving God and other persons. The more people who are involved, the more giving and receiving of love there is. Thus, an ethical decision-maker at work helps people to move forward professionally, and to exercise their creative abilities.

5. *Fragile.* Of course, a realistic understand-ing of humans must recognize the significance of our being finite (having limitations), and the toughness and cohesiveness of our moral failings. Due to our limitations, we can never achieve the good that we often desire. We must learn patience, humility and realism in setting objectives. Refusal to do this rejects our bodily nature. Further, in our freedom we have all refused to participate as we should in giving and receiving love; the image of God in us all thereby is lessened and distorted.

Since we are all prone to our weaknesses and moral inconsistencies, managers should offer employees compassionate oversight, second chances, extra training or even reassignment.

> Question(s) to consider: When you make a mistake at work, do you try to cover it up, or do you own up to it?

6. Equal. Human equality here means that all of us are called to know and to love God; all have certain rights and duties with respect to others; and all should have equal opportunity. Such basic equality is the basis to provide all persons (especially the disadvantaged) with the necessary material and nonmaterial support to achieve the ends of human life. A consequence of this is that we must not discriminate based on non-performance.

Back to Johnson & Johnson

It seems that Johnson & Johnson understood its social responsibility to protect persons, whose unique value is inestimable. Human beings were put before things (money in this case). This action was consistent with the protection of human dignity, and, therefore, the recall was a proper exercise of managerial freedom. Given that human beings are morally inconsistent and shortsighted creatures, there could've been the temptation to do otherwise.

Economic Personalism also includes the wisdom shown in the prior methods. Universal obligation (Kant and Rawls) must be respected because of our equal human dignity, and we must consider carefully the ultimate impact (Utilitarianism) on actual human beings when reaching a judgment. However, Economic Personalism far surpasses utilitarianism in defining what we mean by human beings and their innate dignity.

Recognizing its social obligation, Johnson & Johnson acted to protect people on the material level. Because they, too, were fragile and morally inconsistent, the Johnson & Johnson executives could have chosen otherwise. Spiritually, they maintained our trust. They recognized basic equality by not putting their own good above others. Summing up, they chose the action that most led to the protection and promotion of human dignity.

> Question(s) to consider: When you purchase a product or service, do you consider how ethical the company is? For example, how do they handle layoffs? How truthful is their advertising? Where are their foreign investments? Are they socially responsible by considering the environmental impact of what they do, by hiring the less fortunate, including ex-inmates, and by having a positive impact on their local community?

Given our nature as morally inconsistent and shortsighted creatures, Johnson & Johnson could have been tempted to do otherwise. It is a relief to ethicists and moralists—and a source of deep satisfaction— that Johnson & Johnson fared so well in the long run in the wake of its highly ethical actions. We see that ethical behavior can be consistent with surviving and making money.

The dilemma of our age is the combination of unprecedented material progress and systematic spiritual decline. The decline in public and private morality can be witnessed in the marketplace as well as the forums of international diplomacy. In the past, a man's honor and reputation were his most valuable assets. Business agreements were made with a handshake. Today one might be well advised to check the "bottom line" and read the "small print."

King Hussein (1935–1999), Commencement Forum speech, graduation of his son Prince Feisal, Brown University, May 1985

Group Discussion Questions

- Is the maxim "Let your conscience be your guide" sufficient to provide ethical direction in today's complex world?
- What makes Johnson & Johnson a model for corporate ethical behavior?
- Optional Question: compare and contrast the ethical theories of Kant, Rawls, and Mill.
- What is economic Personalism? Can you add ideas to the table on "Protecting Human Dignity in the Workplace?
- What course of ethical direction does Personalism recommend for Johnson & Johnson?

Chapter 45

• • • • • • • •

Smart Moves for Global Executives in a Multicultural Workplace

by Mary Anne Walsh, Ed.D. , Certified Five
O'Clock Club Coach

If you speak to a man in a language he
understands, you speak to his head.
If you speak to a man in his own
language, you speak to his heart.

Nelson Mandela

Case Study: Mr. Goto Working in a Foreign Land

Now more than a decade into the new millennium, we can see that management styles have been evolving in response to the global context in which most businesses now function. Did we have to worry, even a few years ago, about how to work well with Chinese or Indian counterparts?

Without a lot of preparation for dealing with cultural differences, there can be bad bottom-line consequences. I was once hired to help a company get out of a mess created by lack of cross-cultural awareness. Mr. Goto had been sent to the U.S. from the Japanese division of an American company in Tokyo. He was identified as a high potential. His assignment was

described as developmental, and he was assigned to a team comprised of ten individuals representing many different cultures. This team had been formed to complete a specific project within two years. An American headed the team and was responsible for teaching Mr. Goto, according to objectives jointly developed by the Japanese sending division and the American receiving division. While his assignment was seen as developmental, he did have expertise critical to the success of the project.

After a very short time on the job, his frustrated manager said that Mr. Goto was not working out. His performance was poor and he could not keep up with assignments. She blamed him for some of the problems arising on the team—and even in the division—and claimed that she had done all the right things in terms of being cross-culturally sensitive. She proudly told me that she left him alone, had given him no direct feedback, fearing loss of face for him. When things got really bad she assigned another staff member to help him. I was brought in by a senior manager who asked me to fix the problem. No one wanted Mr. Goto to fail. He had to succeed, as did all members of the team.

When I spoke to Mr. Goto, he said that he was experiencing stress, adjustment difficulties and general dissatisfaction with the content and purpose of his development program. He had a hard time adjusting to the female manager and missed not going out after work with his colleagues. Although there had been specific goals acknowledged by both the sending and receiving divisions, there was a lack of common understanding. The objectives for Mr. Goto, put forward by the Japanese sending division, were clear:

- Learn how things are done in the U.S.
- Improve his ability to communicate in English.
- Contribute his expertise to the project.
- Develop a leadership presence.

While these objectives were readily accepted by the receiving division, the problem was that the American side interpreted the objectives differently. Also, for Mr. Goto, the reality of working in this country did not match his expectations. He had expected to learn by watching, listening and talking to colleagues, especially his U.S. manager. He thought he would have a very supportive relationship with his boss. He expected to be guided, and told exactly the nature of his tasks, as well as the process for completing them. In the role of a subordinate he did not view himself as a self-reliant doer. The U.S. manager, however, considered him an equal: She expected him to take an active, hands-on role, with specific learning objectives. She piled on the assignments since he was the "expert" on the project.

Keeping in mind that perspective drives behavior, it is easy to see how their cultural orientations contributed to the negative experience that unfolded. Both the manager and Mr. Goto had rigid stereotypical perspectives. They were locked into inaccurate and limiting assumptions, as well as judgmental reactions to each other. If the manager had spent time building a relationship with all team members initially—especially regarding the various cultural perspectives and

hot buttons—perhaps she would have been able to read Mr. Goto more accurately. Helping team members understand why people do things is a big step in avoiding misunderstandings.

Here are some of the questions that the manager could have explored to put matters on a more solid footing:

1. What do you need from others on the team? What are you willing to give?
2. What are the tasks that need to be accomplished, and how will the various relationships on the team impact our ability to get there?
3. What are the most desirable behaviors that will move the project forward?
4. What behavior would be intolerable?
5. What is the new culture we are creating together?

I think that this case illustrates that there are layers of complexity in cross-cultural management that are a challenge to understand and thus may inhibit proper and timely execution.

Then and Now

Change has been so rapid that it might be helpful to speak about how a Twentieth Century Manager (prior to 2000) contrasts with a Millennium Manager (post-2000).

- A Twentieth Century Manager who was transplanted outside his or her home country, or given responsibility for staff transferred into the corporate home country, took note of the principle cultural differences in the work environment and tried to manage in light of them. These cultural differences could be compensated for with a management style that could adapt to the task at hand and effectively pursue the business plan of the organization. Goals could be defined in terms of productivity, market share or bottom line, as appropriate.
- A Millennium Manager in the same

position now faces a task that is difficult to define and to execute. A Millennium Manager is challenged to go beyond managing cultural gaps (*i.e.,* understanding how people are different) but must help the organization **itself** to adapt and evolve in response to cross-cultural realities. Organizations themselves must change.

Managers prior to 2000 aimed for adaptation, with little or no thought to assimilation: adaptation to the overall corporate culture, to organizational policies and processes and to strategic goals. Effective management now, in a cross-cultural environment, means facilitating the integration of multiple cultural inputs. Embracing integration requires several competencies, and the move toward a new paradigm of global leadership. "Leaders" include all employees who work in a context of multicultural complexity to achieve business results where everyone is expected to use global leadership skills as they interface with customers and coworkers across the hall or the world.

Appropriate questions for such leaders to ask include:

1. How is my current style of doing business serving me?
2. What style of leadership should I embrace as a leader playing on a global stage?
3. What complementary skills should I cultivate?

Culture is context and perceptions drive behavior. The people working in organizations come from many different backgrounds, are located often in several time zones and have very different ideas about what they expect from leaders. Effective communication and sensitivity to a kaleidoscope of cultures are, therefore, critical to create clarity, direction and effective implementation of work in these complex environments. At the same time, global managers need to lead, inspire and innovate across many barriers of language, culture and technology.

Informed by my senior clients who have made this developmental shift, I offer five *Smart Moves* that have worked for them.

1. Accelerate Out of Your Comfort Zone

By definition, living in a time of change means that all managers are required by circumstance to grapple with new ideas, concepts and relationships. In a time of rapid change, experience is valuable, but precedents may be of limited value. Favorable outcomes will emerge from fresh thinking. It will be up to managers to discount history to create actions that will serve as precedents for the future.

For most managers the need to set new precedents can be a daunting task, since we all are prone to operate largely on the basis of our past experiences, which define our personal comfort zones. Managers in a multi-cultural environment need to step out of these comfort zones, and do so quickly in order to keep pace with global economic change. Appropriate questions include:

1. Am I leading from a too comfortable rut?
2. What new risks do I need to take?
3. How can I challenge myself and others?

2. Become an Adaptive Leader

Managers who operated in a multi-cultural environment prior to 2000, were guided by the standard models of multi-cultural conduct. Managers now must be guided by complex interconnections. The management function itself has to change, which means looking beyond the conventional rulebooks. This is not a matter of wholesale disregard for the rules that have provided a sense of order and process. But now managers must seek a multiplicity of options that will come from diverse perspectives. This is the essence of transitioning from directing and managing change to facilitating the integration of multiple cultural inputs, referred to above. The new-style managers will share leadership with their constituents and assimilate the input received to operate at optimum levels.

The successful manager now will not simply lead with authority, but rather will exercise authority tempered by empathy. An authoritarian approach does not commonly allow for the assimilation of other perspectives or ideas. Seeing the world through the eyes of others can moderate the exercise of authority and help to create a shared sense of purpose within the open architecture of the group. A millennium manager asks:

1. What makes an adaptive leader?
2. What do I need to do differently?
3. How do I know if I am adaptive enough?

3. Develop Multicultural Effectiveness

Today management itself is multicultural in dynamic, complex organizations where the **corporate culture is the context**. Whenever a merger, acquisition or joint-venture is formed, two or more distinct organizational cultures must be blended. This happens with optimum results when both (or all) organizations seek a cultural synergy, as opposed to one company asserting its culture upon others. This requires finesse in the practice of multicultural management.

Especially within a global corporation, one will find cultural diversity in the various departments, divisions and subsidiaries around the world. As a matter of fact, every time a project team is formed, good multicultural management is usually required. When layers of nationalities are added, the leader faces additional challenges because of the various cultures represented. The manager can learn about them from ongoing interactions and gradually reshape his or her thinking. A culturally synergistic mindset, which focuses on how to recognize the value of working together, is vital. The millennial manager welcomes many kinds of differences,

e.g., nationality, gender, ethnicity, age and other sources of social identity.

Multiculturalism and cultural competency are now buzzwords in the business world. Being a true multicultural leader goes beyond being multilingual and successfully completing an assignment or two in a foreign country.

- The first step is to be aware of, and knowledgeable about, your own cultural preferences. Can you articulate your cultural values, beliefs and attitudes and how they are reflected in your behavior? Are you also aware of the cultural preferences of your counterparts and how they are expressed in their behavior? Are you thinking about the third culture of synergy that you can create together?

- The second step is to examine where you are in the process of learning to communicate with and understand people of other cultures or people who are different from you. Most often, the natural reaction to human differences begins with ethnocentrism: you are hostile to differences and want things done your way only.

  As you grow in your level of acceptance of other cultures, you will go through progressive stages:

  ✓ Awareness: "Not everyone does things my way."

  ✓ Understanding: "This is what others do when they do things their way."

  ✓ Acceptance: "It is OK for others to do things their way, but I'll continue to do things my way."

  ✓ Appreciation: "There are some good things about how others do things."

  ✓ Selective adoption: "I'll try doing a few things the way others do them."

This is only a beginning of being multi-culturally effective. While this process might seem relatively simple at first glance, diagnosing one's own position in the journey and moving oneself forward from the us-vs.-them mentality can be challenging—but it doesn't have to be.

By cultivating a multicultural leadership style not only will your company's work environment be better and more enjoyable, but you also will be able to better understand and harness the added value of your multicultural customers and colleagues at home and abroad. The most successful businesses will be those that incorporate the influences, practices, and values of diverse cultures in a respectful and productive manner.

Multicultural leadership encourages an inclusive and adaptable style that brings out the best in a diverse workforce and fashions a sense of a creative collaborative community with people from many parts of the globe. It enables a wide spectrum of people to actively engage, contribute, and reach their potential.

4. Master Dancing with Opposites

Leaders are being asked to navigate rough seas now more than ever, as conflicting styles of leadership are encountered more and more frequently. It's possible to run into ways of doing business that may seem alien and shocking. For example, a client who works primarily in China noted that being successful in China requires skills that not only go beyond those honed working in the U.S., but may even conflict with standard best practices, and it has been an unnerving experience. Global leaders find it hard to deal with the differing and conflicting styles on a consistent basis.

For example, there may be strong pressure to deliver on speed and quality. Both of these are good, but these expectations are often in conflict with each other. How to balance the two may be viewed very differently from one culture to the next.

Another example is managing the tension between the creation of a global culture and yielding to the need for local autonomy. There are usually no easy or right answers. But it is vital to analyze the differences thoroughly and

honestly and become comfortable dancing with opposites. In navigating such rough seas, these are important questions to keep in mind:

1. How am I balancing tough alternatives and being empathetic?
2. What marks would I give myself managing change and coping with transition?
3. How am I balancing being self-reliant and trusting others?

5. Drop the Heroic-Leader Mentality

The traditional view of a strong and effective leader is one who has an assertive personality and who either has a vision of his/her own, or can adopt the vision of another and implement it within an organization. "Leading from the front" and "chain of command" are traditional concepts that have worked well. While they remain valid in some organizations, they no longer remain viable for others. Modern technology, information flow and changing sources of innovation now make a collaborative and fully networked structure the optimal model for many organizations. These have been called "new millennial organizations." In these contexts, leadership needs to be more adaptive and more distributed.

Historical pyramidal organizations operate using vertical access of command and control, with information flowing in parallel, vertical channels. Orders flow down while feedback flows up, filtered or acted upon at each stage in its ascent to senior management. These structures work well, for example, in public utility companies, heavy manufacturing, big retail stores and the military.

In other organizations, however, the pyramid is being supplanted by matrix structures in which command and control are determined by network strength and synergy among departments and divisions. It is difficult to imagine a military operation being directed by anything other than a pyramidal structure. But new millennium companies such as Google, Facebook and others would not have been as productive without collaboration fostered by a matrix structure that ignores traditional hierarchy. The iPhone could not have been designed and produced by the same corporate structure and strategy that designs and produces washing machines. The Boeing 787 Dreamliner would not have been possible without the creation of the first major, distributed design and production network.

Post-2000 managers recognize that contributions of employees are enhanced when they are a part of an assimilative network structure and function in collaboration with their colleagues. These managers foster this collaborative effort with influence, rather than the simple assertion of authority. They share their authority with the members of the group to create an aggregate authority that directs their actions. This is not a trivial development. The work environment needs to be collaborative, but it cannot be unstructured nor undirected. The networking teams within a matrix structure need to be managed to achieve and maintain a close alignment with related teams, within the strategy of the organization.

Thus leaders in new millennial organizations need to encourage and harness the energies of the diverse people they manage, and it must not look like an attempt to herd cats, as the saying goes. The appropriate questions to ask include:

1. Have I taken time to get employees aligned around our organization's vision, values and priorities?
2. Do I empower my leaders to take risks, with failure acknowledged as a possible but acceptable outcome?

3. Do I encourage and support team members to move both horizontally across roles and vertically to connect with the next levels of leadership?

Living and working in a time of extreme uncertainly has implications for leaders immersed in the day-to-day operations of their organizations. My clients who have been able to navigate these waters understand the changes taking place all around them and the demands for remaining competitive. They have been able to develop their capabilities in three dimensions:

- Asking good questions of the world around them, and coming up with answers that lead to the realignment of the organization.
- Leading by using a blend of smarts and emotional and cultural intelligence, changing not only themselves, but also their organizations.
- They look for win-win situations internally and with their external network of stakeholders.

While there is no universal checklist of smart moves for leaders, by focusing on the strategies described here, you will be better equipped to thrive in today's turbulent and unpredictable business environment.

The real voyage of discovering consists not in seeing new lands but in seeing with new eyes.

Marcel Proust, French author

You must be the change you wish to see in the world.

Gandhi

Part Six:

Moving On

Chapter 46

• • • • • • • • •

Career Danger Signals
What to Look for

by Hélène Seiler and Bill Belknap,
Certified Five O'Clock Club Coaches

*Planning is bringing the future into the present
so that you can do something about it now.*

Alan Lakein, Time-Management Expert

Overview

Your career traffic signals…are they green, yellow or red?

What to do when your career light changes color.

When you drive your car and approach a traffic light it tells you how to proceed to the intersection. Wouldn't it be nice if there were a "career traffic light?" Good news, we think there is, but unfortunately, as we have found, most successful managers are paying so much attention to the tasks at hand that they often end up "running their career traffic lights."

- How clearly are you seeing your career danger signals?
- Did you ever get blindsided when your boss said, "We need to make a change"?

Here is a quick guide to reading your personal career traffic light and what to do when you see it change color.

You will know your career is in the Green Light mode if:

- Your career is on track. This means you have written career objectives, including a time line. By the way, studies have shown that people with written career objectives make considerably more income than those who just keep their career objectives in their head.
- You have a good reading on your next one or two moves.
- You have recently been told by your boss or the board, hopefully in writing, that you are exceeding their objectives.
- You enjoy your job.
- Your boss has delegated to you things he or she would normally do.
- You are being considered for a significant promotion.
- You are in good health and are satisfied with your work-life balance.

However, green lights don't stay green for-ever. We encourage you to maintain and develop your internal and external networks, volunteer for the cross-functional task forces and accept those speaking engagements. Do not drop your guard when you are in the Green Light mode and remember, "The best defense is a good offense."

Yellow Light Mode

You know that driving through a yellow light can get you into trouble, but how about at work or at home? Below are situations where you should be prepared to brake. We will also give you some tips on what to do when you see a Yellow Light in the distance.

In our experience two or more of the following mean that you are looking at a Yellow Light for your career:

At Work

- You are not clear about your next move. Here we don't mean the exact title but directionally, such as operations, marketing or finance.
- No one has discussed a long-term career plan with you.
- You haven't had a career discussion with your boss or your boss' boss in the last 12 months.
- You aren't sure whether you fit in with the culture of the company.
- The company is highly leveraged or has cash flow issues, or both!
- The company or division is not perform-ing in the top quartile of its industry or market.
- A merger, takeover, management buyout or sale of your company is materializing. It doesn't matter what side of the deal you are on.
- A re-organization is underway.
- You have a new boss, even if you know her.
- There is a change in the relationship

with your boss. For example, your review just dropped a rating in one category or several categories.
- You have lost key people on your team or new team members have been added without your approval.
- A major new account, client or project has been added to your responsibilities.
- Your mentor or a strong supporter leaves.
- You are assigned to a new position, es-pecially if it requires changes in geogra-phy, function, industry, size of business, nature of your team, or amount of travel required.
- You are no longer invited to some key meetings.
- There are persistent rumors about your department.
- There are key people in the organization who make no secret that they disagree with your direction and style.
- Friends or co-workers are frequently asking, "Is there anything wrong?" "Are you okay?"

At Home

There has been a change in:

- Your mental or physical health.
- Your residence; this can be very decep-tive because on the surface it may appear positive but any relocation is high on the stress scale.
- Your commute.
- Your intimate relationship, such as mar-riage, divorce, or a new relationship.
- Your family life; birth of a child, elder-care, death of a family member or friend.
- Your financial obligations; unexpected expenses, remodeling the house, college expenses.

Okay, so you have a couple of these situ-ations going on in your life. What should you consider doing besides slamming on the brakes?

- First, take your foot off the gas for a second.
- Don't make any quick decisions.
- Talk with people in the company you respect. Ask them how they perceive your potential. Listen to what they think.
- Have a serious career discussion with your boss and his or her boss.
- Get to know more decision-makers and influencers inside the company, especially those outside of your functional or operational area.
- Step back and assess exactly what's going on. Is this event having an impact on your work, your attitude or your motivation?
- Reach out to your boss, mentors, peers and friends. Ask for feedback if you aren't sure how you are coming across.
- Start listing the resources you may need to address the challenges; include both office resources and family resources.
- Begin strengthening your network.
- Stay visible, speak at conferences and industry organizations.
- Help mentor others.
- Consider seeking professional help: an executive coach, a spiritual leader, a psychologist or family counselor.
- If you decide the changes and challenges will lead to a no-win situation, then you may decide it is time to leave the company and begin an aggressive search.
- Make an effort to build bridges to your key detractors. This takes guts but can pay big dividends. The important thing is to understand how much is a perception problem and how much is a strategic or operational difference of opinion.
- Stay current on global trends in your industry and be aware of your market value. The latter can do wonders for your confidence.
- Work harder to have a more balanced life.
- Protect your health with exercise, proper diet, relaxation and fun! While this is last on our list we think it is the most important.

Case Study: Josh How He Dealt with His Yellow Lights

Two years ago, we received a call from Josh, a successful general manager of a $1 billion U.S. subsidiary of a European financial services company. Josh had been with the company for four years and he called because he wanted to know what his market value was and he wanted us to provide him with some benchmark data. We first asked why? He said he thought he was underpaid and wanted to look for a similar job but in another company. We agreed to meet with him and sensed that there was something more going on than just a comp issue.

Josh told us that he was working too hard. On paper he was successful, delivering above expectations, but Josh did not have time for anything but work. In his late forties, he was single but was anxious to start a family. He also had been very athletic but could not find the time to exercise. He said his relationship with his European boss was courteous, but distant. He was uncomfortable bringing up the topic of compensation. He had no mentors or sponsors in the company. In addition, he was not getting along very well with three of his direct reports who were having performance problems and, in fact, he had lost his temper with them several times. He also admitted that he had a fairly negative attitude.

Obviously Josh was facing a bunch of Yellow Lights! No wonder he wanted to leave.

So what did we recommend? First, we discouraged him from leaving prematurely. Then, we encouraged him to work on the relationship challenges with his boss and subordinates. We told him a new company would not be tolerant about his temper and, in fact, would fire him quickly if he had serious relationship issues with new subordinates. Josh agreed and began to prepare a proactive, positive strategy.

He immediately sat down with his direct reports and began to positively coach two of them. The third was not a fit for his area and was transferred.

We also urged him to plan more frequent trips to the European headquarters and other subsidiaries to strengthen his relationships with his boss and other key operating people. This turned out to be a gold mine. He re-connected with a former boss and asked him if he would consider becoming a mentor and, to his pleasant surprise, got agreement.

The ending: After six months Josh went back to his boss and put his hat in the ring for a General Manager spot in a much larger business unit. Yes, he got the job and has now been there for over a year.

The story has a wonderful ending but we must put in a quick disclaimer. The ending is a result of Josh's executing his plan effectively not because we coaches had the answers. We provided some candid feedback and lots of encouragement, but Josh did the heavy lifting.

Another important lesson we can learn from Josh is to first look inside your own company!

Experienced marketers are always telling us that increasing the loyalty of existing customers is much more efficient and cost effective than acquiring new ones. The same goes for a job search. We strongly recommend looking first in your own backyard. Explore all of the areas in the company. The grass may appear greener on the outside, but it seldom is. It is also a thousand times easier to network effectively and schedule meaningful meetings inside your company than to make those dreaded cold calls to people you don't know.

Red Light Mode

Red Lights are the easiest to see. We all know we need to stop immediately. A Career Red Light also calls for immediate action.

Let's look at a few of the most common Red Lights and what to do about them.

At Work

- You are fired from your current position.
- Your boss suddenly resigns.
- Your division or company has a series of bad quarters.
- Your position is eliminated and there are no alternative positions.
- Your company has been acquired and they already have "one of you"!
- You have just received an "average" performance review or worse.

At Home

- You are unable to continue your job because of an illness.
- You have to resign from your job because of a life-changing situation.

Here are a few ideas from a number of Five O'Clock Club clients who found themselves faced with one of the Red Light situations. You will notice the key pattern, in all three cases, is how proactive and immediate their actions were.

- Mary, an experienced Marketing Director, just learned that her company was being acquired by another company which had a major marketing department with an experienced, highly competent Marketing Director. She immediately pulled her family together and described in detail what was going on at work. She asked for their input and shared her "draft" strategy. There was a lot of give and take, but everyone agreed she should immediately begin reaching out to her network and pursue outside opportunities. She also sat down with an old boss and mentor to get his advice.
  1. Immediately pulling your family together may sound like a no brainer but we often have to take our clients kicking and screaming into this step. Yet when you think about it, it is the quickest way to get the family behind you rather than have them wondering why you are

so edgy or why you now get home at 5 P.M.!

- Corey was Director of an equity trading desk at a major bank. The day his boss told him his position had been eliminated, he went back to his office and did three things:
  1. He called home to share the news and put the home renovation project on hold.
  2. He called his major clients to tell them his company had decided to eliminate the trading desk and he would be leaving. The good news was, most of his major clients asked him to be sure and tell them where he was going because they wanted him to continue to manage their accounts.
  3. He reached out to all the Directors and VPs he knew at his current competitors and told them the following: the trading desk has been eliminated and he would like to explore whether there were any similar opportunities with them. And, of course, he mentioned what his major clients had told him.

- Jane, the VP of Finance in a large manufacturing company, had just gotten great news: she was having triplets! Unfortunately, there were some medical complications that required considerable bed rest early in the pregnancy so she couldn't maintain the pace of her demanding job.
  1. Within 24 hours of learning about her pregnancy complications, she sat down and outlined a proposed transition plan to review with her boss and the SVP of HR. Fortunately, she had been developing one of her direct reports, Jeff, who was now considered promotable. Her boss and the SVP of HR agreed with her plan to begin transferring duties to Jeff. They also agreed with her suggestions about her career path once she returned.

Summary

If you are in a Green Light situation:

- Leverage your current position and strengthen it.
- Be visible and build your internal networks.
- Continue to hone your leadership skills.
- Get on high visibility task forces.
- Keep job, family and your health in balance.
- Constantly scan for Yellow and Red Lights.

If you are in a Yellow Light situation:

- Don't think that changing companies will solve your problems.
- History shows most of our problems are ours.
- If you own your problems, history also shows the chances of your fixing them are excellent.

If the light turns Red:

- Be strategic as well as tactical.
- Start immediately.
- Procrastination is guaranteed to bring unhappiness.
- Networking is the key.
- Reach out quickly, build an advisory board, consider a coach and make your

family part of your support system.

Chapter 47

• • • • • • • •

Eight Signs That Say It's Time to Change Jobs

by Kate Wendleton, President, The Five O'Clock Club

All that is gold does not glitter,
Not all those who wander are lost;
The old that is strong does not wither,
Deep roots are not reached by the frost.

From the ashes a fire shall be woken,
A light from the shadows shall spring;
Renewed shall be blade that was broken,
The crownless again shall be king.

J.R.R. Tolkien, *The Fellowship of the Ring*

Most people don't lose their jobs over-night—except for those who have been caught stealing, giving away company secrets or in a compromising position with a subordinate. Even if your company's been bought, sold or reorga-nized, a layoff is not immediately in the cards for everyone. It takes time for top executives to determine how they want to handle downsizing and redeployment. But, if your company is in the news for a period of time, it's likely there are problems that can't be resolved. The longer you stay on a sinking ship, the harder it is to get onto solid land. Prospective employers may look less

favorably on anyone who wasn't smart enough to get out when the getting was good.

But from where *you* sit—without even looking at the bigger corporate picture—there may be signs that another pasture *somewhere else* has to be greener. If you've noticed three or more of these warning signs, it's time to update your résumé and begin mounting a job-search campaign.

1. **You don't fit in.** Your values don't match. The people you work with are uncouth, dishonest, focused on getting ahead regardless of legal or moral barriers. They win by cheating. You are refined, ethical and would never knowingly break the law or hurt another's livelihood.

2. **Your boss doesn't like you, and you don't like him/her.** You don't like your boss' character or style. He/she never solicits your opinion, or invites you into his/her office to chat or out to lunch. You don't support his agenda or initiatives. And if you've ever done something to undermine your boss, you might as well get out now.

"This is Dr. Fredericks, the company's psychiatrist. He's here to determine whether or not your disgruntled."

3. **Your peers don't like you.** You think they are beneath you. You're never included in any of the social outings they plan and you probably wouldn't want to go if invited. You feel isolated, gossiped about, excluded from the inner workings of the organization. For the most part, you don't get along with people at the company. You don't feel like a team player and have no sense of camaraderie at work.

4. **You don't get assignments that demonstrate the full range of your abilities.** All the good assignments go to others, or you get the ones that play to your weaknesses. You feel that the boss doesn't trust your judgment or believe you care enough to do a good job.

5. **You always get called upon to do the "grunt work,"** the tasks nobody else wants to do. If the boss always asks you to do things you feel are beneath you, learn to lobby for better projects and cherry pick the ones that will showcase your skills and heighten your visibility.

6. **You are excluded from meetings your peers are invited to.** You don't feel that your ideas are valued or that your contributions are central to the company.

7. **Everyone at your level has an office; you have a cubicle in the hallway.** This is a blatant sign that you are not thought of as highly as others. It also telegraphs your status in the informal company hierarchy loudly and clearly, despite your title.

8. **You dread going to work and feel like you're developing an ulcer.** The idea of going to work makes you anxious or physically sick. You can't sleep on Sunday nights and you've used up all your sick days. You have a hard time concentrating and count the hours from the time you arrive at the office until the second you leave.

Chapter 48

• • • • • • • •

Time for a Change: Why Not Consider a Nontraditional Career?

by Joan Runnheim Olson, Certified Five O'Clock Club Coach

Two roads diverged in a wood, and I—
I took the one less traveled by,
And that has made all the difference.

Robert Frost (1874–1963), American
poet, *The Road Not Taken*

Have you been blocked in your attempts to move up the career ladder? Or perhaps as a child you dreamt of a career that involved climbing a real ladder. Maybe you're reached the top, but haven't found it as fulfilling as you thought it would be. Or are you in a career that was someone else's dream, not yours? If any of these sound familiar, you may want to consider a nontraditional career.

According to the U.S. Department of Labor, **nontraditional careers are those in which more than 75% of the workers are of the opposite gender.** For women, these careers include everything from aeronautic engineer to wood machinist. For men, they include everything from administrative assistant to nurse.

The Push for Nontraditional Careers

Over the past 10+ years, there have been government initiatives to help encourage men and women to consider nontraditional careers. Initially, the emphasis was on helping more women break into nontraditional careers to level the *paying* field. The Women in Apprenticeship and Nontraditional Occupations Act of 1992 (WANTO) authorized a grant program to award over $8.6 million to 37 community-based organizations. The money provided technical assistance to employers and labor unions to enable them to recruit, hire, and retain women in apprenticeships and nontraditional occupations.

The Carl D. Perkins Act of 1998 provides funds to secondary and postsecondary educational institutions to support collaborative projects to recruit more students, both female and male, to enter nontraditional careers.

Why Nontraditional?

Men and women both want careers they enjoy. In addition, more women pursue jobs traditionally held by men because of the higher wages. For example, women now make up almost half of those in law-school (2010), and almost half of those attending medical school. Many men find more fulfilling careers in the helping fields, which have traditionally attracted women. And with the large number of baby boomers reaching retirement age, as the health-care industry expands to meet their needs, there will be increased opportunities for those wanting to work in healthcare—no matter what their gender. In fact, 13% of those enrolled in college to become an RN are male.

Under-representation

While we may assume that women have shattered some barriers, the fact remains that women still tend to be concentrated in traditionally female occupations. In 2010, women represented 91.1% of all registered nurses and 81.8% of elementary-middle-school teachers. Women make up a small percentage of workers in many male-dominated fields. In 2006, for example, only 7.7% of electrical engineers were women, according to the Bureau of Labor Statistics. In 2010, 5% of airline pilots were women and 2% of aircraft mechanics were women.

The Case for Nontraditional Careers: Pay Differentials and Labor Shortage

According to the organization Chicago Women in Trades, the primary cause of the wage-gap between men and women is occupational segregation, the clustering of women in occupations that pay less. This segregation contributes to the lower earning power of females.

Many nontraditional jobs for women pay 20 to 30% more than traditional jobs and have better career advancement opportunities. An administrative assistant, considered a traditional job for women, has an annual median wage of about $40,000. Compare that to an experi-enced architect, considered nontraditional for women, with an annual median wage of just over $70,000.

The large number of baby boomers reaching retirement age (even if many of them opt for semi-retirement) will continue to create a demand for workers. This will probably mean that the line between traditional and nontraditional will continue to blur or might even eventually be erased. According to the Bureau of Labor Statistics, the demand for computer software engineers is expected to increase 21% between 2008-2018. For architects, there is a 16% projected increase. Women can help fill these anticipated openings.

On the other hand, the need for dental hygienists is expected to increase 36% through 2018, while the demand for registered nurses will see a 22% jump. Men can help fill those openings.

Challenges of Nontraditional Work

Men and women both face isolation and discrimination when entering an industry dominated by the other gender. Women are also more likely to report sexual harassment. During 2011, the Equal Employment Opportunity Commission received 11,364 complaints of sexual harassment, of which 83.7% were filed by women. Being aware of—and being prepared to handle—these types of situations can be the determining factor in a woman's success.

Men in nontraditional careers can also face sex discrimination, making it difficult to land a job in the first place. One young man I know graduated at the top of his class at nursing school, and interviewed for a job at a local hospital. But he was passed over in favor of two female candidates. Of course, many factors can influence hiring decisions, but stereotypes of what's considered women's work and men's work are still entrenched in our society.

The Seven Stories Exercise: A Tool for Deciding

Should you be thinking of a nontraditional career? The simple answer is that you've got a lot of homework to do before making any decisions! So many people are in the wrong careers because they don't make the effort to identify what they're good at and what they enjoy doing. Only assessment and research can help you decide if a nontraditional career *is* right for you. Maybe you feel stuck in your career—that might be because you don't utilize your motivated skills. The Seven Stories Exercise (at the back of this book) can help you identify those motivated skills, i.e., those you enjoy and do well.

This Seven Stories Exercise does require much thought. The first step is to list 25 of your life accomplishments. These can include accomplishments from your childhood along with work-related achievements. For example, perhaps as a kid you earned a Girl Scout or Boy Scout badge. Or maybe you landed a five million dollar contract just this week. But the accomplishment doesn't need to be spectacular or extravagant. However, include only those accomplishments that *you did well and enjoyed doing.* Of the 25 on your list, select the seven that mean the most to you, and rank them according to the satisfaction they provided. On a separate page for each of the seven, write down everything that went into that accomplishment: list the skills and talents required and the types of people you worked with. Look for common themes and denominators. Formal worksheets for analyzing these accomplishments can be found in the back of this book

Another helpful exercise, Your Special Interests, requires listing all the things that you really like to do. List anything that makes you feel good and gives you satisfaction. Think back over typical weeks or years, the places you've been, the people you've worked or played with, courses you've taken, etc. Think of how you spend your free time. Your interests may be a clue as to what you would like in a job, which may include nontraditional possibilities.

The Rewards

After all this careful self-study and reflection, brainstorm possible job targets, with the help of family, friends or a career coach. It's important to consider all of your career options, which may include a look at nontraditional work. The rewards can be great: higher wages, good benefits, advancement opportunities and work you will enjoy.

Chapter 49

Things People Do to Get Fired and How to Avoid These Pitfalls

by Richard Bayer, Ph.D., Chief Operating Officer, The Five O'Clock Club

What man actually needs is not a tensionless state but rather the striving and struggling for some goal worthy of him. What he needs is not the discharge of tension at any cost, but the call of a potential meaning waiting to be fulfilled by him.

Viktor Frankl, *Man's Search for Meaning*

In difficult economic times, job hunters face greater competition for the jobs that are available. Everyone has to work harder and be sharper. Just as your employer cannot be sloppy when competing in world markets, you have to be more serious about the way you conduct yourself at work with colleagues and supervisors and maintain a business-like demeanor at company outings and off-sites.

Actually, job security is an oxymoron. Companies cannot afford to retain employees who are merely competent: They expect people to go above and beyond the responsibilities they were hired to perform and seek out assignments that signal an interest and willingness to move up the ladder. What's more, any mistakes people make

in judgment or comportment are less likely to go unnoticed. In fact, certain gaffes can stall or derail a career.

Here is a list of mistakes people make at work that put them at risk of losing their jobs or being overlooked for a promotion or raise. If you are guilty of any of these snafus, now is the time to stop.

Be Careful How You Use Your Computer

Your computer is company property and the company may be privy to any message in your email box or on your web browser. People often send jokes or inappropriate messages to coworkers. Sometimes these emails end up in the wrong inbox and can cause embarrassment or hurt feelings. If these include racial or sexual slurs, they can be cause for legal action or dismissal. Be careful with your web browser. Some people have been caught shopping too much or browsing pornography sites on company time.

Don't Misbehave at Company Parties

Some people think company parties are merely opportunities to have fun and relax. Wrong. A company party is a business event and it's very likely your behavior is being monitored by everyone—from the company intern to your boss and his or her boss. Watch your body language and don't stand too close or whisper to co-workers or subordinates of the opposite sex. Drinking to excess is inexcusable and will only get you in trouble. Bad reputations are often the result of inappropriate behavior at company parties.

Don't Disagree with your Boss in Public

Don't use meetings or public forums to disagree with your boss. If you have a different approach to a problem, don't question his or her strategy or point of view in front of a group. It won't make you look good and it might make the boss' supervisors question his leadership skills. If you want to present your views to your boss, ask to speak with him privately. If you find that you frequently disagree with your boss, you're probably not in the right position and career advancement is going to be difficult. Your boss will eventually say, "I don't need this person around." It's probably a good idea to start looking for a new position, either inside or outside the company.

Respect Your Company's Culture

In every business there's a corporate culture or value system you need to embrace to fit in and get ahead. If you come in at 8 a.m. and leave exactly at 5 p.m. and everyone else starts later and stays later, adjust your schedule. If you eat at your desk and everyone else puts lunch on a company expense account, do the same as the others. Fit in or you'll be viewed as the odd duck.

Don't Speak to the Press Unless You're a Spokesperson.

Typically, one person or department is charged with the task of speaking to the press and has specific messages prepared to address issues or defuse difficult situations. Even if you say something positive, it might not be the same message the company spokesperson is trying to communicate. So, don't speak to the press unless you're authorized to do so.

Chapter 50

• • • • • • • • •

Why Executives Derail

by Jim Hinthorn, Certified Five O'Clock Club Coach

I've missed over 9,000 shots in my career. I've lost almost 300 games. Twenty-six times I've been trusted to take the game-winning shot . . . and missed. I've failed over and over and over again in my life. And that is why I succeed.

> Michael J. Jordan, former professional NBA basketball player, entrepreneur, and majority owner in the NBA's Charlotte Bobcats.

If you are an executive reading this book, you are probably more interested in reading about how to succeed, rather than about how not to derail. But both perspectives are important, and there are important lessons to be learned from seeing how others have derailed. If nothing else, you will want to avoid the mistakes made by the three executives I'm going to talk about, so read on.

The available literature on this topic is endless. Just do a Google search on "Why Executives Derail" and you will find hundreds of articles and studies on the topic. You will find academic works from universities and studies done by organizations focusing on leadership development. There is much commentary from

consulting firms engaged in executive coaching, and—certainly reflective of our times—chatter in the social media venues.

Companies are very interested in the topic and rightfully so, due to the high cost of executive turnover in terms of time and money. But you should be interested for the same reasons: the time it will take you to find another job, and the risk of having no income if you haven't found a comparable position after your severance runs out, if you got any in the first place. Furthermore, if the derailment results in termination, you and your family will also have to bear the emotional toll that often results.

The Experts Have Spoken

I've relied primarily on two resources for background on this topic. For several decades the Center for Creative Leadership (CCL), a non-profit organization focusing on leadership education and research, has been conducting derailment studies. The 1995 study done by two researchers at CCL, Van Velsor and Leslie, is still considered to be the classic study on derailment.

The second resource is the research reported in the 2009 book, *Real Time Leadership Development* by Yost and Plunkett.

- Van Velsor and Leslie at CCL identified four general themes that accounted for executives failing or derailing. They include: *problems with interpersonal relationships, failure to meet business objectives, failure to build and lead a team, and lastly, the inability to change or adapt during a transition.* ("Why executives derail: Perspectives across time and culture," *Academy of Management Executive*, 1995)
- Yost and Plunkett list "The 10 Deadly Sins" that they believed were the most common causes of executive derailment. They identified the following causes: poor performance, a failure to adapt to change, arrogance, unrecognized blind spots, the failure to build a strong team, the failure to build a strong network, poor working relationships, the inclination to avoid stretch assignments, unethical behavior, and just plain bad luck. (*Real Time Leadership Development*, Wiley-Blackwell, 2009)

Comparing the causes in the two studies shows that many of the causes in the more recent study do fit into the four categories from Van Velsor and Leslie's 1995 work. Of the 10 categories listed by Yost and Plunkett only three do not readily fit into Van Velsor and Leslie's model. These three are: *the inclination to avoid stretch assignments, unethical behavior, and just plain bad luck.*

From my own experience, both as an executive and as the head of H.R. in dealing with executives, I have seen evidence to support Yost and Plunkett's additions.

The "inclination to avoid stretch assignments" signals either a lazy executive or one who is afraid to take chances because they might fail. In either case, these are not traits companies want to see in their executives. Companies want executives who are willing to take calculated risks and take initiative. "Unethical behavior" was not on the radar screens of most companies until the scandals involving executives at Enron, Tyco International, and WorldCom were exposed. Since the Van Velsor and Leslie research was done in the early 1990s, these scandals had not yet been exposed and the Sarbanes-Oxley Act of 2002 (a federal law that created standards for U.S. public company boards, management, and public accounting firms) did not exist. Had circumstances that lead up to the 2002 law been so thoroughly exposed in the early 1990s, Van Veslor and Plunkett would certainly have included unethical behavior as a cause of executive derailment.

And what about "just plain bad luck"? I am a believer that timing is everything—well, maybe not everything, but it counts for a lot. When you've lived a lot of years, you've had the opportunity to witness this phenomenon first-hand. The best, and perhaps the classic example, is the executive who is hired and six months later, the person who hired him leaves the company for better opportunity. The executive now has to adjust to a new boss who turns out to be Attila the Hun.

Van Velsor and Leslie's four themes, combined with Yost and Plunkett's Ten Deadly Sins, seem to cover the major factors that lead to executive derailment. So, let's look at some real cases that resulted in executives being derailed. These three cases all come from my experience as a senior human resources officer.

Case 1: The Failure to Meet Business Objectives

This is one of the most common reasons for executive derailment, because it is quantifiable and objective. Most companies measure and reward executives according to performance: Do they meet objectives? Although business objectives vary widely, financial objectives count more than others: do the metrics show that you're getting the job done? A *New York Times* headline (February 19, 2012) says it all: "Ford's Mr. Inside,

In Sight of the Crown, the Heir Apparent, Yes, As Long As His Numbers Soar." The operative phrase in the headline is "as long as his numbers soar." The article was about Mark Fields, President of Ford's very successful North America division, and his chances of succeeding Mulally as CEO.

Here is a story about a general manager whose numbers didn't soar. In his first year on the job, his division showed mediocre financial performance. Sales had slightly exceeded expenses and a small profit had been generated. In his second year, his objective was to increase sales by 10% and revenues by 15%. He committed to grow sales of existing products, and introduce a new product with significantly higher margins than existing products. At the same time, his goal was to reduce overall manufacturing costs by 10%. Everyone was optimistic that this would be the turn-around year for the division. The new product was released on schedule in April and manufacturing costs were tracking lower than budget, and existing sales seemed to be on target. Good news, after the first quarter of the year.

Unfortunately, by July 1st, it was evident that the new product was not being well received in the marketplace, despite advanced focus-group feedback that it would sell. The general manager insisted that lack of sales was just a fluke and, rather than adjust production downward, he continued to produce large quantities of the product. By end of September, it was obvious that the new product was a failure and it would be difficult to unload the inventory that had been produced.

Not only had the new product failed, but manufacturing costs had increased compared to the previous year, existing product sales were flat, and the division was forecasted to have its largest loss ever. In October, the general manager was informed that he was being terminated, not due to the new product's failure per se, but due to his insistence on continuing to produce the product when there was no tangible evidence to support doing so. The chairman had lost confidence in his ability to run the division. This was a clear case of not meeting business objectives.

Case 2: The Failure to Build a Team

This example illustrates that it is often a combination of factors that leads to an executive's derailment. This senior executive was responsible for product development, reporting directly to the division head. She had been recruited from another company and was well known in the industry for her design talent. We didn't know when we hired her that we had, in fact, hired two people. She was one personality when dealing with people at or above her level, and another personality when dealing with her subordinates.

She had only been with us about six months when one of her staff appeared in my office and wanted to talk. This employee wanted to let me know how abusively he had been treated by his new boss. He wanted to let me know what was going on, but didn't want or expect me to do anything about it. This is always a dilemma for the human resources person—if the boss' behavior is not illegal, unethical or discriminatory. There is not much you can do than but honor the employee's request.

About a month later, another employee showed up at my door with a similar complaint about the boss. She had been screamed at by the executive in front of her colleagues; she felt demeaned and shamed. She had made a product design change that the president of the company did not like. The irony of it all, according to the employee, was that it was actually the boss who had insisted on the design change, but was unwilling to admit this to the president. According to this employee, she felt betrayed by the boss and embarrassed in front of her peers. Unlike her colleague a month earlier, this employee wanted something to be done about the boss' abusive behavior. Now I had two employees with the same complaint, but only one was willing to have it addressed by human resources.

I spoke to the president of the division, but I couldn't get him to deal with his abusive manager. He was afraid she would quit if he confronted her. She was just too valuable and he didn't want to risk loosing her talent. Unfortunately, this is not an uncommon situation in corporate America. Unacceptable behavior is tolerated because an abusive boss is "too valuable." But during the next year, the department suffered a 50% turnover rate and product quality suffered. The executive was provided with a professional coach to help her deal more kindly with subordinates, but her abusive behavior continued. Finally, we moved her to an individual contributor position with no one reporting to her. She was no longer considered for promotional opportunities, and her career prospects were damaged considerably.

Case 3: Be Careful What You Say— or Write

We relocated an executive who was running a small business for us in another country. We brought him to the U.S. as a general manager to run a similar business here. This executive had demonstrated good marketing, product development and management skills. He had P&L responsibilities and had consistently exceeded financial objectives for the small division he was running overseas.

Our company's succession plan had identified him as high potential and he was slated to run one of our largest divisions within one to two years, provided he continued to perform as he had in the past. After nine months in his new job, all indications were very positive, his division was performing well, sales of existing products were up, a new product was about to be released, and more new products were in the pipeline. By any of our financial measurements, he was doing an outstanding job.

As he was approaching the one-year mark, our superstar, high-potential executive did a performance review on his controller and gave the controller a copy of the review. Later that same day, the controller was reading the written review and noted it was his boss' original copy with the boss' hand-written notes. A little while later the controller appeared in my office and

handed me the review. I couldn't believe what I was reading. There was a very derogatory racial slur penciled in the margin. It was a totally inappropriate racist comment. I told the controller that this was a very serious matter and that I would investigate and get back to him by the end of the following day.

I did investigate the matter. Our high-potential executive admitted it was his handwriting and said he had inadvertently given the wrong document to his controller. He was very sorry, but knew the damage had already been done. He knew his career with our organization was over and he resigned.

Recovering from Derailment

It is worth noting that, in two of the three cases, the warning signs for potential problems were present. Had the signs been recognized and action taken early, perhaps derailment could have been avoided. Clearly, in the third case involving the performance evaluation, there were no advance warning signs that this was going to occur.

The good news for executives who derail is that there is life after derailment. If you are an executive who has derailed, you know what I'm talking about. Although painful at the time, many derailed executives—who have bounced back and given serious thought to what went wrong—say they're learned very valuable lessons about themselves and the realities of the workplace.

If you are an executive who has never derailed, consider yourself fortunate, but do not become complacent. My advice is to *do a risk assessment*: how do you stack up against the factors that are the most common causes of derailment? If you do this, you might just head off a situation that could cause you to derail.

I can think of only one factor in the literature I've sited that you are virtually helpless to do anything about—and that is Just Plain Bad Luck. I wish you good luck on that one!

Chapter 51

Get What's Coming to You: Negotiate the Best Possible Severance Package

by Kate Wendleton, President, The Five O'Clock Club

The Five O'Clock Club product is much better, far more useful, than my outplacement package.

—*a Five O'Clock Club Member*

The Club meetings kept the juices flowing. You meet with people weekly, you're told what to do, what not to do. Job hunting can be very lonely. There were fresh ideas. I went through an outplacement service that, frankly, did not help. If they had done as much as the Five O'Clock Club did, I would have landed sooner.

—*another Five O'Clock Clubber*

Case Study: Beth
Short-Timer Gets Outplacement

Beth had worked at Intelliger for less than two years, including working only two days a week for the past month. The company wanted her to leave, but stay on for another month to train a new person. Beth wanted two months' severance, the $60,000 bonus money that was due her, and outplacement help. Following the advice in this chapter, she ended up with

a significant portion of the bonus money, four weeks' severance and outplacement with The Five O'Clock Club.

Even short-timers have negotiated severance.

Case Study: Daniel
Help in Starting His Own Consulting Business

Daniel's case is more typical. Like most people who receive a termination notice, Daniel was stunned when he received the news—and rightly so. Daniel had been given every assurance that his career was on the rise and his job with the company secure. A year earlier, when he received an offer from a competitor, his supervisors begged him to stay on. These professional assurances went beyond words, though. Daniel's compensation was made up of a base salary plus bonuses tied to performance. With his future looking so rosy, Daniel felt comfortable purchasing an expensive home.

. . . .

A traditional outplacement firm cannot help you negotiate severance with your employer (it is a conflict of interest since your employer is their client), but The Five O'Clock Club can help you (because *you* are our client).

. . . .

The ink was scarcely dry on the new deed when Daniel was struck with the news that he had been replaced. The company offered him a severance package consisting of nine months of base pay (which represented a small part of his prior year's compensation) and only three months of traditional executive outplacement. (Companies typically offer outplacement packages that end just when you need them the most—at the three-month mark when you are about to get offers.)

When he called me at The Five O'Clock Club, Daniel was still in a state of shock. He knew that his severance package was inadequate, but he did not feel he would be able to negotiate anything better. Should he just take what they offered and move on?

. . . .

His only strength was to prod company officials until they gave in. He knew they wanted to get him out of their hair.

. . . .

Absolutely not! Many departing employees have more leverage than they think—sometimes simply by asking for fairness—or even sympathy. In Daniel's case, his age (51) raised the specter of age discrimination. We worked

together to develop a strategy and he went back to his company armed with his plan. The result? He walked away with $125,000 more and a commitment for off-site office facilities, as well as a full year of career coaching to help him launch his own business.

Daniel's case is not an unusual one. Here at The Five O'Clock Club, we coach many professionals, managers and executives dissatisfied with their severance packages, but who are hesitant, for a variety of reasons, to say so.

. . . .

Daniel wanted to leave with his dignity and pride intact, and with the ongoing help he would need to move ahead.

. . . .

The first thing I advised Daniel to do was to return to his company and tell his supervisor that he would have trouble accepting what was offered because he would have financial difficulties. "I want to remain whole," was the phrase that Daniel used to express his feelings to anyone he spoke with. The phrase helped Daniel to focus on his goal while sending a message to company officials that he was not just after money. He wanted to leave with his dignity and pride intact, and with the ongoing help he would need to move ahead. After his 12 years of service, the company owed him that.

Why would a company agree to any of Daniel's demands? Because he wasn't going to stop pestering them until he was satisfied. He would prod the company officials until they gave in. They wanted to get him out of their lives. To do that, they soon realized, meant they had to pay his price.

It doesn't mean that Daniel was obnoxious. My advice to him was to be "pleasantly persistent." Of course, Daniel had to make a commitment to go back to these people again and again. He didn't have any trouble holding to that resolve. "Here's what I want," he would say. Concentrating on his purpose spurred him on.

Based on my coaching sessions with Daniel and others, I can offer further guidance on how to negotiate the severance package you deserve. Here are some things to consider:

Deal with each compensation issue separately. A severance package is made up of many items. These may include an actual cash settlement, career coaching help, benefits, office support and other items, depending on the industry and company. Like Daniel, who neglected to scrutinize the outplacement help he was being offered, you need to look at each component individually. A large cash settlement, for example, may quickly be eaten up if you end up paying for outplacement help and benefits.

Decide what you want. List what you think is fair and also what you think you are likely to get. It helps if you have some idea of what others have received. "Company policy" may have nothing to do with what people actually get.

Push to continue your benefits. It costs a company very little to carry employees on its medical plan. But if you try to duplicate that coverage on your own, it would cost a lot.

Develop a mantra. Daniel's was, "I want to remain whole." Find one that succinctly describes your feelings, such as "I just want to be treated fairly." The phrase will keep you focused and give your overall campaign consistency. Then, no matter what they say, you can repeat your mantra.

In addition, it is not out-of-line to talk about the stress you and your family are suffering.

Ask for career coaching services for one year. You should never underestimate the amount of time it will take you—or the help you will need—to find another comparable position. Depending on the complexity of your situation and your own psychological makeup, your search may last a long time—some tough searches have taken more than a year.

You'll need a year because your search may take that long. You may even decide in the

middle of your search to start your own consulting business, then realize that consulting is not for you after all, and resume looking for an on-payroll job instead.

If your company grants you only one to six months' outplacement assistance, you could find yourself cut off in the middle of your job search. Therefore, ask for The Five O'Clock Club service. If your company has a contract with a traditional outplacement firm, ask your company to supplement less-than-full corporate outplacement help with attendance at The Five O'Clock Club.

If you find you do not like your new job—or lose it—you can return to The Five O'Clock Club during that year and continue your search. (Traditional outplacement firms do not allow you to return once you have been "placed.")

Don't take money over outplacement. A cash settlement of $25,000—or even $5,000—sounds like a lot, but on your own you are unlikely to spend what you need for career coaching services. Instead, you are likely to skimp and end up unemployed or taking a lesser job than what you would have landed if you had received all the help you need. Get whatever cash you can and ask for the outplacement help as an added benefit.

Select the career coaching service yourself. Although your firm may have a relationship with an outplacement firm, many companies allow you to select the outplacement service of your choice.

Remember that, with traditional outplacement firms, the "client" is your former employer. With The Five O'Clock Club, the client is you! You will probably be impressed with the plush space and other amenities offered by the outplacement firms. But space does not help you get a job: career coaching does.

Many people in traditional outplacement come to The Five O'Clock Club for the career coaching help—so they can get a job! Some negotiate with their prior employers to pay for The Five O'Clock Club's services in additional to traditional outplacement (which they want for the space), and some pay for The Five O'Clock Club on their own *so they can get a good job.*

It's better to ask for Five O'Clock Club help and get space elsewhere. We can give you some ideas.

In addition, most packages at traditional outplacement firms end at the three-month or six-month mark. Most outplacement packages at The Five O'Clock Club are for a full year. This extra time gives you more breathing room to find the situation that is best for you.

Use outplacement help to launch your own consulting business. Daniel's dream was to have his own business. He was tempted to take a cash settlement, believing that the money was the most important ingredient he needed to form his new company from scratch. I convinced him otherwise. A highly qualified Five O'Clock Club career consultant can help you write a business plan, develop your target list, brochure and verbal "pitch," and serve as a valued advisor until you are on your feet.

Peter, an unemployed actor in his mid-40s, came to The Five O'Clock Club because he was having trouble starting his own consulting business. He wanted to coach senior executives in presentation techniques. After working with The Five O'Clock Club, he landed his first three clients who were senior executives at major corporations. Then we advised him to increase his rates and showed him how to get more business on an ongoing basis. Peter was so successful that his wife quit her job, he ended up buying a 30-acre estate, while keeping an apartment in the city.

. . . .

You can start Five O'Clock Club coaching even though you have not completely come to terms with your employer—we can help with that!

. . . .

You can be looking for another job at the same time you are pushing your company for a better settlement. A traditional outplacement firm cannot help you negotiate with your employer (it is a conflict of interest since your employer is their client), but The Five O'Clock Club can help you (because you are our client).

If your company only offers three months' traditional outplacement and refuses to budge, you could take it—and ask if you could come back and ask for a monthly extension if you are conducting a full and active search and have not landed by that time. Then, right before the three months are up, go in and push for an extra month at a time.

However, if you negotiate for The Five O'Clock Club's services, it is unlikely that you will have to ask for more. At The Five O'Clock Club, you can receive a full year of outplacement help—and negotiate a space allowance as well—for what your company would pay for three months at a traditional outplacement firm.

Find out what other employees have walked away with. Use this information to further your own case.

Daniel discovered that what he was offered was not what he had to settle for. He almost made a mistake—one that would have been very expensive in the short term, as he struggled to make ends meet, and in the long term, because he never would have been able to afford to start his own business in such style.

Make sure you don't settle for less, either. Every situation is unique. Get help negotiating your severance package. The amount you spend on a little bit of coaching can reap enormous benefits. You will end up with what you deserve and need. It may cost your company more, but as the saying goes, you're worth it.

Chapter 52

How to Get Fired: A Review of Smart Exit Strategies

by David Madison, Ph.D., Director, The National Guild of Five O'Clock Club Career Coaches

This article is based on a presentation by two of our senior certified coaches, Bill Belknap and Chip Conlin, to a training session for our National Guild of Career Coaches. Bill and Chip are members of our team of severance coaches—those to whom we refer clients who ask for advice on how to negotiate departure from a job.

Let's see, you could throw a drink in your manager's face at the company picnic. Or perhaps arrive at the office wearing your pajamas. Every morning at your desk—before taking a half-hour coffee break—you could spend a couple of hours surfing the net looking for your next vacation destination. Or during your annual review with your boss, say, "You were serious about all those goals for last year?" In the film *Nine to Five*, when Lily Tomlin's character thinks she's poisoned her boss (Dabney Coleman) by mistake, she laments, "I just killed the boss. You don't think they're not going to fire me for something like this?"

How do you survive with dignity and with as little damage as possible?

"I'm going to have to let you go. Even though you're one of the best computer programmers we've ever had, we just can't tolerate you eating the other employees."

These are surely ways to get fired—or at least come very close. But this chapter isn't really about how to *get* fired—who needs that kind of advice? We want to review a few of the things you can do to survive the process of being fired. That is, how do you survive with dignity, and with as little damage as possible?

This clearly is a topic most of us don't even want to think about. But bear in mind that jobs don't last forever in the modern economy. A generation ago, job security was built into the system. These days, however, it's built *out* of the system. Jobs last an average of 4.5 years. That's why it's important to be very aware of career planning—and it's important to be savvy about being fired. Chances are, you will have to go through it once or twice.

Of course, employers and termination policies differ greatly. We've all heard horror stories about employees being treated like criminals when they're asked to leave. We also know that some organizations get high marks for handling people with care and sensitivity when there's a forced departure. And it's hard to know when you take a job how things may play out when you leave the job.

But it's also very true that employees commonly aren't as skilled as they could be in handling forced exits. There usually is a degree of trauma, confusion and anger—the latter especially, if the circumstances seem to be unfair or arbitrary. Even people who have been through this harrowing experience give far less thought to the process of leaving a job than getting a job. Naturally, at The Five O'Clock Club we focus far more on job search strategies. But we encourage people to look upon being fired as a crucial time for self-protection instincts and strategies to kick in. Being fired may be inevitable now and then, but you don't necessarily have to take it lying down—as in, being run over.

Circumstances will vary enormously, but we're going to review a few key principles to bear in mind. Some of these may apply to your situation, others may not, but keep this list on file to review if it happens to you.

> **Being fired may be inevitable, but you don't have to be run over.**

Find a Coach

Why try to fly solo through an experience that has the potential to cause you damage and loss? Getting good advice can save you a lot of grief.

There are coaches who have helped hundreds of people go through this—and their words of wisdom and emotional support can be invaluable. The rate for such coaching is usually in the $125 to $150 per hour range, but the return on investment can be huge. The strategies, suggestions and scripts offered by a coach could mean that you will walk away with a few thousand dollars more or a few more months of insurance coverage—as well as other substantial advantages. After just a few minutes into a conversation with a coach you may find yourself saying, "Gee, I never thought of that." It's the things you don't think of that can mean big trouble.

At the end of this article we will return to the topic of getting help—in the form of employer-paid outplacement services.

> **Panic will work against making the best of a bad situation.**

Distance Yourself from the Emotions of the Situation

Depending on your temperament, you might react smoothly or hysterically, or anything in between, when you hear the words "you're fired"—even if it's not put that bluntly. But most people can assume that their judgment will be clouded when they get the word that their job is over. By all means, avoid making decisions or signing anything until you've had time to distance yourself from your first reactions.

One of the most difficult emotions to handle is panic, because job loss may feel like the end of the world... if you haven't looked for a job in ages, if you live from paycheck to paycheck, or if your plate is already full with personal problems at home. But panic will work against making the best of a bad situation. Simply reviewing the other points to follow in this article can help you see that there are constructive steps to take— and the situation probably is not as bleak as it may seem.

There may be a lot of anger, too. One Five O'Clock Club client was so filled with rage when she was fired that she couldn't even bear to meet with her boss to work out severance. With the help of her coach she crafted carefully worded emails to present her case—that is, she made sure that her rage and anger didn't come through in what she wrote. In this way she doubled the payout that the company had originally offered. If you try to negotiate from anger, you're probably building toward a lose-lose situation for everyone. Which brings us to the next point.

Try to Be as Non-Confrontational as Possible

One of the most natural reactions to being fired is one variation or another of, "After all I've done for this company...." Almost everyone—on one level or another—wants to think that he or she has done a good job, and doesn't deserve to be fired. Even if an employee is being terminated for performance reasons, there is likely to be disagreement with the boss on the quality of the job done. But it is usually pointless to try to argue your case. For every wonderful accomplishment you can claim, your manager is likely to counter with an example of something you failed to do or how you fell short. An argument about performance is the last thing that will advance your case at this point.

> Most employers want to make the exit graceful.

Believe it or not, most employers want to make the exit as graceful as possible—to keep stress as low as possible for all parties concerned, and to protect the reputation of the organization.

So just accept the fact there will probably not be agreement on whether or not you deserve the forced exit, and focus on negotiating as calmly and pleasantly as possible. As much as anything, a feeling of goodwill (even if it seems strained and artificial!) increases the chances of arriving at a win-win solution. You are vulnerable to damage in these situations, and you want to minimize damage as much as possible.

So how good are you at making nice?

> Negotiate calmly and pleasantly. A feeling of goodwill increases the chances of arriving at a win-win solution.

Sharpen Your Acting Skills

At The Five O'Clock Club we tell job-hunters that interviewing is showtime. Even if you don't feel confident and on top of the world, try to act as if you do. Performance is half the battle in landing a job offer. The same advice applies when you're presenting your case for the best possible exit package. Of course you need to huddle with your coach to plot strategy, perfect your script and note all the points that need to be covered. Have your list of needs and desires (not demands!) and focus on the realities of your situation and the job market. We prod job hunters to perfect their Two-Minute Pitches, and you need a variation of this for the meetings with your boss or HR manager to discuss the terms of your departure. Rehearse it with family members and your coach. This is meant to be a framework for your presentation, but you will act the part when the time comes if you can remember to talk from the heart. If you have firmly in mind the reasons why the package you want makes sense, it will be easier to do that.

It's Not a Done Deal Until It Is Signed: Gear Up to Negotiate and Influence

Being an employee usually means being in a position of minor or inferior power—in comparison to the corporation or boss. The feeling of having power stacked against you usually is intensified by being forced out of a job. It's very common to feel that you're in a take-it-or-leave-it situation. But you'd be surprised how many people get more by asking for more—and by simply being persistent about it. The Five O'Clock Club mantra for finessing salary negotiations—that is, keeping negotiations going while building the case that you're the best person for the job—is, "You're a fair person, I'm a fair person."

That can be your opening volley every time you come back to your employer to try to get more. Most employers assume that people will just go away when the terms of separation have been announced; after all, who (supposedly) holds all the power? But you can come back with reasoned arguments about why the package isn't all that it should be. To put it bluntly, this can be a matter of guts. How often are you willing to go back to the table? They think they've gotten rid of you, but you refuse to go quietly: "I'm a fair person, you're a fair person, and here's what's fair." Don't forget that things don't have to be rushed. By law you usually have 21 days to work out an agreement.

Clearly, if you happen to be part of a massive layoff of dozens or hundreds of people, there may be little room for you to maneuver—com-

pany policy that applies to everyone may appear to be written in stone. But can you make the case that your situation is unique? Have you been on payroll only a short time, after being recruited away from a 10- or 15-year job somewhere else? Did you relocate from a great distance to join the company? Did you play a key role in a major project? Your career coach can help you build the case that you deserve more than is being offered. It may also be good strategy to find allies within the company who are willing to remind management of your contributions and accomplishments—especially if a manager or boss is losing you because of a merger or reorganization. Now is a good time to call in the favors that people may owe you.

Go into negotiations with a firm idea of your priorities—and have the numbers carefully worked out. "I want to remain whole" is a strong argument to make with fair-minded people as you initiate negotiations. That is, as you transition to a new job (and you usually have no idea how long that may take), you don't want your finances or family life to take a hit. Hence, you

"I know you've been waiting for that promotion to V.P., Roberts, but I've decided to give it to my son Timmy. You understand, don't you?"

should know all of the numbers, and be prepared to discuss items in order of priority, e.g., severance, health insurance coverage, unpaid vacation days, the laptop you'd like to take with you.

When to Get the Ball Rolling Yourself—Without Quitting

It's not uncommon for people to see the handwriting on the wall. Perhaps there's a new boss, or a change in management in general. Or the newspapers may be full of stories about an upcoming merger that will impact your company—so it's no secret that jobs will be cut. For a variety of other reasons you may sense that your days on the job may be numbered; you might have been on put on warning for failing to meet goals, mastering a new process or procedure—or even fitting in with the corporate culture. In such cases the daily mood at work can be strained; if you sense that you're just marking time, it might be appropriate to be proactive. The boss or manager might be relieved to hear that you're looking for a separation that will make everyone happy. Some of the possible scripts:

- "Janet, you know this is not working, I know it's not working. Why don't we work something out?"
- "Tom, after really thinking about this situation, I'm afraid that I won't be able to meet these expectations. I'd like to work something out that makes sense for both of us."
- "John, this is not the job we initially discussed. I'm not as motivated as I thought I would be—maybe we'd better discuss how to bring this to a conclusion."

Obviously, situations and reasons differ enormously, but if you've arrived at the point of hating to get up and go to work every day, it may be time to maneuver an exit, without quitting. Resigning because you hate your job can be a very risky strategy—in fact, if it's not thought out carefully, it's an impulse, not a strategy. This

article is aimed at helping you be fired—and working that process to your advantage. Unless you have solid backup plans A, B & C (which include, for example, money in the bank and the means to provide health insurance), quitting is not really an option.

> Resigning because you hate your job
> is an impulse, not a strategy.

The scripts suggested above should be tried only after gauging the political situation at work, which means talking to trusted coworkers to get a reading on how the powers-that-be react to employees who ask for exit packages. Chances are, these waters are not entirely uncharted, and finding out about company history can be useful. And absolutely nothing of this sort should be attempted without talking with your career coach.

Get a Written Statement

At The Five O'Clock Club we advise job hunters to get good at explaining why they left their last jobs. Anyone who asks you on a job interview why you left your last job doesn't really want too much information—in the sense of "all the gory details," if this includes a detailed account of why things didn't work out in your last position. Interviewers want a brief explanation that makes sense and reflects well on you. They don't expect you to give them names of people (as references) who are going to say bad things about you. They expect to hear good things about you. That's why it's important to build a list of former bosses and colleagues who will sing your praises.

And part of a good exit strategy is to get something in writing. Especially if you're leaving a job for performance reasons, or because the job turned out not to be a good fit, it's wise to get a written statement that accentuates the positives that you brought to the job. Even if your employer doesn't want to write a glowing recommendation, negotiate a statement that will help satisfy curiosity in a positive way about why and how you left the job.

....

**A lawsuit will divert you
from your job search.**

....

You can show this document to the people you have asked to be your references. That will help them say the right things when people call them to ask about your personality, reputation and work history. Of course, if you're a student of The Five O'Clock Club methodology, you know that your references should be thoroughly briefed about each job you're a finalist for—so that they can better describe you in terms of the position.

A letter of recommendation or reference from your employer should be kept on file permanently. Ten or fifteen years from now, it may be impossible to find former bosses and managers, so the letter can substitute for talking to the people who have disappeared.

To Sue or Not to Sue: When to Call a Lawyer

Americans are fond of saying—especially when something really wrong or unfair has happened—"I'll take it all the way to the Supreme Court." But, in fact, the period of transitioning from one job to another is probably the worst time to be involved in a lawsuit. It can be very expensive and time consuming—and will divert you from the very thing you should focus on the most, namely, your job search (a full-time job search requires 35 hours a week). Besides,

"Johnson, if you're going to have negative thoughts, I suggest you get rid of that thought balloon!"

the last thing you want prospective employers to find out is that you're suing your former company. The suspicion is that something went terribly wrong, and you are suspected of being a litigious person. So the impulse to sue should be treated like most other impulses: forget about it. Or at least wait until the impulse has cooled, and you've thought about it a lot, before taking action.

That having been said, there may be reasons to consult with your attorney during the exit process. If there is genuinely an issue relating to discrimination or criminal behavior that brought about your dismissal, you may be justified in seeking legal action. Consultation with your lawyer could reveal how strong a case you may have. Of course, the potential benefits of suing would have to far outweigh the aggravation you would have to endure. And what would be the purpose of suing? To get your job back? That would be a good idea only in very rare circumstances.

As you review all of the issues relating to your termination with your career coach, the latter will clearly point out when a matter requiring legal advice comes up. Career coaches are not lawyers and don't have the expertise you need for such issues.

One of the areas for consulting an attorney is non-compete agreements. Most of these are usually imbedded in the hiring agreements that may have been signed months or years ago, but, especially when you lose your job against your will, your employer might be at a disadvantage in trying to enforce a non-compete. You may be able to have a non-compete renegotiated—with the help of your lawyer—when you're settling all the matters relating to your departure.

Getting Your Next Job Soon: The Value of Outplacement

Career coaching that is provided by your employer when you're let go (that is, you don't pay for it) is known as outplacement. Some companies offer this service, others don't—it's a matter of finances and attitude. Once when we made a presentation to an HR officer about Five O'Clock Club outplacement, we stressed that our program (a full year of coaching help) is a way of demonstrating that a company cares. We were shocked to be told bluntly, "But we don't care." This level of insensitivity is rare, and you should include outplacement on your list of requests as you negotiate an exit. Even if you work for a company known for its heartlessness, you should make the case for getting outplacement help.

· ·

Anyone who asks why you left your last job doesn't really want too much information.

· ·

The primary reason for doing this is that people who get job-search coaching land better jobs faster. There's really no mystery about this: most people are not experts on how to find a job.

Even people who have found themselves out of a job several times in their careers say, "Oh no, not again"—because it is stressful and always presents new challenges. There's a lot of conventional job-hunt wisdom floating around—most of it wrong—and if you follow it, you're likely to get stalled or delayed on the way to your next job. Working with a coach means that you can avoid making costly mistakes; coaches have guided hundreds of people through the process and can offer invaluable guidance. Asking your employer for this kind of service is a way to give yourself a boost—which you will come to fully appreciate in the weeks and months ahead.

But what about money instead? Your employer may say, "Here's three months' severance and outplacement service OR four months' severance. Which do you want?" Most employers are astute enough not to offer this option, because the impulse of most people is to say, "Show me the money!" But turning your back on job-search help is simply not a smart move—it could very well translate into several more months of unemployment…which means you've lost money.

· ·

Turning your back on job-search help is simply not a smart move.

· ·

A cushion of money is nice, of course, and who doesn't want the cushion of money to be as big as possible? Ironically, a large cushion of money can work against you: "Wow—I've got six months' severance, I can give myself a break and coast for a while." Many times people have arrived at The Five O'Clock Club in a panic: "I'm just about out of money: I've got to find a job fast." And it turns out that a big severance package is just about exhausted, and the person had been job-hunting half-heartedly; the extra cash had bred complacency and procrastination. It's very hard to get geared up for the hard work of job search if you've just been coasting for a while. Chances are, if you get signed up for outplacement, your coach will prod you out of the coasting mode as soon as possible (at least that's the way we do it at The Five O'Clock Club). Our research shows that people who don't get started on job search right away lose momentum, and end up with much longer searches. Getting outplacement service as part of your exit package is one of the best ways to shorten your between-jobs status.

Chapter 53

• • • • • • • • •

How to Terminate Employees While Respecting Human Dignity

by Richard Bayer, Ph.D., Chief Operating Officer, The Five O'Clock Club

"There is nothing worse than being escorted from your place of work, a place where you have come day after day and given your time and your blood. You missed your kid's soccer games to be there, and now they are saying to you, 'You are so dangerous that you must be escorted from this place. We paid you a salary, we gave you a 401k contribution, we gave you health benefits, we gave you vacation and now today, all of a sudden, you are so awful that we have to remove you as if you were a criminal.'

"Escorting someone out should be reserved for situations in which, if you did not escort the person out, you would be placing the rest of your staff in jeopardy. The circumstances are so rare in which you would need to do that. If an employee threatens to kill people, that's the one who needs to be escorted out."

Denise Z. Kaback, Director, Human Resources, at the law firm Schulte Roth & Zabel LLP

Question(s) to consider: A theme that runs through this chapter is "being a good person." See how this theme underlies the steps that follow.

Termination with dignity helps both the employee and the organization move forward.

- Have you ever had to dismiss someone?
- Have you ever been dismissed yourself?
- How was it handled?
- Could it have been done better?

Overview: A Kind Word Helps

If you lay off one or more staff members, what impact will that have on those who remain? Will productivity—and the bottom line—suffer? Are you likely to lose your best people who

277

will worry about their positions? Or will morale increase, because you handled the terminated employees with dignity?

This chapter can help. Here is what will be covered:

- Allow separated employees a decompression period in familiar surroundings. Let them have some control over how they leave. If possible, let them finish tasks they want to finish and make arrangements for keeping in touch with coworkers.
- A kind word helps during the dismissal meeting.
- Give your employees the kind of outplacement that gives them dignity while positioning them for the future.

The central idea of this chapter is this: The separation should be handled such that both the employee and the organization are empowered to move forward.

Part I:
The Case for Termination with Dignity

Whatever the reason for the separation, few workplace situations are dreaded more than a face-to-face meeting to break the news that an employee is being dismissed. It is not uncommon that the person losing the job has little idea of what's coming—and in all too many cases, unfortunately, the manager has little training in how to handle the situation. We must recognize the difficult business and human problems that involuntary termination presents.

. . . .

Organizations need a termination policy that would apply in all but the most extreme circumstances.

. . . .

Regrettably, the termination process is given far less attention than the hiring process. But there has been a trend in the last few years to correct this imbalance—for the very simple reason that there is much more built-in turbulence in the workplace than there was only a few decades ago. The average American today has been in his or her job for only four years, and, not surprisingly, expects to be in that job for only those four years.

Separations due to downsizings, mergers, relocations and closings are now part of the landscape. Terminations for cause can be on a continuum ranging from an employee's inability to adapt to a new computer system to those situations in which other employees or the organization are put at risk. Although it makes great sense to handle potentially violent or otherwise risk-filled situations with caution, it makes no sense to handle all employees as if they were a threat.

Organizations need termination policies that apply in all but the most egregious circumstances, assuring that:

- The goodwill toward the organization stays intact.
- The remaining employees feel secure.
- The leaving employee(s) feel empowered.

If for no other reason than the good of the workplace itself—the effect that separations have on those who remain—it would be foolhardy to act as if the exit phase of employment doesn't deserve major attention.

. . . .

Today, organizations are faced with an increasingly competitive labor market. It may be more difficult in the long run to recruit workers, as well as keep up productivity, in an organization that fails to *treat its workers with dignity*.

. . . .

Employment in this country is for the most part "at the pleasure of" both parties. Organizations—with some restrictions—can hire and fire at will. However, every employee deserves to be terminated with *dignity*. We have chosen that term after careful consideration. No less a body than the United Nations speaks of treating humans with *dignity,* especially in critical situations.

Employees are clearly resources and they contribute to productivity, but unlike facilities and equipment, humans have intrinsic worth beyond their contribution to the organization. Our goal here is to identify practices that benefit the parties involved, both employee and employer. Put yet another way: The termination should be handled such that both the employee and the organization *are empowered to go forward.*

Progress in this area has been uneven; American leadership should devote increasing attention, energy and dollars to refining and improving the separation process. And while organizations are looking at this issue more closely, mostly because of mergers and downsizings, separation with dignity should apply to *all* situations: the employee who is let go because of poor job performance is no less entitled to decent and respectful treatment consistent with the facts of each situation than someone who is terminated just because of downsizing. Even in the case of an employee's being discharged for willful misconduct, decency should not be suspended.

Why Should the Employer Care?

1. **Termination with dignity increases the organization's ability to hire the right people.** An organization's ability to attract the best talent is influenced by its goodwill in the marketplace, which depends to some extent on how it handles terminated employees.

    The workplace today is circular, not linear. Employees don't come in and stay. They come and go and intermix with people outside who learn how they were treated. When an organization lets someone go, that person touches dozens of others (or hundreds, with the advent of social media) who influence the company's image—and its ability to hire—in the marketplace. If an organization wants to compete and hire well, it must give attention to the way it lets people go.

2. **Termination with dignity is becoming a routine part of doing business in a civilized society.** Not too many decades ago, few practical business people could have been persuaded that the routine cost of business included offering employees paid vacations, health and dental insurance coverage, personal days, matching contributions to pension plans, and so forth.

    Over time, organizational thinking has changed, in part based on the recognition that employees are resources for which there is an increasingly competitive market.

Unlike facilities and equipment, humans have intrinsic worth beyond their present contribution to the organization.

The costs of developing and implementing dignified termination policies should be considered a part of doing business in a civilized society. Dignified termination should be seen as one of many *benefits* provided by the employer. The movement in the past century toward expanding and increasing employee benefits reflects an understanding of the *social contract* or *social covenant*—accepted standards as to what is decent for ordinary working men and women. One of the major components of our social covenant as Americans, as fellow citizens wishing to enjoy the benefits of a vigorous economy, is the understanding that we are obliged to contribute to the *general well-being.*

> As termination with dignity becomes a standard in the workplace, organizations that fail to practice it run the *risk of damaging their reputations.*

Hence, we have no trouble arguing for compassionate termination policies that reduce stress on families, lessen financial hardships, and decrease the chances that discharged employees will suffer emotional crises.

3. **Termination with dignity protects corporate profitability.** Such termination policies do, in fact, protect corporate profitability. Shareholder value will increase and business will profit in the long run by moving vigorously in this direction. At least two arguments can be advanced here:

   a. Organizations do not welcome negative publicity. Notoriety is not good for business, for example, product recalls, boardroom scandals, headlines about embezzlement—or news that 20 executives have been cut from the payroll just three months short of their retirement benefits. An organization's good name is an asset not to be squandered. And organizations do acquire reputations as bad places to work, because of poor benefits or a general perception about the way people are treated. Organizations that earn a reputation for decency in the way they let people go are considered attractive places for competent people to work. As termination with dignity becomes standard in the workplace, organizations that fail to practice it run the risk of damaging their reputations.

   b. The impact on the productivity of the remaining employees is important. The morale of the employees who survive a downsizing—or, for that matter, witness a single separation-for-cause—should be

a primary concern to management. Major layoffs typically result in increased workloads for the remaining employees, which is cause enough for stress and hard feelings. But many factors can come into play: Those who are left behind can feel a loss because familiar faces are suddenly gone, teams are broken up, and officemates have disappeared. There can be anger that things aren't the way they used to be, and fear that the same fate may be in store for those who remain.

Preparedness entails:

- Guidelines for management's behavior on the day of termination.
- Trained managers.
- Carefully prepared (though flexible) positive scripts.
- Plans for taking care of separated employees (including quality monetary packages).
- A full description of career coaching and other services ready to distribute.
- A list of each employee's contributions and strong points that have been valued over the years.
- Thought regarding the method of severance payout.

> Termination with dignity does, in fact, *protect corporate profitability.* **The reputation of the organization and employee morale are protected. Shareholder value will increase and business will profit in the long run by moving vigorously in this direction.**

Resentment and fear can be eased if there is a general perception that the separated employees got a fair deal and that management handled the terminations in a decent and caring fashion. It is in management's interest that:

- People still believe that this is a good place to work.
- Employee energy and focus are put into work and productivity.
- Venting and complaining be kept to a minimum.

Employees who have witnessed termination with dignity will be more inclined to like the organization and support its goals and mission.

There is a growing awareness in the American workforce that mergers and staff reductions are now an inevitable part of the corporate landscape. This should be accompanied by a growing awareness that management will merge and cut with care for human dignity; that it is committed to making the termination as painless as possible and to protecting the well-being of employees as productive resources.

....

The costs of developing and implementing dignified termination policies should be considered a part of doing business correctly in a civilized society.

....

Part II:
How to Terminate With Dignity

In those few cases where the former employee has taken legal action, the reasons for doing so usually revolve around treatment during the termination meeting.

Therefore, during the meeting, consider the following:

- The employee wants to know what went

wrong. People are more likely to be able to go forward if they are given an explanation.
- The employee is listening for a kind word about past performance.
- There is the matter of pride: How will the departure be portrayed to the remaining workforce?
- There are the pragmatics: How am I going to survive? Have available, full written summaries of severance benefits prepared with as much care as the benefit booklets handed to new hires.
- Discuss other issues, such as professional references, so the employee can formulate a strategy to move forward.

Allow people to return to familiar surroundings and share reactions with friends—to proceed with some degree of normalcy for the time being. This is part of the empowering process.

Before, During and After the Termination Meeting

Proper termination is a lengthy process. Many factors come into play, so it's helpful to analyze the method chronologically. To carry it off well, pay attention to the:

- Extensive groundwork required beforehand.
- Protocols and procedures to be followed when it happens.
- Appropriate actions required in the days, weeks or even months after a layoff or termination.

Before the Meeting

Impulse, or letting the chips fall where they may, has no role in affirming and constructing a proper termination policy. Because preparedness is vital, termination procedures must be imbedded in a written policy and, over time, instilled in the organization's culture. These practices must become a part of workplace protocols. In other words, this is not something to be put on the shoulders of untutored managers. The organization's guiding philosophy on the issue must be studied and mastered.

Letting people go is an extraordinarily important and sensitive task. Those entrusted with this responsibility should be trained to handle the termination process.

Managers Must Be Trained

When people are going through a termination process, all parties are moving into the arena of human hurt: great sensitivity will be required. Human lives and futures are at stake and the organization's image is on the line. Accordingly, managers and HR officers must be trained to listen attentively and to respond to human distress.

Preparedness for this role may require, at the very least, attendance at seminars, tutoring by specially trained HR officers, and scripts.

Enlightened organizations have long trained managers to improve their hiring and interviewing skills. This enables them to be more astute in selecting candidates and more aware of legal pitfalls: Who needs a manager who hasn't gotten the word that a female candidate can't be asked blatantly sexist questions? The same degree of training should be given to managers for the hard task of letting people go: Who needs a manager who is too busy to care about feelings and just wants to get the unpleasant business behind him—or worse, who views his task as an opportunity to settle scores? Letting people go is an extraordinarily important and sensitive matter. Those entrusted with this responsibility should have the benefit of professional coaching.

Smaller organizations could at least give their managers selected reading material or perhaps this chapter.

Preparedness is the key factor to ensure that the financial and emotional well-being of the terminated employee are protected.

Develop Positive Scripts

Carefully prepared (though flexible), positive scripts are indispensable to the separation process. Enabling people to pick up the pieces and move on should be the goal; separated employees who have been emotionally battered and damaged by the termination process may be ill-equipped to grapple with the emotional battering that may come next (i.e., a job search). Saying a nice word plays a critical role; the lack of kind words eats at people and erodes morale. The guiding norm, at the very least, should be "to do no harm." In a downsizing or merger, it is easier to assure people that this is a *no-fault situation,* but even here self-esteem can take a beating and positive scripts are essential.

The employee is listening for a kind word about past performance, such as:

- "George, you've been a trooper. You've helped us for 15 years and I'm sorry that the organization has moved in a different direction."
- "Mary, you have excellent people-relations skills and have added a lot to the group."

Termination procedures must be imbedded in written policy and instilled in the organizational culture. Otherwise, people won't want to work there again—or recommend that others do.

Point Out Each Employee's Strengths

The manager should be prepared to review, with each employee, his or her contributions and strong points that have been valued over the years. Even in a termination-for-performance, prompted by the fact that someone's skills were inadequate for a particular situation, the person's assets and abilities can still be acknowledged. A termination-for-performance should not be an occasion for abuse. As will be noted shortly, financial considerations are crucial, but a generous dollar settlement usually cannot erase bitter memories of uncaring or even unkind words. The "sharp stick in the eye" is likely to be remembered long after the separation money has been spent. Indeed, in those few cases in which former employees have taken legal action, the personal reasons for doing so usually have to do with the treatment during the separation process.

"The Package"

Preparedness also means creating plans for taking care of separated employees: An important element in enhancing a corporation's reputation is the quality of the package. The quality of the package is measured by how much the person is able to move forward professionally and personally.

Termination with dignity presumes that the package will include:

- Severance pay.
- Professional support for finding a new position (i.e., career coaching and other such services).
- In-house counseling to help separated employees come to an understanding of what combination of severance pay and support services is appropriate.

Carefully prepared (though flexible) positive scripts are an indispensable element of the process. For example,

---

"George, you've been a trooper. I'm sorry that the organization has moved in a different direction."

Many employees will be unaware of the importance of various transitional support services, and may dismiss them in favor of cash settlements. However, management has an obligation to evaluate separated employees individually, and guide them with sensitivity, based upon their needs and histories. Organizations should devote time and care to reviewing individual profiles and needs to construct separation packages consisting of cash, career coaching and other services in line with the organization's policies, usually in proportion to the employee's level and years of service.

Being prepared means having a full explanation of the termination services ready to hand to the employee—a detailed written explanation of benefits (i.e., career coaching help, educational grants, health insurance continuation, and so on).

Smaller organizations often cannot afford extensive packages. When choices have to be made based on cost, it's usually best to provide employees with ongoing career coaching until they are re-employed (rather than, for example, short-term coaching along with expensive space and other support services).

Preparedness also means deciding upon how severance will be paid out. For example, except for special requests or circumstances, paying a six-month lump sum in November or December—and enormously inflating the W2 for the year—will certainly create resentment. Severance pay is rightly viewed as limited and precious: no more of it than absolutely necessary should be lost to taxes. The costs for bookkeeping and payroll services may be higher if the payout lasts for six months vs. one or two, but this should be done if it is in the best interest of the employee.

Information Sharing

While there may be no way to eliminate the element of surprise, there are ways to reduce shock and humiliation in the wake of a downsizing that has been a closely guarded secret. Except in the most unusual of circumstances, there is little justification for "sudden death" discharges; there are plenty of horror stories of fired employees who are asked to leave the building immediately, even by being escorted from their desks to the door by security. The person is treated as a threat. The trusted employee has suddenly become a danger. This certainly creates the impression that the termination is a punishment, causing humiliation and resentment. Too many managers think that this is simply the way to do it: "It's over, let's make a clean break."

Management must consider the consequences in each case. Most managers would resent an employee's failing to give two weeks' notice, while, of course, the dynamics can be vastly different when the separation is the employer's decision. Organizations should consider the positives of allowing for a decompression period, for an appropriate time in familiar surroundings, allowing discharged employees to finish tasks, complete projects, and make arrangements for keeping in touch with coworkers. This may strike some as being highly idealistic, but carrying it off depends on *how well the reason for the termination has been explained*, about which more will be said later.

··

There is little justification for "sudden death" discharges. These cause humiliation and resentment.

··

Attention should be given to the secrecy that usually surrounds merger negotiations or plans for downsizings. This subject is beyond the scope of this chapter, but it needs to be carefully analyzed because of its impact on the workplace.

It's harder to achieve termination with dignity when people have little or no warning that jobs are about to be cut. There's a need for confidentiality at some level, but there's also a need to evaluate the impact of secrecy on the men and women in the workforce.

During the Meeting

The musical "A Chorus Line" is the story of young Broadway hopefuls trying out for a new production. Near the end of the show, after all have taken their turns at dance and song, they stand in a line on the stage nervously facing the director. He announces, "When I call your name, please step forward." Those called do so; smiles and looks of relief cross their faces. But after calling ten people forward, the director says to them, "Thank you for coming, we appreciate your trying out, but I'm sorry we can't use you. Those who remain will receive contracts in the mail." It was a particularly cruel way to announce his selection.

··

The quality of the package is measured by how much individuals are able to move forward professionally and personally.

··

The Delivery

Much depends on how people get the news— the words that are actually used are important—and on how the events of the day unfold. If it *seems* that the organization is acting cruel or mean, there can be significant harm—both to the individual and to the organization in the form of damaged reputation or even lawsuits. While almost all legal actions brought by terminated employees are unsuccessful—employment law allows either the employer or employee to end the association at will—such actions remain a nuisance. Lawsuits are often emotional reactions to the hurt inflicted during the termination.

It's best, for example, if ten people are to be cut from a staff of 45, that either all ten are called to a special meeting or that the names of all ten are announced as closely together as possible. This is especially true if all 45 are on the same floor or in the same department. The remaining 35 should be told what is happening. Sometimes, management doesn't think far enough ahead to see that this is the best course. On the other hand, when the announcements are spaced out too far, the atmosphere can become unbearable, ruining productivity, while dozens of people are dreading that the phone will ring. If a humane policy is in place, the discharged people can return to their desks when they are ready, discuss events and feelings with co-workers, and sit down for a helpful session with a career or other counselor.

Most managers would resent an employee's failing to give two weeks' notice. Yet, often, employees are simply ushered out the door.

When the time for a termination arrives—manager and employee are face-to-face—termination with dignity requires addressing the employee's needs on two levels. He or she has just received life-changing news and will likely be curious about two things:

- Why has this happened to me?
- What is going to happen to me now—how am I going to survive?

Horror stories abound of fired employees being asked to leave the building immediately, even being escorted by security from their desks to the door.

"Why Has this Happened to Me?"

"Why has this happened to me?" is an emotional, self-esteem question. Representatives of the organization should be prepared to explain, at least generally, why the organization is cutting staff, merging or closing; but they should be sensitive to feelings of the person being singled out. "How did I end up in the group being downsized?" This feeling may be expressed in a variety of ways—or not at all, in the turmoil of the moment—but the underlying plea is, "Please help me to understand what went wrong." As discussed earlier, representatives of the organization should be prepared with positive scripts tailored to each employee. People are more likely to feel empowered if they do understand what went wrong.

Since the primary rationale for termination with dignity is to empower people to move ahead with their lives, putting in a good word for them can play a crucial role—and has been shown not to put the organization at risk.

Further, people's pride must be considered. Separated employees will need to know how their departure will be portrayed to the remaining staff; they should be assured that they will not come off looking like has-beens or part of a defective group that wasn't pulling its weight. Management can:

- Set the tone for the day.
- Preserve an atmosphere of respect. Convey genuine regret that the organization had to make what is a hard decision.

"What is going to happen to me now? How am I going to survive?"

These questions are typically rooted in simple panic. A fair number of people live from paycheck to paycheck, or, at the very most, may have no more than a few weeks or months of savings. Some may be in too much shock to absorb a detailed explanation of the terms of severance, but it is best to work on the assumption that survival information should be conveyed immediately.

Managers should give the employee full written statements of separation benefits and policies, that is, what the separated employee can expect in terms of:

- Money
- Career coaching services
- Health coverage
- 401(k) rollovers
- Pension rights
- Compensation for earned vacation days
- References

These statements should be prepared with as much care as the benefit booklets handed to new hires, as already noted above.

Shock and panic can be reduced if people leave the manager's office with some sense that they are not really on the edge of disaster, that a support system has been put into place.

On-site Liaison

The HR staff should be assigned to liaise with separated workers. The primary message should be, "You have been an important and valued part of the team; we want to help you move on." This means a willingness to help people navigate life during the weeks and months that follow.

After the Meeting

References

Management should seriously consider the issue of references. Since the primary rationale for termination with dignity is to empower people and enable them to move ahead with

their lives, putting in a good word for them can play a crucial role. Does maintaining a wall of silence help?

For years, organizations have believed that references can translate easily into lawsuits. So, most employers do little more than verify the dates of employment—and forbid managers to respond to requests for references. The result, of course, is that information is sought informally and travels by the grapevine—increasing the chances that hearsay or rumors can damage reputations and careers.

Offering references does not, however, put organizations at risk. *The New York Times* (February 21, 1999) reported the following:

"According to C. Patrick Fleener, a management professor at Seattle University, 'the fear of being sued and losing is not well founded.' Professor Fleener, co-author of a study of Federal and state court records nationwide from 1965 to 1970 and 1985 to 1990, found only 16 defamation cases arising from reference checks. And plaintiffs prevailed in only 4 of the 16, he found."

It is worth the effort to reinvent strategies on references and convey good news about people to prospective employers. Even those who are fired for poor performance deserve to have their good points preserved in the record. This is consistent with the philosophy, to do no harm. The policy should be that although today's events involve stress and a significant setback, the organization should act so that these feelings need not be any greater than necessary.

Making it a Reality

A thorough survey of the American employment landscape undoubtedly would reveal wide variations in termination policies; some organizations would get high marks, while others would be seen as brutal. Mostly, it seems that the standards advocated here are already accepted in theory by many, and even offered as written policy by some. Termination with dignity, however, is hard work, requiring a heavy commitment of money and human talent. Writing it up in the policy manual is one thing; true implementation is another. "Our employee manual was heavy with human concern," an executive noted in commenting on an especially bruising departmental layoff. But to save money in the short term, the guidelines were simply ignored.

Further study, research and consultation among leading executives should be undertaken to consider strategies for implementation: How can ideas and ideals be translated into plans of action? Often, this means a significant change in an organization's culture. As was mentioned at the outset, many benefits are now taken for granted as part of the deal that American workers expect (e.g., insurance coverage and paid vacations). Termination with dignity should take its place as a benefit, along with others, to maximize the effectiveness of the workforce and the development of employees as resources, as well as to respect our human dignity. At present, the termination process is frequently crippling both to organizations and workers. Nothing in law or economics requires that this state of affairs be preserved.

HR managers are realizing that Five O'Clock Club outplacement is more effective and less expensive than conventional outplacement. The remaining employees feel better knowing that their fellow workers will receive *a full year of coaching help*.

Conventional outplacement generally lasts only for a short period, and usually provides expensive office space, a phone and a computer—but with limited coaching and outdated job-search techniques. Just about everyone today has a home computer, and either a printer or access to inexpensive printing and copying. There really isn't a need to give a laid off employee an office. What is needed are updated career coaching, support, and practice in the latest job-hunting techniques. That's The Five O'Clock Club method.

Based on over 25 years of research, our cost-effective corporate packages offer a minimum of one year of outplacement including private coaching as well as small-group strategy sessions. That is—again in contrast to traditional

outplacement firms—people may return to us if their new job or consulting assignment has not worked out.

An outplacement package can cost as little as $2,000. Our Premium package, for those earning over $100,000 per year, includes 14 hours of private coaching, as well as one year of small-group coaching for only $5,000.

At traditional outplacement firms, people usually get three months of space and phones, but only five hours of coaching, the service job hunters need most. The quality of traditional outplacement has declined as coaches are overloaded with short-term clients, handling three times the caseload of previous years.

Separated Professionals and Managers Prefer The Five O'Clock Club

Time and again, The Five O'Clock Club is the provider of choice. In a downsizing of 19 professionals and managers (whose salaries ranged from $35,000 to $150,000), all 19 were given a choice between The Five O'Clock Club and a "major" outplacement organization. Fourteen chose The Five O'Clock Club. We were able to offer eight hours of one-to-one coaching and one year of small-group coaching, along with books, CDs and other materials. The major outplacement firm was offering three- and six-month packages depending on seniority. Employees consistently choose expert career coaching over the space provided by traditional outplacement firms. Be sure to tell your friends and those in human resources about the most cost-effective job-search solution available.

Group Discussion Questions

- What does this mean: "The separations should be handled such that both the employee and the organization are empowered to move forward."? How does this apply to a termination? Why is it so very important? How do we interpret "move forward?" Use the entire chapter to answer this.

- Give hints on the proper manner of termination before the meeting, during the meeting, and after the meeting.
- The section below have both quotes and surprisingly similar versions of the Golden Rule. Take some time in evaluating the "Quotations to Inspire You" and "The Golden Rule." What surprises you the most?

Quotations to Inspire You

Difficult terminations and situations involving threatening employees are similar to other volatile social situations: . . . the interests of one party are in direct conflict with the interests of another party. Accordingly, resolutions that are completely satisfactory to all parties are rare. To complicate matters, the difficult employee often has similar problems away from work as well. The good things in his life are like dominos that have started to topple: Confidence has toppled into performance, which topples into identity, which knocks over self-esteem. The loss of his job may knock over the few remaining dominos, but the one that employers must be careful not to topple is the dignity domino because when that falls, violence is most likely.

Gavin DeBecker, *The Gift of Fear and Other Survival Strategies that Protect Us from Violence*

He means well, but he means well feebly.

Theodore Roosevelt (speaking about a political rival)

Since college, I'd always worked at top speed. From a demanding law practice, I'd gone to work in Richard Nixon's White House. Days began at 6 A.M., and I seldom was home before ten at night. Suddenly there was a vacuum in my life. I had nothing productive to do.

John Ehrlichman, former White House Domestic Policy Coordinator, on losing his job

Time-limited contracts will become commoner. Executives have often been hired with contracts that specify some compensation if the arrangement is terminated sooner than planned, and such clauses will become available to other workers as well. All of us are going to move toward some kind of contract with the organizations that pay for our services.

William Bridges, *JobShift: How to Prosper in a Workplace without Jobs*

Heroes come in all sizes, and you don't have to be a giant hero. You can be a very small hero. It's just as important to understand that accepting self-responsibility for the things you do, having good manners, caring about other people—these are heroic acts. Everybody has the choice of being a hero or not being a hero every day of their lives.

George Lucas, film director, as quoted in *Time* magazine, April 26, 1999

To feel that one has a place in life solves half the problem of contentment.

George Edward Woodberry, American poet, critic and educator (1855–1930)

The Golden Rule

Bahá'i: "And if thine eyes be turned towards justice, choose thou for thy neighbor that which thou choosest for thyself."
—*Lawh'i'Ibn'i'Dhib*, "Epistle to the Son of the Wolf", 30

Buddhism: "Hurt not others in ways you yourself would find hurtful."
—*Udana-Varga*, 5:18

Christianity: "In everything do to others as you would have them do to you; for this is the law and the prophets."
—*Matthew*, 7.12

Confuscianism: "Do not unto others what you do not want them to do to you."
—*Analects*, 15.13

Hinduism: "This is the sum of duty: do naught unto others which would cause you pain if done to you."
—*The Maha-bharata, 5:1517*

Islam: "Not one of you is a believer until he loves for his brother what he loves for himself."
—*Fortieth Hadith of an-Nawawi, 13*

Jainism: "A man should wander about treating all creatures as he himself would be treated."
—*Sutrakritanga, 1.11.33*

Judaism: "What is hateful to you, do not do to your neighbor: that is the whole of the Torah; all the rest of it is commentary."
—*Talmud, Shabbat, 31a*

Native American: "Respect for all life is the foundation."
—*The Great Law of Peace*

Sikhism: "Treat others as thou wouldst be treated thyself."
—*Adi Granth*

Taoism: "Regard your neighbor's gain as our own gain and your neighbor's loss as your own loss."
—*T'ai Shang KanYing P'ien*

Zoroastrianism: "That nature alone is good which refrains from doing unto another whatsoever is not good for itself."
—*Dadistan-I-Dinik, 94:5*

Reprinted with permission of the Tanenbaum Center for Interreligious Studies, Union Theological Seminary in the City of New York

Chapter 54

• • • • • • • •

Compassion

by Richard Bayer, Ph.D., Chief Operating Officer, The Five O'Clock Club

We may have uneasy feelings for seeing a creature in distress without compassion; for we have not compassion unless we wish to relieve them.

Samuel Johnson, English author

When we have a job, we spend most of our waking hours in the workplace, and so our virtues must show there if they are going to show anywhere. The workplace can be a dramatic venue to show compassion if you think about it! It is where hopes rise and fall, reputations are formed, fortunes are made and lost, people develop or squander their talents, systems help or oppress people, colleagues are treated justly or unjustly, and so much more. What an arena for compassion to be championed or stifled in! In other words, the workplace is a setting to show whether or not we have compassion. And it is a choice for most of us. For a select few (the Dalai Lama or the Pope come to mind), compassion is a way of life and is not reserved for special cases or situations.

Question(s) to consider: How often do you go out of your way to help someone else? Often? Sometimes? Rarely? Do you look at situations by putting yourself in someone else's shoes?

Perhaps we don't see as much compassion in the workplace as we might like to because the spirit of competition is so highly prized in our market economy. Products compete for consumer attention, businesses compete for market share, and employees compete for promotions and wage increases. Indeed, we often assume that corporate or personal survival is at stake if we fail to beat the competition.

How can compassion coexist with competition? To answer this question, let's begin by looking at some of the definitions of compassion found in dictionaries:

1. Deep awareness of the suffering of another coupled with the wish to relieve it.
2. A deep awareness of and sympathy for another's suffering; the humane quality of

understanding the suffering of others and wanting to do something about it.

So compassion is not incompatible with a moderate sense of competition at the workplace. Two things in particular are important, based on the definition of compassion: (1) awareness and sympathy for another; and (2) doing something about his/her distress, suffering or misfortune. Anyone who is moved by the needs of others, but doesn't do anything to bring relief, is not compassionate.

Bear in mind: We are not only competitors; we are also colleagues. It's not only realistic, but also necessary for a spirit of compassion to prevail among colleagues. Older, experienced workers show compassion when they mentor new hires until they are comfortable in their new positions. A well-run business requires people and departments to collaborate. Careers and lives can be set back or ruined by cutthroat tactics that lack compassion.

Businesses also show compassion when they donate funds or employee time to charities— and, indeed, thousands of charities benefit from corporate giving. This creates a corporate culture (or character) that makes for a more pleasant world.

What is the alternative to compassion? It is competition run wild without boundaries. People would either cease caring for others or stop acting based on caring. Serious damage would be done, given the importance of economic life for all of us. His Holiness The Dalai Lama points out how we all depend on each other to live; some of us grow crops, some make our clothes, some build our homes, some teach our children, and on and on. Without others, our society as it is could not exist.

To sum up, in the often-dramatic world of the workplace, compassion brings us to sympathize with others and actively intervene and help when we see suffering. This not only does much to determine our character (we have to live with ourselves!), but it also creates a constructive environment in which we spend so many of our waking hours.

This is not a matter for theorizing. It's a matter of common sense. There is no denying that consideration of others is worthwhile. There is no denying that our happiness is totally woven in with the happiness of others. There is no denying that if society suffers, we suffer. And there is no denying that the more our hearts and minds are afflicted with ill will, the more miserable we become.

Compassion is what makes our lives meaningful. It is the source of all lasting happiness and joy. And it is the foundation of a good heart, the heart of one who acts out of a desire to help others. Through kindness, through affection, through honesty, through truth and justice toward all others we ensure our own benefit. Thus we can reject everything else: religion, ideology, all received wisdom. But we cannot escape the necessity of love and compassion.

His Holiness The Dalai Lama, *Ethics for the New Millennium*

True compassion is more than throwing a coin to a beggar. It demands of our humanity that if we live in a society that produces beggars, we are morally commanded to restructure that society.

Rev. Martin Luther King, Jr.

Group Discussion Questions

- Is compassion incompatible with a sense of competition at the workplace or in our private lives? State why or why not.
- How can compassion create a constructive environment?

Appendix 1

• • • • • • • •

Exercises to Analyze Your Past and Present: The Seven Stories Exercise®

by Kate Wendleton, President, The Five O'Clock Club

The direction of change to seek is not in our four dimensions: it is getting deeper into what you are, where you are, like turning up the volume on the amplifier.

Thaddeus Golas, *Lazy Man's Guide to Enlightenment*

In this exercise, you will examine your accomplishments, looking at your strongest and most enjoyable skills. The core of most coaching exercises is some version of the Seven Stories Exercise. A coach may give you lots of tests and exercises, but this one requires work on your part and will yield the most important results. An interest or personality test is not enough. There is no easy way. Remember, busy executives take the time to complete this exercise—if it's good enough for them, it's good enough for you.

Do not skip the Seven Stories Exercise. It will provide you with important information about yourself for the direction of your personal life as well as your career. If you're like most people, you have never taken the time to sort out

the things you're good at and also are motivated to accomplish. As a result, you probably don't use these talents as completely or as effectively as you could. Too often, we do things to please someone else or to survive in a job. Then we get stuck in a rut—that is, we're always trying to please someone else or always trying to survive in a job. We lose sight of what could satisfy us, and work becomes drudgery rather than fun. When we become so enmeshed in survival or in trying to please others, it may be difficult to figure out what we would rather be doing.

When you uncover your motivated skills, you'll be better able to identify jobs that allow you to use them, and recognize other jobs that don't quite fit the bill. Motivated skills are patterns that run through our lives. Since they are skills from which we get satisfaction, we'll find ways to do them even if we don't get to do them at work. We still might not know what these skills are—for us, they're just something we do, and we take them for granted.

Tracking down these patterns takes some thought. The payoff is that our motivated skills do not change. They run throughout our lives and indicate what will keep us motivated for the rest of our lives.

Look at Donald Trump. He knows that he enjoys—and is good at—real estate and self-promotion, and that's what he concentrates on. You can identify commonalities in your accomplishments—aspects that you must have that will make you happier and more successful. In my case, for example, whether I was a computer programmer, a chief financial officer or a career coach, I've always found a way to teach others and often ran small groups — even in my childhood!

One's prime is elusive....You must be on the alert to recognize your prime at whatever time of life it may occur.

Muriel Spark, *The Prime of Miss Jean Brodie*

The Seven Stories Approach:

Background

This technique for identifying what people do well and enjoy doing has its roots in the work of Bernard Haldane, who, in his job with the U.S. government in the 1940s, helped military personnel transition their skills to civilian life. Its overwhelming success in this area won the attention of Harvard Business School where it went on to become a significant part of its Manual for Alumni Placement. Haldane's work is being carried on today all over the world through DependableStrenghts.org. They have brought Haldane's method to places as diverse as South Africa and China, to colleges and universities and in their work with young people.

The Seven Stories (or enjoyable accomplishments) approach, now quite common, was taught to me by George Hafner, who used to work for Bernard Haldane.

The exercise is this: Make a list of all the enjoyable accomplishments of your life, those things you enjoyed doing and also did well. List at least 25 enjoyable accomplishments from all parts of your life: work, from your youth, your school years, your early career up to the present. Don't forget volunteer work, your hobbies and your personal life. Other people may have gotten credit or under-appreciated what you did. Or the result may not have been a roaring success. For example, perhaps you were assigned to develop a new product and take it to market. Let's say you worked on a project for two years, loved every minute of it, but it failed in the market. It doesn't matter. What matters is that you enjoyed doing it and did it well.

Examine those episodes that gave you a sense of accomplishment. You are asked to name 25 accomplishments so you will not be too judgmental—just list anything that occurs to you. Don't expect to sit down and think of everything. Expect to think of enjoyable accomplishments over the course of four or five days. Be sure to ask others to help you think of your accomplishments. Most people carry around a piece of paper so they can jot ideas down as they occur to them. When you have 25, select the seven that are most important to you by however you define important. Then rank them: List the most important first, and so on.

Starting with your first story, write a paragraph about each accomplishment. Then find out what your accomplishments have in common. If you are having trouble doing the exercises, ask a friend to help you talk them through. Friends tend to be more objective and will probably point out strengths you never realized.

You will probably be surprised. For example, you may be especially good interacting with people, but it's something you've always done and therefore take for granted. This may be a thread that runs through your life and may be one of your motivated skills. It may be that you'll be unhappy in a career that doesn't allow you to deal with people.

When I did the Seven Stories Exercise, one of the first stories I listed was from when I was 10 years old, when I wrote a play to be put on by the kids in the neighborhood. I rehearsed everyone, sold tickets to the adults for two cents apiece, and served cookies and milk with the proceeds. You might say that my direction as a general manager—running the whole show, thinking things up, getting everybody working together—was set in the fourth grade. I saw these traits over and over again in each of my stories.

After I saw those threads running through my life, it became easy for me to see the elements I must have in a career to be satisfied. When I would interview for a job or think of business ideas for myself (or when other people made suggestions), I could find out in short order whether the job or the business idea would address my motivated skills (running small groups, writing books, public speaking, and so on). If it didn't, I wouldn't be as happy as I could be, even though I may decide to take certain positions as an interim step toward a long-term goal. The fact is, people won't do as well in the long run in positions that don't satisfy their motivated skills.

Sometimes I don't pay attention to my own motivated skills, and I wind up doing things I regret. For example, in high school I scored the highest in the state in math. I was as surprised as everyone else, but I felt I finally had some direction in my life. I felt I had to use it to do something constructive. When I went to college, I majored in math. I almost flunked because I was bored with it. The fact is that I didn't enjoy math, I was simply good at it.

There are lots of things we're good at, but they may not be the same things we really enjoy. The trick is to find those things we are good at, enjoy doing, and feel a sense of accomplishment from doing.

To sum up: Discovering your motivated skills is the first step in career planning. I was a general manager when I was 10, but I didn't realize it. I'm a general manager now, and I love it. In between, I've done some things that have helped me toward my long-range goals, and other things that have not helped at all.

It is important to realize that the Seven Stories Exercise will not tell you exactly which career you should have, but the elements to look for in a career that you will find satisfying. You'll have a range to consider, and you'll know the elements you must have to keep you happy. Once you've selected a few career possibilities that might satisfy you, talk to people in those fields to find out if a particular field or industry is really what you want, and the possibilities for someone with your experience. That's one way to test if your aspirations are realistic.

After you have narrowed your choices down to a few fields with some possibilities that will satisfy your motivated skills, the next step is to figure out how to get there.

. . . be patient toward all that is unsolved
in your heart and try to love the questions
themselves like locked rooms and like books
that are written in a foreign tongue.

Rainer Maria Rilke, *Letters to a Young Poet*

A Demonstration of the Seven Stories Exercise

To get clients started, I sometimes walk them through two or three of their achievement stories, and tell them the patterns I see. They can then go off and think of the seven or eight accomplishments they enjoyed the most and also performed well. This final list is ranked and analyzed in depth to get a more accurate picture of the person's motivated skills. I spend the most time analyzing those accomplishments a client sees as most important. Some accomplishments are more obvious than others. But all stories can be analyzed.

Here is Suzanne, as an example: "When I was nine years old, I was living with my three sisters. There was a fire in our house and our cat had hidden under the bed. We were all outside, but I decided to run back in and save the cat. And I did it."

No matter what the story is, I probe a little by asking questions: What was the accomplishment for you? and What about that made you proud? These questions give me a quick fix on the person.

The full exercise is a little more involved than this. Suzanne said at first: "I was proud because I did what I thought was right." I probed a little, and she added: "I had a sense of accomplishment because I was able to make an instant decision under pressure. I was proud because I overcame my fear."

I asked Suzanne for a second story; I wanted to see what patterns might emerge when we put the two together: "Ten years ago, I was laid off from a large company where I had worked for nine years.

"I soon got a job as a secretary in a Wall Street company. I loved the excitement and loved that job. Six weeks later, a position opened up on the trading floor, but I didn't get it at first. I eventually was one of three finalists, and they tried to discourage me from taking the job. I wanted to be given a chance. So I sold myself because I was determined to get that job. I went back for three interviews, said all the right things, and eventually got it."

What was the accomplishment?

What made her proud?

"I fought to win."

"I was able to sell myself. I was able to overcome their objections."

"I was interviewed by three people at once. I amazed myself by saying, 'I know I can do this job.'"

"I determined who the real decision-maker was, and said things that would make him want to hire me."

"I loved that job—loved the energy, the upness, the fun."

Here it was, 10 years later, and that job still stood out as a highlight in her life. Since then she'd been miserable and bored, and that's why she came to me. Normally after a client tells two stories, we can quickly name the patterns we see in both stories. What were Suzanne's patterns?

Suzanne showed that she was good at making decisions in tense situations—both when saving the cat and when interviewing for that job. She showed a good intuitive sense (such as when she determined who the decision-maker was and how to win him over). She's decisive and likes fast-paced, energetic situations. She likes it when she overcomes her own fears as well as the objections of others.

We needed more than two stories to see if these patterns ran throughout Suzanne's life and to see what other patterns might emerge. After the full exercise, Suzanne felt for sure that she wanted excitement in her career, a sense of urgency—that she wanted to be in a position where she had a chance to be decisive and operate intuitively. Those are the conditions she enjoys and under which she operates the best.

Armed with this information, Suzanne can confidently say that she thrives on excitement, high pressure, and quick decision-making. And, she'll probably make more money than she would in safe environments. She can move her life in a different direction—whenever she is ready.

Pay attention to those stories that were most important to you. The elements in these stories may be worth repeating. If none of your enjoyable accomplishments were work related, it may take great courage to eventually move into a field where you will be happier.

People have to be ready to change. Fifteen years ago, when I first examined my own motivated skills, I saw possibilities I was not ready to handle. Although I suffered from extreme shyness, my stories—especially those that occurred when I was young—gave me hope. As I emerged from my shyness, I was eventually able to act on what my stories said was true about me.

People sometimes take immediate steps after learning what their motivated skills are. Or sometimes this new knowledge can work inside them until they are ready to take action—maybe 10 years later. All the while internal changes can be happening, and people can eventually blossom.

If one advances confidently in the direction of his dreams, and endeavors to live the life which he has imagined, he will meet with success unexpected in common hours.

Henry David Thoreau, American writer and philosopher

Motivated Skills—Your Anchor in a Changing World

Your motivated skills are your anchor in a world of uncertainty. The world will change, but your motivated skills remain constant.

Write them down. Save the list. Over the years, refer to them to make sure you are still on target—doing things that you do well and are motivated to do. As you refer to them, they will influence your life. Five years from now, an opportunity may present itself. In reviewing your list, you will have every confidence that this opportunity is right for you. After all, you have been doing these things since you were a child, you know that you enjoy them, and you do them well!

Knowing our patterns gives us a sense of stability and helps us understand what we have done so far. It also gives us the freedom to try new things regardless of risk or of what others may say, because we can be absolutely sure that this is the way we are. Knowing your patterns gives you both security and flexibility—and you need both to cope in this changing world.

Now think about your own stories. Write down everything that occurs to you.

The Ugly Duckling was so happy and in some way he was glad that he had experienced so much hardship and misery; for now he could fully appreciate his tremendous luck and the great beauty that greeted him....And he rustled his feathers, held his long neck high, and with deep emotion he said: "I never dreamt of so much happiness, when I was the Ugly Duckling!"

Hans Christian Andersen, *The Ugly Duckling*

The Seven Stories Exercise® Worksheet

This exercise is an opportunity to examine the most satisfying experiences of your life and to discover those skills you will want to use as you go forward. You will be looking at the times when you feel you did something particularly well that you also enjoyed doing. Compete this sentence: "There was a time when I..." List enjoyable accomplishments from all parts of your life: from your youth, your school years, your early career up to the present. Don't forget volunteer work, your hobbies and your personal life. Other people may have gotten credit or under-appreciated what you did. Or the result may not have been a roaring success. None of that matters. What matters is that you enjoyed doing it and did it well.

List anything that occurs to you, however insignificant. When I did my own Seven Stories Exercise, I remembered the time when I was 10 years old and led a group of kids in the neighborhood, enjoyed it, and did it well.

When you have 25, select the seven that are most important to you by however you define important. Then rank them: List the most important first, and so on. Starting with your first story, write a paragraph about each accomplishment. Then find out what your accomplishments have in common. If you are having trouble doing the exercises, ask a friend to help you talk them through. Friends tend to be more objective and will probably point out strengths you never realized.

Section I

Briefly outline below all the work/personal/life experiences that meet the above definition. Come up with at least 25. We ask for 25 stories so you won't be too selective. Just write down anything that occurs to you, no matter how insignificant it may seem. Complete this sentence, "There was a time when I ..." You may start with, for example, "Threw a fiftieth birthday party for my father," "Wrote a press release that resulted in extensive media coverage," and "Came in third in the Nassau bike race."

Don't just write that you enjoy "cooking." That's an activity, not an accomplishment. An accomplishment occurs at a specific time. You may wind up with many cooking accomplishments, for example. But if you simply write "cooking," "writing" or "managing," you will have a hard time thinking of 20 enjoyable accomplishments.

Complete this sentence, "There was a time when I …"

1. _____
   _____

2. _____
   _____

3. _____
   _____

4. _____
   _____

5. _____
   _____

6. _____
   _____

7. _____
   _____

8. _____
   _____

9. _____
   _____

10. _____
    _____

11. _____
    _____

12. _____

_____

13. _____
    _____

14. _____
    _____

15. _____
    _____

16. _____
    _____

17. _____
    _____

18. _____
    _____

19. _____
    _____

20. _____
    _____

21. _____
    _____

22. _____
    _____

23. _____
    _____

24. _____
    _____

25. _____
    _____

Section II

Choose the seven experiences from the above that you enjoyed the most and felt the most sense of accomplishment about. (Be sure to include non-job-related experiences also.) Then rank them. Then, for each accomplishment, describe what you did. Be specific, listing each step in detail. Use a separate sheet of paper for each.

Here's how you might begin:

Experience #1: Planned product launch that resulted in 450 letters of intent from 1,500 participants.

a. Worked with president and product managers to discuss product potential and details.

b. Developed promotional plan.

c. Conducted five-week direct-mail campaign prior to conference to create aura of excitement about product.

d. Trained all product demonstrators to make sure they each presented product in same way.

e. Had great product booth built; rented best suite to entertain prospects; conducted campaign at conference by having teasers put under everyone's door every day of conference. Most people wanted to come to our booth.

—and so on—

Analyzing Your
Seven Stories®

Now it is time to analyze your stories. You are trying to look for the patterns that run through them so that you will know the things you do well that also give you satisfaction. Some of the questions below sound similar. That's okay. They are a catalyst to make you think more deeply about the experience. The questions don't have any hidden psychological significance.

For now, simply go through each story without trying to force it to come out any particular way. Just think hard about yourself. And be as honest as you can. When you have completed this analysis, the words in the next exercise may help you think of additional things. Do this page first.

Story #1.

What was the accomplishment?

_____

What about it did you enjoy most?

_____

What did you do best?

_____

What motivated you to do this?

_____

What about it made you proud? What prompted you to do this?

_____

What enjoyable skills did you demonstrate?

_____

Story #2.

The accomplisment?

_____

Enjoyed most?

_____

Did best?

_____

A motivator?

_____

Made you proud?

_____

Prompted you to do this?

_____

Enjoyable skills demonstrated?

_____

Story #3.

The accompliment?

_____

Enjoyed most?

_____

Did best?

_____

A motivator?

_____

Made you proud?

_____

Prompted you to do this?

_____

Enjoyable skills demonstrated?

_____

Story #4.

The accomplishment?

_____

Enjoyed most?

_____

Did best?

_____

A motivator?

_____

Made you proud?

_____

Prompted you to do this?

_____

Enjoyable skills demonstrated?

_____

Story #5.

The accomplishment?

_____

Enjoyed most?

_____

Did best?

_____

A motivator?

_____

Made you proud?

_____

Prompted you to do this?

_____

Enjoyable skills demonstrated?

_____

Story #6.

The accomplishment?

_____

Enjoyed most?

_____

Did best?

_____

A motivator?

_____

Made you proud?

_____

Prompted you to do this?

_____

Enjoyable skills demonstrated?

_____

Story #7.

The accomplishment?

_____

Enjoyed most?

_____

Did best?

_____

A motivator?

_____

Made you proud?

_____

Prompted you to do this?

_____

Enjoyable skills demonstrated?

_____

We are here to be excited from youth to old age, to have an insatiable curiosity about the world. ...We are also here to help others by practicing a friendly attitude. And every person is born for a purpose. Everyone has a God-given potential, in essence, built into them. And if we are to live life to its fullest, we must realize that potential.

Norman Vincent Peale, theologian

Let me listen to me and not to them.

Gertrude Stein, author

What seems different in yourself; that's the rare thing you possess. The one thing that gives each of us his worth, and that's just what we try to suppress. And we claim to love life.

André Gide, author

Stick with the optimists, Niftie. It's going to be tough enough even if they're right.

James Reston, journalist

Optimism Emerges As Best Predictor To Success In Life

"Hope has proven a powerful predictor of outcome in every study we've done so far," said Dr. Charles R. Snyder, a psychologist at the University of Kansas. "Having hope means believing you have both the will and the way to accomplish your goals, whatever they may be. . . . It's not enough to just have the wish for something. You need the means, too. On the other hand, all the skills to solve a problem won't help if you don't have the willpower to do it."

Daniel Goleman, *The New York Times*, Dec. 24, 1991

Appendix 2

• • • • • • • • •

Your Fifteen-Year Vision® and Your Forty-Year Vision®

by Kate Wendleton, President, The Five O'Clock Club

In my practice as a psychiatrist, I have found that helping people to develop personal goals has proved to be the most effective way to help them cope with problems.

Ari Kiev, M.D., *A Strategy for Daily Living*

By recording your dreams and goals on paper, you set in motion the process of becoming the person you most want to be. Put your future in good hands—your own.

Mark Victor Hansen, American inspirational and motivational speaker

If you could imagine your ideal life five years from now, what would it be like? How would it be different from the way it is now? If you made new friends during the next five years, what would they be like? Where would you be living? What would your hobbies and interests be? How about 10 years from now? Twenty? Thirty? Forty? Think about it!

Some people feel locked in by their present circumstances. Many say it is too late for them. But a lot can happen in 5, 10, 20, 30, or 40 years.

Reverend King had a dream. His dream helped all of us, but his dream helped him too. He was living according to a vision (which he thought was God's plan for him). It gave him a purpose in life. Most successful people have a vision.

A lot can happen to you over the next few decades—and most of what happens is up to you. If you see the rest of your life as boring, I'm sure you will be right. Some people pick the "sensible" route or the one that fits in with how others see them, rather than the one that is best for them.

On the other hand, you can come up with a few scenarios of how your life could unfold. In that case, you will have to do a lot of thinking and a lot of research to figure out which path makes most sense for you and will make you happiest.

When a person finds a vision that is right, the most common reaction is fear. It is often safer to wish a better life than to actually go after it.

I know what that's like. It took me two years of thinking and research to figure out the right path for myself—one that included my motivated abilities (Seven Stories Exercise) as well as the sketchy vision I had for myself. Then it took 10 more years to finally take the plunge and commit to that path—running The Five O'Clock Club. I was 40 years old when I finally took a baby step in the right direction, and I was terrified.

You may be lucky and find it easy to write out your vision of your future.

Or you may be more like me: It may take a while and a lot of hard work. You can speed up the process by reviewing your assessment results with a Five O'Clock Club career counselor. He or she will guide you along. Remember, when I was struggling, the country didn't have Five O'Clock Club counselors or even these exercises to guide us.

Test your vision and see if that path seems right for you. Plunge in by researching it and meeting with people in the field. If it is what you want, chances are you will find some way to make it happen. If it is not exactly right, you can modify it later—after you have gathered more information and perhaps gotten more experience.

Start with the Present

Write down, in the present tense, the way your life is right now, and the way you see yourself at each of the time frames listed. This exercise should take no more than one hour. Allow your unconscious to tell you what you will be doing in the future. Just quickly comment on each of the questions listed on the following page, and then move on to the next. If you kill yourself off too early (say, at age 60), push it 10 more years to see what would have happened if you had lived. Then push it another 10, just for fun.

When you have finished the exercise, ask yourself how you feel about your entire life as you laid it out in your vision. Some people feel depressed when they see on paper how their lives are going, and they cannot think of a way out. But they feel better when a good friend or a Five O'Clock Club counselor helps them think of a better future to work toward. If you don't like your vision, you are allowed to change it—it's your life. Do what you want with it. Pick the kind of life you want.

Start the exercise with the way things are now so you will be realistic about your future. Now, relax and have a good time going through the years. Don't think too hard. Let's see where you wind up. You have plenty of time to get things done.

· ·

The 15-year mark proves to be the most important for most people. It's far enough away from the present to allow you to dream.

· ·

There are more things in heaven and earth, Horatio, than are dreamt of in your philosophy.

William Shakespeare, *Hamlet*

Your Fifteen-and Forty-Year-Vision® Worksheet

1. The year is_____(current year).

    You are _____ years old right now.

    - Tell me what your life is like right now.

    - (Say anything you want about your life as it is now.)

    - Who are your friends? What do they do for a living?

    - What is your relationship with your family, however you define "family"?

    - Are you married? Single? Children? (list ages.)

    - Where are you living? What does it look like?

    - What are your hobbies and interests?

    - What do you do for exercise?

    - How is your health?

    - How do you take care of your spiritual needs?

    - What kind of work are you doing?

    - What else would you like to note about your life right now?

Year: _____ Your Age_____

_____

_____

_____

_____

_____

_____

_____

_____

_____

_____

_____

_____

Don't worry if you don't like everything about your life right now. Most people do this exercise because they want to improve themselves. They want to change something? What do you want to change? Please continue . .

2. The year is_____(current year + 5).   Year: _____   Your Age _____

    You are _____years old right now.
    (Add 5 to present age.)

    Things are going well for you.

    • What is your life like now at this age?   _____
      (Say anything you want about your life
      as it is now.)   _____

    • Who are your friends? What do they do
      for a living?   _____

    • What is your relationship with your
      "family"?   _____

    • Are you married? Single? Children?
      (List their ages now.)   _____

    • Where are you living? What does it look
      like?   _____

    • What are your hobbies and interests?   _____

    • What do you do for exercise?   _____

    • How is your health?   _____

    • How do you take care of your spiritual
      needs?   _____

    • What kind of work are you doing?   _____

    • What else would you like to note about
      your life right now?   _____

3. The year is_____(current year + 15).

    You are _____years old right now.
    (Add 15 to present age.)

    Things are going well for you.

    - What is your life like now at this age?
      (Say anything you want about your life
      as it is now.)

    - Who are your friends? What do they do
      for a living?

    - What is your relationship with your
      "family"?

    - Are you married? Single? Children?
      (List their ages now.)

    - Where are you living? What does it look
      like?

    - What are your hobbies and interests?

    - What do you do for exercise?

    - How is your health?

    - How do you take care of your spiritual
      needs?

    - What kind of work are you doing?

    - What else would you like to note about
      your life right now?

Year: _____   Your Age _____

_____

_____

_____

_____

_____

_____

_____

_____

_____

_____

_____

The 15-year mark is an especially important one. This age is far enough away from the present that people often loosen up a bit. It's so far away that it's not threatening. Imagine your ideal life. What is it like? Why were you put here on this earth? What were you meant to do here? What kind of life were you meant to live? Give it a try and see what you come up with. If you can't think of anything now, try it again in a week or so. On the other hand, if you got to the 1 -year mark, why not keep going?

4. The year is xxxx (current year + 25).

You are _____ years old!

(Current age plus 25.)

Keep going. How do you feel about your life? You are allowed to change the parts you don't like.

5. The year is xxxx (current year + 35).

You are _____ years old!

(Current age plus 35.)

6. The year is xxxx (current year + 45).

You are _____ years old!

(Current age plus 45.)

7. The year is xxxx (current year + 55).

You are _____ years old!

(Current age plus 55.)

(Keep going—don't die until you are past 80!)

8. Year: _____ Your Age _____

Using a blank piece of paper, answer all of the questions for this stage of your life.

You have plenty of time to get done everything you want to do. Imagine wonderful things for yourself. You have plenty of time. Get rid of any "negative programming." For example, if you imagine yourself having poor health because your parents suffered from poor health, see what you can do about that. If you imagine yourself dying early because that runs in your family, see what would have happened had you lived longer. It's your life—your only one. As they say, "This is the real thing. It's not a dress rehearsal."

Index

About the Authors: Kate Wendleton and David Madison, Ph.D.

Kate Wendleton, President, The Five O'Clock Club

Kate is a nationally recognized authority on career development. She founded The Five O'Clock Club in 1978, and developed its methodology to help employees of all levels, making The Five O'Clock Club the only organization to conduct ongoing research on behalf of employees, as well as job hunters.

Kate was a nationally syndicated columnist for eight years and a speaker on career develop-

ment, having appeared on the *Today Show*, CNN, CNBC, *Larry King,* National Public Radio and CBS, and in the *Economist, The New York Times, The Chicago Tribune, The Wall Street Journal, Fortune* magazine, *Business Week* and other national media.

For the past two years, Kate has spent every Saturday with young adults who have aged out of foster care, trying to give them the opportunity to make the most of their lives. This organization, Remington Achievers, is a not-for-profit arm of The Five O'Clock Club.

Kate also founded Workforce America, a not-for-profit affiliate of The Five O'Clock Club, that served adults in Harlem who were not yet in the professional or managerial ranks. For ten years, Workforce America helped each person move into better-paying, higher-level positions, as each improved in educational level and work experience.

Kate founded, and directed for seven years, The Career Center at The New School for Social Research in New York. She also advises major corporations about leadership and career-development programs. A former CFO of two small companies, she has 20 years of business-management experience in both manufacturing and service businesses.

Kate attended Chestnut Hill College in Philadelphia and received her M.B.A. from Drexel University. She is a popular speaker with groups that include associations, corporations and colleges.

While living in Philadelphia, Kate did long-term volunteer work for the Philadelphia Museum of Art, the Walnut Street Theatre Art Gallery, United Way, and the YMCA. She currently lives in Manhattan and Wynnewood, PA, with her husband, and has three step-children.

Kate is the author of The Five O'Clock Club's five-part career-development and job-hunting series for professionals, managers and executives, as well as *Launching the Right Career*, and *Your Great Business Idea: The Truth About Making It Happen*, as well as The Five O'Clock Club's boxed set of 16 lectures on audio CDs.

David Madison, National Director, The Five O'Clock Club Guild of Career Coaches

David Madison, Ph.D. has been Director of The Five O'Clock Club Guild of Career Coaches since 1997. In this capacity, he oversees the

Coach Certification Program. This includes re-cruiting, screening, training and testing coaches. His department coordinates matching clients to coaches when The Five O'Clock Club is given executive-coaching, leadership-coaching or outplacement assignments by organizations, and when individuals join the Club on their own and request private coaching.

David wrote the *Coach Training Manual*, and, on an on-going basis, he has guided the evolution and tightening of the certification process itself to insure that our coaches meet the highest standards of performance, practice and ethics.

For many years, the Associate Editor of *The Five O'Clock News*—the Club's monthly magazine—he has written numerous articles on job search and career management. He is the author of The Five O'Clock Club book, *Report from the Front Lines: Job Hunters and Career Counselors Tell You How to Have a Successful Search.*

Prior to his work at The Five O'Clock Club, David worked as a senior recruiter for two personnel agencies that serviced the banking industry, being the owner of one in the early 1990s. In the mid-1990s he decided to move into the career-coaching field and met Kate Wendleton, the President of the Club, at a professional association meeting. He accepted her invitation to study to become a Five O'Clock Club coach and speaker, and within a year he was asked to become Director of the Guild.

Prior to David's move into the personnel field, he spent ten years in the United Methodist ministry in Massachusetts, serving churches in Rockport and Shrewsbury. Heavily focused on the educational and pastoral aspects of the parish ministry, he did extensive small-group teaching and established a network of support groups for widows and widowers.

A native of a small town in northern Indiana, he holds a B.A. in Political Science from Indiana University and a Master's in Sacred Theology from Boston University School of Theology. In 1975, he received his Ph.D. in Biblical Studies, majoring in Old Testament Studies, from the Boston University Graduate School.

The Five O'Clock Club®

Intensive, 3-MONTH Business Coaching Program for:

- newly promoted managers or mid-level new hires
- high-potentials
- those wanting to make a lateral move
- those you want to reward or make an investment in

Intensive, 9-MONTH Executive Development Program includes:

- extensive assessment instruments
- 360-feedback (structured interviewing and LSI 1 and 2)
- ongoing coaching and feedback to insure permanent change
- a written action plan, reviewed by a second coach

Ask for our brochures and a sampling of our executive coach bios.

Great change means great opportunity. Whether you are in HR or are a staff manager elsewhere in your organization, these are exciting times. People are a company's greatest asset, and it's time to make the most of your people.

Employee performance and retention are the name of the game. Typically, many employees who feel stuck during a recession say they will leave when the market gets better. By taking steps now that the economy is on the verge of recovery, you can prevent this from happening to your organization.

Both HR and executive management have a role in driving the required change and making sure every executive and manager has bought into the new direction, understands why it's important, and knows what to do next. Executive coaching can serve an important function in supporting these efforts.

The Five O'Clock Club Business Coaching and Development Programs are designed for the employees you value and want to keep. These programs are meant to increase:
- leadership/managerial effectiveness
- productivity
- retention

The Return on Investment

Among the most pressing needs facing management today are the development and retention of top talent, as well as the development of methods to enhance managerial productivity. In fact, a high percentage of managers in a new position will not make it:
- The "jury is out on them"; They often essentially struggle on their own.
- They may not quickly grasp the corporate culture or the informal organization.
- They may feel the pressure to prove themselves and produce results too quickly, thus making mistakes.

Affordable Business Coaching

Most Business Coaching programs are enormously expensive, even when the situation does not require a program of extended duration. In keeping with the Five

The Five O'Clock Club Business Coaching Advantage

❶ **A Team Effort:** Our tightly-knit Guild of senior career coaches works closely together. We turn to each other for guidance. After the primary coach has worked with your employee for four or five hours, **a coaching peer will review the situation**: assess the direction of the coaching, brainstorm the situation, and help develop a course correction, if called for.

❷ **A Proven Methodology** that is the industry standard—based on over 25 years of research. Employees better understand themselves and their organizations, how they fit in, and what they can do to improve their relationships with bosses, peers, subordinates and clients, and how they can most effectively help the organization move ahead. **Our texts, *Navigating Your Career* and *WorkSmarts*,** are used by professionals, managers and executives in for-profit and not-for-profit organizations of all sizes.

❸ **Devoted Coaches** who truly care what happens to the individual. Unlike firms where the coaches are over-burdened with a too-heavy client load, our coaches are responsive to their clients, use best practices, brainstorm with other coaches about their clients, and are **excited about each assignment because it means an opportunity to do the best for each client.**

continued

O'Clock Club's approach of providing high-quality programs at affordable prices, we offer Business Coaching and Development Programs that provide intensive coaching without the sticker shock.

The 3-month Business Coaching Program ($5,500), Business Coaching, is meant for:

* mid-level outside hires and those newly promoted
* high-potential employees
* employees making a lateral move

The 9-month Executive Development Program ($13,500) includes intensive 360 feedback, both through structured interviews (one-on-one interviews with peers, bosses and subordinates, or whoever is appropriate), and through the LSI, a computer-based feedback mechanism. It is appropriate when you want to effect change, and change takes a while. You'll see how thorough the program is when you look at the outline.

Highly Experienced Coaches

A coach must have the ability to quickly assess the situation, ask the hard questions, and provide guidance to effect positive change. Our coaches are skilled in doing just that and providing the structure needed. What's more, Five O'Clock Club business coaches have business, as well as extensive coaching experience helping clients to:
* assess themselves, the culture and the situation,
* identify areas that need to be addressed,
* develop a strategy for achieving business results quickly,
* anticipate problems, develop tentative solutions, and review the employee's performance in key situations, and
* create a development plan to follow after he or she no longer has the ongoing help of the coach.

You'll be very impressed with all of our coaches. Not only are they each top business coaches, as you will see from their bios, but they also all follow The Five O'Clock Club methodology and have worked together for years. Because they are all using the same methodology:

* they speak the same language,
* conduct regular and smooth peer reviews, and
* there is an inherent element of quality control.

Without a strong methodology, one coach may start with a core assessment, while another coach may just plunge in with a situational analysis. All of our coaches start with assessment, as one example of our structured approach. What's more, they are well-disciplined in the research-based, Five O'Clock Club model.

The Business Coaching Program starts with assigned exercises in our **150-page *Navigating Your Career*** and **300-page *WorkSmarts* manuals**. These exercises form the basis for understanding the executive and his or her strengths, weaknesses and goals in a uniform way.

Quality Control of Business Coaching Programs

Five O'Clock Club Business Coaches are of the highest quality. Most have been Business Coaches for over a dozen years. Just as with our outplacement program, our Business Coaching program is one you can trust. Our quality control includes:
* Coaching Circles, where groups of coaches meet every 6 weeks — in person or by teleconference to learn new techniques, exchange information, and conduct

peer supervision on specific (but anonymous) cases.
* One-on-one support to coaches — to review cases and get suggestions and support.
* Client progress reviews with headquarters — to assess the progress of each Business Coaching client.
* A quality-control call from our Client Services Manager to the client directly to assess how the coaching is going, and to HR to review client progress in accordance with ground rules and confidentiality agreements.

Business Coaching for Five O'Clock Club Members

If you are a Five O'Clock Club member, you may meet with your coach after you land your new job — and regularly over the years to plan your career, handle any issues that may come up, and make sure you are on track. You will pay your coach directly on an hourly basis as you go along. No heavy up-front fees are allowed.

If you would like to be matched up with an business coach, just fill out the Coach Request Form in the Coaches section of our website or email: Guild@fiveoclockclub.com.

Customized Coaching Solutions

Feel free to contact us if you would like to explore other options including tailored seminars and workshops. Email Guild@fiveoclockclub.com or call 212-286-4500.

The Five O'Clock Club ... a name you can trust

The Five O'Clock Club has been privately owned by its founders since 1978. We are a dedicated team of individuals who care about each other and our clients.